A PERFECTLY IMPERFECT LIFE

A PERFECTLY IMPERFECT LIFE

DEBRA WILLIAMS

Copyright © First Printing 2023, by Debra Williams.
Copyright © Second Edition 2025, by Debra Williams, includes additional content for clarification where needed, elimination of two chapters (Moving Forward and Remember the Unicorns), and editorial corrections.

A special note of gratitude to all seen and unseen who helped to make this publication a reality.

All rights reserved. No part of this book may be reproduced in any manner whatsoever without written permission except in the case of brief quotations embodied in critical articles and reviews.

The author of this book does not dispense medical advice or prescribe the use of any technique as a form of treatment for physical, emotional, or medical problems directly or indirectly. Please consult a professional licensed physician for any health concerns.

The intent of this book is to only offer information of a general nature to aid you in your quest for emotional and spiritual well-being. In the event you use any of the information in this book for yourself or others, the authors and the publisher assume no responsibility for your actions.

Peer Review Quotes

Loved reading the book. The amazing journey that Debra traveled through and her bursting out into the bright light of her new world view. These words gives me the courage to also take my individual journey. I am extremely honored, to see a way for me to experience the same outcome. Thank you deeply dear one.
--Michael

Wow!!! What a journey Debra's life began with. The many extreme life events that unfolded within her life is what you would see on the movie screen. It was an intriguing read as she found self healing on her way to discover the divine within herself. Through her AURA & RAAH sessions Debra gained knowledge and curiosity of the many things happening in and around her. I found her stories activating as the energy from the pages went tingling through my senses. Debra has opened herself up and is sharing with us how we can also grow by entering this beautiful work of self healing. I see her as the strong Divine Feminine and am thankful for all that she is for she is love.
--DebRa E

Beautiful heart expanding book...When you feel like giving up. This Beautiful book gives you hope to push forward. We think our life is hard until we read what other people have endured, and it's so heart expanding to see how much wisdom and soul expansion they've gained from their journey. Thank you for sharing your perfectly imperfect life.
--Maria

This book is Phenomenal. It will rock your world in the most beautiful heart and soul rhythm of a divine life well lived. A beautiful story of being love and expressing love. Reminding us to dance bravely and live well. These pages bring so much wisdom, compassion, and joy. One of the hardest things we can face is the letting go and forgiving when life disappoints us. The challenges we face can be overwhelming. This story and wisdom reminds us the divine power we carry to connect with our spirit, our selves and each other. I am sure and hope this is just the first in Debra's beautiful wisdom share of life and spirit and living our best with all the bumps and questions elegantly understood and transformed into love, peace and divine expression.

--Aggie

So I've just finished your book- and it's so wonderful. I do think part of the activation I am feeling through this book might be also remembering the feeling you've inspired but there is also such magic in your words. Right from the beginning there was such a comforting gentle and loving embrace. The way you talk about your life is so beautiful and brave and I felt your love and gentleness in every word. And what a life, what a remarkable, remarkable life- I remember being on page 32, putting the book down for a minute to think, wow, and this is only the beginning. And even now, the book might have ended but it also feels like such a beautiful new beginning. There is so much life to live! It's quite breathtaking – and I do hope for a sequel . Thank you for sharing your experiences so bravely and elegantly. And it's amazing how your words feel much more than mere words but actual gentle touches. And there is so much light!

--Anja

PREFACE - The Lotus Effect

Over the years I have found the lotus flower and its connection to each of us particularly fascinating. The secret of its self-cleaning surface is especially intriguing. It grows in muddy water emerging unblemished and untouched by pollution. For

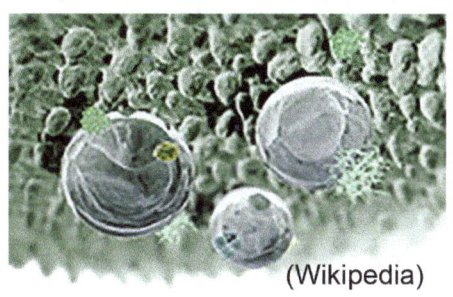
(Wikipedia)

thousands of years, the lotus flower has symbolized spiritual enlightenment.

Botanist Wilhelm Barthlott and his students at the University of Bonn in Germany spent twenty years scanning the surface of some 10,000 plants at the micro level. The magnifications of their images ranged from 90 to 6,000 diameters. When looking at a lotus flower, from casual observation, it has a slick smooth surface. As illustrated by the image on the right, these researchers were able to show that at the micro-level, the surface of the lotus leaf is covered with a dense layer of pointy little mogules. Dense enough that they repeal foreign matter. Barthlott refers to this as the Lotus Effect. (Hans Christian, January/February 2000)

Barthlott enjoyed demonstrating the Lotus Effect by smearing water-soluble glue and many other contaminants on the surface to watch them bead up and roll off the plant. No wonder this magnificent flower represents spiritual enlightenment. And no wonder some of us who may have undergone some pretty rough life experiences are so excited to learn we too can with our intent, have whatsoever dark energies and infringements we may have, roll right off, no longer defining who we are. For we are sovereign with limitless potential and do not consent to anything less. Magnify that by a group of us together. Simply phenomenal.

The story you are about to hear is an intimate account of my own journey of discovering my private Lotus Effect. My intent is that sharing these experiences may help others to evolve out of the muddy waters they may find themselves in.

Sending you the infinite love of the Universe,
Debra

Contents

1	Through My Eyes	1
2	Finding and Losing Religion	61
3	First Hypnosis Experience	73
4	Getting Certified	101
5	It's Not Safe to Move	117
6	Positively Polarizing 2,000 Dark Ones	147
7	Sensing Mars	179
8	Like Layers of an Onion	205
9	Jump, Debra, Jump	243
10	Indigenous Connections	273
11	Argentina: Being of One Heart	305
12	Priestess of Hathor	315
13	A Conversation with Source	337
14	Epiphanies	345
15	Who I Have Been All Along	371
16	Mind Expanding	401

Introduction

Just before turning sixty-five, I received the message from my inner voice, or Higher Self, that I was to write a book about my journey toward remembering who I am. Talk about going out of my comfort zone. Who would want to read of such an unremarkable life? The calm sweet answer I received from this internal argument was that the everyday mundane is the building block of the whole. What does it matter if no one other than yourself reads this work? What you share is to be transparent in every way vulnerable, and an honest account of this time and space. From grade school, you have kept journals. Some were so dark that you threw them away. That's the way it was meant to be. Keep the mundane within your story as the cellular structural patterns they are. Jump Debra, and allow all to unfold.

I find it noteworthy that this book is written by a person who in her mid-thirties was too illiterate to write a complete sentence. Someone who was marginalized and not allowed to take many high school classes by teachers who felt she was a waste of their time. Learned behaviors from bullying, it was safer to be a loner of sorts. Put me in a crowd of more than three people and I'll unconsciously find a way to disappear. I'm okay to be in the crowd if I have a task or find myself facilitating what is going on, but otherwise, the conversations seem to be something I'm either not able to relate to or the topic moves along so fast that by the time I find thoughts to add, the topic changed. Adding to this disappearing act, several decades of my life have been within a culture where I don't speak the language. That's when I really become invisible and legitimately outside of the conversation. Plus, in my mind, I often felt that they've got it covered and that their perspective carries more weight.

What compiling my thoughts into this work has revealed to me is the chaos that has been going on deep inside my consciousness. The chaos of being dyslexic and transposing things so bad that it just takes more effort to be coherent and is so time-consuming that my thoughts become lost. This realization reminded me of when I was working at the University of New Hampshire and had the opportunity in 2008 to talk to a brilliant math professor. He was receiving an unprecedented Grammy Award for his chaos theory and it was my role within the college to write a spotlight on him. What a fun interview. The part that sticks out in my mind is his explanation of discovering order within chaos. Our Universe is a universe of order. He shared that it was about tediously taking all the tiny bits of information from the smaller parts of the equation and combining them with the other smaller parts and their tiny bits to look at them all together within the much bigger picture. When you do that, you start to see a pattern. A pattern you once may have assumed was simply chaos. There is no chaos; not when your perspective is the whole.

As I mentioned, some of my journal entries were so dark that I threw them away. Revisiting that level of detail was more than I could bear at that time. My intent of sharing a portion of some of those harder experiences is not for recognition, but rather as markers that you may also relate to. Many of these darker, deeper struggles were slow to heal. Chapters one and two of this book lay the foundation, while subsequent chapters add needed puzzle pieces that loosen and pull the layers away, allowing me time and space to consider a bigger picture.

This formula of introspection and reviewing our various experiences is what is known as our shadow work. Once we see it and learn the lesson or purpose from each experience, we are able to thank it and let it go. In that respect, this book has been extremely healing for me. It has allowed me to coherently recognize and pay tribute to all these incredible aspects of myself so that I can let them go as I remember my lotus effect. Remembering the beauty and the infinite love that I am, allows all these tiny bits to flow through and off of my petals.

In gratitude and love, it is my intent that my story may be of assistance in your journey toward remembering.

1

Through My Eyes

From a very young age, my dear Grandma groomed me to carry on the role of family historian which has been a fascinating and revealing ride. A person's story begins long before their birth. Dating back to the 1600s, I have in my possession personal histories of my mother's ancestors. The histories tell of tender moments of hardships, and miracles. Overall, they were hardworking people dedicated to their God, families, and community. I learned from these histories that I am a direct descendant of the original founding members of the Mormon Church, correctly referred to as The Church of Jesus Christ of Latter-Day-Saints. The religion is known for its own set of scriptures called the "Book of Mormon," dietary restrictions, and large families, but mostly for the practice by many until 1890, of polygamy. Polygamy within the then-Mormon teachings was when a man took on more than one wife. My mother's side of the family included two generations of polygamists, otherwise, the family didn't practice that part of the religion.

The peculiar Mormon lifestyle was upsetting enough that my forefathers were forcefully driven out of settlement after settlement in Ohio, Illinois, Missouri, and more, earning them the distinction of being called the Mormon Pioneers. Historically, many of the Mormon Pioneers roamed from settlement to settlement until they reached

Utah. At the time the only people living in the Utah area were the Ute, Goshute, Shoshone, Paiute, and Navajo Native American Indians. Mormon scouts would be sent ahead to eliminate what they would refer to as the Indian problem. When new Mormon immigrants entered the Salt Lake Valley, church leadership assigned them to an area of the state to build their new homes. This is exactly how my family first immigrated to Manti, Utah on August 25, 1863.

Years after building their homes, the Indian threat continued. Sightings of Indians were met with deadly force on both sides. One great, great, uncle was a leader of a patrol assigned to keep the area safe. Indians not killed were imprisoned under deplorable conditions in a cow barn located south of town. This was the state of affairs when my mother was a young girl. It was just after the Great Depression and World War II. Many were destitute. My grandmother recorded how her group of other married-with-young-children friends chose to meet at least once a week to play cards together or find some other activity. If one of the couples chose to not show up for the activity, the rest of the group would go to their home and finding them with all the lights off and doors locked, would break in through a window and pull them out of their depression.

Imagine if you will, the mindset of this white Mormon town of Ephraim, Utah (Located six miles north of Manti), when in 1947 a worn-out noisy filthy overloaded truck similar to the one pictured, rolled into town filled with a non-English speaking brown-skinned family of seven, along with what was obviously all of their earthy possessions hanging out on all sides. These new immigrants weren't welcome and they knew it. The eleven-year-old boy, and second to the youngest, in that truck, would be my father.

His father moved his family to the area for a job and a home promised to him for tending a man's sheep. They were coming from the Jicarilla Apache Reservation out of Farmington New Mexico, where their home was an adobe house, with a dirt floor, no electricity, plumbing, or even glass windows. Worse yet, they were Catholic. Some years ago, in a quest to better understand my history, I visited the Jicarilla Tribal Headquarters in Dulce, New Mexico. There I was greeted warmly and an Elder took time out of his day to walk me through the grounds inside and outside of the facility. We walked up to a wild plant. He invited me to pick a leaf off of the plant, which I did. He taught me to memorize this plant, how it looks, where it grows, how it feels to your touch and your heart, how it smells, and how it tastes. Learn its value and properties. Once you have welcomed this plant into your family, you are ready to meet the next plant or aspect of Mother Earth. This Elder was a genuine teacher, not only giving me space but also respect. At the time, I didn't feel that respect was earned due to my not having been part of the Reservation life. When expressing my unworthiness, he taught that The People talk of a time when the hearts of those lost to the Tribe will, in time, remember their roots. He taught me many such things, which I hold close to my heart. Held in great esteem was a book by Veronica E. Velarde Tiller, "The Jicarilla Apache Tribe: A History." Written by one of their own, this is a book the people stand behind. A book I soon read cover to cover more than once.

It doesn't take much imagination to guess what drove my father's young family to relocate to the foreign harsh environment of Utah. It was about providing for the family and something even more critical. As recorded in Tiller's book, back on the Jicarilla Reservation authorities were forcibly taking very young children away from their families and placing them in horrific boarding schools. Boarding schools are run by the government with the motto 'Kill the Indian, save the child.'

Children were forcefully ripped from their families and often transported to unknown locations hundreds of miles from their homes. Their long hair was cut and they were dressed like their abductors. Plus they were forced to forsake their traditional ways and language. Emotional, mental, and physical punishment for speaking their native tongue or other such infractions, was quick and harsh.

In those days the Jicarilla boarding school had a seventy percent attrition rate. It was essentially a death sentence for the children. As you might imagine, the surviving thirty percent's torturous childhoods carried forward affecting generations. Speaking today from the time and place of 2023, empty boarding school facilities still exist throughout the United States and Canada. There's a darkness shrouding those areas along with discoveries of mass gravesites. I have firsthand experience driving past empty boarding schools like the one in the northern Utah area, which has always sent the deepest sadness throughout my heart and soul. Additionally, I have listened in person to several survivors my age. Their tales are horrific.

A Mohican woman allowed me to park my RV on her property in Farmington, New Hampshire. That RV was my temporary home while looking for a house when I first moved to the area. I met my Mohican friend while shopping in the area, and we instantly hit it off. She was an associate professor at one of the local colleges. At the age of seven, she was sent to a boarding school in Maine. Her back bowed a bit, so they placed her in a body cast and left her lying like that for years. Consequently, she's lived a life full of unspeakable physical and mental pain. Whereas her bones had no room to grow, they fractured within that cast and became infected with disease upon disease. Once released from the cast, she was bound to this day to be in a wheelchair. Hers is just one of the thousands and thousands of stories. Should you happen to come by documentaries on the topic, they are worthy of your time and respect. Some of these Indigenous children were sent to live with Anglo families rather than a boarding school. Again, they would have been hundreds of miles from their families. I went to school with several of these children through my high school years. As a reminder, I graduated in 1975.

There are several excellent movies and documentaries on the topic. I highly recommend the film, "Older Than America," written and produced by Georgina Lightning, of the Samson Cree Nation of Canada. Lightning, who is also a prominent actress in the film, based her 2008 film on her father's experience with the Canadian boarding school system and other personal family stories. I met her when she visited the University of New Hampshire while I worked there. She was holding a promotional talking circle on the topic. Sitting next to her in a group of about twenty people, I found her delightfully beautiful, personable, serious, knowledgeable, and passionate about bringing awareness of these darker issues to the light.

It's no wonder my father's family hid our Jicarilla Apache ancestry even from me. In my family's case, because they spoke Spanish, it was easy to hide their Native American ancestry. If asked, we were Spaniards. I was a young mother before my father confessed our heritage. Years later, I discovered that even what he knew, being raised as a boy on the reservation, was limited. Avoiding the heritage topic between parents and their children feels multigenerational. It's possibly a survival tactic. Still, pondering this notion of multigenerational trauma, from the personal histories I've gathered on my mother's side, I discovered a trend. Like my Grandma, my Mom, and myself, at least one hundred years of my direct lineage of ancestors broke the status quo of their time by marrying "outsiders!" They married someone who was not accepted by their community socially. Going back two generations, which is all I've accomplished so far, the same is true on my father's side. I find that very interesting. But that's a story for another time.

Getting back to the topic of my parents; in the school system of the neighboring towns of Manti and Ephraim, all the children attended junior high in Ephraim and high school in Manti. Being a year apart, my parents knew of each other but not closely. As a teenager, my mother was the life of any party and had an endless supply of boyfriends. Mom's older sister jealously recorded in her journal how my mom was the bell of the ball. One day my father attracted an extra bit of attention from being in a college shop accident where he lost part of his thumb. That day happened to be the day of one of my mother's senior-year high school dances. My father attended the dance with his hand all bandaged and held above his head. That was the first day that my parents got together. They later became engaged on the day my mother graduated from high school.

With this engagement, my father disrupted his family by leaving the Catholic Church and becoming Mormon. It couldn't have been an easy time as he was thrown out of his family's home and for a time while attending his college classes and working part-time, lived under a lean-to. A year later I entered the picture. My claim to fame is that my cradle was a cardboard box up in Utah's Manti La Sal Mountains where like his father, my father herded sheep. I love that about me. Before starting kindergarten, we moved away from my mountains and into the city. However, most weekends and all childhood summer vacations were spent right back there camping close to streams and lakes of plentiful fish, never-ending aspen and evergreen trees, big boulders to climb, abundant wildlife, and marvelous blue sunny skies in all directions. Being a free spirit who found comfort in the solitude of mother nature, I often wandered off away from the campsite onto my

Debra as a child

own adventures. I especially loved hiking to a certain pond that was home to several beavers. Just before I arrived, I could hear them slapping their tails on the water to warn each other of an intruder. My favorite part was finding a spot close to the water and holding still long enough, that they could sense I wasn't a threat. The beavers would come out from hiding and go about their daily activities fixing their homes.

One family activity was up Ephraim Canyon, which is part of the Manti La Sal Mountains. It was with extended family from both my father's and my mother's side of the family. I was probably seven or eight and went off on one of my solo hiking adventures. Losing track of time I walked back into camp close to sunset to find an alarmed family. They had been out searching for me and were in the middle of creating an organized effort. My biggest mistake was excitedly telling them that I found and climbed up a beautiful waterfall but slipped and fell so I had to stop and turn around back to camp. That's when I really got a talking to.

Regarding grade school, I was extremely shy and liked to cover my face with my hair. Plus, I was one of the slower learners. Learning to read felt out of reach which spilled over to all the other subjects. The one thing I enjoyed was art. I remember making spirals and spirals. Everything had spirals. My family moved around a lot. By the time I was in fourth grade, I had been in six different schools. But that is somewhat of an exaggeration because three of those schools were due to living in a new neighborhood and the school was still being built. Can you imagine the headache it created having to find places for an entire school grades kindergarten through six? For that first year, school number four, I was bused to a neighboring town. During the first two months of the next year, fourth grade and school number five, I was bused to an even further away town. Along with about twenty kids in my class, we didn't have chairs or desks during the school day. The regular students in that class were forced to crunch their desks closer to make room for us to sit on the floor on one side of the room.

Making friends is harder when you're not in one place very long and especially hard if you're an introvert. Still, I had good friends here and there, which was wonderful. There is one particular first-grade memory I'm not proud of. I was that little girl who messed her pants in class. It was pretty traumatic. I kept raising my hand asking permission to go to the restroom but my teacher insisted I wait for recess. Not wanting to ever go back to school, I somehow lived through it with my mom's help.

Another childhood memory that became the subject of a grade-school written report happened over the summer at my grandparents. My cousin, Mike, and I were very close and for a few years, spent our summers living with our grandparents on my mom's side of the family. Mike was about fourteen and worked with Grampa on the farm. I was eight or nine. As previously mentioned, my grandparents lived in Manti, a couple of hours south of where we lived in the city. It was a treat to go to the farm, usually with Gramma to take Grampa this or that. She was forever answering my questions and explaining how things work. My best friend those days was my small Pekinese dog, Lang, who also spent those summers with us. Lang was never allowed to go to the farm, but one happy day, Grampa finally told me Lang and I could go with him and my cousin Mike as long as I held on to her tight the entire time.

There was a cow that just birthed a calf. Mike went to tend to it. A herd of cows was near it but not too close. My Grampa had to move the herd away from the cow with the calf so that Mike could drive the cow and calf into a separate coral. It was a special thing to witness. Suddenly Lang jumped out of my arms, under the fence, and headed for the cows. I was screaming and trying to get to Lang. All Grampa cared about was getting to me and keeping me from going inside the fence after Lang. He told me, "There's nothing we can do for Lang! She's a goner! This is why she doesn't belong on the farm!"

I'm out of control sobbing and screaming. It started out with this little tiny seven-pound brown furry barking dog chasing this big herd of probably fifty head of Black Angus cows before all at once the cows turned around at the same time and started chasing the noisy ball of fluff. I'm really screaming now and Grampa has a tight hold on me. The cows were just a few feet away when Lang flew under the fence to safety. Grampa later said it was amazing the herd didn't bust through the fence and trample us all. Both Lang and I sat in the cab of the truck completely out of breath holding each other grateful to be alive until Mike and Grampa were finished doing what they went there to do. That was a quiet ride home. What an experience!

As hard as Grampa worked those long hot sunny days at the farm, each night after supper he got up to do the dishes. My job was to clear, rinse, dry, and take care of them. While doing the dishes Grampa took the time to hear about my day or get my opinions on things. That was our time together and I always felt important around him. After the dishes were done, we all often played cards or another game. Grampa was vicious at cards. Gramma was pretty awesome too. Besides having a blast together he would explain that playing cards will help you in life to deal with numbers and think on your feet. Regularly, they would ask me to read the family's personal histories to them. This is when Gramma instilled the importance of my keeping a journal of my own.

Do you know that I was born on Friday the thirteenth? Since I can remember, as a little girl my Gramma and Grampa celebrated every Friday the thirteenth of whatever month as my birthday complete with presents, cake, and ice cream. And if I wasn't there, a present would be sent through the mail along with a special phone call and song. They continued that tradition through their entire lives even after I was raising children of my own. That day finally came when kids in school teased me for being born on Friday the thirteenth. It didn't matter what the world believed. To me, it's the best day of all. Two of my daughters and one granddaughter were also born on the thirteenth.

I'd like to share one more of my tenderest memories of my mom which was from a time when I was in a dark place emotionally. During one of her meetings at the elementary school, my teacher informed Mom that I had climbed into a shell far away from my classmates and that I may need help. That night when it was time for us kids to go to bed, Mom turned the TV off and asked me to stay up and talk to her. My younger sister and brother complained that it wasn't fair that I got to stay up and they didn't. Mom explained that this was the way it was going to be for the next while. Once she felt like the two of us were alone, she shared what my teacher had told her and assured me that every night she and I would spend some time talking until I felt better about things. Those were precious discussions that I will forever treasure. After saying that I could always go to her she counseled me that whenever I feel there isn't anyone I can talk to or ask for help, there is always my Heavenly Father.

Unrelated, several weeks afterward, our dad's dad, Grampa Williams who as previously mentioned lived in Ephraim, a couple of hours south of us, was diagnosed with aggressive prostate cancer. He was scheduled for potentially life-saving surgery at the Holy Cross Hospital located in Salt Lake City, close to where we lived. Grampa was a down-winder, meaning he was out in the Mesquite desert herding sheep when the government tested their atomic bombs. When talking about it, he was full of all these emotions angrily sharing what he witnessed. He witnessed firsthand an atomic bomb with its mushroom clouds of fallout destruction. All his sheep died from it. The government never took responsibility for the lives lost during those years. At least not for the Native Americans who lived and worked in the area.

Gramma Williams stayed with us so that she could spend her days at the hospital with Grampa. Our dad's sister wasn't staying with us but was staying in the area. My bedroom was in the unfinished basement directly under my parent's bedroom. One night I kept waking up because my parents were talking all night long. That morning after Gramma Williams and my aunt left for the hospital, Mom called us kids to come into the house from where we were outside playing with the neighbors. My little brother wouldn't come in. It was just my sister and me. We could tell our mom had been crying about something. I figured it was something about Grampa. She said that she needed to talk to all three of us together and to again go and get our brother. We went back and forth like this for a while until my brother finally came in.

Once she got the three of us to sit around the kitchen table, she informed us that our dad was leaving her for another woman. She said it had nothing to do with us kids, and that our dad loved us. He just didn't love her anymore, and she had to move out. My younger sister and I were crying that we wanted to be with her. Mom was explaining that she didn't know what was next for her and that she wouldn't have much in the way of being able to take care of us. My sister and I didn't care. Our brother, who was the youngest, didn't show much emotion about it. He was only seven years old. The decision was made that she wanted to be out of the house before Gramma and our aunt returned and she wasn't sure if they'd be back for lunch or not. Gramma had enough to worry about with Grampa. Our mom called our dad on the phone at work and told us, kids, to tell him that we loved him. This was an extremely emotional call. She then gave both of our dogs fresh water and a piece of bologna and a hot dog. This was an unheard-of treat. As a rule, the dogs only ate dog food.

Soon after we were on the road, it was announced over the car radio that it would reach 102 degrees outside. Our small economy car didn't have air conditioning. Mom pulled into an Arctic Circle (Fast-food place) on 900 East and about 5300 South (A suburb of Salt Lake City) and bought each of us kids a vanilla ice cream cone. She didn't get anything for herself, and we didn't take any water or anything with us on this trip. We kept asking where we were going, but all she could say was that she didn't know, she just needed to keep driving. She suggested that we try to sleep while she works it out. We woke up when she slowed down to make a U-turn. Looking out the car window, we were in the middle of the salt flats with nothing in sight other than miles and miles of flat white salt. We asked her where we were and if we were going to California. She responded that we were in the middle of nowhere. "Wendover was a few miles ahead, but we were turning around to go back home to figure things out from there and that we might as well go back to sleep."

The next thing I knew there was some strange man standing over me telling me everything is going to be all right, everything is all right, everything is all right, like a broken record. I had been knocked unconscious and woke to find I was laying down in some sort of strange vehicle with all sorts of equipment and I could hear my sister screaming about we can't leave our Mommie. I couldn't see my sister. She was upfront with the driver, which was behind me. A man's voice who was upfront with her was telling her, "We're not going to leave your Mommie. See that other ambulance? That ambulance is just for your Mommie." She kept screaming and crying, "Mommie!" The man told her she had to settle down because she was scaring her sister and brother. I assume she turned around in the seat and saw me because she screamed, "Debi! What's wrong with Debi?" My face felt wet and tickly. This man next to me kept repeatedly telling me everything was okay when I knew it wasn't. Why couldn't I move? I gave it my all to painfully sit up to see what was going on. The man was freaking out that I was moving. I looked around and saw nothing that made sense until I looked down. On a different stretcher below me was my little brother all covered in blood not making a sound with his frightened wide eyes looking straight into mine. My sister is non-stop screaming, "Debi, what are you doing to Debi?" And on and on. I realized that the wet tickly feeling on my face must be blood and then just laid back down. The siren went on for a bit longer before we arrived at the hospital in Tooele, Utah.

Dark trauma followed my sister, brother, and me throughout our remaining childhood. Today, having known that level of betrayal by my own beloved husband, my best friend, the love of my life, and the father of my children, it was a shocking inexplicable excruciatingly painful knife in the heart that our mom was processing that day. The circumstantial evidence leads one to believe that the accident was intentional. I know most of my life I believed it was. She even said before we left the house that morning that she wanted to get run over by a truck. But using my gift of heart discernment, her saying that was just something people said without really meaning it. The moment she made that U-turn to go back home, she stood her ground against the betrayal. It was in that place of peace that one finds from such a realization, that she was returning to HER home, the home she created. The rest is conjecture. Pure exhaustion from the emotional devastation and having little to no sleep the night before complicated by several hours of the intense heat of the day out in the desert without rest or water, took its toll. I honestly don't believe the accident was intentional. Her dying last words witnessed by my sister were that she loved us. Sitting in the front passenger seat, my brother had been ejected from the car on impact receiving severe burns from the car's exhaust pipe and a deep gash to his head. Sitting in the back seat behind our mother while sleeping, I was knocked unconscious. My face went through the car window shattering the glass causing multiple lacerations all over my face and legs requiring about thirty stitches on my face, plus my left femur had a compound fracture, splitting up the middle from the impact. My sister, who had been sitting in the backseat behind my brother, is who received the brunt of the emotional trauma for she was awake and witnessed it all. My little brother also witnessed more than I know.

My mom was and is my hero in every sense of the word. It is sufficient to note that at 1:17 p.m. (The time her wristwatch broke) on July 27, 1968, east of Delle, Utah, my mother, age 29, fell asleep at the wheel causing her car to cross the median and into oncoming traffic where her car ricocheted off of a double trailer semi-truck, killing her and leaving her three young children motherless, who were also inside the vehicle at the time and who suffered minor physical injuries. I was nine at the time, my sister eight, and my brother was seven years old. Against the wishes of our mother's parents, who asked to raise us, we were left in the hands of a proud clueless father who year after year would be gone for weeks and months at a time. We each endured a pretty rough loveless childhood of hunger, neglect, abuse, and intense degradation before finishing high school and moving out on our own.

Still, there were a few fond memories from those days. Directly following the funeral, Dad took us three kids on a drive to California to get away from it all. We intended to spend some time with his oldest sister, who lived there, but we never found her. It made us cut our trip short. My favorite part of that trip was visiting SeaWorld in San Diego. When we were at the Whale tank, I met an eternal friend who, once our eyes connected, I wanted to stay with forever. She was a huge Whale. There was so much love and comfort in her gaze that I desperately wanted and needed. Tourists came and went, but my new companion, Whale, and I stayed locked on the other. It was as though she knew the heartache I was experiencing. Dad kept getting after me to stay together. His words were, "That Whale doesn't know anything. It's just a dumb Whale." I cried and said, "Look, she hasn't left my side this entire time. She's talking to me!"

I'm the kid with a long history of things like having to be locked in a bedroom while they butchered a sheep because I was screaming at them that they were hurting the sheep. My dad gave in as long as I promised to stay there with the reassurance that he would come back to check on me. From time to time, my Friend would leave for the surface and then return to be with me. About an hour later, Dad returned in unbelief that my Friend and I were still gazing at each other. He warned me that our time here was limited and that I would miss seeing the rest of the aquarium with many other magnificent things. That was okay with me. Hours later, my dad returned, saying that we were leaving. I still cried, looking back at my Friend. My Friend lovingly looked me in the eye, telling me she understood along with the reassurance that I was going to be okay. Then she turned, and as I watched her floating to the surface for her much-needed breath of air, I knew our time was over. That afternoon with my Friend, the Whale, has never left my heart.

Other tender memories during those first weeks and months without Mom are of the family reaching out to do what they could. Mom's sister invited each of us one at a time to spend a week with her and her family. During my visit, she made me a dress and a personalized loose-leaf binder for school. Plus, I remember fun picnics up in the mountains and playing with my cousins.

Journal entry June 2, 1985: A couple of months ago, while visiting my mother's parents, I read over some old letters Gramma saved that I had written her not too long after I lost my mother. I can't forget the gloom of my youth but after reading those letters, I was much more depressed and alone than I remember. Gramma always encouraged me to write her or write in my journal to get whatever I was going through out on paper so that I could let it go. I was so patient and sensitive. It has always been my nature to have a pure heart. By this I mean, I never judged anyone or held grudges. I merely wanted to please and to love and be loved. I remember my father not coming home for weeks, none of which was job-related. Gramma and Grampa gifted us with half of a beef so that we would have plenty to eat. However, not paying the bills, the electricity would often be turned off for extended periods of time, and all the food spoiled. When our father did come home, we wouldn't tell him how hungry we were because we were sure he had a lot of more important and serious problems. He didn't say anything as he filled the garbage cans with all that food. I remember a treat was to find a slice of stale bread and dip it in old grease drippings. The three of us kids would split that one slice. We wouldn't be satisfied but it helped for that day. We loved our father and were very loyal to him. We rarely if ever complained about our circumstances. —End of journal entry.

Looking back, I now know that those weeks away were with various women, even married women. And that the trips he took to places like Mexico were with the insurance money he received from our mother's death. With that money, he literally bought a huge diamond ring for a married woman who ended up not leaving her husband. So while we kids went hungry and without nurturing or even electricity, he was out doing his thing. My father avoided contact with our mother's family and in most cases wouldn't allow us kids to visit them. Maybe it had to do with the guilt of spoiling all that meat but more likely a combination of that and his extravagant love affairs. In my heart, I don't think he understood our suffering. At least I hope not. Things like nurturing and caring for your children or even paying the bills were things he was clueless about.

We eventually lost our house and after a quick marriage moved in with one of his girlfriends. That's when my sister, brother, and my true hell of abuse and terror really began. Our new stepmother had some deep-rooted traumas of her own that she took out on us three. Daily physical beatings for things like talking to one another became part of our lives. Once she beat my little eight-year-old brother to a bloody mess while holding a wrench in her hand. However, it was the verbal demeaning mental, and emotional abuse that left the deepest scars.

One of my coping mechanisms was riding my ten-speed bike. While a teenager in high school, I was out riding my bike and happened to ride past the town's park. The baseball team, which my older step-brother was a member of, was practicing at the time. Before I was able to ride past the park, the entire team turned and started barking at me and calling me a dog. Many of those boys were my age and in some of my classes. You can imagine the humiliation.

All three of us left home at a very young age. My brother moved out and married before finishing high school. But before getting into when I left home, it is only fair that I mention my high school years. My circle or click of friends included Nancy, who had been held back a grade, her sister Sherry, Carol, and myself. Carol's mother passed from a massive stroke not long after our click became a thing. The traumas of our mothers' deaths bonded us together. One day while at Nancy and Sherry's house, the four of us decided to play around with an Ouija board. Not knowing what we were doing, we darkened the room and lit a candle. Before long we were playing around, taking turns with one of us laying down in the center and the rest sitting around her in a circle. We placed both of our pinky fingers evenly spaced under the person lying down and then chanted a few made-up words. It was all giggles until it was my turn to lie down in the center. My eyes were closed when the chanting began but suddenly, my friends were quiet. I waited a few moments before opening my eyes and questioning, "What's wrong?" They were surprised that I hadn't sensed anything because I had levitated and it terrified them. We never considered looking at, or playing with, mystical things ever again!

Between a messed up abusive stepmother, an absent father, and two privileged, demeaning step-brothers, things were pretty bad at home for my sister, my brother, and me. There were some pretty low days. My friends were worried that I might do something to hurt myself. I practically lived at Nancy and Sherry's house. Their mother told me I was always welcome to go there even if they weren't at home. Once, when we were sitting around the kitchen table, their mom suggested that we get involved in a school activity. That way I would have an excuse to regularly be away from home. Barely knowing how to swim, we all joined the high school swimming team. Sadly, not long afterward Nancy and Sherry moved to Eugene, Oregon. However, Carol and I stuck with the swimming team.

This was also when I started working at a local hamburger drive-in called the Iceberg, located in Draper where I lived. At first, I was earning a dollar per hour and gradually built up to somewhere in the neighborhood of three dollars per hour. I rode my bike or took the bus to and from the eight miles to school and the two miles to work. Swim practice was held at a middle school one mile from my high school. Swim practice was every weekday from 5:00 a.m. until school started, and then again immediately after school until 4:30 p.m. From school, I caught the activity bus straight to work from 5:00-10:00 p.m. I was definitely away from my family and home. Weekly home chores had to be done but it worked. That is how I survived high school.

Carol and I started hanging out with Karen and Kathy, who were twins. We became a new tight click. Not long after beginning our senior year, we decided to check out a place that had a DJ and dancing in Salt Lake City called the Wrecking Crew (Sugarhouse area off of 2100 S 1050 E). We were all wearing cute short dresses that we helped each other pick out. I remember wearing my shiny black go-go boots that went up to just under my knees. The place was packed full of people and loud music. We were just getting settled when this guy asked me to dance. It was hard to figure him out. He had a cool long afro but weird old-man-type white shiny shoes, old-man fitted white and blue plaid polyester pants, and a mismatched colorful green and yellow button-up aloha shirt. I think I only agreed to dance with him because I was so caught off guard.

It was a somewhat rebellious move on my part because my father had recently given me the talk that I was not to be with any Black boys. That happened after I received a call at home and my father answered. This was the early 70s when civil rights issues and university sit-ins all over the country headlined the news. To give you an idea of the demographics, all through my junior high and high school years there was only one Black kid, about ten Native kids forcibly living with white foster families, and no other Hispanics other than myself. I was raised to believe I was a half-breed Hispanic who didn't fit in. Getting back to the dance, this unusual guy with the big fro and I ended up dancing every dance together until my friends needed to leave. He said he was nineteen. As my friends and I were pulling out of the parking lot, we were talking about my dance partner when who else and his group of friends/cousins walked over to stop our car. He was asking for my phone number. I was hesitant but my friends were on his side.

At the time I was dating about five other guys. When he called, I didn't give him my home address. Rather I met him down the street from my house. We went to a hockey game in Salt Lake City. The big excitement at the hockey game was the players got into a couple of fights leaving blood on the ice. My date had a pretty heavy accent making him hard to understand but he was pleasant and respectful. As we sat watching the game, anytime a group of other Black men walked by, my date jumped up and greeted them with a LOUD energetic high-five.

After that date, he started planning out dates a couple of weeks in advance. Pretty soon the other guys I was dating stopped calling because I kept saying I wasn't available. On one particular date with this same dance partner, he took me out for a Sunday lunch and I ordered coffee. That's when things shifted.

In my heart I knew I didn't want to see him anymore. I told everyone at home, "If he called, I wasn't there." I don't remember who answered the phone but their eyes told me it was him. My family owned one phone attached to the wall in the kitchen. It had a long cord to the receiver, which for privacy, I took across the hall and into the bathroom. Hesitantly taking the call, I started with, "There is something I need to tell you." He said, "There is something I need to tell you too." We argued about who was going to go first until he convinced me to start it off. That's when I told him that I can't see him anymore because I'm of the Mormon religion and Mormons can't be with Blacks. He chuckled and said he was calling to tell me he couldn't see me anymore because he's Mormon and can't be with someone who drinks coffee.

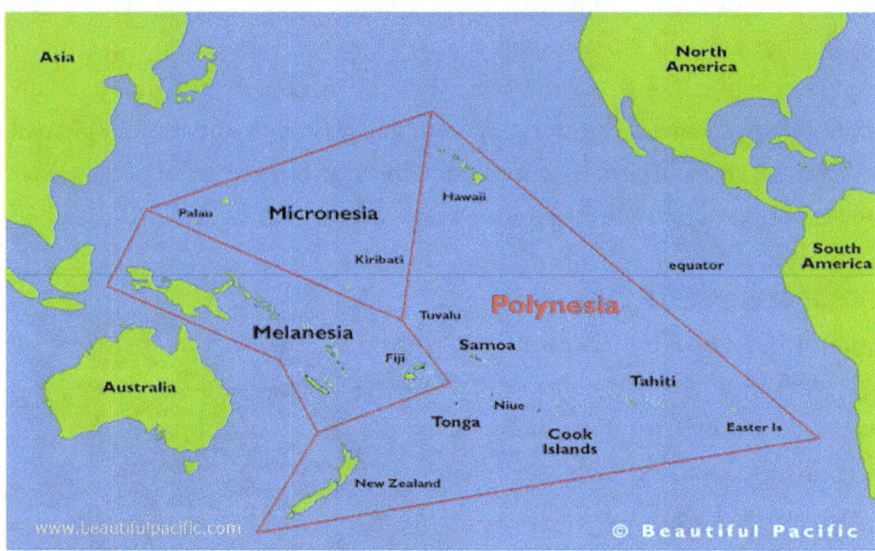

A good laugh later, he shared with me that he wasn't from Africa. Rather he is from the South Pacific Island of Tonga, which is like Hawaii. I had never heard of Tonga or any of the other island countries in the South Pacific other than just a little bit about Hawaii. He had moved to Utah two years earlier from Tonga and was living with his older brother's family. For the most part, Tongans were moving to Utah because of the Mormon Church. The church sends missionaries out all over the world. He shared that his family was one of the first to be converted to the Mormon religion and in fact, he served two years as a missionary himself. That's when he shared that he really wasn't nineteen, rather he was twenty-one. His family's goal was to work toward bringing their entire family to Utah so that they could live close to the prophet. Two weeks after that phone call, which was about six or so weeks after that first dance, it was New Year's Eve. That New Year's Eve we attended a church dance held at the Cottonwood Mall, where we were engaged to be married in the Salt Lake Mormon Temple for all time and eternity.

Between people not wanting to hire my fiancé saying he was either underqualified or overqualified, we discovered beyond race discrimination, people were genuinely disgusted by his and my mixed-race relationship. Wherever we went I witnessed the ugly come out on all sides, American and Tongan. Reflecting on those memories, decades have passed. Today's hindsight includes the knowing that bridges were being built. Bridges that our children and grandchildren solidified. Getting back to 1975 and my engagement, as I mentioned, his accent was pretty heavy. So much so that I had been engaged three months before knowing what my new last name was going to be. One red-letter day was my high school senior prom. My fiancé experienced car troubles, so picked me up driving a very old rickety yard work truck full of the day's branches and garbage. He dressed nicely though and was an okay dancer. I was later surprised to see a picture of us dancing together included in my Jordan High School Class of 1975 Year Book. That following August, at the time of our marriage I was seventeen and he was twenty-six.

Before going further, it should be understood that although I married into a Tongan family, it is a very complex culture that I do not claim to start to comprehend. For the most part, I honor and respect the Tongan traditions and find them a breath of fresh air. From what I know, to really grasp a culture is to be raised with mentors or elders who live and practice their traditional ways not only through your childhood but also through your adulthood. Even then there are going to be natural variations between families and the elders. Shared in these pages is simply my perspective as an outsider. Tongans are people who take great pride in treating people with the utmost respect. That respect, hid the realization from me of my being an outsider, for years.

Our first apartment was in Salt Lake City off 700 East. I found a minimum-wage part-time job working a cash register at a department store, and he found a job selling on commission. His job resulted in a multitude of expenses including parking tickets and zero income. Not able to pay those parking tickets with an arrest warrant hanging over his head, he decided we needed to move out of state. So, after a month of marriage, we landed in Idaho Falls, Idaho, sleeping on church lawns those first few nights. With several different types of churches scattered throughout the area, it was a very different environment from the dominant Mormon religion of Utah. Both of us quickly found jobs, me at a laundry mat and him as a supervisor at the sugar plant.

This was one instance where the dark color of his skin came in handy. I don't remember seeing any people of color in Idaho Falls. That resulted in a lot of eyes watching our every move. Interestingly, other than at work, that attention was positive. At work, there were ill feelings from deserving competent employees being passed over by this individual being paid more for knowing and doing nothing. On the flip side, within the community, we were invited to speak at activities all over town, mostly Mormon Church-related. Folks were curious and wanted him to share some of his life experiences, coming from the South Pacific. It was a sweet time.

However, having never been away from his family or the Tongan community, it wasn't six months before my husband became seriously homesick. All it took was one visit back to Salt Lake for the holidays, to discover that family was much more important than whatever financial solutions we found in Idaho Falls. Plus Idaho Falls was bitter cold. Much colder than Salt Lake. To top it off my husband's older brother got him an application to work at the Salt Lake Union Pacific Railroad. While waiting for the job results, we found an apartment building that was looking for a live-in manager instead of rent. Two antique stores occupied the main level of the building. Furnished apartments took up the next three levels with rent starting at eighty-five dollars per month for a one-bedroom.

The major drawback was that this particular building was located within a rundown slum area in the inner-city block frequented by prostitutes, drug traffic, and all that comes with it (240 Pierpont Ave). I can't tell you how many times I called the police due to a body lying on the sidewalk outside of our building. Nevertheless, we made it work. That is until one day like so many others, we planned to visit his family. As I was getting into the car, I remembered I forgot to lock the door to our apartment. He was angry but I went in anyway. When I returned, my husband was gone. It wasn't safe to stand there. I had no choice but to start walking toward his family. That meant walking four miles through the downtown area to the other side of the city.

After making it through the inner city and only a little more than halfway there, as bad as I wanted to get out from under the sun and rest for a bit, I noticed a man following me. He was about a block away. I kept walking as briskly as I could without revealing the terror I was feeling. Eventually, this man caught up to me and started a conversation. He had a very heavy accent. I soon learned he was part of an experimental work-core program and was here from Atlanta, Georgia. Going along with the small talk, I calmly stayed on course as though I had all the time in the world.

Several blocks later he started getting sexually aggressive, completely disregarding the fact that I was married and five months pregnant. I joked past his advances all the way until finally walking up to my brother-in-law's house in the Sugarhouse area. Another brother-in-law happened to be outside working on his car with his wife. I greeted my in-laws and the man quickly turned and started running. My brother-in-law asked me if I was okay before taking off in his car after the guy. We listened to the news a little more carefully after that because when my brother-in-law returned, he had left the guy unconscious in the gutter.

Meanwhile, it was one of the hotter days of summer and I was very dehydrated, flushed, and swollen. I think it helped that I was only eighteen. The family hurried and cooled me down with liquids and rest. Three hours later, it was dark when my husband finally showed up. He received a thorough tongue-lashing from his mother, his sisters, and his brothers. Although it was all in Tongan, a language I do not understand, it was obvious that he was in bigger trouble than he had ever before that moment been in.

When it came time to give birth, I ended up in the intensive care unit (ICU) with a serious previously unknown heart problem. I remember being wheeled on the stretcher away from my baby to the ICU past my sister and her saying, "What's wrong with her? She looks horrible." Twelve hours later, due to my concern about the possibility of my hospital visit not being covered by health insurance, I was able to convince my doctor to release me. My heart had stabilized but was unresolved. When my husband returned to the hospital after going home to sleep, he forgot to bring my lovingly packed bag of baby things: clothes, blankets, and a handmade quilt, all meant for our newborn son to go home in.

Luckily, our son was a bicentennial baby and received a special onesie t-shirt from the hospital otherwise he would have gone home with nothing more than his diaper. When we left the hospital, it was in the middle of a bitterly cold and windy snowstorm. I had no choice but to wrap my precious newborn in my filthy old coat. Holding him close helped to keep me from freezing too. The nurse wheeling me and my baby out to the car said you need your coat more than your husband. I nodded agreeing that we would just dash into the hopefully warm car.

How do I adequately share the roller coaster of emotions I went through those days? Before our son's arrival, my husband talked about how he wanted twelve kids and I always countered with nope, no more than two. As time grew close to giving birth, my fears and feelings of inadequacy dominated my entire being. The labor and delivery itself were pretty brutal not only landing me in Intensive Care but separating me from my newborn. As soon as I was allowed to hold my son, I asked to be released from the hospital. Once I held him in my arms, I couldn't stop looking at him in amazement and awe. Before that moment I had never felt that level of genuine deep unconditional love.

Nothing, I mean nothing else mattered more than him. We had created a precious new life more perfect and beautiful than I had ever before that moment comprehended possible. I couldn't take my eyes off of him even when he slept. In fact, that first night at home I stayed up all night just staring at and admiring him.

On the second day after breastfeeding him, he still seemed to be hungry so I made him a bottle of the formula that the hospital sent us home with. Huge mistake! He drank the formula and was sound asleep, then shortly after my milk came in, in full force. Live and learn as they say.

How my children survived all my bumbling shortcomings as a young mother at nineteen without examples to follow or guidance along the way, is beyond me. My motto was to raise my children with the opposite of what I experienced after losing my mother. Each child would wake up in the morning of their birthday with the house newly decorated celebrating their birth full of balloons, colorful crate paper streamers, and their name prominent in the space. Every holiday would be somehow personalized with our unique traditional decorations and gifts. We would bake all sorts of goodies together and I would tutor them with their schoolwork to the best of my ability.

From my perspective becoming a family was magical. Being a mother brought unimaginable joy and satisfaction as my world revolved around first, my son and then each child afterward. Their first smile and first giggle, their loving and soothing eye contact while nursing, and their beautiful spirits continually unfold revealing the best of us.

It was when my firstborn was six months old that I found myself again pregnant which was confirmed after a visit to the doctor. A few weeks later, I miscarried. This miscarriage broke my heart. Having discovered so much joy and love with my son, I now was on the same page as my husband in wanting twelve children. I loved and cherished every magical moment of being a mother. After the miscarriage, a couple of years passed of not getting pregnant. Then a short time after agreeing that we could be happy with one child, I again conceived. We were more than happy about the news. This pregnancy was different from my first. I was really sick not able to hold any food down, catching every virus that went around, including bronchitis with endless painful coughing, and to top it off, wrought with nightmares. Plus I developed a new fear. Would I be able to love this baby as much as I love my son?

The Universe provided us with an extra special gift. My beautiful tender-hearted new daughter was born on my birthday. Her birth was revelatory and glorious. The revelation I experienced was that I didn't have to divide my love between my new precious baby girl and her fearless older brother. Love magically multiplies bigger than ever! Imagine that, love not only multiplies, it becomes stronger as the most powerful force against all odds. Much like my firstborn, I was in awe of her perfection and beauty. It was extra fun getting to know and witness how her sensitive loving personality was a stark change from her brother who was the center of the Universe. Each new baby transformed the family dynamics making no two days the same and each arrived with their own amazing personality full of a love that again, only multiplied. By the time my thirdborn arrived, she was also her older brother and sister's baby.

Through the upcoming years, my heart continued to be an issue with episodes of beating in the range of one hundred eighty beats per minute. The real struggle was that it would get stuck there for hours or days. Triggers were unpredictable, often coming from being startled or even from bending over to pick up a piece of paper. Episodes lasting hours had little effect on my daily life and responsibilities. However, episodes lasting days would land me in bed or the emergency room. All in all, my heart condition was just part of our active happy life.

Like previously mentioned, I kept a moderate journal that I'd like to share a few selections of. Entries about my children's childhood reflect a healthy involved growing loving family. At least that is my perspective. My kids were my life. Memories of my married life, and raising our children are filled with love and joy and are among my happiest. Belatedly, I took a step back to reflect deeply on various patterns having to do with a few of my adult struggles that led to my divorce from my children's father. To help me untangle some of these darker struggles I pulled a few of those journal entries to share. Writing about these things is simply how I process them. Before writing them out, they live as chaos in my mind. Once I put them on paper, I can move forward and let it all go. Again, I can't emphasize enough that the majority of my journal and my memories are filled with love and pride in my children and the magnificent people they have become. Although not all are a part of this work, those entries are available to members of my family with the desire to see them.

-- Journal entry October 5, 1984: *It's 11:00 at night, and all five kids, including my five-month-old, are peacefully sleeping. I want to make a note of how much happier our family is now than it has been in a long time. I'm proud to say I'm truly happily married. I love my husband with all my heart. I have forgiven him for the hard times before and decided that sure I had a difficult time the last two months of this last pregnancy; sure five little ones are a lot of hard work, quite a bit more than planned but I was not going to add any more pressures to my husband. He is on-call with his job and only has a couple of hours' notice. The hours were never consistent and often took him away from home days if not a week or more at a time.*

After some unhappiness and contention, I made the decision that when he is home, it would be a pleasant, loving home with his kids happy to see him. He would not be asked to do one thing around the house or yard. It worked. Because I didn't expect any help from him, I stopped being disappointed or unexpectedly overloaded, and I became a much happier person. I learned to manage myself better and take care of priorities. Then, when or if he did come home and did help out, it was a bonus. Our life is continually improving. A couple of days ago I had some kind of flu bug where I couldn't even get out of bed. My husband came home with a pizza and stayed with the kids. The next morning he washed the dishes and cleaned the kitchen. That was truly a miracle. Last night we went out on a date to a movie, "Sam's Son," on the motorcycle with the baby who was a sweetheart. It was uplifting, refreshing, and enjoyable fun. I do love my man and respect him. Note: Our car, truck, TV, and oven all died on us, plus the clothes washer is leaving messages of dying soon but we're making it. – End of journal entry.

-- Journal entry February 15, 1985: A sad thing has happened in my heart. Years into the beautiful Tongan culture, I learned I had the mistaken illusion that marriage and birthing children in the family made me part of my husband's family. The harsh reality is that I will always be an outsider. My sisters-in-law and mother-in-law publicly say that I am raising my kids to disrespect their Tongan heritage.

This was shocking to me because it couldn't be further from the truth. In the Tongan culture, the sisters name their brother's children. My husband was one of the youngest in his family having six older brothers and sisters and two younger sisters. My kids have over fifty (First) cousins just on their father's side. At the time of my fifthborn's birth, his aunties gave him his first name and asked me to give him a middle name. Disappointedly, they gave my son the same name they gave his older brother. Two first cousins in the family also carried that name, making four first cousins with the same name, plus an uncle, and a large number of second cousins.

These aren't cousins who live in different parts of the world, they are cousins in the same close-knit community. As allowed, I gave my baby the middle name after my father's father who had no namesakes. The same grandfather who lost his life as a consequence of choosing to attend my mother's funeral rather than have the scheduled surgery to remove his prostate cancer. Naming my son after my grandfather, my grandmother quilted a yellow quilt with appliqued brown bears on it and a brown ruffled border for him. It's the only quilt she ever made for any of her grandchildren or great-grandchildren. Additionally of note, my oldest daughter's middle name is after this same grandmother, yet no quilt for her.

My maternal grandmother also quilted a brown teddy bear quilt for this son. Surrounding the teddy bears were navy blue bandanas. Bears are a symbol of strength and courage that this young son exemplified throughout his life. *At any rate, at every family gathering since his birth, my son's nickname literally became the four-hundredth 'name withheld.' Having my beautiful baby boy called the four-hundredth, bothered me so I chose to use both his first name from the aunties and his middle name after my Grandpa Williams.*

Believe it or not, what ended up happening was that my kids and I were shunned from their cousin's homes and given the silent treatment. The public pretense stemmed from one sister-in-law witnessing me refer to my baby by both the name they named him and the middle name that I gave him. Days earlier this same sister-in-law forbade me from calling my son by the name they gave him because that was her son's name and we live too close together for them to have the same name. Of course, once I was excommunicated from the family, I only referred to my son by the name I gave him. – End of journal entry.

Years later, reading between the lines and putting some puzzle pieces together of comments made here and there, I think there was more to my being excommunicated from the family than the issue with my son's name. The accusations were merely the groundwork and cover story for what the women in the family assumed was coming once the world knew of my husband's illicit affairs with various women. They obviously knew more than I did about my own husband.

A few months later, on August 1, 1985, I suffered my third miscarriage. The other two miscarriages were before and after my firstborn. My maternal gramma stopped in for a brief visit and looking for sympathy, I told her about my miscarriage. I was complaining about how busy I was having to teach this emergency preparedness class along with my doing Cub Scouts and caring for my family. Gramma surprised me with her response. She said, "It's probably a good thing that you're so busy. I've seen many women go to a dark place from having a miscarriage." As I said her response caught me off guard but flowed with infinite wisdom. She was right and I knew it. With respect, how could I complain after that?

-- Journal entry August 11, 1985: *I really feel our marriage is starting to bond together again. It doesn't seem to take much for the bottom to fall out but we are blessed.* – End of journal entry

-- Journal entry July 27, 1988: *July 27, is typically a somber day for me as it's the anniversary of my mother's traumatic death. Today I would like to reflect back to last July 27. Last July 27 was not only this gloomy anniversary but it was also the day I never expected to live past. I never expected to live longer than my mother who died at the age of twenty-nine. I was twenty-nine and my oldest kids were the same ages, as my sister, brother, and I, at the time of the accident.*

It's hard to express the mixture of emotions that were going through me. In somber reflection, I was looking out the kitchen window doing dishes when the phone rang. It was my husband's older sister. In a frantic voice, she asked for her brother and when I told her he wasn't home she hung up on me. The window I was standing at looked out on our backyard and had a view of the front of this sister's home. Those were the first words she spoke to me in three years since my being excommunicated from the family over my son's name.

I saw someone running into her home. The phone rang again and it was this same sister. I could hear screaming in the background. She told me this was serious and she needed to talk to her brother. I responded that I was telling the truth, he wasn't home and I didn't know where he was. And then I screamed back, what is going on? She said that something was wrong with their younger sister. (Before my ex-communication, this younger sister and I were the best of friends.) I hung up the phone and ran over to find a house in crisis.

My husband's mother and older sister were in the living room hysterically screaming and crying. They told me that an ambulance was on the way. Their younger sister had put a knife through her chest downstairs in the basement

and was dead. I asked where the kids were. This was the first time I had been in the house in three years since being shunned from the family. I told them that I didn't care what they said, I was taking the kids to my house for popsicles. They don't need to be here to watch their mother put on a stretcher and taken away! They'll never unsee it!

Standing tall, I walked through the house and went in to find all eight frightened children (Five of one sister whose home this was and three who were now motherless) silently looking at me to know what was next. The oldest was about fourteen, and the youngest was about four. I gently told them to come with me to my house for some popsicles. As we were filing down the hall, then down the stairs and out the front door, my husband's mother and sister asked if they could come too. Just that fast, we were back to being family, helping each other through the tenderest of times. – end of journal entry. Note: My sixthborn was three months old at the time.

My family and my entire neighborhood of newer starter homes of young families were immediately immersed in a cultural experience, unlike anything I had ever known. Although married into it, my understanding of the Tongan culture only scratches the surface of its complexities. Within the hour word spread of my sister-in-law's devastating death and families started arriving to show their support. It had been my experience with my mother and grandfather's deaths that family and neighbors show up with a casserole or baked item to leave with the mourning family and give their condolences. I soon learned that in the Tongan culture, families drop everything, run over, and stay for as long as it takes in support.

Soon there were literally hundreds of people of all ages in and around my home, and everyone seemed to know their role. I was surprised at how organized it was and learned to appreciate and value these traditional roles. My six children happily gave up their bedrooms for these new guests and moved into my husband's and my bedroom. The older women occupied the living room, the young women were in the kitchen, where it seemed to be non-stop cooking because all of the guests needed to be fed. The children played in the backyard and the majority of the teenagers hung out sitting on parked cars that now lined the entire neighborhood.

After considering space needs, a group of men erected an arch-shaped altar out of wood that was probably about eight feet wide by six or seven feet high, on the grass of our front yard. This new temporary altar was further marked with hand-woven mats under and in front of it. To one side of our property was a cement pad we used as a double basketball court. That was soon filled with canopies, portable banquet tables, and folding chairs.

The following day after things were set up, an older man whose role was to represent the family of the deceased, sat on the ground cross-legged on the mats under the wooden arch-shaped altar where guests lined up to pay their respects and make offerings. Guests didn't line up randomly, rather they lined up in family groups according to their relationship with the deceased. Then after making their presentations, many sat on the surrounding grass. Speeches and some reverent singing happened ceremoniously. Additional speeches and sounds of comforting songs were held in our downstairs family room which was the location for the men. The men's singing in the family room were all-nighters. The daytime outside ceremony lasted about three days, while the inside downstairs all-nighters lasted several weeks.

One morning about two or three days into it, when all was quiet, I looked out at the neighborhood to find garbage in the streets. Grabbing a garbage bag and broom I started cleaning it up. This is when several neighbors started coming out to talk to me. I was sure between the noise levels, dense traffic, garbage, and all of it, they were angry but instead, I was met with the deepest condolences of love. Even the garbage was a nonissue. As curious as they were, they were waiting for the right moment to respectfully ask about what was happening. Afterward and for the duration of those weeks, several of my neighbors dropped by with cases, literally cases of soda and other perishables for the crowd. I think my exchange with the neighbors caught my guests' attention for afterward teenagers maintained the garbage around the neighborhood. The best word I can find to describe it is 'harmony.'

Before this experience, I felt sorry for people with multiple families living together under one roof. To top it off, we only had one bathroom. Then as abruptly as it all started, they were all gone. The first day of public school marked the end of that portion of the mourning period. During it all, I would look out and see our ten-foot by ten-foot sandbox tightly filled with very young children playing together. I don't remember tantrums or screaming, only respect and giggles. The grass area of the backyard is where older children played various outdoor games. The grass area of both the backyard and front yard became bare from this event but soon grew back, and the neighborhood soon returned to the quiet place it had previously known.

To my shock, I missed it and I missed everyone. As I recall, one of the first nights after my sister-in-law's death, or rather very early in the morning because activities and singing went on all night, I got up to go in the kitchen. What I discovered were sleeping bodies all down the hallway, the living room was filled to the max with sleeping bodies as well as the stairs leading to the downstairs family room. Can you imagine sleeping on stairs? Whatever complaint I had in my mind about my family of eight being in one room, we actually enjoyed the most comfortable arrangement of anyone. At least we had a king-size bed. Two of the other rooms had bunk beds and the downstairs boy's room had a queen bed. My deep respect and love for so many of the Tongan traditions grew even deeper through this experience.

Life tends to keep moving. Sadly, shortly afterward, one of my husband's older brothers and father to five children was hit by a drunk driver and killed a few blocks from his home.

-- Journal April 16, 1990: Snapshot Children Spotlight
*My firstborn has chosen not to play baseball this season which is a surprise. He says he wants to devote his energy to basketball and is

playing on three different teams. He's a great player. He is also in an experimental class of seventh-grade algebra and getting straight A's. Next year he'll be in geometry. He sure is a nice young man.

*My secondborn seems to have always been my right hand. After all, she was born on my birthday. She has the tenderest of hearts and gives her whole self to please or make everyone's life around her better. To summarize, she's extremely creative, fearless, always thinking ahead, as smart as can be, and of all of us, is the responsible one. When I broke down at my grandfather's death, she was just as broken. Today she turned in her Girl Scout cookie money. At first accounting, she was short ninety-one dollars. You can imagine the stress and tears. She wouldn't receive any allowance until December. After closer inspection, she is only short twenty dollars, will go without allowance for two months, and is currently very happy with that. Many lessons were learned for all of us this cookie season. The good news is that the reward for all her efforts is that she'll be going to Girl Scout Camp this summer. She's my sweetheart, always pleasant and helpful. I really love her.

*My thirdborn, oh where do I begin? What a joy, what a character, what a tease. So many times just because she cares, she does the thorough clean-up of the bathroom or the kitchen or whatever without being asked or helped or noticed. On her own, she takes care of the little ones, makes up games or goodies, or takes a shower complete with shampoo. She does excellent in school too. One of her dearest traits is that she doesn't care who people are, she treats, or I should say, teases them all equally. She has a great ability to comprehend the whole picture of life. I was nineteen before I could do that and actually have yet to master it.

*My fourthborn was involved in an accident at school a couple of weeks ago. The school children were in the auditorium/cafeteria watching an assembly. My daughter happened to be sitting by the kitchen serving station which was closed off with one of those metal dividers that pull down from the top. The cook was pouring hot grease down the garbage disposal and then turned on the cold water causing it all to explode. My daughter received a large third-degree burn on her shoulder and two smaller ones on her waist. It was a panic-ridden situation that the teachers handled wonderfully. I cried all the way to the school fearful of what I would find. It's so hard to have your little one hurt so badly like that.

*My fifthborn is in kindergarten. I was worried about how he would do in school because he was a little slower in speech and in understanding discipline. In fact, he received a very low entry test score and would have failed to go into kindergarten had the school not been so familiar with me and our family, but he's doing excellent. He is one hundred percent aggressive and always competitive. He has a pure heart and tries to be good. What more could a mother ask of a son? I do love him. (Hindsight, by the end of the year he received the highest test score, and halfway through the next year of school we discovered that my son was ninety-five percent deaf. It wasn't until the surgery that we learned he had been deaf since he was a baby. He was so high functioning that none of us picked up on his deafness, including doctors, school teachers, family, and the myriad of normal social interactions. All this time, he had somehow taught himself how to lip read. I remember spending extra time helping him correctly pronounce words and intuitively having him place the palm of his hand on my cheek as I say a word and then on his own. Phenomenal!)

*My sixthborn just celebrated her third birthday three days ago. Is life ever so magic through those sparkling eyes? We sure needed her. Of course, everything she does is cute. Yesterday the girls were letting her boss them around and discipline them as though she were the mother. Last week, without even knocking, she walked right into the neighbor's house, up the stairs, and into the kitchen. My phone rang, with this dad on the other end. He says, "Are you missing anyone?" I looked around and hesitantly responded, ah apparently I am. He came back with, "Let me just put it this way, there's a naked little girl sitting on my lap eating my food." Yikes, I'm on my way. Yeah, this little girl is a handful but she sees herself as a big person. She's a character and a joy. – End of journal entry.

-- Journal April 17, 1990: Today my heart is at peace with the sorrows in my life; my mother's death, my crazy teenage years, Grampa's death, marriage problems, as well as my husband's sister and brother's deaths. I'm a different person today than I was before those experiences and I feel somewhat stronger thanks to them.

Currently, my dad is going through a divorce. In a strange way my sister, brother, and I are each happy about it. Just before Christmas, my sister, my kids and I went over to my brother's. My dad was there too. My brother started talking to our dad which he hadn't done since our mother's death twenty-two years earlier (He always gave our father the silent treatment). Everything fell like dominoes. We kids had and continued to endure an unhappy childhood for the sake of our dad's marriage. Our dad on the other hand, claimed he had been enduring an unhappy marriage for us kids.

Each one of us individually suffered over twenty years of lonely unhappiness for the sake of the other. All this time we felt terribly unloved. What a surprise to discover how deep down we really really loved each other. My sister and I enjoyed several heartfelt wonderful talks since that time. That emptiness and disappointment I've had towards my own family are finally gone.

Before I forget, the major big news of the year is that my husband got his job at the railroad back. He was out of work for one year and ten days. We actually lived through it. It's been a good year of bonding our marriage, supporting each other and building each other up. I believe for the first time he has been able to see how hard I work each day and that he finally might see or find some respect for me.

I'm in my third year as a Girl Scout Leader, my second year as Cub Master, the Girl Scout Family Event Chairman, and the Girl Scout Day Camp Director. Plus it's my sixth year earning an income doing full-time daycare for several children in addition to caring for six of my own. During the summer months, I serve lunches for about eighteen children. It's a busy household and it's our home too. I'm very happy with things and very grateful for my husband's job back. – End of journal entry.

On the lighter side, I just had a memory I'd like to share of how the kids would hold weekly dance competitions in our living room. They would take turns picking songs and performing their solo routines and then all at once, everyone would get up and show their stuff. It was a hoot and something we couldn't get enough of. I should also explain that I was one of those moms who missed each of her kids when they were in school or any time they were away. I wondered if they missed me too. Along this line of thinking came the idea to create fond memories. What can I do to help them be excited about coming home? Of course that meant a well-kept home they could be proud of but the best way is through their stomachs. Paying close attention to the clock, I would time it so that just as the kids were walking home from school, they would smell freshly baked cinnamon rolls meant just for them. That was such a hit that it became a regular occurrence.

Another fun memory that comes to mind is when my oldest was in the fifth or sixth grade. We sat around brainstorming ideas of what he could do to enter the school's talent show. They came up with the idea to choreograph a dance to a children's song we loved called, "The Gorilla Rap." "The Gorilla Rap" is a lesser-known song with fun jungle sounds and exaggerated comical lyrics. My son had one huge restriction to this idea of his going on stage and dancing. He would only do this if he could wear an actual Gorilla costume with his face covered. The girls wanted in on this too and loved the idea of dressing up like Jane in the Tarzan cartoon and dancing on each side of the Gorilla.

The kids created and practiced their dance while I figured out costumes. Unfortunately, there was no Gorilla costume to be found. I had to special order one but the cost was so prohibitive that I could only order the mask. The company I worked with was sympathetic and suggested that I buy the fur sending them enough for the mask and simply making the body suit portion myself. With my son's help in choosing it, we picked out an oak brown long-haired fur. As I recall, that mask was in the neighborhood of seventy-five dollars. It cost as much as the entire piece of fur but turned out awesomely realistic. For the girls, I used a large leopard print flannel fabric. Their dresses were tied over one shoulder, leaving the other shoulder bare, plus they had the stereotypical jagged hemline. Making their long hair messy and going on stage barefoot worked out perfectly. The Gorilla, however, wore white athletic shoes.

I have to say, my son was the envy of the school. He totally nailed some pretty fancy dance moves and my daughters were as cute and polished with their routine as could be. Few in the audience, including his best friends, knew who the Gorilla was. But some recognized his sisters and the word quickly spread. It was crazy fun and an absolutely hilarious hit for the talent show. The extravagant expense of that Gorilla suit was so worth every penny. Plus, over the years almost every kid including cousins and neighbors had a turn being the Gorilla for Halloween and however many costume parties. The outfit had its own waiting list.

Moving on, at the age of five, my fifthborn asked me to teach him how to ride his hand-me-down bike. This is the same son who we didn't realize at the time that he was deaf. I explained ro him that I couldn't run beside him without triggering my heart but let's go ask our neighbor. This particular neighbor lived several houses away and had three boys who were part of my daycare. He's also the very same neighbor who called me about a naked girl sitting on his lap eating his dinner. In fact, this dad was the bishop of our church, and our families were close friends. The timing was perfect and this dad was happy to come over and teach my son. Holding the bike for him as my son got on it, this neighbor started explaining how riding a bike works and how he would run beside him as many times as it took while he figured it out. Attentively, my son listened but before our neighbor was finished explaining things, my son took off riding with no assistance or even so much as a push. He rode that bike as though he had been riding all along. Both my stunned neighbor and I looked each other in the eye just grinning.

Oh, and how can I not share what happened that Christmas Eve that was like no other? The kids and I were in the kitchen and adjoining living room busy happily finishing up with holiday preparations when my four-year-old youngest daughter ran into the space and hid under the kitchen table. We knew something was up but she wouldn't tell us. She just looked at us with huge scared eyes, trembling as she held her knees tight to her chest. Alarmed, I hollered at everyone, "Search the house!" What we discovered was a bedroom closet engulfed in huge hot flames!

Before the Fire Department arrived with sirens blasting, the kids and I were able to extinguish the fire. The only damage that happened was my oldest daughter's loss of all her clothes. The closet was so disheveled that the fire didn't even reach the carpet or walls and woodwork. Still, the Fire Department had to stick around to inspect each electrical outlet and wall to ensure there weren't any hidden active embers. Thank goodness for messy bedrooms, at least in this case. The firemen were extra friendly and playful too. To this day, we never learned what was going on in my young daughter's curious mind or even what she used to start that fire. We had a wood-burning stove in the downstairs family room, so even at four, she knew about fire safety. One thing is for sure, it gave us each something to talk about, especially each Christmas Eve.

While we're on the subject of memories, there was the day my oldest, who must have been about seventeen, came busting in my bedroom door after hearing me and my youngest, ugly out loud sobbing in my room. He burst in with, "WHAT'S WRONG?" We were both sitting up on my bed next to each other sharing an open book in our laps. We were crying so hard we couldn't speak. All we could do was look at him while mumbling incoherently and pointing at the book. He was like, "All of this over a book!" Then turned around and left closing the door hard behind him. To this day reflecting on that moment triggers hysterical laughter. Totally comical.

Previously mentioned is my heart condition and how it just became a part of our life. The truth is there were times when it became center stage. This is probably a good place to pause a minute and talk about that. One such time was when I was a no-show to a Cub Scout Pack Meeting that I was facilitating as the Pack Cubmaster. A pack is a cluster of dens. Dens are determined by age and the number of boys. Often there is more than one den per age group determined by the number of boys. Our Pack Meeting was held at the church on a weeknight and included about twenty boys plus their leaders and families. We're talking about around sixty to seventy-five people. Several of the boys weren't members of the Church but were full members of their den and pack.

This particular Pack Meeting was a rather extravagant event with a number of interactive activities planned. The only problem was that the only person running these activities was absent. Calling my home they only found my kids. Not wanting to alarm my kids, nothing further was said. Patiently waiting as long as possible, the bishop of our ward causally called and talked to my oldest daughter who told him that I had to stop by the Emergency Room before the Pack Meeting. Straight away the bishop called the Emergency Room. Pretty soon a phone was brought in where I was hooked up with all these wires and my bishop needing to talk to me. I apologetically informed my bishop that what started out only needing no more than a couple of hours four hours ago, got a little more complicated.

The doctor just informed me that they weren't going to release me anytime soon and that we needed to postpone the Pack Meeting. What a mess. I was out of the tachycardia but my t-wave was upside-down, which whatever that meant, was something they didn't like. A few hours later I convinced the doctor that I would take it easy if they let me go home to be with my kids who were alone and growing more anxious. That two-hour hospital visit turned into eight hours and a little Pack Meeting drama. I couldn't apologize enough to my kids for the scare I gave them but reminded them that in my case some people freak out more than needed when talking about heart conditions. Years later we learned that I had a hole in the lower left ventricle of my heart from a birth defect. It's something that runs on my mother's side of the family.

Another incident was private between me and my two oldest daughters. My tachycardia was a longer-lasting episode, so much so that my body wasn't getting the oxygen needed and depleted my strength beyond clammy and weak. Laying on the loveseat in our living room my daughters were at my side counting the beats for me so that I could let my cardiologist know when I called him. While one daughter watches the time the other places her ear to my heart and taps with a pen on paper for every beat within that given time. It's a nice system. For good measure, they typically do it more than once.

As trained as they were, on this particular occasion, they struggled to find a heartbeat. It was at that moment that I was lovingly looking down at them and my body. I was completely filled with love and bliss and instantly surrounded by glorious gold and white light. It was indiscernibly fantastic, so much so that I didn't want this totally blissed-out experience to ever end. Nevertheless, my love for my kids was greater. I knew I needed to go back. The funny thing is, at that moment I knew it was my choice. The entire experience was a beautiful gift impossible to forget and a reminder that my purpose in this life is far from over. I later learned that this incident is described by the term, near-death experience or NDE. My NDE was simply magical.

Moving on to more day-to-day things, it was important to me that my kids were proud of their heritage. I wasn't taught about my Hispanic or Native American heritage, so little could be done there, but we could learn about my kid's Tongan heritage. In my search to learn more about Tongans, I turned to their traditional dances. Their dances typically tell of an ancestor or their personal story, hence retaining history. Through this quest, I found my dearest friend. She was

Samoan and married to a Tongan. A Tongan man we soon learned my kids were related to.

Tonga and Samoa are small island countries in the South Pacific Ocean that, along with Hawaii, and other countries, create Polynesia (Refer to the map of Polynesia on page 20). Before her marriage, this new Samoan friend was a professional Polynesian dancer who traveled the world performing with her family. We were like-minded and able to attract about twenty elementary-aged children to learn the dances and perform at their and other local elementary schools. Part of the performance was educating others about the different island countries in the South Pacific. This new friend/sister was the creator of the dances and designer of their authentic outfits. My role was coordinating/emceeing shows, financing, and sewing all the costumes.

Practices were held in and outside of my home. Those were days of charred circular spots on the lawn from my thirdborn learning and practicing her fire poi-ball routine. Poi-balls are traditional among the Māori people of New Zealand. They are typically stuffed fabric balls about the size of an orange, connected to a piece of about thirty inches of braided yarn in which the user twirls multiple balls performing various acts of coordination to match the lyrics and music. Fire poi-balls are a little more complex to create but you get the picture. We all enjoyed watching her practice her fire poi, especially when it was dark. This same daughter later became the Poi-ball dancer of the year for the State of Utah. This was a bonding time not only for this new best friend/sister and me but for our kids. Our two families naturally blended into one. This beautiful relationship carried my family through rough times ahead.

Before long, while at my oldest daughter's middle school graduation, the pure weight of the stress I was under found its way to my back. The pain was so excruciating I could no longer stand. I ended up missing her graduation; just lying on the grass outside of the school. It was two weeks before I could stand and function.

Fast forward a few years, in 1995 I found myself an abandoned single mother making about five hundred dollars a month working long graveyard nights doing data entry for UPS and having little marketable skills. I was illiterate. Plus I had this chronic heart problem. My twenty-year marriage was over. My husband once mockingly asked me "What will you do if I left, shovel snow to feed the kids because you won't get a cent out of me!" My response was if that was what I had to do, I would. Till the night that my husband left, I figured he and I would work whatever out like we always had before. I loved him with all my heart and planned on growing old with him. Devastatingly, on that day the truth came out. He no longer was just twisting that sharp knife through my heart; he had sexually violated our daughter!

While we were married, my husband wasn't around much so when he abandoned us, there was little change in our lives. Telling the kids that their father had left us, was a painful dark time. How could I ever soothe, comfort, nourish, and support these precious ones entrusted in my care? Mind you I was still deeply in love with my husband. Yet, reflecting, really reflecting, I began to see the pattern. A pattern I had before that moment, been too overworked and distracted from seeing. A pattern of my being betrayed by my beloved, only for him to betray me, time and time and time again, and each betrayal becoming more and more destructive.

The first time my husband cheated on me was when I was expecting our firstborn. I was barely eighteen and it was only a few months into our marriage. I was eighteen then but didn't learn of it until some church requirement came up when my firstborn was six months old. He claimed it was a one-night stand. This truth hurt me like no other. I took off in the car and because I was breastfeeding, I took my baby with me. So this is what my mother was going through at the time of the accident.

My first thought was to drive off a cliff. Then I looked over at my beautiful son and thought who can I leave him with? While looking at him, my heart filled with my overwhelming love for my son. Along with the realization that if he needed me in his tiny little pinky as much as my entire being needed my mother, driving off a cliff wasn't an option. From that moment on I never again had such thoughts.

So I called my sister who welcomed me into her home and allowed me the space to grieve and talk things through. She and my son were my heroes that dark day. Within a few hours, I returned home and worked through the process of the damage it did to our new marriage.

A few years later after giving birth to our secondborn, I received an overdue notice saying our electricity would be disconnected along with added charges if I didn't pay some strange Jenny's bill. Imagine that! Having to use my grocery money, not extra money, grocery money to pay some strange woman's bills! At another time I received a call from Blockbuster (A video rental store) asking why I hadn't returned the VCR equipment that I checked out. I responded that this was the first that I heard of it, we owned a VCR and didn't need to rent one. The lady from Blockbuster became alarmed about potential fraud and described the man and woman who rented the machine. I agreed with her that the man fit my husband's description but so did a lot of other men. And my having just given birth to my fourth baby, I definitely didn't match that woman's characteristics of being scantly dressed. She said, well, I'm sure even after just giving birth you would probably look better than that woman. We laughed about it then when my husband came home, I told him. He said not to worry about it and that he'd look into it. Weeks later when I went into a Blockbuster to check out some videos, or actually often when going to the bank or various places, the teller or the cashier would look at the name and questionably ask, "You're HIS wife?" It's worth noting that wherever he is, my husband has a loud often obnoxious way of making his presence known.

One Thanksgiving was held at our home with all of my husband's side of the family. It was a sit-down formal dinner for over seventy people with the entire space decorated complete with place settings, party favors and organized to include family updates and a talent showcase. We videoed it. This was meant to be a teaching moment for the majority who had never experienced a traditional American Thanksgiving or even traditional Thanksgiving foods. All through the day and on video, my husband was vocally rushing everyone. When the phone rang, we just let it go as a nuisance. This is long before cell phones. The caller kept calling back and calling back until I reluctantly picked it up. The caller said, "Hi this is Sharon. Where is 'my husband's *name withheld*?' My mom and everyone have been waiting for him for over an hour for our Thanksgiving!"

In front of my husband and his entire family, I loudly responded, "Sharon, I'm sorry you and your mother and family have been waiting. My husband is here with his wife, his children, HIS mother, his sisters, his brothers, and his nieces and nephews enjoying OUR Thanksgiving Dinner!"

Another glorious moment happened about the time of our fifteenth anniversary when the love of my life gifted me with gonorrhea. Even the church knew about this but took his side that there must be another explanation of how he passed it on to me that didn't involve sex with another person. Still, I'm the one having to go through government health clinic treatments. I have plenty more examples but you get the point. His lies over the years were more and more cunning as well as less and less discernable. His latest act of sexually violating our beautiful daughter was inconceivably heart-wrenching and couldn't be erased. It was now time to do whatever I needed to protect my children.

My Mormon church advised me against a rushed divorce. The church leaders and our kids were hopeful the marriage could be saved. I was scared to death with no money in the bank, bills piling up, and no way to support my family. My husband was true to his promise even during our year-long separation, of not giving us a cent. Finding part-time work paying seven dollars an hour with no benefits, as well as taking in sewing projects, I somehow managed to meagerly feed my large family and keep up with the mortgage.

As luck would have it, that part-time job was at a university. My illiteracy had to be my best-kept secret. At the time I literally couldn't spell or write a complete sentence. What this job required above a formal education was someone who could look at the bigger picture and think ahead about how things should be organized, structured, and acted on. Between life experiences raising a family and my years of volunteer church and scout activities, those were skills I had in spades.

-- Journal entry November 29, 1998: *A couple of nights ago my ex-husband dropped by the house to try and talk me into taking him to our son's basketball game. Instead of finding me, he was confronted by our oldest, who let his father know that his mom wasn't going with him. Neither one had talked more than a few words with the other over the past three years. (Legally, their father was not allowed to be in the proximity of the kids unsupervised.) During this visit, I was in the bathroom listening while cutting a child's hair and felt that it was better for me to stay out of it and let the two of them work it out. Unfortunately, things were said that were hurtful. For my ex, this was a fight for his position as the head of the family rather than what was best for the kids. Before this visit, my ex had gone over and fought with the husband of my best friend, whose family the kids and I had grown very close to. The guy is fifty years old and a total mess trying to convince anyone who would listen that if I would just forgive him and take him back everything would be okay.* – End of journal entry.

For seven years, which is how long Financial Aid lasts, I took a night class each trimester and learned what was needed professionally. By the end of that first year, I was not only full-time at my job but had benefits for my family. Eventually, I was even able to get my corrective heart surgery. As luck would have it, my surgery failed. The surgeon told me I was inoperable, but after changing doctors, my second surgery was a complete success. Things continued to be tight financially. However, for the most part, we were doing all right. One huge mistake I made with the divorce was keeping my married last name. At the time, I thought it would be easier for the kids if I were to have the same last name as them. Another mistake I made at that time was living in the same house and keeping things much the same as before the divorce.

A house is more than a house. In our case, it was a home filled with my, and my kid's sweet childhood memories. Those mistakes cast a glimmer of hope for some of the kids that our family would one day return to the way it was. More than once, I told my kids that we needed to start thinking of moving out of this house and making new memories. Over the next several years, I used my tax returns to fix it up. I painted the interior and the exterior, replaced the kitchen cabinets, bedroom doors, and fixtures, and installed new flooring. For the most part, my oldest daughter was a great help but in general, my kids didn't support the idea of moving.

The real trouble happened about the time the house was finished. It had been nine years since the divorce and I met someone. My kids stood firm against this second marriage. Talking with several others who experienced a second marriage, they assured me that it was normal for kids to behave this way about their mother and it would pass. Even my church leadership said as much. I also know of women who chose to live a life alone because of their kid's feelings on the matter. At the time of the divorce, I was in my thirties. I postponed the marriage two times before finally just ripping the bandage off and marrying this man I had fallen in love with.

What was intended to be full of love and the moving forward of our family, became a shipwreck. Initially, this second marriage started in our same home. My children's childhood home. Each day my new husband was made to feel more and more unwelcome. A year into this second marriage, things continued to crumble rather than improve. It was apparent that the hard decision made years earlier to move, needed to happen. That move really hurt the kids. My youngest at the time was seventeen halfway through her senior year in high school. I fixed up a bedroom for her and invited her to move to the new home with me and this second husband but she wouldn't consider it.

Things continued to deteriorate. It went from my being uninvited to attend my youngest son's high school graduation and being uninvited to attend my daughter's newborn's naming ceremony to a year later being uninvited to attend another daughter's wedding. The daggers to my heart just kept coming. Then out of the blue sky, four years into this second marriage, I received an offer to apply for a job clear on the other side of the country at the University of New Hampshire. I had never traveled more than a few hundred miles from Salt Lake City and didn't even know where New Hampshire was.

Getting the job, I let my kids know of my forthcoming move and invited them to get together for dinner. My mother's sister even offered to host the dinner to help make it more comfortable for everyone. At the time we all lived separately but within minutes of one another. After waiting several days to hear back from my kids about the dinner plans, the phone rang. Representing all six of my kids, my younger son informed me that they were sorry but the only day they all had available was October 13, and they were using that day to take their father to dinner for his birthday. His birthday was on October 21. My move was scheduled for November 6.

During the job interview visit on-site in New Hampshire, my husband and I fell in love with this beautiful property located in Maine, close to the border and only a ten-minute drive to my new job. Asking around, living in one state while working in another, was common in that area. It was just a trailer home, but it sat on two acres of beautiful woodlands secluded from the road and not far from the ocean. Plus it was well within my price range. We contacted the Realtor, expressing our interest. The Realtor noted that the property had been on the market for months and that the seller may be interested in renting it while waiting for the closing. He promised to follow up with the seller and recommended I get back to him once my Utah home was sold. Having a nineteen-foot trailer, we also found several trailer parks in case we needed something in the interim. Feeling comfortable about having a place to live once our move took place, things started to fall into place. My new job included moving expenses, plus the house in Salt Lake sold quickly.

Moving about three thousand miles, from Utah to New Hampshire, the distance from my kids and my sister hurt deeply while at the same time, it strengthened me in ways I didn't know I had. Part of the reason for my move was to have distance from the pain of being within minutes of the kids and yet not a part of their lives. Another part was to see if this second marriage had a chance. But the deciding reason was for a new adventure. It was time to do something in my best interest professionally and emotionally. It felt right in my heart.

Having closed on our Salt Lake home, with light hearts my husband and I embarked on our move across the country along with our German Shepherd dog, Liberty. The trip was slower due to stopping as frequently as possible to take Liberty for walks. By day three, Liberty was done with being couped up in our tight quarters but she was forgiving and sweet at the same time. Then we received a call from my Realtor in Salt Lake that the bank changed its mind. Our Salt Lake home was no longer sold. How is that possible? The bank uncovered something they didn't like about the buyer. I immediately placed the house back on the market and it sold the following day. But that meant four to six weeks before the next closing. Contacting the Realtor in Maine, he came back with oh, sorry that property you were interested in sold already. Having just lost the bulk of my moving expenses I called my credit union in Salt Lake sharing my predicament and requested a signature loan to hold me through the interim of this new closing date. My loan officer agreed to make it happen.

At the same time all this was going on, my husband's health deteriorated forcing me to stop at an Emergency Room along the route. There was little they could do for him due to our transient situation. This meant all the driving and overall arrangements continued to rest on my shoulders. The further east I got the more tangled roads seemed to be pulling a trailer. This was before GPS navigation was a thing. I had never seen so many lanes of bumper-to-bumper traffic or confusing toll roads. Traffic was fast-moving and fast to honk at you. It was as though everyone hated each other.

Before my move, the professors from my job at the University of Utah took up a collection. Little did I know that over three hundred dollars of that cash would go toward tolls. What a gift that was. To top it off all this extra stress made my dog throwing up sick.

A few hundred miles from our destination, the rain started. It wasn't raining like I was used to. It was a downpour. Unheard of to me coming from the west desert, this downpour ended up lasting all day and night for two solid weeks. Next, I needed to find a place to park my trailer. Reaching out to my church bishop back in Salt Lake, he was able to connect me with a local bishop in New Hampshire who granted me permission to park my trailer in the church parking lot for three nights or until church that Sunday.

Adding to the list was the need to get my husband's medical issues addressed. He was admitted to the hospital with blood clots in his lungs. So now, it's raining cats and dogs, my husband is in serious shape in the hospital, and my dog is sick and not able to get out much due to the rain, my interim living space vanished into thin air, and I have a moving truck arriving with no funds in the bank to pay for it.

Following up with my new job regarding the moving expenses, I learned it would be added to my first paycheck after I was in the system which they anticipate taking several weeks. Hearing my story, the accountant agreed to push through an advance for me but even that would take several days.

Next was finding a new home. My Realtor in Salt Lake hooked me up with a new Realtor in New Hampshire. The next day I was conditionally pre-approved for a new home loan. I also had to find another location to live once my three days in the church parking lot expired. All of that had to wait because the moving truck arrived and I had yet to find the funds. The mover informed me that he was charging me forty dollars an hour up to 4:00 pm the next day, after that my things would be placed in storage and the fees would be ten times more painful.

Being homeless you soon learn how limited your choices are. Still, I decided I needed to start growing roots somewhere in my new community. Up against the impossible I drove around and decided that that somewhere would be at a bank. The bank that stood out to me was TD Bank in Dover. Walking in I asked to speak to a loan officer. Showing my offer letter for my new job mentioning the paid moving expenses, my closing papers, and the correspondence from my Utah Credit Union for a loan, and from my movers with the clock ticking at forty dollars per hour as we speak, and hearing that upon arrival my husband was admitted in the hospital for blood clots, she said she wouldn't believe so many things could go wrong for one person is such a short amount of time if she didn't see it in black and white right in front of her eyes. She called my Salt Lake Credit Union who confirmed my money was sitting there but that it required another signature from someone who wasn't there.

Here I am, a stranger off the street sitting across the desk from this beautiful loan officer, when she suddenly said, "This is ridiculous!" Right then, and there, she wrote out a bank check to the movers for the exact amount required! With tears of gratitude, I hurried off to the movers. While on the way my new job called to tell me I could stop by at my convenience and pick up my moving allowance check. What should have taken days or weeks took a few hours. With minutes to spare the movers left and I had my possessions. Within two hours I was able to stop back at the bank and deposit my check to cover what this beautiful loan officer advanced me. While at the bank, my Salt Lake Credit Union wire transfer came through. From a humble leap of faith, what felt impossible that morning transformed into miracle upon miracle that afternoon.

Time to breathe.

Moving forward, the success at my job in New Hampshire and in making some beautiful new friends made things bearable and even wonderful. I found and bought a cute little home in Rochester, New Hampshire, on an acre lot in the middle of the woods. It had a fenced-in backyard for Liberty, and a huge secluded pond within a ten-minute hike. Even the twenty-minute drive to work each morning and back home each night was magically surrounded by endless tall vibrant trees, flowers, hills, curves, ponds, and wildlife. Imagine being the only car driving down a steep curvy mountainous hill to find a flock of wild turkeys caught off guard and clumsily trying to scoot out of your way. That same hill wasn't so fun in the winter when I spun out of control and thought I would end up at the bottom of the pond with no one finding me before spring. Happily, that particular adventure just cost me the need to replace a tire. But overall the people were the best part. They were welcoming and supportive.

Soon after moving to New Hampshire a friend from work invited me to participate in a healing sweat located about an hour from me in Maine. It has been my teaching that a traditional sweat lodge is run by a Lodge Keeper who not only has been chosen but has endured a number of vision quests over years of teaching ceremonies from an Elder Sweat Lodge Keeper. I joined this friend and found a sweat lodge run by several Anglos. They were given some Native teachings in exchange for financial support. The entire experience felt artificial and was more like going into a steam room of adult children playing house. I never returned.

As I mentioned earlier, one of the reasons for moving away from my kids was to see if this marriage was salvageable. It wasn't, and it had little to do with the kids. He now had become addicted to prescription painkiller medications. His outbursts were violent. Eight months after our move to New Hampshire, I could no longer walk the path of this second marriage. He moved back to Salt Lake while I continued on in New Hampshire. However, New Hampshire didn't accept my application for a divorce before living there for at least a year. One more hurdle or at least that's what I thought. I say that because when I did go to court requesting my divorce it took several extra months in addition to the year because they lost my paperwork. You can't make this stuff up. If you did, who would believe you?

This was the day when alone and on the other side of the country, that in my perception, I turned my back on the judgmental jealous vengeful God I loved, the church I dedicated so much of my life to, and simply all of it! It was during this turbulent time of what I perceived as my emotional and mental rock bottom, that I started to question the limiting, narrow-minded dogma of my situation. At the same time, my job flourished and my new lifelong relationships within the Native community deepened. It was one of those things where you meet someone and feel like you've known this person your entire life. This happened over and over for me in New Hampshire. It felt like I was home. Weekends during the warmer months were filled with days and nights spent at various powwows, campouts, gatherings, sweat lodges, ceremonies, and making new friends. One of my dearest friends was Pat Lilly.

I soon learned that not only was Pat the organizer of the Medicine Bear Pow Wow but she was an esteemed Elder of the Native community, a Pipe Carrier, a Sweat Lodge Keeper, and a Drum Keeper. It is no small feat to be called to fill just one of those roles. Each role requires years of apprenticeship and multiple vision quests. Not all teachings are identical across the tribes. Essentially, a vision quest is typically when an individual works for several months, years, or however long it takes with their mentor toward a particular purpose. This objective is completed upon a series of four-day hard fasts abstaining from food and water out in solitude while maintaining their sacred fire. In the advent their fire goes out before the four days are up, the quest is considered incomplete. I once supported a friend who went out on a vision quest. By support, I mean small things like gathering supplies beforehand and organizing the feast afterward. The day after he started, we had a downpour of rain that lasted two days. Can you imagine keeping your fire going through all of that? Somehow he was successful with a newfound inner strength to be admired. It took Pat about ten years of persistent teachings and vision quests before being called to be a Lodge Keeper. Likewise separately for each of her roles.

When asked for assistance in a good way with a gift of tobacco, a Pipe Carrier/Lodge Keeper Elder is obligated to fulfill that request, which is the role Pat filled for the community. It wasn't long before I became Pat's helper in collecting supplies and supporting her in these ceremonies. As a Drum Keeper, the Drum would be invited to various Pow Wows throughout the New England states. I became part of the Drum as a singer, standing behind the drum and shaking my Turtle rattle. Pat and I literally traveled much of Maine, New Hampshire, and Massachusetts weekly. One particular week we held four sweats, each spaced a

Debra dancing in traditional regalia at the Medicine Bear Pow Wow (Rochester, NH 2010)

day or two apart from the other, three with Pipe Ceremonies. All of this was while Pat and I worked full-time at our respective challenging jobs, homes, and dogs.

On my way home at 2:00 am, driving forty miles after that Wednesday evening fourth sweat and pipe ceremony, I was a few houses from my home when blue lights started flashing. I was being pulled over for crossing the middle line. I think I looked down to change the radio station as the road curved. I responded honestly when the officer asked why I was out this late. "I'm on my way home from a Native American sweat lodge." He accused me of doing drugs and alcohol. I felt he was trying to offend me for my reaction. When I calmly denied doing alcohol or drugs, he asked me to stay in the car and wait. The calm still voice inside me said there was nothing to do but be silent and still.

You can imagine how dehydrated and exhausted I am after a long day at work from my full-time job, plus the work involved in the preliminary ceremony, sweat, and closing ceremony, and the fact that I had to wake up in three hours at 5:00 am to get ready for my next day at work.

Ten minutes later spotlights were on me when this officer returned with another officer. They both started badgering me with derogatory accusations against Native Americans. It felt as though for whatever reason they were trying to arrest me. I remained silent. The original officer told me he had been following me since I got off the highway and making a right turn I crossed the line on the right curbside of the road. Note, this meant he had been following me for seven miles. Seven miles of varying speed limits, two red traffic light intersections, and three stop signs. Yet, the only infraction he has on me is momentarily crossing the middle lane while looking down to change the radio station in the middle of the night with no traffic.

The officer asked if I would agree to a breath test, which I did. He got angry with me because I had a hard time figuring out how to do it plus as dehydrated as I was, I didn't have the strength. This was a new experience for me. Upon threat of being arrested and multiple tries, I finally got enough air in the thing. He hollered at me because it registered zero as though I would be surprised. For anyone else reading this who might be curious, sweat lodge ceremonies are sacred and only filled with love and healing energies. No Native American ceremony or activity I have been associated with has ever included any alcohol or drugs.

Okay, back to my so very important breath test. After it registered zero, the officer asked me to step out of my car. To my surprise, four police cars were circling me with their headlights, plus all these additional officers and their spotlights. I'm realizing the entertainment factor of my predicament. They wanted to look through my bag in the backseat which I agreed noting that it was just my stinky wet sweat dress and towel. I'm wearing a simple midi-length denim skirt, pastel-colored t-shirt, and flip-flops. The cultural bashing continued as they had me walk the line and hop on one foot, etc. before asking if I would submit to go to the station for a drug test. Still remaining silent through all of this, I rolled my eyes and agreed to go have the drug test. That's when they released me to drive the three houses to my comfortable bed and two hours of sleep.

A few hours later, at work, my boss, the dean, came in complaining about something on his way into the office. I returned the favor and told him about my morning. He looked me in the eye in disbelief and said, "You win."

Working at the University of New Hampshire (UNH) I received an occasional unsolicited visit from people in the Native community requesting that I organize a Pow Wow for the University and that I start a club for the Native students. My job at UNH was intense enough as it was with fifty-hour weeks, plus I wouldn't know where to begin. Several years passed before I finally agreed to attend one of the student meetings. The Student Diversity Counselor coordinated the group. Receiving a warm welcome, I soon fell in love with the students. By the third meeting, I was the new student advisor. Our meetings became a cherished part of my week. We created a website and calendared activities we entitled Wisdom Keepers. Local Native guests were invited to share their wisdom teachings either through stories or the arts of basket weaving, making Dreamcatchers, Indigenous recipes, etc. And then sure enough the students wanted their own UNH Pow Wow.

I quickly discovered that a few years prior to my arrival, UNH held a powwow that resulted in a huge blowup between UNH and the Native Community. Here I am oblivious to all of that and simply moving forward through the minutia of required red tape. Walking a fine line, I personally shouldered the many meetings between the UNH administration, including all the various facilities with parking and vendor needs. It was crazy and more and more obvious that it required an outsider such as myself without history on either side of the fence. Learning as we went, my students too, were working feverishly through all of this.

Then, having a handle on the powwow, I made a trip back home to Salt Lake City to visit my kids and grandchildren. There, I learned that my younger son qualified to compete in a worldwide event in his sport and that it was being held a few hours away from Salt Lake City in Mesquite, Nevada. You can imagine my pride and excitement when he asked me to be there. In my heart of hearts, I would do whatever it takes to be there. This is after years of silence between us. Then he told me the date.

As you probably predicted, yup, it was the same day as the UNH Pow Wow. Sadly, I had to turn down my son's only invitation to one of his professional competitions. Call it what you may, but I have a thing about following through with what I say I will do. It was one of those moments where there were no do-overs. That hurt cut deep. I was so disappointed that I started clenching my teeth and broke a back molar in the middle of the powwow. But thinking it through, I had already used up my vacation time. Had I tried to return for my son's competition, it might have cost me my job. It is what it is. No regrets, right?

Up to this point, I was able to take a week or two to vacation in Salt Lake for Thanksgiving or Christmas. My first Thanksgiving back was spent with cousins, as my kids had other plans. Years later, my most memorable visit was when I stayed at my youngest son's home and enjoyed several family gatherings. The day before returning home to New Hampshire, I had the warmest, most loving phone conversation with my newlywed daughter, who lived in California with her husband and new baby. The two of us figured out where I could fly into California the next morning and spend three hours with her and meet my new son-in-law and grandson, then fly back to Salt Lake in time to catch my flight home to New Hampshire. What a blast that was. More importantly, I finally got to meet my beautiful six-month-old grandson. It was a time of great healing for both my daughter and me.

On my next visit to Long Beach, California, New Hampshire was in the middle of a devastating ice storm with power outages and frigid temperatures causing trees to fall onto buildings. The widespread power outages meant the gas pumps didn't work. I witnessed my neighboring regularly generously kind people become fearfully defensive. It was ugly. What a change to arrive in sunny California. This particular trip was to spend a couple of weeks with this same daughter to help out when she gave birth to her secondborn. What a gift.

These precious little ones and their pure hearts are simply magical. They love so deeply with all that they are, so much so that they mourn and cry real tears when you leave. Each time one of my grandchildren cried after a brief annual visit, it became harder and harder for me to endure. Six years after moving to New Hampshire, I moved back to Utah. The timing of my move couldn't have been at a worse time financially. It was 2012, and my home's value crashed. All across the country, people were losing their homes. Even if I could sell my house at top dollar, I would owe the bank thirty thousand. As it turned out,

I walked away from my cute little home in the woods. Losing everything of material value while gaining my heart. A decision I never for an instant regretted.

It was a misty Sunday morning on Mother's Day when I drove away from my cute little home in the woods, driving a twenty-one-foot moving truck with a trailer to pull my car for a four-day drive across the country. On day three shortly after entering Wyoming, I stopped off for a late breakfast. You should have seen the waitress' shock at my reaction to her question, "What kind?" when I asked for hot sauce. I swear no one in New Hampshire uses hot sauce. That was a savored breakfast for sure. Making it to the other side of Wyoming, I slept in the cab of the truck at the Utah Welcome Center Westbound I-80 rest stop. Then, just after noon of the next day, I arrived at my fourthborn daughter's apartment with her husband and two kids whom I had planned to live with for a short term while she had her brain surgery to remove a tumor.

Talk about a happy reunion! The very next night after my arrival, my thirdborn gave birth to her fourthborn. Devastatingly the baby didn't survive. Our hearts were shredded. I can't imagine what it would have been like had I not been there.

Over the next several years each of my kids living out-of-state returned to Utah to again live minutes from one another. They've been years filled with birthday parties and holiday traditions. One of my favorite traditions has been the Grammy sleepovers with all the grandkids hanging out together. I love that my grandkids are just so happy just being with one another. It was no secret that those Grammy sleepovers had less to do with Grammy and more to do with all of them. Of course, filling their tummies up with all-you-can-eat animal-shaped chocolate chip pancakes became a tradition that helped too. We can all attest, especially their mothers, that little sleeping happened at those sleepovers. All too soon those days became rarer and rarer as everyone got older going their different ways. Still, the fond memories are irreplaceable.

I started this chapter concerned about writing about an unremarkable life but now find it has been a rewarding experience. I can't wait to see how the remaining chapters unfold.

2

Finding and Losing Religion

I woke this morning knowing that it was time to face writing about my relationship with religion. It's not a chapter I'm looking forward to unraveling which is probably exactly why I need to. For context, I finished the Argentina chapter of this book a few weeks ago. Somehow, I figured I could just quickly brush past religion as I did in the previous chapter by saying, "I turned my back on the judgmental jealous vengeful God I loved, the church I dedicated so much of my life to, and simply all of it!"

That explosive emotional choice came after years of deep often anguishing introspection and a great deal of external research. It was a big deal because for decades I believed in the church with all that I was, and it didn't come easy finding that belief. Once I did, I lived it one hundred percent. As a child, I don't remember attending church with my family. We were active churchgoers before I started elementary school, but the only church-related memory I had while my mother was alive was when I got baptized at eight. My arm floated to the top, so I had to get dunked under the water twice. Some of our inactivity had to do with my father blaming the church for the death of my infant brother. My mother was asked to give a talk in church when pregnant and, not long afterward, went into labor prematurely.

My baby brother lived only a few hours. I was eight months old at the time.

It was during the summers staying with my mother's parents that I went to church with my Gramma. After my mother's death, Gramma was all about creating opportunities for me to make friends, and going to church with her would help. She was right. Soon, I was engaged in several of the town's social gatherings and made the best of friends. And likewise, accepting invitations to attend some activities when living back home in the city. There were a few occasions when my father and his second wife, along with the entire family, attended church. For the most part, I independently got myself to the various meetings and activities. It's not that I believed in the church, but rather the goodness of it that resonated with me. When I was asked to give talks, I made sure not to say anything about believing in the gospel like everyone else. My talks were more about instances of people doing the right thing. As a teenager in high school, my best friends weren't churchgoers and often made fun of people who were. That didn't seem to matter; I still went.

As previously mentioned, at seventeen years old, I met my husband-to-be. He and his family had this absolute knowledge about the truth of the gospel that was so bluntly simple that it caught me off-guard. After all, my fiance's family came to America from Tonga to be close to the church headquarters and leadership. They unquestioningly walked and breathed the church. We were engaged within weeks of our first meeting. His family expected a Mormon temple wedding. It caused me to question what was true and to do some soulful scripture studies of the Book of Mormon. I can still remember the morning I woke up feeling like my heart was about to explode. The sun was shining brighter than I had ever seen it shine before. I felt so much hope, love, and joy knowing that God lived, Jesus was my Savior, and the Book of Mormon and the Church of Jesus Christ of Latter-Day-Saints were true. It's a worldwide church structured with neighborhood sections called wards and groups of wards called stakes. The membership in 2022 is approaching eighteen million.

Not long after, while still seventeen, I was married for all time and eternity to the love of my life in the Salt Lake City Temple of the Church of Jesus Christ of Latter-Day-Saints. Since the morning I found my testimony of the truthfulness of the church, I never wavered in giving my all to whatever the church asked of me. It's a church of volunteer commitments, several hours of meetings and activities at least twice a week, living the required modest lifestyle, limiting what we eat or drink, and giving ten percent of our income. It becomes an exclusive way of living. From my perspective, this was a loving atmosphere of growth and service to one another and how I wanted to raise my six children. We were immersed in the church. That is except for my husband, who was often out of town with work or so I believed.

I shared in the previous chapter about how my childhood after the accident was within a dysfunctional, hateful family without a proper education or support system. Plus, my children's father was from the third-world country of Tonga, and we lived on the poorer west side of Salt Lake City. Some would label our neighborhood as the scary part of town. Statistically, the odds were stacked against my children that they would even finish high school, let alone contribute to society. Now, add to my kids' struggle that they were coming from a broken home with an unsupported single mother with few income-making opportunities. This was a pretty overwhelming time for me.

Thankfully, my association with other young mothers at church helped. Through these church interactions, I was forever coming up with ways to discipline my children that didn't have to do with beatings and rage. Rather, their early childhood consequences for misbehavior were typically things like having to put their nose in a corner or having to touch their toes. Additionally, I believed that attending church would help my children's confidence in themselves grow. There they had opportunities to give talks in front of large groups and otherwise engage in service and leadership roles which I felt helped them in school.

However, I don't know if anyone grew more than me during those years. Those volunteer assignments and being placed in many stressful leadership roles prepared me to handle my journey in the workforce. All in all, my religion was much more than learning and reciting scriptures. It was people I learned to love like brothers and sisters with all of my heart, and a safe place to discover more about my potential gifts and abilities.

As alluded to earlier and as in love with God, my Savior, and the church that I was, there were things about the church that didn't sit right. They were small things that I could easily rationalize as not being systematic. After all, the church is run by people and if we were perfect, we wouldn't be here, right? An example of something that bothered me was so many judgmental people. Maybe that is something that happens across the board with all religions or belief systems, but still, that doesn't make it okay. There were other things about the church like the never-ending volunteer commitments and the inconsistencies.

There's a saying, if you want something done give it to the busiest person. That's the short game. It's hard to understand why people take advantage of overusing people this way when the long game is what we might want to consider. It might take a few more minutes to find someone else from the sidelines. Consider being inclusive, respecting all, loving all, and lifting each other up, by bringing someone less involved into the mix.

Oh, and I especially didn't like the teachings of a jealous and vengeful God or the teachings of places like Heaven and Hell. If we are children of God and I as an imperfect mother have nothing less than all the love in the world for each of my children, how is it that our perfect Father in Heaven can be so judgmental and absolute?

Moving on to the topic of spirituality, since the time I was a child, I was gifted with the ability to hear and listen to my heart. One instance that comes to mind happened on one of those nights when after sending all of the kids to bed only for them to find this and that excuse not to go to sleep; this kid needed a drink of water, and another needed to use the bathroom, another complained it wasn't fair that he can have a drink of water. Well, you get the picture. This went on and on until I finally drew the firm line of no more talking; everyone needs to go to sleep, now! Minutes after that final command, one more little girl knocked on my bedroom door, "Mommy?" I'm about to explode but that small quiet voice in me said, "Be calm." My sweet young daughter gently and lovingly approached me to share a sacred spiritual moment, which continues to be one of my most treasured memories.

One day at church before the meeting started there were a few of us talking about an upcoming change in our local church leadership. People were guessing who would be called to that position. I piped in to say who it would be. My prediction was someone totally off the radar who days later filled that spot. This gift I have of picking up on little things like that is just who I am. But now this is where it gets harder to articulate my relationship with the church. I started to have questions but nothing that warranted leaving the church and the people I loved. Nor did I, at least not right away. The next few years are when the movie "The Matrix" (Lana Wachowski, 1999) came out, 9/11 happened (Attacks, 2001), I remarried, and among other things, the movie "Passions of the Christ," (Gibson, 2004) came out. Each was loaded with emotions and controversy. And each played a part in my being more open to other possible explanations.

I previously mentioned what a nightmare my second marriage was for my kids. What I didn't mention was how odd this man was. When it was just the two of us, we enjoyed hours and hours of high-level conversations but around others, he was void of emotions. He had severe ADHD (Attention Deficit and Hyperactive Disorder) which he took a prescribed medication for. Before our marriage, I met with his doctor who had been seeing him for years.

This doctor alleviated my concerns medically speaking about any probability of his not being a stable husband or trustworthy with my kids. It's my nature to respect people equally. Thereby I was open and accepting of his quirks. My heart felt good around him and I really loved him. Plus he and my oldest daughter shared this remarkable ability to see and talk to various Guardian Angels such as my mother. Each day was filled with sacred moments but nothing that anyone else other than for a short time this one daughter, could feel or understand.

A secret side project that my husband was working on was translating ancient records. From my perspective as a faithful member of the Mormon church, ancient records needing to be translated in a quiet unassuming manner isn't something that was totally out of the question. In fact, that is exactly how Joseph Smith, the founder of the church, translated our primary book of scriptures, the Book of Mormon. Who is to say that no additional ancient histories need the same?

Plus, I had the confirmation in my heart that this was sacred work to be shared in due time with the world. I never witnessed the records nor was I concerned that I hadn't. The sacred confirmation in my heart was enough. However, I did witness a page of the symbols in which my husband translated the meanings for me.

Then one day, out of the blue, I received an email while at work. Reading the first word of the email filled my entire being with blissful love. Today, I don't recall the content, but rather the feeling. It was from a being not of this world who my husband was working with to translate the records. Who do you talk to about this stuff? I didn't feel I could talk to anyone other than my husband. My husband had constant communications with these beings telepathically.

That email was the first of many such communications sent directly to me. Some of these communications told me things that no one else should know such as what I did five minutes earlier or the night before. Regarding the example of five minutes before, I had my own office. No one else was around. It was wild! It was more than the physical confirmations; there were the spiritual confirmations. Confirmations I was feeling in my heart and my gut. Over the next few years, I copied and printed a bulging three-inch binder full of these email communications with first, this being and then two other beings. They represented themselves as deity. A couple of years into this type of work and correspondence, my move to New Hampshire happened.

Not long after settling in New Hampshire inconsistencies in these sacred moments started creeping in. So much so, that they began to be filled with hateful rage condemning me of blasphemy for my questions beyond what I could bear. In my heart of hearts, I loudly decided that no matter the consequence, I had to turn my back on anything further to do with my husband, these deities claiming to be God, Divine Mother, Jesus Christ, and all of it! I built a bonfire in my backyard and burned every page of that binder. Those pages were time-stamped, small print single-spaced, and double-sided. Often three communications fit on one page. At other times one communication filled three pages. At any rate, that emotional moment was in 2007, seven months after moving to New Hampshire.

As I write about that moment it's been sixteen years. Since that time I've had little to nothing to do with religion. They've been years of continued subtle searching. Not for God per se but for other perspectives while not attaching to any of them. It is my inner standing that Jesus' teachings are not a religion nor were they meant to be religion. They are love. He taught us to love all equally. The concept of rising from religion and spreading seeds of love feels right. I resonated with the sweat lodge ceremonies and many people within the Native American community. It took finding the modality of past life regression hypnosis before I discovered who those out-of-this-world entities so dominant in my second marriage factually were, but I'm getting ahead of myself.

My tumultuous experience with these entities and my unpredictable second husband caused me to question what else might be going on under the surface that I wasn't aware of. I was forever looking for clues in movies and books. Anything about Egypt was sure to catch my eye. It was about this time (2013-2016), that I enjoyed watching the TV History Channel's episodes of "Ancient Aliens." The questions posed in those episodes helped me better understand my personal experiences with entities. From there I started following the Gaia Channel and the 'Flower of Life' series with Drunvalo Melchizedek. One of Drunvalo's Guides is Thoth of ancient Egypt.

Drunvalo shares his story of coming from a different galaxy and teaches about going within your heart to remember who you are. He has written several interesting books. I was intrigued by Drunvalo's loving soul and his teachings. So much so that I found an in-person four-day workshop located a few minutes from my home in Salt Lake City facilitated by one of his certified trainees. This workshop was the third revision from his "Flower of Life" workshop entitled "Awakening the Illuminated Heart." It was a profound experience where I learned the art of meditation, finding the galaxy within the tiny space in my heart, and activating my Merkabah. From here I continued to broaden my perspective reading all his books and several others that were questioning the mainstream.

Along with researching books, I paid attention to various others who too were questioning things. There are fascinating series of episodes on the Gaia Channel such as "Cosmic Disclosure," "Wisdom Teachings," "Mystery Teachings," and "Initiation." Fast forward several years, it was in December 2020, while watching one of Laura Eisenhower's live YouTube videos that I experienced a huge paradigm shift.

Laura was interviewing Rising Phoenix AuroRa. They were talking about Galactic Wars and Archons. I had never heard of AuroRa or Archons and was hungry for more. Before this very moment, I had never considered such a thing as reincarnation as a possibility. It was my Mormon teaching that this life is our one and only life. Plus, what's with artificial attachments or literally any of what AuroRa was talking about?

What is an Archon? Archons are beings from an alternate universe void of light. They are also known as the Custodians. Currently, AuroRa has met with over four hundred AURA (Angelic Universal Regression Alchemy) clients, many of whose sessions are posted on social media. Her book, Galactic Soul History of the Universe, is a compilation of transcripts from select clients under hypnosis, along with her channeled messages. In hypnosis, clients are able to connect to their Higher Selves, meaning their subconscious. This is done to learn and address the root cause of a client's disease or concern.

After working with so many clients, patterns started to emerge of dark beings attaching to people. These beings were causing all manner of issues. Have you ever lost control of your temper and wondered why it went as far as it did? I know I had. That is one of the ways that these dark beings feed off of us. What we learned is that these dark beings are Archons. They are artificial intelligent parasites who after depleting their world, infested our world without our permission or knowledge. Their energy source is light, and light is the very Life Force within us as humans.

I think the animated movie, "Monsters, Inc." (Docter, 2001), was spot on when portraying this relationship of a parasitic race secretly creating nightmares in children to rob them of their light. This robbery or virus is something that has been going on in the shadows for thousands of years and they are very good at what they do. Additionally, it's important to note that Archons are known to have enslaved Draconians and Reptilians to serve them in this effort, all of whom feed off of us daily. Draconians and Reptilians are races that we meet during the body scans of these AURA hypnosis sessions.

Resonating, I immediately ordered AuroRa's book, which I read cover-to-cover in just over a week. Over the following months, I binge-watched AuroRa video after video and channeling after channeling. I'd like to quote a little something here that Divine Mother taught during an AURA session recorded in the Galactic Soul History of the Universe, page 683. "Know, when you shield thyself, you're shielding the innocent. When you don't consent and you're shielding your energy, you're balancing your energy, you're healing yourself, your energy; and you're doing that for your inner child, for the Collective of Children, for the Earth. You and only you can save yourself."

Reading this was huge. This book not only opens your mind to a multiverse of perspectives, but it's also a forum of profound teachings. Teachings that seem to relate to exactly what is going on in the world today as well as what is going on in my personal life at the very moment I read and inner-stand what is being shared.

Moving forward I came across a transcript from one of AuroRa's AURA past life regression sessions, "Abducted from Within the Womb," Session 332 on January 2021 (Found within www.risingphonenixaurora.com). The chapter was about the AI (Artificial Intelligence) infringements that happen in hospitals at the time of birth. These infringements have been traced back to Reptilians, Archons, and more. Reading this information triggered things deep inside me raw and painful. Part of me didn't want to believe or know this was happening or that it had happened to me and my babies!

AuroRa writes, "The Archons know that if a mother has grief, anger, or sadness, that they become a matching vibration to the possibility of abductions or infringement of some kind on the baby they are cultivating and carrying. A simple ill thought or intent from a family member or friend directed towards the mother energetically can harm the carrying child."

Resonating, I became devastated and distraught. It was heart-wrenching. I was a total dysfunctional mess. After much reflection, processing, tears, and sleep, I sat outside at sunrise directly on Mother Earth. I called on my Angels for help in healing and forgiving the unforgivable. Not having been able to speak to God or any Heavenly beings for so many years, I struggled to even think of them in my mind. After more intense grieving, I was finally filled with calming peace and infinite love for the gift of this knowledge. I felt the gentle loving arms of my Divine Mother and my Divine Father, whose love I recognize as who I AM.

Although not completely healed, my anger against God was transitioning. Pieces of this transition come from bits of inner standing found within the following chapters. No one is more surprised than me by what's forthcoming but that puzzle requires the entire book to piece it together.

Soon after this shift in my relationship with God, during one of her live channeling YouTube videos, Rising Phoenix AuroRa announced her live in-person Chicago retreat for AURA Hypnosis and RAAH Reiki Certification. I was already enrolled and taking her ISIS Priestess online class. With urgency, before she finished making that first announcement, I immediately registered to attend the certification retreat. Before that moment I hadn't considered myself an AURA hypnosis practitioner but felt compelled to jump. Jump I did. The ongoing knowledge and beautiful healing I receive from this practice are immeasurable.

The following chapters are layers of my intimate journey. We really are like onions with several layers and like a lotus flower to allow these layers to be released as we uncover or integrate what we are receiving in the gentlest most loving manner. My first session organically without preplanning turned into another and another which I transcribed for my additional healing. It was while transcribing my May 2022 session, that I felt impressed that these sessions may be useful to others. It is with utmost humility that I share my journey with you with the intent of your greatest healing.

Fast forward several months after being certified as an AURA practitioner, the opportunity presented itself for me to attend an 11-22-11 event in Argentina, more of which I talk about in the chapter entitled, *Argentina: Being of One Heart*. Through my experience in Argentina, I met other attendees from all over the world. One of those attendees was Anja Richter (Consciousness Coaching and Education) from Germany. I love how Anja so clearly expresses herself. I feel her remarks are a perfect conclusion to this chapter. Note, that this quote is taken verbatim from one of Anja's recorded Zoom meetings which I happened to attend. It's cited at the end of this book. Reading and hearing her words is one thing, but listening to the energy with which she spoke is a whole new level. I encourage you to look up this recording on YouTube.

"The simple secret to healing yourself is possible only when you are open to the greater consciousness of yourself and at least intend and be willing and ready to completely surrender to that and to open up to that and to identify with that. In that space, in that eternity, you are actually recognizing yourself again as something that can't die, that can't be destroyed, that is immortal, and that is unconditionally allowed and loved. In that space in that wisdom in that recognition, everything heals because everything that is hurting is hurting because it is calling for that consciousness. Another word for this consciousness is actually Light. It is calling for that Light. It is calling for that Love, for that Welcoming, for that Embrace. Everything that is hurting, whether mental, emotional, or physical, is a call on whatever level for your consciousness, for your recognition as that Light, as that Eternity, as Consciousness." – *Anja (Richter, 2022)*

Debra (Far left) meditating at pond by her home in NH. Photo credit: Debra's youngest daughter.

3

First Hypnosis Experience

AURA (Angelic Universal Regression Alchemy)
Hypnosis Healing by Rising Phoenix AuroRa
July 10, 2021

Soon after starting to read AuroRa's book, <u>The Galactic Soul History of the Universe</u>, I sought an AURA hypnosis session from AuroRa herself. Seven months later, the time of my long-awaited session arrived. In preparation, I watched hundreds of AURA sessions on YouTube, read the book twice, and completed the Rising Phoenix Mystery School ISIS Priestess course and the prerequisites of her AURA Hypnosis Practitioner Certification course. I had spent several years becoming a vegetarian and learning to meditate. Preparing through the modality of AURA hypnosis I went from vegetarian to vegan and eliminated coffee, sugar, and processed foods including white flour. That is except for some fish items. Additionally, I surround myself with crystals and candles along with morning and night alchemy shielding and grounding.

 I felt prepared to surrender going in for my AURA session. No one was more shocked than me by how blocked I was. I mean, why wasn't I seeing all these beautiful images similar to the sessions that are online or in the book? Why am I not allowing my Higher Self or my past self, to speak?

But then again, maybe I'm not as blocked as I thought. Each time I've revisited this, my first AURA hypnosis experience, I've learned even more deeply how each session provides yet another puzzle piece towards my remembering the bigger picture of who I am. We are different people today than we were yesterday. Revisiting this first AURA I find new treasures woven into this session that I hadn't seen before. There were puzzle pieces right there in plain sight that at the time, I wasn't ready for. How glorious is that?

Session begins.

A [AuroRa]: Tell me what you see and sense, you've landed on the ground. Higher Self, move her mic piece closer to her mouth.

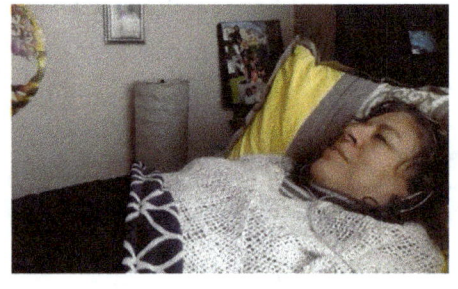

D [Debra]: It's like psychedelic variegated colors of light and dark purple, and I feel my body is very heavy.

A: *Good, that's how it feels. How does it feel to be in this space?*

D: Very peaceful, safe (whimpering) it does feel safe.

A: *Good. Do you feel that you have a body?*

D: I don't feel anything different than the colors.

A: *Okay, go ahead and enjoy the different colors and shapes that you're seeing. Enjoy it and let me know when something changes.*

D: There's a different depth perspective.

A: *Explain.*

D: I feel like I'm moving.

A: *Let's keep moving time and space, moving time and space through this space of yours, let's deal with it when something changes, something changes. You are there now. Tell me what's going on now.*

D: More dominantly purple.

A: *How does it feel to be in that space?*

D: (Illegible response)

A: *Very good, let's leave that space. Let's go to another important time, another important time for your highest healing. You are there now. You are able to see, sense, and feel what is going on and very clearly, you are there now. You are able to see, sense, and feel very clearly, very clearly. Tell me what you see and sense now.*

D: The colors have darkened and are more solid. Not as cheery.

A: *Allow yourself to experience these different colors and sensations now. You are being taken to this space for an important reason; to begin the energy healing. Just allow what this space is meant to do. Allow it to continue to heal you and enjoy it. Let's keep moving the scene along, moving the scene along. See if we are able to go to any other space besides here. Let's go ahead and leave this scene, let's leave this scene and move to another important time, another important time when we will find the answers that we seek for your highest healing. You are there now. You are there now, tell me what you see and sense.*

D: There's a little bit more brightness. The purple is coming back somewhat. I thought something started happening in the top right of my sight, but it faded away. Long pause. The waves are back and more of the waves and colors.

A: *Beautiful. Higher Self, I know you've brought her to this space for an important reason to begin her energy work. Since she is not moving past this space, this is where we will begin her energy work. Higher Self, I would like to speak to you now, please. I would like to speak to the Higher Self of Debra, speak to you now.*

The Higher Self is called in and the body scan begins.

Higher Self: Greetings.

A: *Greetings. Thank you for speaking to us. I love you, honor you, and respect you. May I ask you questions?*

Higher Self: Yes.

A: *Beautiful. Thank you. Thank you for bringing Debra to this time and space to do an AURA hypnosis healing session. It is such an honor. You have her in this beautiful space that seems so magical, with different colors and a kaleidoscope of energy shifting going on, why is it that you've taken her to this space?*

Higher Self: (No response. In my mind, I was digging around for answers or knowing but nothing was coming. It felt empty.)

A: *Higher Self, let's go ahead and begin the body scan. Which Archangel would you like us to assist you or any other benevolent being during the body scan?*

Higher Self: Archangel Michael would be wonderful.

A: *Beautiful. Higher Self, connect us to Archangel Michael now, please we would like to speak to him now. Greetings, Michael.*

AA Michael: Greetings.

A: *Thank you. We love you, honor you, and respect you for all the aid you have given us so far. The Higher Self has requested your assistance right now to begin her body scan if the Higher Self and you, Archangel Michael, can work together to begin scanning her body from head to toe looking for any negative energies, entities, technologies, or anything that we can heal that you would like to begin at first. Where would you like to begin first?*

AA Michael and Higher Self: (Weakly) Head to toe, head.

A: *Okay, what kind of entity is that earthbound, Archon or Reptilian? (no response) What kind of entity is that Michael, Archon, Reptilian, or earthbound? Help her see, sense, feel, and know exactly what everything is. Keep giving her the messages, Higher Self, and Archangel Michael. What is that on her head? What kind of entity is that?*

AA Michael and Higher Self: Archon.

A: *Archon, very good, go ahead and contain that with the alchemy symbols and let me know when it's contained.*

AA Michael and Higher Self: It's contained.

A: *Good, let's start neutralizing, neutralizing that Archon out of the top of her head. Can you all do that?*

AA Michael and Higher Self: Yes.

A: *Good, let me know when the Archon attached there on the top of her head. When did this Archon attach?*

AA Michael and Higher Self: Searching . . . not seeing it.

A: *She's able to know exactly she's able to see, sense, feel, hear, and know exactly. Show her a number, perhaps an age, was it another life? Help her know exactly Archangel Michael and Higher Self when it was that this Archon attached to her.*

Higher Self: (No response. Everything felt emotionless and blank. I wasn't receiving any information and the doubt of my abilities kept growing.)

A: *Was it this life, or was it another?*

Higher Self: (No response. More doubt crept in. I gently told my ego to step to the side.)

A: *Was it this life or another?*

AA Michael and Higher Self: It feels like another.

A: *Okay, let's start healing any trauma that happened when this Archon attached and we are eradicating, neutralizing that Archon inside her head. Let's continue scanning her. Let's continue scanning her. Does she have any dark portals? Michael, please scan her, does she have any dark portals?*

AA Michael: (No response.)

A: *Let me know Michael if you see any dark portals in her.*

AA Michael: (No response.)

A: *Does she have any dark portals, Michael?*

AA Michael: (No response.)

A: *Tell me what's going on. Higher Self, would you like us to call on anyone else; a divine being, Divine Mother, Divine Father, or Source during this body scan? (AuroRa lighting palo santo)*

AA Michael and Higher Self: (This session happened shortly after the event from the previous chapter where I shared going from turning my back on God, Divine Mother, and all of it, to being softened after reading and resonating so deeply with the AURA session, "Abducted from Within the Womb." At the moment, my relationship with deities still wasn't clear. Hearing AuroRa's suggestion about asking for Divine Mother's assistance felt warm and comforting. Almost in tears, my voice broke as I meekly whimpered . . .) Could I have the help of Divine Mother?

A: (It was as though AuroRa sensed my relationship with the divine had been traumatized. AuroRa's tone changed. She gently said . . .) Yes. Higher Self, connect us to Divine Mother. We would like to speak to Divine Mother now.

D: She's so wonderful! (This was my response to feeling Divine Mother's energy; hence the D: notation when transcribing this session. But again, from the perspective of the now, in my heart, I know it was both my and Divine Mother's reaction to that initial conscious greeting. The confirmation of this knowing is an emotional one for me.)

A: Yes, Divine Mother, greetings.

Divine Mother: Greetings.

A: Thank you for being here. If you could assist us for the rest of her healing today. Divine Mother, Archangel Michael, Higher Self, if you could scan her now. Does she have any dark portals in her?

Divine Mother, AA Michael, and Higher Self: We're seeing something in the heart.

A: What's in her heart? Is it an implant, portal, or entity? What is it?

Divine Mother: (No response. I'm trying to listen or know the right answer but everything is blank.)

A: What is in her heart? Higher Self, Divine Mother, help her know what's in her heart. Implant, portal, entity?

Divine Mother, AA Michael, and Higher Self: (No response.)

A: What is it, Divine Mother? What's in her heart?

Divine Mother: I feel it's an entity.

A: Good, what kind of entity is it? Is that an Archon, Reptilian or earthbound?

Divine Mother: Reptilian.

A: Okay, contain it now in the alchemy symbols. Divine Mother let me know when it's contained.

Divine Mother: It's contained.

A: Let's go ahead and find all entities in her. We want to find them all and contain them all now. Scan her deeply, thoroughly. We want to make sure we do not want to miss any entities. Where else does she have entities at?

Divine Mother: Throat.

A: What's in the throat? What kind of entity is that, Archon, Reptilian or earthbound?

Divine Mother: Archon.

A: Okay, contain that now in the throat. Let me know when it's contained.

Divine Mother: It's contained.

A: Good, let's start eradicating that Archon out of her throat now. Neutralizing it out. Can you all do that?

Divine Mother, AA Michael, and Higher Self: Yes.

A: Let me know when that Archon came into her throat. Was it this life or another?

Divine Mother, AA Michael, and Higher Self: This life.

A: What happened to her? What was going on that allowed this Archon to enter her throat?

Divine Mother, AA Michael, and Higher Self: Not able to speak her mind.

A: Okay, good we're neutralizing, we're neutralizing that Archon now, so let's continue scanning her. Where else does she have entities that we can contain? Anywhere else she has entities; we want to find them all. Scan her deeply, thoroughly, Divine Mother where else does she have any entities? (Aurora continues smudging with palo santo.)

Divine Mother, AA Michael, and Higher Self: Third Eye.

A: Third Eye. What kind of entity is that? Is it an Archon, Reptilian or earthbound?

Divine Mother, AA Michael, and Higher Self: (No response.)

A: *What kind of entity is that? Divine Mother, help her know exactly what she has that is within her. She's doing great. What kind of entity is that?*

Divine Mother, AA Michael, and Higher Self: It's Reptilian.

A: *It's a Reptilian. Where is it at?*

Divine Mother, AA Michael, and Higher Self: In the third eye.

A: *Okay, let's contain it in alchemy symbols. Let me know when it's contained.*

Divine Mother, AA Michael, and Higher Self: It's contained.

A: *Okay, now that it's contained, where else does she have entities at?*

Divine Mother, AA Michael, and Higher Self: Sacral area.

A: *What kind of entity is it – Archon, Reptilian or earthbound?*

Divine Mother, AA Michael, and Higher Self: Reptilian.

A: *Contain it now with the alchemy symbols. Let me know when it's contained.*

Divine Mother, AA Michael, and Higher Self: It's contained.

A: *Wonderful. Let's scan her again. Where else does she have entities? We want to make sure we do not want to miss any. Where else does she have entities at?*

Divine Mother, AA Michael, and Higher Self: It feels like the left ankle.

A: *Let's scan that area now and see what is it? What kind of entity is it – Archon, Reptilian or earthbound?*

Divine Mother, AA Michael, and Higher Self: Archon.

A: *Contain that now in her left ankle and let me know when it's contained.*

Divine Mother, AA Michael, and Higher Self: It's contained.

A: *Good, let's start eradicating that Archon there in her left ankle, neutralizing it out. Let me know when it is that this Archon attached to her left ankle.*

Divine Mother, AA Michael, and Higher Self: Fear, transitioning from the workforce into retirement. A lot of changes going on.

A: *Very good, let's eradicate that. While we continue to work on those Archons there, let's continue to scan her. Does she have any other entities in her? We want to make sure we don't miss any.*

Divine Mother, AA Michael, and Higher Self: There's something in the left shoulder.

A: *What is it – an Archon, a Reptilian, an entity, or something else? Where else does she have entities at?*

Divine Mother, AA Michael, and Higher Self: (No response.)

A: *Scan her again, where else does she have entities?*

Divine Mother, AA Michael, and Higher Self: In the spine, upper back.

A: *Okay, what kind of entity is that?*

Divine Mother, AA Michael, and Higher Self: Reptilian keeps coming to mind.

A: *Contain it now within the spine and let me know when it's contained.*

Divine Mother, AA Michael, and Higher Self: It's contained.

A: *Good, let's continue scanning her. Again, where else does she have entities? Does she have any other entities in her Divine Mother?*

Divine Mother, AA Michael, and Higher Self: The bladder comes to mind.

A: *Okay, Divine Mother, let's scan that area. What is there? Is it an implant, hook, portal, or entity?*

Divine Mother, AA Michael, and Higher Self: It's an implant.

A: *Okay, let's go ahead and start eradicating it. We are using Phoenix Fire to remove that implant now. Can we do that?*

Divine Mother, AA Michael, and Higher Self: Yes.

A: *Good, it was in the bladder. Okay, transmuting that out of her bladder now.*

Divine Mother, could you scan her one more time? I want to make sure she doesn't have any dark portals in her. Does she have any?

Divine Mother: Looks like the center of the chest.

A: *What's going on in the center of her chest?*

Divine Mother, AA Michael, and Higher Self: You asked about dark portals, there's a dark portal there.

A: *Divine Mother and Archangel Michael, could you go ahead and close that for her?*

Divine Mother, AA Michael, and Higher Self: Yes.

A: *Good. Let me know when it's closed.*

Divine Mother, AA Michael, and Higher Self: It's closed.

A: *Very good, let's start healing that space, the center of her chest where that portal was at. Healing, filling it in with Love-Light. Divine Mother and Higher Self, can you do that?*

Divine Mother, AA Michael, and Higher Self: Yes.

A: *Good, and can you tell me what was that portal causing by being there at the center of her chest?*

Divine Mother, AA Michael, and Higher Self: Access.

A: *Access to her?*

Divine Mother, AA Michael, and Higher Self: Yes.

A: *Very good, we are healing any trauma and damage, that caused. Are there any other portals in her? Scan her deeply, thoroughly, are there any more?*

Divine Mother, AA Michael, and Higher Self: Something is going on with the right shoulder.

A: *Okay, let's scan and see what's going on with the right shoulder. Is it an implant, portal, hook, or entity? What is that there in that area? You are able to see, sense, and feel, very clearly, very clearly. What is that?*

Divine Mother, AA Michael, and Higher Self: It's just pain.

A: *Okay, let's soothe that pain, soothe that pain. There isn't anything attached to it, correct?*

Divine Mother, AA Michael, and Higher Self: It's a sharp pain moving from shoulder to elbow.

A: *Can we use Phoenix Fire to get rid of the pain?*

Divine Mother, AA Michael, and Higher Self: Yes, please.

A: *What is causing the pain?*

Divine Mother, AA Michael, and Higher Self: It's random.

A: *Is there anything else behind the energy?*

Divine Mother, AA Michael, and Higher Self: Yeah, there's an entity.

A: *What kind of entity is it – Archon, Reptilian or earthbound?*

Divine Mother, AA Michael, and Higher Self: (No response.)

A: *Archangel Michael, Divine Mother, what kind of entity is that?*

Divine Mother, AA Michael, and Higher Self: It moves around a little bit.

A: *It moves, okay let's figure out what it is so we can contain it. What does it look like?*

Divine Mother, AA Michael, and Higher Self: It doesn't feel like Reptilian.

A: *Is it like a snake or something else? What is it?*

Divine Mother, AA Michael, and Higher Self: (No response.)

A: *Tell me what's going on Higher Self?*

Divine Mother, AA Michael, and Higher Self: Well, it's no longer a sharp pain, it's a dull pain. Trying to discern.

A: *Okay, help her know exactly what it is – Archon, Reptilian, earthbound, or some other kind of entity.*

Divine Mother, AA Michael, and Higher Self: I'm thinking it could be a snake.

A: *What is it Michael, Divine Mother? Anything else within that space?*

Divine Mother, AA Michael, and Higher Self: (No response.)

A: *Tell me what's going on.*

Divine Mother, AA Michael, and Higher Self: It's got our attention.

A: *Do you feel it's organic or artificial Michael, Divine Mother?*

Divine Mother, AA Michael, and Higher Self: I'm going to say artificial.

A: *Does it feel organic or artificial?*

Divine Mother, AA Michael, and Higher Self: Artificial.

A: *Let's contain it now in the alchemy symbols. Let me know when it's contained.*

Divine Mother, AA Michael, and Higher Self: It's contained.

A: Good, eradicating the artificial entity from within her right shoulder and elbow now. Okay, where else does she have entities? We want to find them all.

Divine Mother, AA Michael, and Higher Self: I'm not sensing anything anywhere else.

A: Wonderful, let's scan her DNA now. In the DNA we are looking for any negative fractals within it, making sure it is organic. Let me know how it looks, Divine Mother. How does her DNA look? Is it fully organic?

Divine Mother, AA Michael, and Higher Self: Yeah.

A: Looks good?

Divine Mother, AA Michael, and Higher Self: Looks good.

A: While you're looking at it, if you could start working on it, making sure it's at its full crystalline formation as well as if there is any deprogramming needed within her DNA, deprogramming any false, anything that no longer serves her for her highest good. Can you all work on that for her?

Divine Mother, AA Michael, and Higher Self: Yes.

A: Good. One more time I want to scan her deeply, as we know they can hide, the entities, so we don't want to miss any before we start talking to them. Are there any other entities in her Archangel Michael, Divine Mother, and Higher Self? Scan her deeply for any others. Does she have anything more in her?

Divine Mother, AA Michael, and Higher Self: We're not finding anything else.

A: Very good. Okay, the Archons in her head, throat, and left ankle. Are they all gone?

Divine Mother, AA Michael, and Higher Self: Yes.

A: Wonderful. Go ahead and fill in Love-Light for all parts of those areas, repairing any damage that they caused. Higher Self, Divine Mother, and Michael, can you do that for her?

Divine Mother, AA Michael, and Higher Self: Yes.

A: Beautiful. Let's see what else is here. What about the implant in her bladder? Is that gone?

Divine Mother, AA Michael, and Higher Self: Yes.

A: *Good, let's start healing any damage to her bladder as we know she's been having issues with that all her life, so healing her bladder completely. One more last time, does she have any more implants, hooks, or portals in her before we start talking to the Reptilians?*

Divine Mother, AA Michael, and Higher Self: Feels clear.

A: *Wonderful. Let's go ahead and talk to the Reptilians. She has some in her heart, her third eye, her sacral, and her spine. Are any of them connected to one another?*

Divine Mother, AA Michael, and Higher Self: (No response.)

A: *Are any of them connected to one another?*

Divine Mother, AA Michael, and Higher Self: (No response.)

A: *Are we able to speak to them collectively or do we speak to them individually?*

Divine Mother, AA Michael, and Higher Self: Collectively.

A: *Very good, let's go ahead and speak to the Reptilians there in her heart, third eye, sacral, and spine. We would like to speak to you now, if you all can come up, up, up, up now, please. Greetings.*

Reptilians: Hello.

A: *Thank you for speaking to us. We love you, honor you, and respect you. May we ask you some questions?*

Reptilians: Yes.

A: *Thank you. Okay, if you can tell me when did you all attach to the heart, third eye, sacral, and spine? Did you all attach together, or at different times?*

Reptilians: Different times.

A: *Okay, so did any of you attach together at the same time?*

Reptilians: (No response.)

A: *Okay, let's go ahead and speak to the one in the heart. Speaking to you now. When was it when you attached to her in her heart?*

Reptilian in the heart: When she was about ten.

A: *What was going on when she was about ten that allowed you to attach to her?*

Reptilian: She was broken, and lost, spending a lot of time after the loss of her mother, secluded in cemeteries. She stayed at cemeteries a lot.

A: *Okay, what kind of damage, what kind of discomfort have you been causing her by being there in her heart?*

Reptilian: Confusion between what's genuine.

A: *Okay, thank you, and do you have a Reptilian body that you're connected to somewhere else? Do you have a Reptilian body somewhere else or are you just a consciousness here in her heart?*

Reptilian: (No response.)

A: *Divine Mother does this Reptilian have a body somewhere else or is it just a consciousness?*

Divine Mother: Just a consciousness.

A: *Speaking to that Reptilian there in her heart, are there any other Reptilians that are just a consciousness, like the one in her third eye, sacral, her spine? Are they just consciousnesses or do they have Reptilian bodies somewhere else Divine Mother?*

Divine Mother: (No response.)

Are they just consciousness' or do they have Reptilian bodies somewhere else, the other Reptilians that are in her third eye, her sacral, and her spine? Divine Mother we just need to know which ones are just consciousness. We know that the one in her heart is just a consciousness. How about the ones in the third eye, sacral, and spine? Are they also just consciousnesses or do they have Reptilians connected to them as well?

Divine Mother: I'm not sensing that any of them have bodies associated with them.

A: *How about the one in the heart, did it have a body?*

Divine Mother: No, I'm not sensing a body there.

A: *Very good. So talking to the Reptilian in her heart now. We are looking to assist you today so that you no longer have to play this negative polarized role. You can choose to ascend to a positive polarity and keep your memories. You know once the earth ascends parasitic entities like you will be transmuted, returned straight to Source. You will lose the memories that you gained and the experiences you gained. Instead of doing that we would love to be able to help you just spread your light. Would you allow for us to help you spread your light and positive ascend?*

Reptilian in the heart: Yes!

A: Good. Find the light within you, find the light within you, and spread it to all that is you, every root, every chord, every part of you, and let us know once you are fully light.

Positively Polarized Reptilian: I am light.

A: Beautiful. Go ahead and remove yourself, remove yourself from her body and let us know once you are removed.

Positively Polarized Reptilian: I'm out.

A: Wonderful. Do you have a message for her before you go?

Positively Polarized Reptilian: I'm sorry.

A: Thank you. Go ahead and go with the Love-Light of the Universe. We call forth on Archangel Azrael. Archangel Azrael brother?

AA Azrael: Yes.

A: Thank you for being here brother. We honor you, love you, and respect you. If you could guide this now positive polarized consciousness Reptilian to where it is meant to go for his positive ascension, thank you.

AA Azrael: Thank you.

A: Wonderful. Go ahead and go with the Love-Light of the universe. Blessings to you. Archangel Azrael will ensure your safe passage. Now let me go ahead and speak to the Reptilian in her third eye. If you could come up, up, up, up now, please. Greetings.

Reptilian in the third eye: Greetings.

A: Thank you for speaking to us. Love you, honor you, and respect you. May we ask you questions?

Reptilian: Yes.

A: Thank you. If you can tell me when was it that you attached there to her third eye?

Reptilian: Previous life.

A: What was going on with her then that allowed you to attach?

Reptilian: She's sensitive and able to see things.

A: *Very good. Okay, now do you have a Reptilian body somewhere else?*

Reptilian: (No response.)

A: *Do you have a Reptilian body somewhere else?*

Reptilian: Yes.

A: *Okay, let me speak to that Reptilian body that you are connected to. Please I would like to speak to it now. Greetings.*

Reptilian body: Greetings.

A: *Thank you. Thank you for speaking to us, love you, honor you, and respect you. May we ask you questions?*

Reptilian body: Okay.

A: *Thank you. If you can tell me where is it that you are located at.*

Reptilian body: Off planet.

A: *Where are you at exactly off-planet?*

Reptilian body: In a ship.

A: *In this ship how many more Reptilians are there with you?*

Reptilian body: (No response.)

A: *Are there any more Reptilians there with you on the ship?*

Reptilian body: The number five comes up.

A: *Okay, thank you. As we spoke to the other Reptilian consciousness, the same thing for you. We would love to assist you to positively ascend, no longer having to play this parasitic role. Would you allow us to help you positively polarize and spread your light and be free? All five of you there, all of you there on the ship. Do you say yes?*

Reptilian body: Yes.

A: *Beautiful. Go ahead and spread your light to all that is you within that Reptilian body. Divine Mother did they attach to any others besides Debra?*

Divine Mother: (No response.)

A: *Did they attach to anyone else besides her?*

Divine Mother: (No response.)

A: *Did they attach to any more Divine Mother? How many more did they attach to?*

Divine Mother: Thirteen.

A: Thirteen, okay, can you ask those Higher Selves if they will allow for us to help and remove those attachments, consciousness' that are attached to them?

Divine Mother: Agreed.

A: Beautiful. Go ahead and help them start spreading those consciousness' to light as well as the consciousness that they have attached to her third eye. Let me know once all the consciousnesses are light and they have been turned back to these Reptilians on the ship and they are whole once more and all light.

Reptilians: We are light.

A: Beautiful. Do they have a message for her before they go?

Reptilians: No.

A: That's okay, beautiful. Go ahead and go with the Love-Light of the Universe. Blessings to all of you. Archangel Azrael will ensure your safe passageway. Thank you. Let's fill in the third eye now. Start healing, Divine Mother and Higher Self, with Love-Light, repairing any damage that was caused in her third eye. Repairing it now and opening it up to the biggest it can be as the Higher Self allows as well as activating her abilities. Higher Self, can you do that? Can you do that Higher Self?

Higher Self: Yes.

A: Good, as well as expanding her heart. I know we already worked on her heart right before, so expanding her heart to the biggest it can be and refilling her light there. Thank you. Can you do that?

Higher Self: Yes.

A: Beautiful. Let's go ahead and talk to the Reptilian in her sacral. If you can come up, up, up now, please. Greetings.

Reptilian in sacral: Hello.

A: Thank you for speaking to us. We honor, love you, and respect you. May we ask you some questions?

Reptilian: Yes.

A: If you could tell us when was it that you attached to her sacral?

Reptilian: She was about ten.

A: What was going on that allowed you to come in?

Reptilian: One of the older neighbor boys got too close to her sexually.

A: Okay, let's go ahead and start healing this trauma for her now. Can we do that for her Divine Mother?

Divine Mother: Yes.

A: So you entered into her that way. Do you have a Reptilian body somewhere else?

Reptilian: No.

A: Okay, you don't have a Reptilian body somewhere else. Same for you, we would like to help you spread your light so that you no longer have to play this negative polarized role. Would you allow us to help you do that and release yourself?

Reptilian: Yes.

A: Good. Find the light within you and spread it to all that is you, every root, every chord, there in her sacral. Let us know when you are fully light.

Positively Polarized Reptilian: I am light.

A: Beautiful. Release yourself out from her sacral and let us know when you are fully out. Make sure you don't leave any piece of yourself.

Positively Polarized Reptilian: I'm out.

A: Very good. Now, do you have a message for her before you go?

Positively Polarized Reptilian: Thank you. I'm sorry.

A: Very good, thank you. Go ahead and go with the Love-Light of the universe. Blessings to you. Archangel Azrael will ensure your safe passageway. Thank you. Okay and then her spine the Reptilian in her spine, does that have a Reptilian body somewhere else? I'd like to speak to the Reptilian in her spine. If you could come up, up, up, up now, please. Greetings.

Reptilian in the spine: Greetings.

A: If you can tell me when was it that you attached there to her spine? When did you attach there to her spine?

Reptilian: She was about probably in her early thirties.

A: What was going on then, that allowed for you to attach?

Reptilian: She was neglecting herself. Doing everything for everybody else.

A: Very good, and tell me do you have a Reptilian body somewhere else?

Reptilian: I can't remember.

A: That's okay. Divine Mother does he have a Reptilian body somewhere else or is he just a consciousness?

Divine Mother: I think he's just consciousness.

A: Wonderful, thank you. Okay, the same thing for you as the other Reptilian consciousnesses, we would love to assist you to spread your light no longer playing this parasitic role, you could be free. Would you like to free yourself and spread your light?

Reptilian: Yes!

A: Okay, go ahead and spread your light, every root, every chord, every part of you and let us know once you are fully light.

Positively Polarized Reptilian: Okay, I am light!

A: Before you release yourself out, make sure you are fully out. Don't leave any piece of yourself behind.

Positively Polarized Reptilian: I'm out.

A: Healing her entire spine now from any damage. If you can all do that, filling in Love-Light, please.

Divine Mother, AA Michael, Higher Self: Yes.

A: Thank you. Okay now the A.I. in her right shoulder and elbow, has that been completely removed?

AA Michael: Almost.

A: Okay, wonderful. While you continue to work on that I want to ensure we took care of the reasons of what was attached to some of the illnesses that she needs to be healed. She wants to make sure she has no negative side effects from all of the doctor visits, vaccinations and surgeries. Can you scan her? Does she need any healing for any of that? Especially her pregnancies and hospital delivery experiences and the multiple surgeries that she's had. Did we heal all of that?

Higher Self: Yes, she's got that taken care of.

A: Beautiful, good. She wants to make sure her issues with acid reflux, sleep apnea, and high cholesterol are healed. She still needs to take medication for these ailments. Can we assure her that she is completely healed so that she no longer needs to take these medications?

Higher Self: Yes.

A: Good. Were any of these entities causing that? Any of that?

Higher Self: Yeah.

A: What were some of these entities that were the root of some of these things that she has?

Higher Self: They were causing a lot of fear. A lot of self-doubt, anxiety, lack of self-love, and self-worth.

A: Okay, all these lacks, let's go ahead and start helping them heal, please. Can we do that for her Higher Self?

Higher Self: Yes.

A: Good. She wants her metabolism and digestive system normalized for a healthy activity and ideal weight control, please. Can we do that?

Higher Self: Yes.

A: And also her negative relationship with kidneys and her bladder as well. We already know that we found an implant there, but we want to make sure that we heal all that, plus she had various life experiences and surgeries within that.

Higher Self: Yes.

A: Specifically her trauma related to the beginning of her life, when she just lay in a crib with no one attending to her. Can we heal any trauma that caused her soul and her essence? (During the interview before this session, AuroRa asked this great question which surprised me how relevant it was. She asked about what it was like when I was a baby. The only reason I knew the answer to this question is that my clueless father continually bragged about what a hero he was coming home every four or so hours between work and school to the dread of changing my disgusting diapers. Diapers that always made him throw up. The hero-of-the-day would then hurriedly prop a bottle in my mouth before heading to his next job. My mother was too sickly to care for me and my father was too proud to let my mother's parents help. That was until I was seven months old when my mother was hospitalized.)

Higher Self: Yes.

A: *Good, Divine Mother start healing her for that. Okay, she wants her teeth healed to avoid future root canals, cavities, fillings, and crowns. Can we heal her teeth, please?*

Higher Self: Yes.

A: *Good. And also the habit of chewing her tongue. Can that be transmuted, please?*

Higher Self: Yes.

A: *Why does she chew on her tongue?*

Higher Self: It was an internal way to pacify herself.

A: *And also the clenching of her teeth. Why does she do that? And are they connected to one another – clenching of the teeth and chewing of the tongue?*

Higher Self: No, they are not connected.

A: *Okay, so why does she clench her teeth?*

Higher Self: Just the frustration and unhappiness of not feeling like she is able to be everything her kids expected her to be along with her career going in different directions. Just undue heavy loads. Heavy stress.

A: *Okay, can we start healing that now to help her stop clenching her teeth and chewing on her tongue? Can we help her with that?*

Higher Self: Yes.

A: *Thank you. She also wants to discover the root fear causing her constant muscle and breathing tenseness. What is the root of that? As well as her arthritis?*

Higher Self: Yeah, that's to do with the traumatic loss of her mother and her perspective of the way it happened and the possibility it wasn't an accidental accident. There was possible suicide involved. Just the ripple effects.

A: *Okay, let's start healing that for her now so that she no longer has that. Can we do that? Are we able to do that for her?*

Higher Self: Yes.

A: *Good. She wants to have her left ankle healed. I know she had an Archon in her left ankle and we already healed that. If there is any healing needed further for that also, please do so. Does she have any negative chords having to do with her negative association with exercise and well-being?*

Higher Self: Yeah, her stepmother and stepbrothers bullied her anytime she took care of herself. It was wrong to do anything for herself.

A: *Okay, let's start healing that for her now, please.*

Higher Self: It is done.

A: *Good, she wants to know if she has any remaining contracts. Does she have any negative contracts overall, but specifically she wants to know if she has any to religion and chords as well?*

AA Michael: No, she's cut those?

A: *Good. Michael, can you scan her for any negative contracts and chords? Does she have any? Does she have any negative chords, Michael, or contracts?*

AA Michael: She should have plenty, but I'm not seeing any.

A: *Did she remove them?*

AA Michael: Well, she's been working on them.

A: *Thank you, Michael. Let us know if you see anything else. Okay, she wanted to know if we could age-regress her. How many years can we age regress her?*

Higher Self: Thirteen comes to mind, thirteen years.

A: *Beautiful, let's start that process now. Can we do that for her?*

Higher Self: Yes.

A: *Good. Scan her, Divine Mother and Higher Self, to see if she has any blocked or misaligned chakras. Can you both heal them and balance them out for her? Can you do that?*

Divine Mother and Higher Self: Yes.

A: *Thank you. As well as scan her auric field to see if it needs any repairs to it. Can you heal that?*

Divine Mother and Higher Self: It looks good.

A: *Good. Very good, repairing it to organic formation. Now can you scan her for any negative technologies or wires in her? Does she have any?*

Divine Mother: I think she's burned them off. (One of the tools we receive when learning to be AURA practitioners is the use of Phoenix Fire. This is an etheric fire that I was using on myself through my coursework.)

A: *Good. Okay, one last time does she have anything else negative within her? Anything else, implants, hooks, portals, or entities of any kind? Because we know she's coming to the retreat soon, and we want to make sure she is fully clear. Michael, Divine Mother, and Higher Self, scan her one last time. Does she have anything else?*

AA Michael, Divine Mother, and Higher Self: Looks good.

A: *Beautiful. Michael, does she have any fragmented soul pieces that she needs to have regained to her? Does she have any?*

AA Michael: I'm not sensing any.

A: *Okay. Divine Mother and Higher Self ensuring that her soul is fully whole. Can you confirm that?*

Divine Mother and Higher Self: Yes.

A: *And that is all. Higher Self, have we set her up for her most highest organic timeline and path?*

Higher Self: Yes.

A: *Beautiful. Thank you. Now she has a couple of questions. How is she holding up? I know she's been in there a while.*

Higher Self: Good.

A: *Good. She wants to know about her husband, of twenty years, and father to her six children, was he Archon influenced? You know he sexually abused the children and he was a womanizer. Who was he really?*

Higher Self: Yeah, he was obviously Archon-influenced, but he was Reptilian.

A: *Okay, okay, thank you. We want to make sure that any connection to him is completely severed from her and is no longer infringing on her in any way. Can we ensure that?*

Higher Self: Yes.

A: *Good. Then her second husband of six years, was he a Reptilian?*

Higher Self: Yes.

A: *Were those communications she received during those years with him, from negative beings playing the part of Divine Mother, Father, and Jesus?*

Higher Self: Absolutely!

A: *They were?*

Higher Self: Yes!

A: *Does she have any remaining contracts or chords to any one of those exes of hers?*

Higher Self: No.

A: *Good. So we just want to make sure we completely eradicate any connection to them, transmuting it thank you. Okay. She wants to know how many current fractals does she have?*

Higher Self: That's not important.

A: *Okay, and what about her Galactic history, and how is that influencing her spiritual path?*

Higher Self: *She's a mix. Arcturian comes up. Her need for detail.*

A: *Okay, anything else you want to tell her about her Galactic history?*

Higher Self: Enjoy the ride.

A: *Beautiful. Okay, and then who are her main guides?*

Higher Self: (Shaky voice) Divine Mother.

A: *Beautiful. And then Divine Mother, she wants to know if there is any assistance we can give to her children, you know as far as entities or Archons that are attached to them? Are we allowed to remove anything from them? Specifically, her oldest daughter who hasn't been able to carry her babies full-term. Is there something that can be healed at this time? Higher Self, are we able to assist them in any way?*

Divine Mother and Higher Self: Yes.

A: *How can we assist this daughter? Does she have anything in her womb or sacral area that is causing her to miscarry? Divine Mother let me know.*

Divine Mother: Yes, there is something there.

A: *Okay, what is it? Does her Higher Self allow for us to help it remove?*

Divine Mother: Yes.

A: *Okay, what is it, an entity, an implant, a hook? What is it?*

Divine Mother: Reptilian.

A: Okay, does her Higher Self allow for us to help it remove?
Divine Mother: Yes.
A: Thank you. Thank you, Higher Self. If we can go ahead and contain that Reptilian in her sacral now and then if you all can do the process on your own separately help it remove. Can you all do that?
Divine Mother and Higher Self: Yes.
A: Anything else we can do for her to ensure she is able to carry children?
Divine Mother: Sending Love-Light.
A: Sending Love-Light now. Wonderful. Now, what about her fourthborn daughter? She's on hospice and anxious to exit. Is there anything we can do to assist her to help her not pass away? Divine Mother let me know.
Divine Mother: She's made her mind up.
A: Okay. Is there anything we can do for her at all?
Divine Mother: Help her distinguish what's real and what's not. The hallucinations are preparing her to exhale that last breath and that it is okay. It's okay to go.
A: Okay, let's do that for her. And we will send her Love-Light. Is that okay? Sending Love-Light to her and her family, thank you. Okay, Higher Self at this point we have asked all the questions and conducted the body scan. Is there anything else that I could have asked that I haven't?
Higher Self: No.
A: Beautiful. Thank you. I want to thank Higher Self, Divine Mother, and Archangel Michael. Thank you for your beautiful assistance, Archangel Azrael, and anyone else who assisted with her healing today. We love you, honor you, thank you, and respect you. Thank you.
Divine Mother, AA Michael, and Higher Self: Thank you.
A: Thank you. And Higher Self before we bring her back is there a name that you go by?
Higher Self: Not at this time.
A: Okay, beautiful, very good. Are we all set? Can I bring her back now?
Higher Self: Yes.

The client is brought back.

I was disappointed that it was such a struggle to find the simplest answers to the questions being asked. In between those questions when there was no response. there were embarrassing long pauses. And I was disappointed that there were no fun earth-shattering revelations. At the same time, I was thrilled with the healings I had received especially for my daughters who were each on my mind. Still, this was my first experience with hypnosis and there was much to process. The more time that passes, the more I have grown to love and cherish this, my first hypnosis experience.

The energies continued to stay with me after this session. That night I had a vivid dream of being abducted. It would take me several months and sessions to unwrap and process the vision of that dream. All in divine timing as they say.

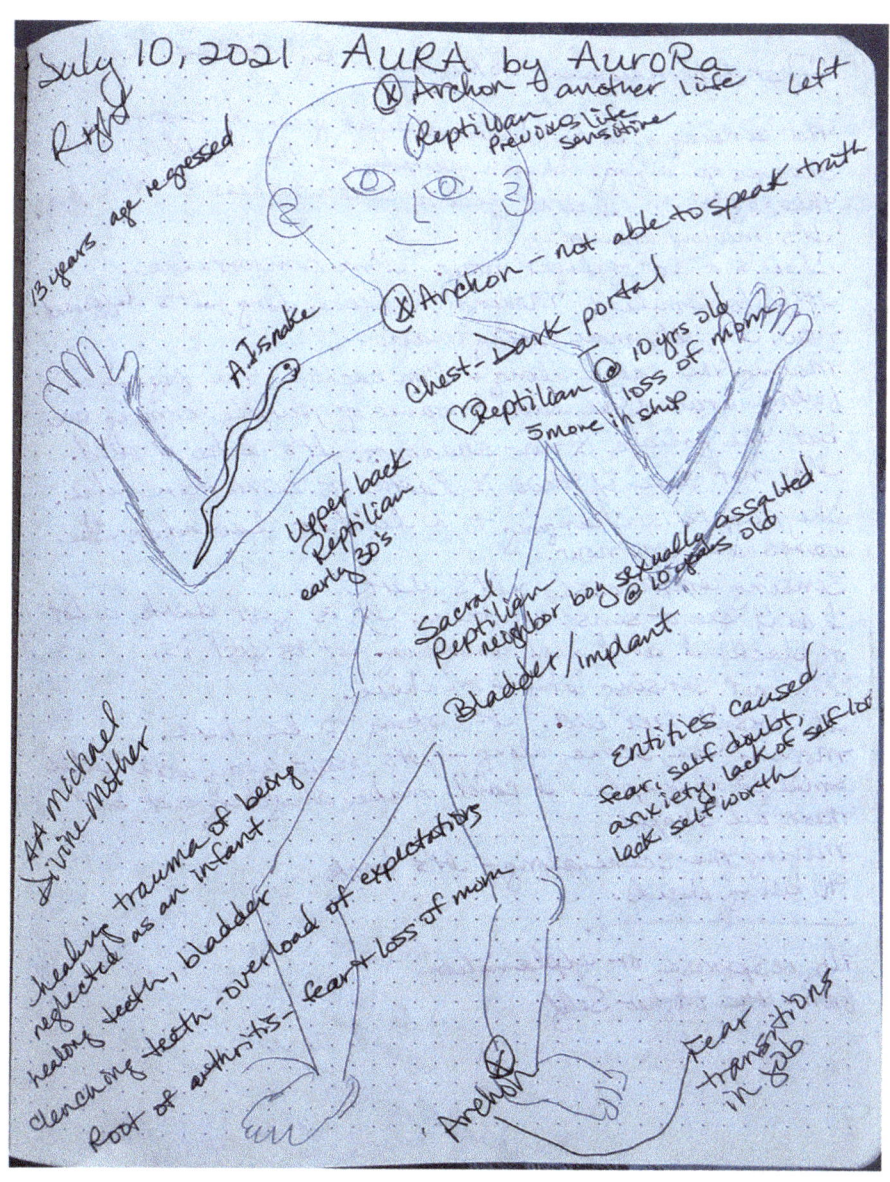

4

Getting Certified

AURA Hypnosis Healing by Alexia
AURA/RAAH Certification Retreat
Chicago Illinois
August 12, 2021

Phenomenal doesn't feel adequate to describe my experience attending an intimate in-person certification retreat with AuroRa and eight other students. The whole concept of becoming a sovereign powerful being was foreign to me. It was a paradigm shift in my belief patterns that I continue to work on. I was grateful for the amount of and the depth of homework required in advance of the retreat. When I say homework, I'm talking about months of intense study including over two hundred hours of videos, monthly live Zoom training meetings with new alchemy to learn, and much more. These are videos not found on the Rising Phoenix Aurora website.

Plus, I have to mention how amazing it was to meet this group of my newly found soul family. Each person is such a beautiful being. We even met AuroRa's husband, Zen, in person, who channeled a bit for us. Zen gifted me with a reading telling me that there was an army standing behind me. Wow! It was a magical experience that opened my mind and heart to this tangible concept of love being the answer. Everything around me was about the concept that there's much more going on than what we've been led to believe.

Feeling like I've done my due diligence in research and assimilating the teachings plus receiving a beautiful healing AURA from AuroRa, I felt sure to be clear and able to surrender for this planned class AURA certification. It is part of the last full day of the retreat for students to perform an AURA healing hypnosis on another student. An important part of this modality is the preliminary interview between the practitioner and the client. In addition to the interview, clients receive full body RAAH (Reiki Angelic Alchemy Healing) before the AURA past life regression hypnosis and body scan. The transcript of this and other sessions in this book begins after the interview and RAAH when the client is under hypnosis for what the Higher Self feels the client is ready to receive in this time and space along with the body scan. We also record and transcribe questions that the client has for their Higher Self.

Getting back to today's session, my partner was Alexia who was gentle, patient, and loving. During the interview, I shared with her a little of my session with AuroRa and how afterward the healing seemed to continue. It felt like I had a dark portal in my back which I addressed by connecting with my Higher Self and using my newly acquired alchemy Reiki energy work tools. I asked Alexia if she could look at my back to confirm the portal was closed which she did admirably. I thank, honor, respect, and love her infinitely.

The following is the transcript of my session which would be Alexia's first session as a practitioner.

Session begins.

A [Alexia]: Do you feel like you have a body?

D [Debra]: I'm sensing light green and brown. I'm not sensing a body.

A: What else do you see around you?

D: It's changed. Now it's like a fog, a fog. There's a purple color in the middle of this fog and . . .

A: This purple color, does it have a consciousness?

D: I don't know. It's moving around.

A: Remember to trust your very first impression. Let's move time along now. Move time along and see if something else changes within this space. Let's keep moving through this fog, moving through the fog, and let me know when something changes.

D: There's a lot of light now.

A: What does it feel like to be in this space?

D: I'm comfortable.

A: Do you feel at home in this space?

D: It feels familiar.

A: You have been taken to this space for a reason. Just be in this space and allow for time to move. Why is it that you have been brought to this space? You know exactly why you are here.

D: Searching. It's different now. It feels more earthy towards . . .

A: You are able to see and sense everything very clearly, very clearly. Why is it that you feel you have been taken to this space?

D: I'm not sure.

A: Do you feel like you have a body?

D: I'm not sensing a body.

A: *Go ahead and continue moving the scene along, move it along until we reach another important time. Another important time where we will find the answers we seek for your highest healing. We are there now. Tell me what you see.*

D: I'm back to the fog. There is foliage around the edges and there are waves of purple coming back, but the foliage is not shadows. It's like it died.

A: *Does this space feel like Earth or somewhere else?*

D: I'm not sure. The purple is changing to a lighter lavender. The waves are gone.

A: *You said they are gone now?*

D: Yeah.

A: *What are you sensing and seeing now?*

D: Emptiness.

A: *These images that you are receiving are an important part of this healing process. Continue to move along and tell me when something changes. Just be patient and allow for what is meant to be shown. Let's go into a space now where we can begin this healing.*

D: It's dark.

A: *Are you in the cave again?*

D: I don't see or sense anything. It is just dark, a lot of black all around me. I don't feel anything, it just is.

A: *Why is it that you have been brought back to this space? You know exactly why you are here. What are you sensing brought you here?*

D: I'm not sensing anything.

A: *What does it feel like to be in this darkness?*

D: It's not bad. It's okay.

A: *Do you like being here?*

D: Yeah, it's okay.

A: *Let's continue to move time along. Move time along and see if something changes within this space. Continue moving time along and let me know what you see.*

D: It's now gray with a little smidge of purple. I can't make out anything. There are shapes.

A: *Remember to trust your very first impression. Let's keep moving through this fog, keep moving through the fog. Trust your very first impression. Do you have a body now?*

D: I'm not sensing a body.

A: *Let's go ahead and leave that life now. Moving away, moving away from that life, leaving that being there so that it can continue on its own path. We send them on their way with love and peace. We now leave that scene with gratitude. Let's go now to a time and space where we can begin this healing. Let me know what you are seeing and sensing.*

D: It is back to being dark.

The Higher Self is called forth.

A: *May I please ask for the Higher Self of Debra? Will you please allow the Higher Self to speak now?*

D: Yes.

A: *Thank you. I love you, respect you, and honor you. Thank you for all the aid you have given us today. May we ask you questions, please?*

Higher Self: Yes.

A: *The life that we went to with the purple waves and foliage, what was the purpose for showing this? Where was she in this life?*

Higher Self: I'm not sensing anything

A: *Higher Self, would this be a good time to begin the body scan?*

Higher Self: Okay.

The body scan begins.

A: *Wonderful. Thank you. Higher Self, please scan the body for any entities, energies, or anything that is not part of her body that we need to heal today. Do we need any assistance from any of the Angels or any other benevolent beings?*

Higher Self: Yes, please.

A: *Who may we call forth for your assistance?*

Higher Self: Can we ask for Archangel Michael?

A: *Yes, of course. Higher Self, if you could please connect us to Archangel Michael, please. Greetings.*

Archangel Michael: Greetings.

A: *It is an honor to be working with you. I am speaking with you because the Higher Self would like assistance with the body scan. Would you be able to assist us with the body scan today?*

AA Michael: Yes.

A: *Thank you. Archangel Michael, please now scan the body for any entities, energies, or anything that is not part of her that we need to heal today.*

AA Michael: I'm scanning. Nothing is popping up. I am still scanning.

A: *She had mentioned a dark portal that she had found in her back. Can we check and make sure this portal has been closed?*

AA Michael: Scanning it now.

A: *Thank you.*

AA Michael: It looks pretty good. It is closed.

A: *Thank you. Are you seeing any other dark portals that need to be closed?*

AA Michael: I am not sensing any portals. There is something going on with her right hip.

A: *What are you sensing? What is going on there? Is it an entity? Does it have a consciousness?*

AA Michael: I'm not sensing a consciousness.

A: *Is it artificial technology?*

AA Michael: It's moving.

A: *It's moving? What does this look like?*

AA Michael: It's energy. It's not dark energy.

A: *It's good energy? Is it causing her any pain?*

AA Michael: Initially but it moved through her hip up through her sacral.

A: *Is it part of her organic blueprint or is it something that needs to be removed?*

AA Michael: It feels organic. It worked itself out allowing it to flow through like it is supposed to.

A: *Can we help this energy with any Love-Light?*

AA Michael: Yes, that would be welcome.

A: *Let's go back to the dark portal in her back for a minute. Can we call in Archangel Raphael to fill in Love-Light where that dark portal was?*

AA Michael: Yes, that would be wonderful. Thank you.

A: *Okay. Archangel Michael, please continue scanning. We would like to make sure she is crystal clear and that there is nothing artificial or inorganic or not of her highest timeline within her. Let's continue scanning for any hooks, portals, implants or anything else that is not meant to be within her.*

AA Michael: I am not sensing anything.

A: *Okay. She says that her knees have arthritis and have been giving her trouble. Is there a way that we can heal her knees back to the healthiest crystalline organic structure that they can be, fully regenerated and not causing her pain?*

AA Michael: We can send them Love-Light.

A: *Is there any entities or implants there perhaps causing this arthritis?*

AA Michael: I'm not sensing anything.

A: *Okay, let's send Love-Light to her knees so that they can be fully restored and no longer cause her pain. Archangel Michael, let's scan her digestive system now. She has been having trouble with her digestive system lately. Let's scan her digestive system for anything that is not meant to be within her.*

AA Michael: It's healing.

A: *What is the cause of this digestive system disruption?*

AA Michael: Emotional traumas.

A: *Are there any implants, hooks, or portals causing this or have they been healed?*

AA Michael: I'm not sensing anything there.

A: *So it is in the process of healing?*

AA Michael: Yeah.

A: *Can we send Love-Light to it to help it heal?*

AA Michael: Yes, that would be lovely.

A: *Archangel Michael, can we go back to her knees for a moment? I want to just double-check and make sure we have removed everything from her knees causing the pain and the arthritis. Scan very deeply. We want to make sure there are no hooks, portals, or anything that is not meant to be within her.*

AA Michael: Scanning now. There is something in the left knee.

A: *What are you sensing in the left knee?*

AA Michael: It has a different feel.

A: *Do you feel that it has a consciousness?*

AA Michael: I'm not sure.

A: *Archangel Michael, is this an entity trying to be something that it is not? Or is it perhaps an artificial technology?*

AA Michael: This is the knee involved in a car accident when she was a child so there is some trauma there.

A: *Can we start repairing that trauma there, please?*

AA Michael: Yes.

A: *Can I send Phoenix Fire and Love-Light to the knee?*

AA Michael: Yes, that would be wonderful.

A: *Phoenix Fire or Love-Light?*

AA Michael: Phoenix Fire.

A: *Sending Phoenix Fire now. Have we removed everything from the knee?*

AA Michael: It feels much lighter, much lighter.

A: *Archangel Michael, let's continue scanning the body. First, we want to make sure the knee is completely healed. That there is nothing there that needs to be removed. Let's double, and triple check the knees so that they can heal and no longer cause her pain.*

AA Michael: It is much better, thank you. There is something going on with the right big toe area.

A: *What is going on there?*

AA Michael: It's heavy there.

A: Does it feel like it has a consciousness?

AA Michael: No, I'm not sensing one.

A: Can you remove this from her big toe? Is it a hook, an implant, or something else?

AA Michael: It's a hook.

A: Archangel Michael can you remove that now? Do you need help with Phoenix Fire?

AA Michael: Yes, please.

A: Sending Phoenix Fire to the hook in the big toe. May I call on Raphael to fill in with Love-Light once that is removed?

AA Michael: Yes.

A: What allowed this hook to come into her big toe?

AA Michael: I'm not sensing where she picked it up. It was recent though.

A: Very good. Has this hook in her big toe been removed now or are you still working on it?

AA Michael: Yes, it is fully removed.

A: Good. Let's scan her heart now. She says her heart has been beating rapidly for the past couple of weeks and she wants to know what is going on with it. Can you scan her heart now and tell us what may be causing her heart to beat rapidly?

AA Michael: It looks pretty healthy.

A: Wonderful. Is there a reason why it was beating quickly?

AA Michael: She may want to relocate her quartz crystal and change that frequency in her room.

A: Why would that crystal make her heart beat quickly?

AA Michael: It is very powerful. If she would just move it over a few feet in a different direction. She currently has it practically over her head when she sleeps.

A: Wonderful. I'm sure she will appreciate that information. She says that she has had surgery on her heart. Scan her heart now and make sure it is thoroughly healthy and regenerated, and that no trauma exists. Can we heal her heart now? Fully heal it.

AA Michael: Yes, send it Love-Light.

A: Sending Love-Light to her heart. She also wants to know if she has any fragmented soul pieces that she can retrieve so that she can be her most full self. Are there any pieces of her that we need to integrate back so that we can make her whole again?

AA Michael: I am not sensing any.

A: Very good. Now let's scan her body one more time, making sure she is crystal clear. Making sure there is nothing hiding in her. And making sure there are no entities, no negative technology, nothing that is not part of her most organic highest timeline. Let's scan her body now. Is there anything else?

AA Michael: I'm not sensing anything.

A: Archangel Michael, is there potential something in her third eye area that might be hiding from us?

AA Michael: There's like tentacles going down above and below the physical eyes.

A: Do you feel that they have consciousness or is this negative technology?

AA Michael: It feels like A.I. without a consciousness.

A: Archangel Michael, let's please contain these in the symbols now and let's begin removing these tentacles from her third eye and crown area. Are these tentacles anywhere else?

AA Michael: It is kind of like a web that just spreads out like this (spreading fingers across her forehead, eyes, and top of her head).

A: Is it all over?

AA Michael: All over this area.

A: What was going on with her? When did these tentacles come into her?

AA Michael: It feels like they have been there a while.

A: Are these tentacles possibly the reason why she has been blocked?

AA Michael: Very possibly, yes.

A: Let's keep removing these tentacles. May I help with Phoenix Fire?

AA Michael: Yes, please.

A: *Wonderful. Directing Phoenix Fire. Have these tentacles been completely removed?*

AA Michael: Not yet.

A: *Okay. Continue working on those tentacles and let's continue scanning the body. We don't want to miss anything and want to make sure that she is crystal clear.*

AA Michael: There's something in the right shoulder. It feels like A.I.

A: *A.I. Let's contain that now in the symbols. Can I direct Phoenix Fire?*

AA Michael: Yes, please.

A: *Directing Phoenix Fire now to the right shoulder. Let me know when that A.I. has been completely removed. What was going with her when it attached to her right shoulder?*

AA Michael: It's been there a while. It was mostly removed during her last session but this little bit was hidden.

A: *Let's continue scanning. Let's scan her throat area very well, very well. Look deep in her throat area and make sure there is nothing there.*

AA Michael: I'm not sensing anything.

A: *Are we still working on the tentacles in her crown and the A.I. in her right shoulder?*

AA Michael: They have been removed.

A: *Wonderful. May we fill in those areas with Love-Light to those areas?*

AA Michael: Yes, please.

A: *Doing that now. We want to make sure that there are no dark portals anywhere in her body or in the homes that she stays in. Are we able to close any dark portals in her body or in those homes? Scan her body very deeply for dark portals.*

AA Michael: Something is going on again in her right shoulder.

A: *Let's contain that artificial technology in her right shoulder in the alchemy symbols. What does this technology look like?*

AA Michael: It is shooting sharp pain.

A: *Higher Self, please make sure she is not feeling any pain. Let's contain this negative technology in her right shoulder now. What does this negative technology look like?*

AA Michael: I'm not seeing what it looks like.

A: *Let's make sure we get every piece of this negative technology out of her shoulder so that it no longer causes her any pain, remove it fully and completely out of her right shoulder, please. May I direct Phoenix Fire to help?*

AA Michael: Yes, please.

A: *Directing Phoenix Fire there now. I just want to double-check on the tentacles in her crown area, are they completely removed?*

AA Michael: Yes, that feels clear.

A: *Wonderful. Are these tentacles perhaps the cause of dyslexia that she mentioned that she has?*

AA Michael: I'm not sensing that.

A: *Are we able to heal the cause of dyslexia so that she no longer feels backward?*

AA Michael: Not at this time.

A: *Okay. May we send Love-Light?*

AA Michael: Yes, please.

A: *Sending Love-Light. Let's continue looking for all the dark portals. Have we closed all the dark portals within her?*

AA Michael: I can't sense any. The dark portal that was in her back is something we worked on a couple of weeks ago. It looks good.

A: *Okay, are there any dark portals in the homes or lands where she is staying? Can we close those as well?*

AA Michael: I am not sensing any portals there.

A: *Very good. Let's scan her DNA now. Let's scan it for any negative fractals or any negative consciousness that has been integrated into her DNA, let's scan this now. Are you sensing anything that has been integrated into her DNA that we can remove today?*

AA Michael: There's the programming of lack, lack of self-confidence mostly.

A: Let's remove this negative programming from her DNA now so that she can feel confident, and that she no longer feels she is in lack. Let's remove these programs from her DNA. Can I send Love-Light or Phoenix Fire to help?

AA Michael: Love-Light, please.

A: Sending Love-Light.

AA Michael: Thank you.

A: My pleasure. Thank you. Let's look for any negative chords. Can you see any negative chords or wires?

AA Michael: No, I'm not seeing any.

A: Beautiful. Let's scan her chakras now. Are there any imbalances that we can realign at this time?

AA Michael: No. You did a beautiful job with your energy work.

A: Wonderful. Thank you. Are there any physical illnesses that we can heal at this time?

AA Michael: No. She looks good.

A: Beautiful. Can we age-regress her, please?

AA Michael: Sure.

A: How many years are we able to age regress?

AA Michael: Five.

A: Wonderful, thank you. Is there anything in her aura that needs to be repaired? Any tears, rips, or dark energy fields that we can heal?

AA Michael: No, it looks good.

A: Thank you. Are there any fragmented soul contracts or trauma from a current or past life that we can heal now?

AA Michael: I'm not seeing any.

A: Thank you, Archangel Michael. We greatly appreciate your assistance with the body scan today. We love you, honor you, and respect you.

AA Michael: We love you and respect you. You have done a beautiful job. Beautiful, beautiful.

A: Thank you very much. Are we able to speak back to the Higher Self, please?

AA Michael: Yes.

The Higher Self is called back in.

A: *Higher Self, may we please ask you questions?*
Higher Self: Yes.
A: *Wonderful. Thank you. Debra would like to know if she has any Dragons or magical creatures that she can connect with.*
Higher Self: Yes, of course.
A: *Beautiful. Who are these magical creatures?*
Higher Self: I'm sensing a white Dragon.
A: *Beautiful. Is this Dragon male or female?*
Higher Self: I'm not sensing anything further.
A: *Does this white Dragon have a message for Debra?*
Higher Self: Life is going to get more and more interesting. Enjoy the ride.
A: *We know that Debra's Higher Self is Archangel Jophiel. Is there a crystal that you suggest that she get to connect with you?*
AA Jophiel: Amethyst comes to mind.
A: *Thank you. Higher Self, do you have a message for Debra?*
AA Jophiel: You are on the right path.
A: *Higher Self, is there anything that I could have asked that I haven't asked?*
AA Jophiel: No. You have done a wonderful job.
A: *Thank you. Higher Self, we are going to wait for AuroRa who will be here shortly and we will conclude the session.*
AA Jophiel: Okay. Thank you. You are amazing. Your spirit is so gentle and caring. We love you, honor you, and respect you.
A: *Thank you. I love you, honor you, and respect you.*

End of the session.

As blocked as I was, my practitioner gently guided me as the client to sense experiencing varying colors of energies before going to this scene of foliage that died, which then transitioned into a dark void. That puzzle piece feels like a trauma I wasn't ready to face at that time and space. Looking at it closer, this trauma surfaces in subsequent sessions. Alexia was also able to guide me on how to further sense the Archangels' voice in finding and removing the web of tentacles and the other negative infringements plaguing me, for which I'm so very grateful. Note her use of specific questions. There is always more to recognize and know. Isn't life grand?

I'd like to add that going into this session, my knees were in excruciating pain. Afterward, I was pain-free. Wow! And how can I forget the absolutely fun bonus, of learning I have a white Dragon? Fantastic!

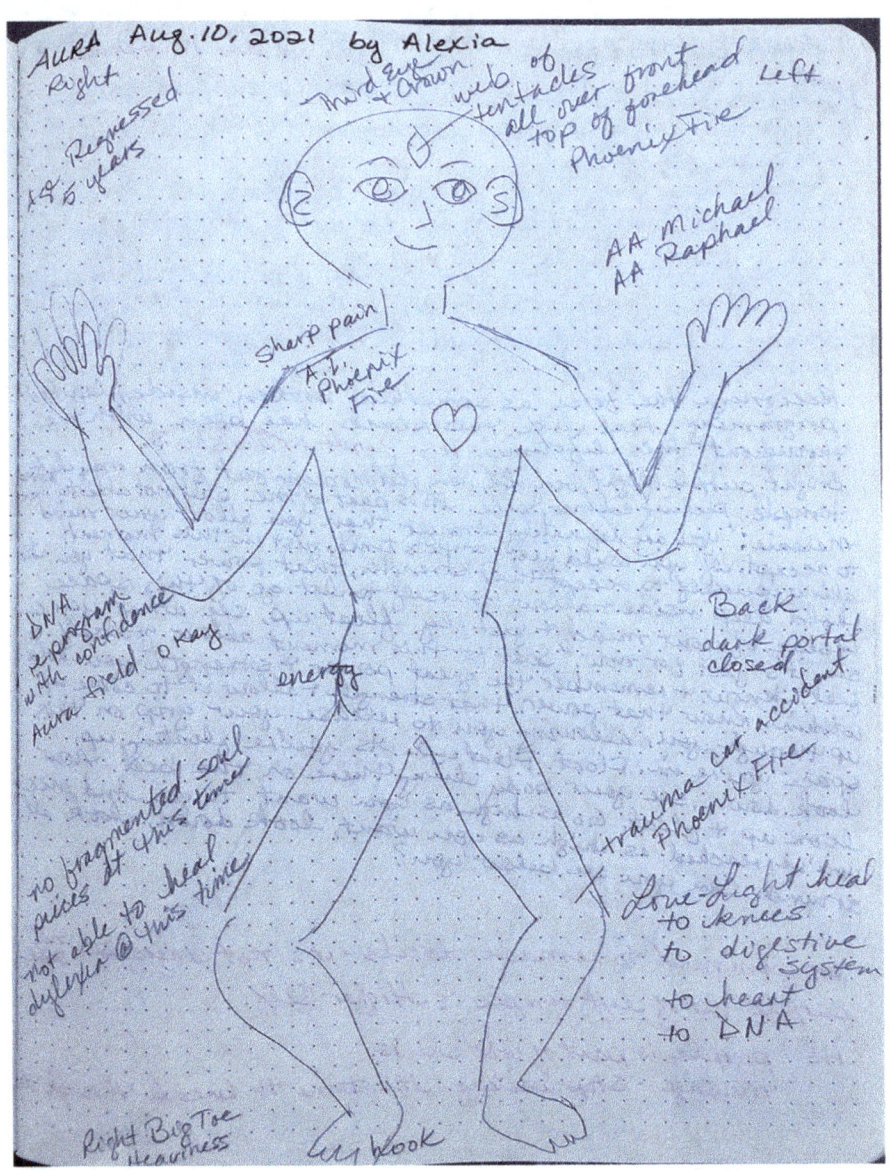

5

It's Not Safe to Move

AURA Hypnosis Healing by Melanie
October 11, 2021

I met Melanie in Chicago at the in-person AURA Practitioners' Certification retreat, who was also getting certified. We were both working on our websites and bouncing ideas past one another. Knowing full well that there were more layers of shadow work that I needed when Melanie asked if she could do a session on me, it was an easy yes, please, and in the greatest of gratitude. Melanie was amazing and so dang creative, patient, loving, and knowledgeable. Love, love, love her.

Session begins.

> M [Melanie]: *Have you landed yet?*
> D [Debra]: *I'm not sensing anything.*
> M: *Tell me how you feel. What does your energy feel like?*
> D: *I feel heavy.*
> M: *You feel heavy. What else do you feel?*
> D: *I feel safe. I feel good.*

M: Look around you, do you notice any colors, any sensations? Just go with the very first thing that comes to you.

D: There are no colors, just the weight.

M: Just feeling heavy?

D: Yeah.

M: The space that you're in, is it dark?

D: Yes, but not pitch-black dark.

M: Describe it.

D: It is kind of like charcoal gray.

M: If you look at yourself in this charcoal gray darkness, can you make anything out? Do you have a body?

D: I don't sense a body.

M: Do you still feel the heavy energy?

D: Yes.

M: With your mind, scan yourself. Do you have a shape?

D: I'm not sensing anything. No shape.

M: This space that you are in, does it feel at all familiar? Have you been here before?

D: Yeah.

M: When were you there before?

D: I don't know.

M: Does it feel recent or has it been a long time since you have been back there?

D: It feels like it is a place I go to escape or I go to have quiet time.

M: Where you sense that you are, you are meant to be here. Let's feel into it some more. You remember that you have been here before, you feel heavy but you don't have a form, it is not quite pitch black, it is more like charcoal. Can you see where this source of light is that is making it not pitch black?

D: Yeah, it is changing now to be variegations of purple coming in.

M: Is there a direction that this purple is coming from?

D: Off-center, left.

M: How do you feel as this purple emerges?

D: Gone.

M: You feel gone?

D: No the purple is gone.

M: What is there now?

D: It is back to just dark, dark gray.

M: Do you feel like you are alone in this space?

D: Yeah.

M: Does it feel like a big vast space or a small area?

D: A small area but I can still move around.

M: If you had to guess where do you think this is located? Is it on Earth or outer space, is it interdimensional, is it in your mind?

D: I think it's in my mind. When you said, "In your mind," my third eye became really heavy so there is that. And the color purple came in.

M: You are right where you are meant to be and we are here to find the answers that you seek and your highest healing. Has anything changed since we first arrived in this place? Any feelings or senses or knowing? You can feel and sense everything very clearly, very clearly.

D: It's comforting knowing we are in the right place that is meant to be.

M: Yes, you are definitely right where you need to be. You said that you are in a small space but you can still move around. How are you moving?

D: It's like floating. Some areas are grayer and some areas are more purple.

M: Are you drawn in any specific direction?

D: Just lounging around.

M: Do you feel like if you wanted to you could leave this space and go anywhere?

D: No.

M: How come? What does it feel like?

D: I don't know. I'm trying to leave and I'm not able to.

M: Walk me through it when you attempt to leave, what does that look like? How does that feel?

D: Feels tighter.

M: You are floating and it feels tighter if you try to move away?

D: Yeah.

M: *What is making it tighter? Does it feel tighter all the way around or just in certain areas?*

D: It's not okay.

M: *What is not okay?*

D: It's not okay to move around, it's not, it's not okay.

M: *Is someone telling you that?*

D: It's a feeling. It's wrong.

M: *So you said that in this space it's small but you can move around except for if you try to leave and then you feel restricted like it is not okay?*

D: Yeah.

M: *Does this space get smaller or does some invisible force start clamping down on you?*

D: I think something happens. It feels . . . a reminder you can't do that. It is a force.

M: *Do you recognize this force or is this the first time that you have sensed it?*

D: I recognize it as something that has been broken in me, it is learned that it is not okay.

M: *You think that it is learned programming and that it is not okay for you?*

D: Yeah, I don't feel safe anymore.

M: *What changed? When you first arrived you were feeling safe and comfortable and now you are not safe. Can you tell me what changed?*

D: Trying to move away from it.

M: *Oh. So you were okay as long as you stayed there but when you thought about leaving it became unsafe and constricting?*

D: Yeah, and very cold, very cold. I'm shivering.

M: *Very cold, Higher Self please make her comfortable that she may witness while not enduring the feeling of discomfort, please. How often do you think that you visit this place?*

D: I don't know.

M: *In the beginning, you thought you went there by choice to get away. Do you still feel like that? That when you go to this space it's a choice?*

D: No. (Very emotional.) I don't think it's a choice.

M: *Can you remember the first time you ended up in this place?*

D: No I can't remember.

M: *You are doing wonderful. Just keep telling me the first thing that pops into your mind when I ask you stuff.*

D: All right.

M: *Do you feel like this has always been with you, this lifetime, this place inside your mind?*

D: Yeah.

M: *Try to feel further. Do you feel like maybe you have had this longer than this lifetime?*

D: Yeah. I feel the stream of purple from the left coming in.

M: *You see a stream of purple coming in from the left? Can you tell how the purple light was able to get in?*

D: It's lighter.

M: *Say that again.*

D: A large huge stream seems to be lighter on the other side of the purple.

M: *Can you go towards it?*

D: I'm not able to move.

M: *You're not able to move?*

D: No.

M: *But you can see the purple light and you can see that it is streaming in from the left?*

D: Yeah.

M: *How do you feel when you see the purple light?*

D: Like there is an urgency.

M: *What for, what's the urgency?*

D: There's an urgency of need, help.

M: *Can you say that again? I heard urgency of need . . .*

D: It's like there is some possible help.

M: *Is the help trying to get in or are you trying to send out help?*

D: It's very old, very old.

M: *The purple light?*

D: Yeah. It's . . .

M: *You said there's a feeling of urgency when you see the purple light, like help. Are you trying to send to get help or is that help, trying to get to you?*

D: I think it's both.

M: *That purple light, does it feel like it's part of you, you are part of it, or is it separate?*

D: (Speaking gentle and softly) Yeah, it's part of me.

M: *It's part of you?*

D: Yeah (Softly).

M: *That's what I saw too.*

D: It is coming up from my left temple.

M: *The purple light is coming in from your left temple?*

D: Out of my left temple.

M: *Oh, it is going out. Are you able to follow it? Did you follow the light?*

D: It feels safer again. I'm calmer. It has some different colors in it and then it fades. It has a streak of red coming through it and then it fades.

M: *Very good. You are definitely stronger than you allow your mind to accept. If you could, just for this time, just at this moment, allow yourself to accept that strength, that power that you hold deep inside. And allow yourself to let go of this space inside of your mind and just fly. Float up. See what you can see. Just for now.*

D: (As Melonie was speaking a new vibration started literally shaking things up inside me - in a hopeful voice I asked) Can you repeat that?

M: (Melanie could sense the breakthrough happening and in a tone of celebration said) *Yeah. For just right now, just this moment, allow yourself to feel, know, and remember, the great power and strength you hold within. And allow that power and that strength to come up, up through you, allowing you to release your grip on this space you are in. Float, float up. As you are float-*

ing up, look down. See your body there lying on the bed. Now look up and float, go as high as you want to go, and keep going. Once you have reached as high as you want, look down. Look all around. Can you see below you?

D: I feel like I started pulling out and then got pulled back in. I'm really tight and cold and shaking all over.

M: Higher Self, I ask for you to please make Debra as comfortable as possible. Debra, are you able to just in your mind feel like you are hovering over your body and see yourself laying right where you are? Can you see that? See your face, the shirt that you have on, the blanket that you have over you, can you see that?

D: Yeah (Meekly).

M: Very good. Can you look around the room? Are you able to see some of the objects that are in here with you?

D: Yeah.

M: What do you see?

D: I see my selenite crystals and my candle.

M: Very good. What else can you see in your room? Can you locate the door in your room?

D: Yeah.

M: Imagine yourself standing near that door while your physical you is laying there. Can you see yourself standing by the door?

D: Yeah. I don't see it but I sense it.

M: You sense it, that is very good. You are doing great. Imagine in your mind, you have done it a thousand times, what it feels like to put your hand on that doorknob. Hold it, feel the cold metal in your hand. Let me know when you can feel it.

D: I can feel it as you say it.

M: Perfect. Now, turn the knob and pull that door open or push.

D: Pull.

M: Pull the door open and stand in that place that you know what is on the other side of this door. Describe it to me.

D: It's a hallway to the restroom, the other bedrooms and to go downstairs to the main level.

M: *Tell me what way do you have to go if you want to go to the restroom?*
D: To the left.
M: *What way do you have to go if you want to go downstairs?*
D: To the right.
M: *Step out of the door and go to the right. Remember to envision exactly the way you know this hallway looks, you've done it a thousand times. Do you see it?*
D: Yeah, yeah.
M: *Go towards the stairs.*
D: All right. I'm there.
M: *You are standing at the top. When you look down, what do you see?*
D: The foyer, the chandelier, the front door, and the front room. It's an open area.
M: *Very good. Start walking down the stairs. Walk as you normally would. What foot first, the right or the left?*
D: The right.
M: *Okay, starting with the right foot, let me know when you have reached the bottom.*
D: Okay, I'm at the bottom.
M: *Very good. What is straight in front of you?*
D: The front door and the front room.
M: *Walk to the front door, and place your hand on the handle. Open the front door, can you see outside?*
D: Yeah.
M: *How do you feel now that the door is open?*
D: I love it out here.
M: *Do you want to go out there?*
D: Sure, okay.
M: *Okay, walk out the door and tell me where you go.*
D: Hmmm, for a walk around the neighborhood.
M: *Very nice. Do you live in track homes or is everybody kind of spread out?*
D: I don't know what track homes are.

M: *Track homes basically look like they are in a track and every other home looks exactly like the two homes before and are pretty close together.*

D: No there are some older homes, some newer, some bigger, some smaller with varied lot sizes. They're varied but not on large, large-sized lots. Some are bigger than others but they are all different. A lot of them have trailers to go camping with that are either parked on the side of their home or in the front. There are many with Halloween decorations up for this time of the year.

M: *Where do you usually go on your walk?*

D: I try to change it up, different directions, like around the back through the elementary school area and along that way.

M: *Which path do you want to take today, right now?*

D: I'll go left through the neighborhood. The elementary kids are having recess so they are having a blast out there. We won't bother them.

M: *Tell me what you see and hear while you are walking, whatever stands out.*

D: One home has this huge, huge, rock right in the corner of their property right off the sidewalk that I love to just go and greet. I'm placing my hand on it. It's beautiful. It has layers of white through it. And I'm just enjoying the air, the crispness of the air.

M: *The house with the beautiful rock, how far from your house is it?*

D: It's around the curve and down the next corner so it's like four minutes or less.

M: *Very good. Where do you go now?*

D: I just zig-zag around the circles and the offshoots that go down to the main road that connects to all of them.

M: *What's the weather like while you are walking around?*

D: It's sunny. It's been raining lately but it's sunny today. It's still crisp, cool not hot.

M: *As you walk, do you have a destination in mind or are you just walking?*

D: Just walking.

M: I just want to say, congratulations! You made it out of that space. That space where you felt like you couldn't leave or even move. You made it out. You are that strong and brave! You took the steps to get out. Now that you're out is there anything else you want to do or that you want to go and see? Is there any place you want to visit? Tell me the first place that comes to mind.

D: No, I don't have any special places around here. I haven't lived here that long.

M: No worries. We're not walking. You can just imagine in your mind just like you imagined leaving the house.

D: Sure, I'd love to go visit the mountains.

M: We're going there now. We're traveling to that place. Tell me what does it look like?

D: It is kind of small with short little trails around it. On one side it's sandy and on the other side it's full of trees. You're going to have to work to get through those trees.

M: Very good. What else is up there?

D: Just Mother Nature with beautiful air, crisp air, the breeze, the sun . . .

M: When you breathe in, what do you smell?

D: I smell water, I smell the fragrant bushes and some sunflowers too but they're not that great smelling.

M: How does it make you feel when you are up there?

D: This is my happy place, being in the mountains outside and in nature. Not so much when it's full of snow.

M: You don't like being in the snow?

D: Not too much. I always had a heart condition and it didn't go well with the cold. I had to stay away from the cold with my heart.

M: Did you ever get a chance as a kid before your heart problems to enjoy the snow?

D: Yeah. I did some skiing. I went picnicking and camping with my family and our grandparents. My grampa threw me up on top of a glacier to grab ice from that glacier to make homemade ice cream. It was warm outside but there were still glaciers left.

M: *How did that feel when your grampa put you up on that glacier?*

D: I felt important because I was the one that was the right size to be able to be thrown up there and strong enough to scrape the ice.

M: *I bet it made that ice cream taste even better.*

D: Yeah (Lovingly).

M: *You're doing great. Is there anywhere else you want to go?*

D: No, not really. I need to do more of these trips though.

M: *You and me both. Know that any time you have a quiet moment where you can close your eyes you can go there again just like you did right now. Okay, let's start the body scan.*

The Higher Self is called forth.

Higher Self: Hello.

M: *Am I speaking to Debra's Higher Self now?*

Higher Self: Yes.

M: *Thank you. I love you, honor you, and respect you. And I thank you.*

Higher Self: And I thank you and honor you.

M: *When we started this, Debra felt like she was in a charcoal gray-colored space, that was small but she could still move around but she couldn't leave. She felt constricted whenever she thought about leaving but she did say she saw a purple light coming in from the left. Are you able to explain this place to her?*

Higher Self: No, I'm not able to.

M: *Okay. The purple light. Are you able to tell her what that was?*

Higher Self: Purple is part of who she is. Anything purple in her life that is familiar to her, she recognizes that.

M: *Was that you reaching out to her in this place?*

Higher Self: Yeah.

M: *She said she felt urgency when looking at this purple light. Like needing help. Can you explain that?*

Higher Self: Stop waiting. It's time. It's time to break through this.

M: *What does she need to break through? Can you explain it to her?*

Higher Self: The powerlessness feeling.

M: *She needs to break through the powerlessness feeling that she has?*

Higher Self: Yes.

M: *Can you tell her how that started?*

Higher Self: I'm not seeing any answers right now.

M: *That's okay. We have a good start. Higher Self you stated that she needs to break through this helplessness. Higher Self, do you feel she is ready for her body scan at this time?*

The body scan begins.

M: *Are you able to do the body scan or would you like any help from the Archangels or any benevolent beings?*

Higher Self: Archangels, please.

M: *Archangels. Sure, which one or which ones?*

Higher Self: Could we ask for Archangel Jophiel?

M: *Anyone else or is that it? It's okay. If you think of more let me know. Higher Self, if you could please call in Archangel Jophiel. Greetings, is this Archangel Jophiel?*

AA Jophiel: Greetings. Yes.

M: *I love you, honor you, respect you, and thank you so much for joining us. The Higher Self has requested your assistance with the body scan.*

AA Jophiel: Greetings. Thank you for having me here.

M: *You are most welcome. Thank you for being here. Are you able to help us with the body scan here today?*

AA Jophiel: Yes.

M: *Beautiful. If you could please begin starting from the top moving your way down, scanning her whole body for any technologies, energies, entities, or anything that is within here that is not organic. Let me know what you find.*

AA Jophiel: There is some tightness around her front rib cage that goes all the way around her back.

M: *Archangel Jophiel, what's there?*

AA Jophiel: It is like it's a hook that hooked all the way around like a clamp.

M: Are you able to see what is attached to this hook?

AA Jophiel: I'm not seeing it.

M: That's okay. This hook that goes all the way around, does it kind of look like barbed wire wrapping around?

AA Jophiel: It has a barb right into the middle of her chest and then it goes around the right side to her back. It is not on the left, just on the right.

M: How long has this been here?

AA Jophiel: It's fairly new. I think it's from all this not being able to keep the Love-Light with some family members where her sick daughter is.

M: So within the last year?

AA Jophiel: Within the last month. Her granddaughter has a lot of darkness around her. A lot of anger and hatred.

M: Is this one of her daughter's kids?

AA Jophiel: Yes. And they have had the vaccines.

M: Is that what is affecting Debra?

AA Jophiel: Yeah. She is allowing it to affect her.

M: Is she doing her shielding?

AA Jophiel: Yes, she shielding but she is so disappointed. She continually sends this granddaughter love but receives abuse in return. It's a sensitive situation with the mom (Debra's daughter) being on hospice dying from breast cancer. The granddaughter is abusive to her mom too. It's wrong but it's understandable. While Debra is living there caring for this troubled family, she has got to stand up more to the granddaughter. It is not right the way she behaves.

M: Can you tell her exactly how this hook came in during these times?

AA Jophiel: It was when asking her granddaughter to help with dishes.

M: Besides the tightness what other discomfort has this hook caused her?

AA Jophiel: Lack of focus. Her attention span is short. I think she is learning her lesson.

M: Are we allowed to use Phoenix Fire to transmute that hook out?

AA Jophiel: Yes, please.

M: Thank you. You said it's hooking in the middle and it wraps around her right side?

AA Jophiel: Yeah.

M: Sending Phoenix Fire. As we do this, Archangel Jophiel, what else do you find?

AA Jophiel: There is a snake partially in her back hanging there.

M: You were able to see a snake in her back partially hanging there?

AA Jophiel: Yes.

M: Where in her back?

AA Jophiel: High upper back right in the middle.

M: Between the shoulder blades?

AA Jophiel: Yes, along the spine. You're right, it's right between the shoulder blades. Is that what you are seeing?

M: Hmmm. Debra said she could see this and it had hands. Is this what you are seeing Archangel Jophiel?

AA Jophiel: Yes. They have gotten inside her, parts are in her.

M: When did this happen?

AA Jophiel: It would have been about six weeks ago.

M: What was going on that allowed this snake being to get in there? Before you answer, could you please place it in the alchemy symbols?

AA Jophiel: Yes. It's contained. There was a lot of contradiction between what she is learning and knowing and what she is able to share and not share. It is the not sharing that is a contradiction with her loved ones.

M: Are you able to give her a specific example so that she can understand clearly what you mean?

AA Jophiel: Well, she tried to clear up her relationship with her son, and he is telling her that he can't have a relationship with her until she can specifically say what she did wrong as a mother. All of her responses to him were too general for him. He needs specific words. In her heart, she knows what is going on is infringements from Archons and Reptilians.

M: *To clarify, you are saying that the son has infringements and those infringements are what is asking for specific examples from her about what he feels she was a bad mother?*

AA Jophiel: Exactly. He doesn't think she is or was a bad mother but he doesn't want anything to do with her because of her second marriage and her first marriage. He doesn't trust her judgment. She was a good mother. Their father molested his sisters.

M: *Which daughters were these?*

AA Jophiel: The secondborn and fourthborn.

M: *And they share the same father as this son?*

AA Jophiel: Yes. All six kids have the same father. They were married for twenty years, so yeah, all six kids.

M: *Does the son know about this?*

AA Jophiel: Yes. That is why they got divorced. The older daughter finally told Debra which is when Debra divorced their father. The younger daughter never said anything until she was terminal with cancer. She had flashbacks after that. For years the younger daughter who had also been molested pulled herself away from the family which we now know is common when you have that situation going on.

M: *Do you have any advice for Debra on this specific situation with the contradiction?*

AA Jophiel: Cleaning the chord with her son but not severe it. Just clean it.

M: *Okay, let's do that now. Are you able to clear that chord or do you need any assistance?*

AA Jophiel: Yes, we can clean it. Let's clean it and surround it with Love-Light.

M: *Okay, good. Just to step back real quick. The hook that was connected to her chest and wrapped around her, has that been transmuted?*

AA Jophiel: Yes. It feels good.

M: Higher Self and Archangel Raphael, I love you, honor you and respect you. Please send Love-Light to the place where the hook was removed from. Back to the snake that was partially inside of her directly into her spine between her shoulder blades, how was it able to penetrate her shields?

Higher Self: She's been broken many times making it easy to crack. When her son told her no, he couldn't have a relationship with her.

M: So it lowered her vibration?

AA Jophiel: Not for long, but long enough that it cracked. Her Love-Light frequency went down.

M: This snake being, is it organic?

AA Jophiel: No.

M: Does it have consciousness?

AA Jophiel: There is no light, nothing, no light, just mechanical.

M: Is it an Archon?

AA Jophiel: It's an Archon.

M: Let's put it in the correct alchemy now and let's start transmuting it. As you work on that please let me know once it is completed. Higher Self and Archangel Raphael, please stand by to fill that area in with Love-Light once it is completed.

AA Jophiel: Please send Phoenix Fire to it.

M: Phoenix Fire, got it. While we are working on that, Archangel Jophiel, what else do you see?

AA Jophiel: I'm not sensing anything else. It is looking clear.

M: When I was doing her energy work, I thought I sensed a couple of things and want to ask your opinion. Can you take a deep dive into her crown and tell me how does her crown look and the area around it?

AA Jophiel: I sense an Archon spider there.

M: You do?

AA Jophiel: What do you see there?

M: Did you say that no, you don't see that?

AA Jophiel: Yeah, there is a darkness there, yes.

M: *I find it very interesting that you said, do you see an Archon spider because that is what I saw but you're feeling just a darkness there? Can you try to . . .*

AA Jophiel: I'm not sure if the darkness was a spider.

M: *Let me shine some Source Light in there and see if you can see it better. Let me know what you see.*

AA Jophiel: Yeah, it is a spider.

M: *Okay, Archangel Jophiel can you put it in the alchemy symbols, please?*

AA Jophiel: It is done.

M: *Are we still transmuting the snake in her back?*

AA Jophiel: Yes.

M: *The Archon spider in her crown, how long has it been there?*

AA Jophiel: This one has been here longer. We've been getting parts of it but we haven't gotten all of it.

M: *You are still trying to encase it?*

AA Jophiel: Yeah, let's put Phoenix Fire on it and get rid of it. There is no light there.

M: *Okay. Did it come in this lifetime or another?*

AA Jophiel: It's old. They have removed it before but not completely.

M: *Say that one more time.*

AA Jophiel: They removed it before but left a piece that grew back.

M: *Are we able to completely transmute that piece?*

AA Jophiel: Yes.

M: *Just let me know whenever it is done. We want to make sure we clear that all out so that it doesn't come back again. Can you look into her third eye and tell me what you see? How does her third eye look?*

AA Jophiel: I don't see anything.

M: *Moving on to her throat, taking a deep dive and scanning her throat area. Do you see anything going on in her throat? How does it look?*

AA Jophiel: I don't sense any energies or darkness there. Are you sensing something?

M: In the energy work of her third eye, it kind of lines up with the first place that she went when we started this. She said that it was charcoal-colored, there was space to move around but it was tight if she left. What I saw was kind of like a bell going over her third eye. It was covering it, a big heavy bell.

AA Jophiel: Interesting.

M: And for her throat, what I saw was almost like a glass case surrounding her third chakra, stopping her from being able to put out the energy that she has in it. Archangel Jophiel, can you see any of this stuff?

AA Jophiel: Can we call on Archangel Michael?

M: Higher Self, please connect us now with Archangel Michael. Archangel Michael, thank you brother for joining us. I love you, honor you, and respect you. Greetings. Am I speaking to Michael?

AA Michael: Greetings. Yes, you are.

M: Thank you, brother. The Higher Self and Archangel Jophiel have called on you to help us with the body scan. Are you able to help us?

AA Michael: Yes.

M: Beautiful. I know you do this all the time. If you could just start the body scan and let me know what you find and we will go from there.

Archangels: There is something gray over her right temple, her eye area there.

M: Okay, what is there, Archangel Michael?

AA Michael: There is no light.

M: Is it an entity, a technology, a portal, a chord, a hook? What do you see?

AA Michael: It's a dark portal.

M: When did it get there, this dark portal?

AA Michael: It hasn't been there long.

M: What was going on to allow for that portal to open?

AA Michael: Lack of balance. Not doing anything fun or for herself.

M: So imbalance, basically not taking care of herself.

AA Michael: Being overwhelmed.

M: *Do you have any advice for her so that once we close this portal it doesn't come back?*

AA Michael: Try to give service to herself too.

M: *Higher Self, do you want to contribute any ideas there of what she can do?*

Higher Self: Yeah, find two days of the week to either do your lap swim or the like.

M: *Beautiful. Archangel Michael, are we able to close that portal?*

AA Michael: Yes, definitely.

M: *Perfect. Let me know once it's done.*

AA Michael: It's closed.

M: *Are we still transmuting that Archon snake in her back?*

AA Michael: Yeah, it looks good though.

M: *Good. It's a feisty thing. Were we able to completely transmute that last piece of the Archon spider in her crown?*

AA Michael: Yes. That has been transmuted.

M: *Archangel Michael, tell me what else have you found? Any entities, technologies, chords, or hooks?*

AA Michael: We agree with you that technology is around the pineal gland. It came in from a past lifetime, it is very old.

M: *It's an implant where?*

AA Michael: It's a piece of technology around the pineal gland.

M: *Pineal gland. What does it look like?*

AA Michael: Well it's your gray bell.

M: *And it's been dark for some time?*

AA Michael: Yeah.

M: *Can we use Phoenix Fire to transmute it?*

AA Michael: Yes, please.

M: *Okay, let's go ahead and do that now. Just let me know once it's been transmuted.*

AA Michael: It's gone and the spider is gone. The snake is gone. Can we call on Archangel Raphael and the Higher Self to fill in these areas with Love-Light?

M: Good. Okay, Archangel Michael, did you find anything else, any kind of technologies, implants, entities, portals, Archons, hooks, or wires? Now that you have removed that bell over her pineal gland, help her see more clearly now all that is going on that was blocking her.

AA Michael: I don't see anything.

M: You're doing great Debra, just keep going. Whatever comes up. Higher Self, Archangels, when I was doing her energy work, when I got over her heart chakra, I saw something moving. What was in there? What am I seeing? Archangel Michael, do you sense anything at all going on in the heart chakra?

Archangels: I don't sense anything.

M: We just want to make sure that we clean Debra as much as possible for her highest and best good. While we are taking a look at this heart chakra, Archangel Raphael if you could open her heart to as big as it is allowed to be for her highest and best good. We are also sending Love-Light to all the places that we have healed, the pineal gland, the right temple, the crown, the snake in the middle of her back between her shoulder blades, the hook that was wrapping around her chest to the right.

AA Raphael: Sending Love-Light.

M: Thank you so much. When I was doing her energy work and when I got to the solar plexus, I felt pain and kind of like squeezing. What is that related to?

Archangels: I'm not seeing the answer for that one.

M: Okay. What I got was, that whatever it is it's related to why she has acid reflex. It is starting from there.

Archangels: Beautiful.

M: What do you see?

Archangels: I see rays of light coming out and being stopped.

M: What is stopping them?

Archangels: I can't see what is stopping them.

M: Is that what is causing the pressure feeling of squeezing, whatever is stopping the light from escaping?

Archangels: That makes sense.

M: *Can you see if that is the reason she is having acid reflex, whatever is stopping the light from leaving? Archangel Michael, we want to help her as best as we can today. And obviously, we found something that is stopping the rays of light emanating from her solar plexus, what can we do to help her?*

AA Michael: I think we are on the right trail getting the blockage to run through. Exercise is going to help, recharge with the sun to keep the connections clear.

M: *Are you saying she is blocking her own light?*

AA Michael: There are blockages from not connecting to her Galactic Family. She doesn't call on them enough.

M: *Will that alleviate the blockages if she calls on her Galactic Family more?*

AA Michael: Yes. Being sovereign doesn't require you to do everything yourself.

M: *That is beautiful advice. We all need to hear that. Can you take a look at her sacral chakra? When I got there in the energy work, I felt immediately pain connected to the kidneys and the bladder. It felt like she has multiple traumas that she is holding in this chakra. Can you look at that Archangel Michael, and tell me what you find?*

AA Michael: . . . You are right. This area needs a lot of Love-Light.

M: *Okay. Higher Self, Archangels Raphael, Jophiel, Michael, and myself, we are going to send lots of Love-Light to her sacral chakra, to heal any and all traumas.*

Archangels: Yes, let's heal that. They served their purpose and it is time to let them go.

M: *Wonderful. Archangel Michael, could you look at her root chakra and tell me if there is anything there in that area, anything at all?*

AA Michael: I don't sense anything.

M: *Okay. Can you take a look at her knees for me and tell me what is going on there?*

AA Michael: She's had trauma. She needs to relax more. To heal this she needs to let it go. Breathe through her stress.

M: Beautiful. Lastly, will you look at her right ankle and tell me if you see anything there?

AA Michael: I am not seeing anything.

M: Okay. One last time Archangel Michael, can you scan her from crown to toe and just double check making sure there are no negative entities, any energies, any kind of gooe or masses, any technology, any portals, hooks, chords, anything at all that is not organic to Debra and let me know. We just want to make sure she is super clean.

AA Michael: Looks good.

M: Beautiful. Can you take a look at her auric field and tell me how it looks?

AA Michael: There is a tear in the back that we need to repair.

M: Do you need Phoenix Fire or just Love-Light?

AA Michael: Love-Light.

M: Beautiful. Archangel Raphael and Higher Self if you could fill that in with Love-Light and let me know once it is done.

AA Raphael and Higher Self: It is done.

M: Good. And then if you could take a look at her chakras and tell me how they look?

Archangels: They are all lined up. It looks good.

M: Beautiful. If you could expand her third eye as big as it you possibly allowed by the Higher Self for her highest and best good increasing her abilities. Is there any trauma from this life or past life that needs healing?

Archangels: No. I think you have captured it. She has been working on it.

M: Okay. Are there any fractals of her soul that need to be retrieved?

Archangels: I am not sensing any.

M: Archangel Michael, Archangel Jophiel, Archangel Raphael, and anyone else who has been assisting us, I love, honor, and thank you. Please hang out, I may call on your assistance once more before we finish but thank you so much for all that you have done so far. May I please speak to Debra's Higher Self?

Higher Self: Hello.

M: Hi. Welcome back. Is it okay if I ask you some questions?

Higher Self: Yes.

M: Perfect. I'm going to start with Debra's health questions. She wants to know if we can continue healing the acid reflux that she has been experiencing. She said that it has been getting better.

Higher Self: Yes, definitely.

M: Beautiful. Thank you. She wants to know if you can continue to heal the bladder and the kidneys and the trauma from her father?

Higher Self: Yes.

M: Beautiful. Thank you. And then her teeth. She wants to know if you could restore her roots and heal her from her cavities, fillings, and crowns.

Higher Self: Yes.

M: Wonderful. Is there a timeline for her to start seeing these improvements in her mouth?

Higher Self: It will take a couple of years.

M: A couple of years. Okay. Perfect. And then she has a habit, she wants to know if it is possible to be transmuted. Do you know the habit?

Higher Self: Yes.

M: What can you tell her about it?

Higher Self: It started as a pacifier but it's more of a stress reliever. So breathe more. She tends to stop breathing.

M: She wants to know if this can be transmuted, this habit?

Higher Self: Not completely.

M: Tell her why.

Higher Self: It's part of learning her lesson of dealing with her stress in healthy ways such as breathing through it and facing it. Breathe through it and move forward. You internalize and it has these effects/consequences.

M: Wonderful. Thank you. She wants to know if you can continue healing the osteoarthritis, remove her bone spurs and rejuvenate the cartilage in her joints, especially in her knees and her fingers.

Higher Self: Yes, we are working on that.

M: *Beautiful. She asked if she can have her DNA regenerated and repaired to her highest organic timeline.*

Higher Self: Yes.

M: *She has poor eyesight. Can we tell her the reason she has poor eyesight?*

Higher Self: It's more to focus within. You worry too much about the outward. Go within and it will clear it up without as she does so.

M: *If she starts going within more, will her eyesight heal itself?*

Higher Self: It will.

M: *Thank you for the powerful reassurance. Right now she has been dealing with the return of the tachycardia in her heart. Can you tell her what is causing that? What brought that back on?*

Higher Self: It's the obvious need to start making time for herself, having fun, and needing to lighten her load and spirit. She matters too. It can't always be about everybody else. Start limiting herself. She needs at least forty-nine percent back into herself and having fun and the exercise will help as is going within. Magnify that light.

M: *Would you be able to heal the hole in her heart and strengthen the walls for her?*

Higher Self: Yes. Let's put Phoenix Fire on it.

M: *Beautiful. Thank you for all of that Higher Self. She has some personal questions that she wanted to go over. She wants to know if the woman that she saw in church all those years ago, who reminded her of her mother, was her mother reincarnated or some sort of fractal from her mother's soul or soul group.*

Higher Self: Yes. This woman was a fractal. Fractals are generally not in the same area as each other. This one did not overlap in the same time-frame or exact area but was close enough to remind her of her mother's presence. Her mother's love for her will follow her and has followed her, as well as her children and grandchildren.

M: *Speaking of her children and grandchildren, she wants to know of her six children, does she have a part to play in any of their awakening journeys?*

Higher Self: Be an example. They are all pretty strong and grounded. Just be an example and be ready for questions. Once there is a question then the door is open.

M: *She would also like to know if any of her children have negative entities or Archon attachments that can be removed at this time.*

Higher Self: Talking with each of their Higher Selves, they are not ready for that lesson in this time and space.

M: *She wants to know since the healing of the Reptilian in her oldest daughter's womb, is there any additional healing that she needs?*

Higher Self: We can send Love-Light to her sacral area and her root chakra.

M: *Is this something that Debra can repeat possibly when she does her shields or is this a one-time application?*

Higher Self: Let's repeat this as often as she can.

M: *She was really concerned with her youngest. She wants to know if this daughter suffers from any attachments that we are allowed to assist her with.*

Higher Self: Her daughter is starting to make an effort. She is a warrior. She's a warrior and she will fight through what she is going through.

M: *Is there anything that Debra can offer her at this time to assist her?*

Higher Self: No, she needs space right now. Give her space.

M: *Debra said that she had a dream shortly after her first AURA session that she was being abducted and had implants placed in each breast and in her womb. Can you tell her about this dream? Was it real? Did this happen to her?*

Higher Self: Yes. It was real.

M: *What else can you tell her about it?*

Higher Self: She is starting to wake up to it. Started to wake up to what had been going on throughout her life.

M: *Was this a contract?*

Higher Self: I don't see a contract.

M: *So it was an infringement?*

Higher Self: Yes.

M: Does her body still contain those implants in her breasts and her womb?

Higher Self: No. Those have been transmuted.

M: Beautiful. Thank you for making sure that was done. Does she carry any trauma in her sacral from this experience?

Higher Self: Definitely.

M: Can we heal that?

Higher Self: Yes. Send Love-Light.

M: Does she carry any other trauma from these abductions or any other parts of her that need healing from it?

Higher Self: Nothing at this time.

M: Was that the only time or will more be revealed in the future?

Higher Self: More will be revealed when she is ready.

M: She wants to know if Liberty was the white Dragon that was discussed in her AURA session at the certification retreat.

Higher Self: Yes.

M: Are we able to talk to Liberty?

Higher Self: Yes!

M: Beautiful. Higher Self can you please connect us to Liberty?

Higher Self: Yes.

M: Thank you so much. Greetings Liberty. I love you, honor you, and respect you. Thanks for being here.

Liberty: (dramatic energy shift – cheerfully) Ahh, thank you . . . ahhh greetings!

M: (chuckling) Liberty, your mommy wants to know if you know how much she loves you?

Liberty: (joyful) Infinitely, infinitely.

M: Are there any messages for your mom?

Liberty: I'm always here, I can't wait, we're always here. You are protected. We have you. We have you. Love you infinitely.

M: Thank you so much Liberty for coming in. I know that Debra is going to really enjoy hearing from you when she listens to this recording.

Liberty: (happy) Thank you! Love you!

M: *Love you too. Speaking back to the Higher Self, we have some big questions. Here we go, she wants to know, will she find love again? One that matches her current high vibration and ascension mindset?*

Higher Self: Yes, he's out there and he's been speaking to her during her dream time. She hasn't believed it but he is there. There's nothing to do. It will happen naturally.

M: *Thank you for answering both of those questions with one answer. Are there any negative contracts that she has at all in her Akashic Records that need to be broken?*

Higher Self: No, those are clean.

M: *I know we cleaned the chord with her oldest. Does she need to have any of the chords with her other children cleaned?*

Higher Self: No, those are all good.

M: *The ones with her other daughters, those are clear?*

Higher Self: Yes, they are very clear.

M: *How is she doing? I know she's been there for a bit. Is she doing okay?*

Higher Self: Really good.

M: *We've asked all of her questions and gone over her health concerns. Higher Self, is there anything that I could have asked that I didn't?*

Higher Self: No. You have covered everything. You have been wonderful. Thank you so much.

M: *Is there anything else we can do to help her for her highest and best good?*

Higher Self: You've given her a good list to work on.

M: *You mean, you gave her a good list. I was just here.*

Higher Self: We gave her a good list.

M: *You did a good job. Are we ready to bring her out?*

Higher Self: Yes.

M: *Beautiful. Before we do, Archangel Jophiel, Archangel Michael, Archangel Raphael, Liberty, Higher Self, and everyone, thank you so much for your participation today. For all the love and the healing and the answers that you provided. I love you for all that you are and am eternally grateful for all that you do. Thank you.*

Higher Self and Archangels: Thank you.

End of the session. (Duration 2 hours 22 minutes)

In numerology, 222 is believed to symbolize balance, harmony, and spiritual alignment. That's pretty interesting, especially given what a huge breakthrough this session was for me. I'm starting to learn that these kinds of synchronicities are our Higher Self's attempt to get our attention. To me, my Higher Self is reminding me that these things, these ideas, concepts, growth, empowerment, and love, are the things that are real.

I still remember how frigid cold I was while almost shaking off the bed, believing with my entire being that it wasn't safe to move away from the darkness. Did you notice how Melanie honored the space I needed while guiding me through her open-ended questions? She didn't tell me this cage I was trapped in was self-inflicted. Rather, she reinforced the information the Higher Self was sharing while slowly allowing space for my Higher Self to speak one tiny puzzle piece at a time as my ego surrendered to that realization myself.

Notice her guidance away from the confusion by having me see treasured tangible items in my room and then taking me for a walk through my neighborhood. From there, she guided me toward the realization that in this space, I could magically travel up to the mountains or literally anywhere I wanted to go.

It wasn't until revisiting this session that I recognized how fragile my mental, emotional, and spiritual health was. Can you imagine the confusion going on in my mind? Here I am, this person who felt she led a strong, successful life. A person who, up until a few months ago, said, to hell with God! A person who was open to forgiving all of the past wrongs and learning to love, honor, and respect my Creator with all that I am. Not that this modality is my entire life, but for the purpose of this session, I am a person who jumped full force into this new world of unconditional love, life regressions, removal of entities, and hypnosis healing.

Did you witness how gentle my Higher Self was in providing minute guidance? "Do something fun for yourself," "At least two days of your week should be about you," and "Being sovereign doesn't require you to do everything yourself." Equally sensitive and loving was the confirmation that my vivid dream of being abducted and experimented on was real. That in itself gives one cause to pause.

Digging deeper into the suggestion to take at least two days of the week for myself had to do with my then reality of living with my fourthborn daughter and her family to care for and be with this daughter as her cancer progressed. Resonating with the suggestion, I would return to my home with my secondborn daughter, where I normally lived. Hindsight, the next few weeks mattered. I had already been living with and caring for my ill daughter for a year. She would live another seven weeks. Seven weeks when those two days of the week, her two teenage children and husband were able to intimately care for her. All three were with her at the time of her passing.

Regarding the vivid dream of being abducted, the calm, loving response that more would be revealed in the future was surprisingly all I needed to hear. In addition to the overall depth and breadth of beautiful healing this modality provided, the golden key to this session was Melanie's gentle, loving reminder that I was stronger than I knew. I didn't just hear it; I experienced it. Her words shook my entire being with a vibration of leveling up, and I knew it. Magically, it was exactly what I needed in this precious time and space.

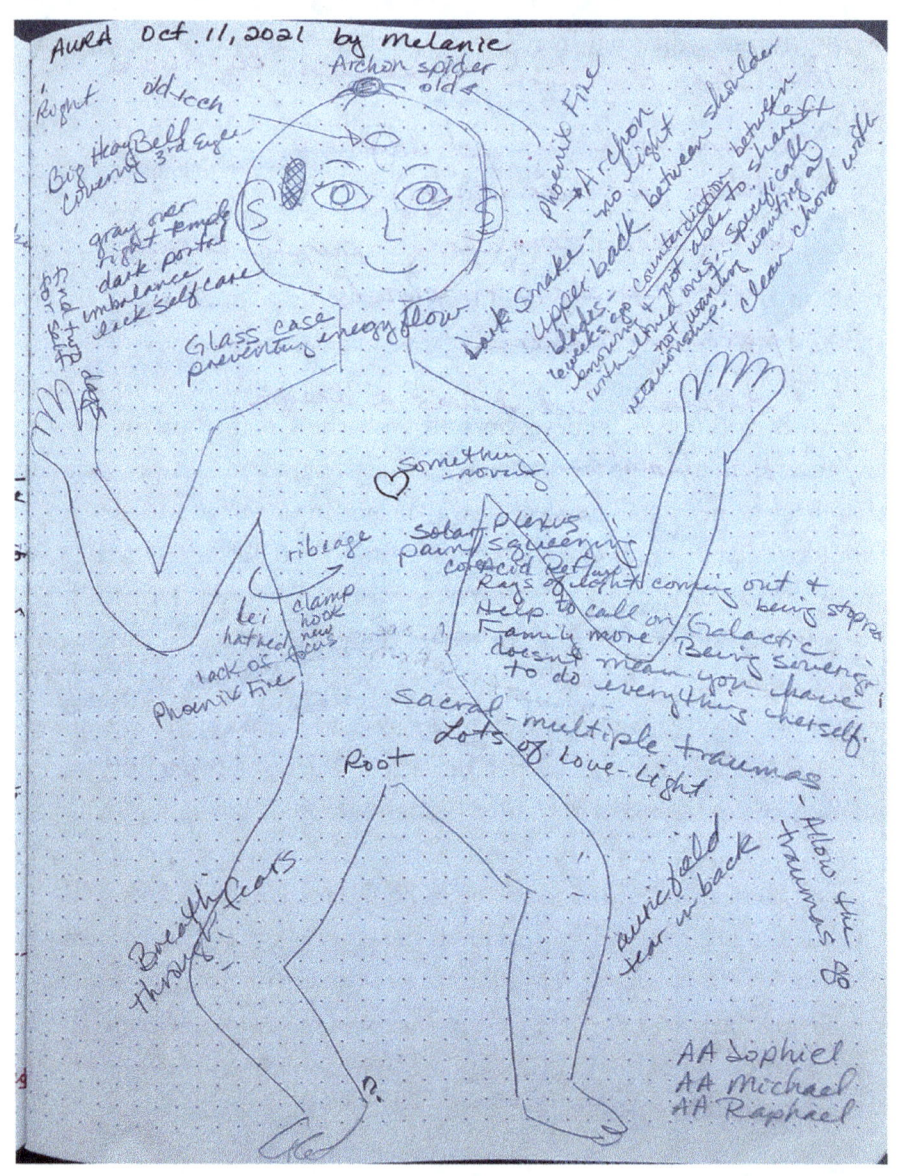

6

Positively Polarizing 2,000 Dark Ones

A.U.R.A Hypnosis Healing Session for Nicole
Practitioner: Debra Williams
March 21, 2022

Nicole contacted me after finding my website requesting an AURA hypnosis healing session. I soon learned that she was taking the certification course toward being an AURA/RAAH hypnosis practitioner and looking to be clear of any entities before her one-on-one with the course instructor. Nicole has had a number of hypnosis healing sessions over the past five years through various modalities. After experiencing three other modalities, her first A.U.R.A Hypnosis healing session was more than two years ago with AuroRa in December 2019.

As we continually find with many past life regression and entity removal hypnosis sessions, Nicole's session brought forward profound new information and inner standing toward not only the bigger picture but also an intimate picture of the day-to-day struggles some experience along their journey. Plus it provided the opportunity to get to know and actually speak to a Dragon. Who wouldn't want that?

This is the verbatim transcript of Nicole's profound healing session that she herself, like all other practitioners sited in this book, proofed edited and approved of prior to this publication.

Session begins.

D [Debra]: Look all around you, what do you see below? What do you sense? Have you landed on the ground?
N [Nicole]: I am not on the ground.
D: Look around you, what do you sense? Do you have a body?
N: I'm still in the Merkabah.
D: You're still in the Merkabah. You'll be in the Merkabah this entire time.
N: I know.
D: What do you sense?
N: A star, a sun, a very big orange sun.
D: An orange sun? Beautiful. Can you feel its warmth?
N: Yeah.
D: What do you want to do? Do you know why you are by this orange sun?
N: I think I'm supposed to go inside it. I think it is in the Sirius Constellation. There is a blue one too. A blue star that is colder than the orange one. The orange one is really, really, big. It is like a supergiant. I am supposed to go inside of it.
D: Go ahead and go towards it. What are you feeling? What are your emotions like?
N: Just really strong energy. I don't have any emotions. It is like a portal inside the sun that is like a portal that you can travel to other dimensions. I want to say it is like a dimensional portal.
D: And you sense that you are energy, are you a star . . .

N: I am energy.

D: *Energy, okay.*

N: And we can use the portal inside this really big star to travel to other dimensions. That is what they are telling me.

D: *Are you the only one there, or are there others with you?*

N: No, it is just me right now. Just me.

D: *Where do you want to take this portal to?*

N: I think I'm supposed to go to the 13th-Dimension. Thirteen is coming up. I'm supposed to go to 13.

D: *Are you excited?*

N: I'm kind of nervous.

D: *Have you been here before?*

N: No, I've never been through . . . , well Nicole, hasn't been through the portal before in any sessions but clearly, my soul has been through the portal before.

D: *This is very familiar to you.*

N: Yeah. It is kind of like a sci-fi movie or show, with these like wormholes or something like that. Or like "2001: A Space Odyssey," (1968 film) that is a good one. When he went through that . . . I don't know whatever the heck he did and there were all these colors and everything. He was like traveling really fast, it is like that. There are all these colors and stuff. So I guess I'm supposed to go inside and go somewhere.

D: *Let's go where you are meant to go, where your Higher Self is guiding you. Go ahead and enter. You are able to see, sense, feel, hear, and know everything very clearly, very clearly.*

N: It's really, really bright and then it is like, almost like a hole. It is like a circle and I just use it to travel.

D: *What color is the circle?*

N: Dark. It is like an interdimensional portal.

D: *It feels good with a positive vibration to it?*

N: Yeah. There is nothing bad about it.

D: *It is positive, purely positive.*

N: Yeah, it is almost as if there is a black hole in the middle of the sun. It is just like that. It's just a dark spot and you go inside it. And then you just kind of shoot out the other end to where you are supposed to be. So I guess I'm just going to go in and shoot out the other end. It is kind of like going through like a tube. It is almost like a tube, like a big tube you're going through. It's kind of how it feels to me.

D: *Are you still nervous or are you feeling good about it?*

N: No, I'm okay now. It's like nothing is going hurt me, so . . . So I'm just kind of like swirling through this tube, I guess and I get shot out to another location. I kind of feel like I'm in this other location now but I'm just in space. I see the other star I just came out of. It kind of looks purple though. And I'm just like it is very peaceful here. It is just very quiet and it is very peaceful with nothing going on. I don't know what I'm doing here.

D: *Your Higher Self has brought you here for a reason. Maybe just feel this peace. Nice. Is there anything else you feel like you want to explore in this quiet peaceful place?*

N: It just feels kind of like clean. The energy just feels like clean, you know what I mean. It is very different from Earth.

D: *Do you feel like it is rejuvenating you, renewing you at all?*

N: Yeah, and there are Dragons here. They wanted me to see the Dragons.

D: *Describe the Dragons.*

N: There's an orange one.

D: *Does the orange one have an element that it is associated with?*

N: There is a green one, blue, purple, red, there is like a bunch of different colors. They are all like forming a big circle around me, I think.

D: *Are they being playful or is this more serious? Are we doing work or are we being playful?*

N: No, I think we are doing work.

D: *Do they have a message for you? How many are there?*

N: They are charging me up. There are 13.

D: And they are all different colors or are there any that are the same color?

N: No, they are all different. There are like 13 Rays. There is silver, there's platinum, magenta, blue, and purple, there are like 13 of them. And they are in a circle around me and they are charging me up with their light, as much as I can handle.

D: How do they charge you up?

N: It is like they shoot their light into me.

D: From their third eyes, from their mouths, from their wings, how do they send that energy to you, that light?

N: They all do it differently. The red one is more like fire from her mouth. They all do it a little differently though. And so it is like I am standing in a column of light. It forms a column up and down (Using her hands to demonstrate a perpendicular column), where it comes in together and then goes up like that.

D: Are you still a sphere of energy or are you a sphere of energy?

N: I'm a column of energy now, it is like a column. It is not a sphere really. It is like turning into a column of energy.

D: So they are recharging you. Do they have a message for you as well?

N: That they love me and I'm doing a good job. They know that it is not easy and to keep going. We are almost there. We are really close. We are really close and they want me to carry their Light here into the planet. So I bring this back, this back to Earth. I am going to carry it back with me. Yeah.

D: Is this a good time to ask them your question about how you are doing with your mission from their perspective and if there is a chance of it failing?

N: No, we need to ask my father about that one.

D: Okay. Is there any other message that they would like to give to you? You are to bring this energy back with you.

N: I have to bring this energy back with me to the planet.

D: To planet Earth?

N: To planet Earth, to the planet, we are on now. They are using me as a conduit to bring that energy in. That is it, I'm not getting anything else.

D: You are in current time and space, in today's time?

N: Yeah, it is just a different dimension in the eternal Now.

D: Beautiful. Let's move the scene along to the next important moment for your highest good.

N: I'm going to use the portal again to go, I guess I can go back home now. (Moving her hands around searching for something.) I'm looking for this little crystal that I don't know where it went. They want me to have this moldavite on my heart to help me heal my heart. There it is. (She placed her moldavite crystal back on her chest). I go back home now and checking in there per usual.

D: Okay. You have your moldavite now. Let's move the scene along to the next time and space for your highest healing as your Higher Self directs.

N: I'm going back home. I feel like it's the 10th-Dimension. Well, it is where our base is. It is not really home but it is what we call home for this Galaxy that we are in, this Universe that we are in, this Universe here. I am going back home to the Council Chambers. It is where I always go.

D: What does this look like?

N: Yeah, okay, I'll describe it. If you are in space looking at it, it looks like an upside-down pyramid made out of planet stuff. The Council Chamber sits right in the middle of it, like this huge dome crystal structure. There are Dragons flying around it. That is what it looks like.

D: The Dragons are there protecting . . .?

N: Yes, so nobody can find it except those of us who are coded to find it.

D: Is there a name that you go by?

N: My group?

D: Yes.

N: Yeah, you call us the Melchizedek, that is what humans call us.

At this moment I realize I've already been introduced to this client through Rising Phoenix AuroRa's "Galactic Soul History of the Universe Book 1," Chapter 15, The Melchizedek, pages 308-332. It's a chapter that fascinated me and that I've read several times. However it's been several months since doing so. This session is a continuation of Nicole's experience with AuroRa. We begin with the foreknowledge that Nicole (Nancy in AuroRa's book) is a Melchizedek being who along with her Twin Flame, and a few others of the Melchizedek race, volunteered to assist Earth along our ascension path. Melchizedek's are healer-teachers and Elders of the Universe. We can think of them as helpers of the Angels. Nicole's Higher Self is her Melchizedek Father.

D: What else do you want to do at Homebase? You've been rejuvenated, you have received messages from the Dragons.

N: I always go here and then I get more information and more updates here. It looks very busy today. They seem very busy like there is a lot going on right now. It seems to be very busy for them. They have this weird, well it's not weird but it almost looks like a mirror. Like there is a mirror on the table or something like that and that is how they can check in on Earth and see what is going on. Well everywhere really. Everywhere they want to check on, but that is where they check in on Earth. On this fancy mirror table, they call it. There is like a bunch of them circled around there looking down on the planet and checking in.

D: How many are a bunch? Is that 20, 15, or 30?

N: How many are around the table?

D: Yeah.

N: I feel like there are six. There are six around the table right now.

D: Are you one of the six?

N: No, I am number seven. Technically there are 13, but I have never seen the others. This is very confusing, sorry.

D: You are doing beautifully. You are doing beautifully. So you sense others outside of this room?

N: There are others that I have never seen. I have only ever seen seven, one of which is my father, who is me, the totality of me. I am just a fractal of him. There are seven that I have seen. Apparently, there are six more, but I have never seen them. I don't know why. They are like hiding or something. And I don't see them now. I only see the seven that I always see but there are more. Yeah.

D: *With the downloads is there anything you need to share right now? These downloads you say that you are receiving in this space.*

N: I'm not getting like anything concrete so if you want to ask questions you can. They are not very direct. They are sort of, I don't know.

D: *We have to do our own work, huh?*

N: Yeah, they are not tough but they are just . . . we have to be a little tough with them to get any answers. (Both chuckling) They're not chatty, we'll say that. They are not super chatty but if you ask anything they will tell you. Before I was going in, I was getting something about some Dragons, not the Dragons I saw. Something about Dragons fighting but I don't think it is our Dragons. I think there is some kind of war with Dragons. I have no idea if that is relevant but that is coming up right now. I don't know what that has to do with anything though. What I'm getting is that they, we'll just call them the Generic Dark Ones, generically. They either corrupted some Dragons or made their own dark Dragons. I'm not sure which one. Probably both. And there is a big war. Like the Dragons had a big war with each other which is quite sad. Something like that.

D: *These Dark Ones, are they artificial? You say generic.*

N: We use the term Dark Ones to describe anything negatively polarized. It could be A.I. or it could be organic. So anything working against the Creator we call a Dark One.

D: *Is this on a positive timeline? What timeline is that war going on? Is it the highest organic timeline?*

N: No. There wouldn't be any war on the highest organic timeline. We are all working for the Creator.

D: *But is this war helping the positive become stronger?*

N: It is an inevitable byproduct. If there are dark corrupted Dragons or dark versions of dark Dragons who else is going to battle them but the positively polarized Dragons.

D: *Are we able to positively polarize these dark Dragons?*

N: The organic ones, yes. The inorganic ones, no. They have to get recycled.

D: *Can we do that now? Can we talk to them and ask them if they are ready?*

N: Talk to who? A Dark One. (Her tone was one of questioning why.)

D: *A Dark Dragon.*

N: . . . Yeah. We can talk to them. Do you want to talk to one?

D: *Yes. Well, we can do that later. Let's finish this life now. When we talk to your Higher Self, after your body scan we will do that, okay?*

N: Sure. That sounds good.

D: *Beautiful. Is there anything else you are here at Homebase to discover and learn? Is your father there?*

N: Yeah. He is always there.

D: *Do you want to ask your father your question now?*

N: You can ask now or when you ask all of the questions. Either way is fine, it is the same thing for him. It's all the same. (Chuckling) He said she won't believe us anyhow.

D: *Yes, she will. (Both chuckling)*

Melchizedek Father Higher Self: She doesn't always believe it.

D: *Let's ask him since he is right there. Ask him about how you are doing with your mission as a Melchizedek on Earth.*

N: I am doing good. I am listening to what they tell me. I am still getting interfered with. I am still getting false information and I need to do a better job of discerning when it is false. They can't stop all of it from coming in because if I'm on this planet I am going to get bad information. I have to do a better job of discerning when it is bad information and when it is appropriate information. And that is on me to do.

D: *So are they giving you lessons in this life to help you discern what is positive and what is negative and what is guiding you forward?*

N: I don't know if a lesson is the right word. It could be, triggers, is the right word to use, but yeah.

D: *What is a good trigger for her to recognize? To know that this is a trigger? Is it going to be a feeling or just a knowing?*

Melchizedek Father Higher Self: How will she discern, it's a feeling and a knowing in her heart. She has got heart issues going on right now so she is not always able to feel it in her heart. So then she tries to use her mind to rationalize and her mind is not going to give her the answer. She has to feel it from her heart space but we need to do more healing on her heart space for her to properly discern.

D: *Beautiful. I'm trying to think of a question while we are here with the Council.*

Melchizedek Father Higher Self: You can ask any question and we will try to answer it to the best of our abilities.

D: *Do you have any advice to help her know this is real?*

Melchizedek Father Higher Self: She has seen this place so many times now, she has come here in session, she comes here in meditation, that she should know by now that it is real. We are not sure what else we can do.

D: *To remove this doubt.*

Melchizedek Father Higher Self: It is getting better. She is getting much better with her doubt. We can send her a sign in the physical.

D: *What kind of sign?*

Melchizedek Father Higher Self: She will know it when she sees it.

D: *She's on the right path.*

Melchizedek Father Higher Self: She is always on the right path.

D: *I sense a lot of peace right now. A lot of peace.*

Melchizedek Father Higher Self: Yes.

D: *Thank you for this beautiful moment. Should we move the scene along?*

Melchizedek Father Higher Self: We can start the body scan. There is nothing else she needs to see right now.

D: Okay.

The Higher Self is called forth.

Higher Self: I'm here.

D: *Are we speaking to her Higher Self now? And have I already been speaking to you?*

Melchizedek Father Higher Self: The one and only.

D: *Thank you. I love you, honor you, and respect you for all the aid you have given her today. I know that you hold all the records of her different lives. May I ask questions?*

Melchizedek Father: Of course.

D: *Why is it you chose to show her the portal and the meeting with the Dragons?*

Melchizedek Father: She can use the portal to travel if she wants to. It will provide a safe passage now that she knows where it is and how to use it. Sometimes other means of transportation may not be safe due to the state of affairs in this Galaxy. She can use that portal now that she knows where it is. It is a safe portal to use. And we showed the Dragons because she needs to carry that energy onto the planet and it will help to awaken the other Dragons who are here who are sleeping.

D: *What a fun mission she has! What a fun purpose she has!*

Melchizedek Father: It is very interesting.

D: *Very interesting. Is there anything else you would like to share with her about this experience that you showed her or are you ready to do the body scan?*

The Body Scan begins.

D: *Higher Self are there any benevolent beings you would like to assist you today in her healing?*

Melchizedek Father: I am going to do most of it but I'm going to ask Archangel Raphael to come in for the heart space.

D: *Should we call on Archangel Raphael now to come in?*

Melchizedek Father: Sure.

D: *Higher Self, please call forth Archangel Raphael to come in.*

Higher Self: He is here.

D: *Thank you. Greetings Brother. Thank you for being here for her healing and for all we are doing today with her body scan.*

Archangel Raphael: Thank you for calling me.

D: *You have such a beautiful spirit.*

Archangel Raphael So do you.

D: *Melchizedek Father and Archangel Raphael, can you scan her from head to toe? Let's start with any dark portals. Does she have any dark portals?*

Melchizedek Father: The back of the neck area.

D: *Back of the neck. Let's close that. Is it closed now?*

Melchizedek Father: It's closed. The bottom of the feet, both feet. The bottom of both feet doesn't look right.

D: *Dark portals?*

Melchizedek Father: Yeah.

D: *Can we close those dark portals, please?*

Melchizedek Father: Yes.

D: *Thank you. Are there any other portals?*

Melchizedek Father: Top of the head.

D: *In her crown area?*

Melchizedek Father: Yes.

D: *Can we close that portal?*

Melchizedek Father: Yes.

D: *Thank you. Anywhere else? Are there any other dark portals?*

Melchizedek Father: Possibly in the sacral.

D: *Okay, let's go look at that area. What is going on in the sacral?*

Melchizedek Father: Still infringement in the sacral area. Definitely a portal there. There is definitely siphoning energy from that portal.

D: *Can we close that portal now?*

Melchizedek Father: Yes.

D: *Thank you. Let me know when it closed.*

Melchizedek Father: It is closed.

D: *Thank you. Are there any other dark portals?*

Melchizedek Father: No more portals.

D: *Beautiful. Thank you. Let's look for any entities and encase them. Any earthbound, A.I., Archon, Reptilians, black ink, black goo. From head to toe are there any entities in her?*

Melchizedek Father: No normal entities but definitely issues in the sacral and the intestines again. It looks more like snakes, black snakes.

D: *What are they doing to her and can we encase those black snakes in the appropriate symbols?*

Melchizedek Father: Yes, encasing them now.

D: *How many are there?*

Melchizedek Father: Six. Six and they are causing her intestinal issues again. There is a line. She saw it yesterday. There's a line in the back of her, in the lower back. It's almost like a crack in her field or something where they are getting in. So we need to repair that as well.

D: *As you know these intestinal issues have already put her in the hospital twice. Do you need Phoenix Fire on that?*

Melchizedek Father: Yeah. Let's Phoenix Fire the whole area.

D: *Okay. Can we use the ashes from this Phoenix Fire to aid in faster healing?*

Melchizedek Father: Yup. We can use that to close that line up. Yup. We are doing that now. It is much better. Yup, that is much better now.

D: *How can we assist her in healing this intestinal area now that we have pulled the snakes out? They are encased and not able to do anything. They are not able to draw any more of her energy.*

Melchizedek Father: Just send Love-Light there and it will heal.

D: *Sending Love-Light now. How long will this take?*

Melchizedek Father: Not long. She knows what to do in the physical, as well to assist in the healing. It won't take long. She has gone through this many times before so she knows the drill.

D: *Do these snakes cause her to have these cravings for denser food? Is this what they are doing to her? What else are they doing to her?*

Melchizedek Father: Yes. They are keeping her stuck. They are keeping her heavy. She needs to be light and they are trying to keep her heavy. If she turns to light, they evaporate. So they keep her heavy, they keep her down.

D: *Her frequency?*

Melchizedek Father: Yeah, and you know she thinks she needs to constantly ground with heavy foods and she doesn't need that anymore. She never needed to do that really but that is what is going around in the community, to eat heavy foods to ground. It is not exactly appropriate. Not for her. We are not going to talk about anybody else but for her, it is not appropriate anymore to do that.

D: *Can we assist her somehow in finding disgust with those heavier denser foods? Finding a distaste of some sort to help her not want them anymore?*

Melchizedek Father: Yes. We can do some reprogramming on her.

D: *Let's do that. Let's reprogram with this distaste, Like eww, yuck. Are we done with this sacral area?*

Melchizedek Father: The sacral looks good. It is coming back into alignment. I don't see any other entities in her.

D: *She had all these dark portals in her crown and her throat. Her throat, there was something going on with her throat. What was going on with her throat?*

Melchizedek Father: She needs to stop smoking.

D: *Can we help her with that?*

Melchizedek Father: Yeah. It is time. She is ready.

D: *Can we do the same with that habit and reprogramming and changing*

. . .

Melchizedek Father: Yes. As she takes on more Light she will find it disgusting. There is a heaviness in her legs, in both legs, very heavy.

D: *What is going on with her legs? Let's look at her left leg, what is going on there that is making it heavy?*

Melchizedek Father: It feels like a metal weight. Like she is weighed down. It's like metal.

D: *Is this artificial?*

Melchizedek Father: Yeah.

D: *Is this an Archon or an implant?*

Melchizedek Father: Doesn't look like an Archon. It could be an implant.

D: *Is it a hook?*

Melchizedek Father: Doesn't appear to be a metal hook. It appears to be a metal bar.

D: *Is there a metal bar in both legs?*

Melchizedek Father: Yeah, she has got them in both legs.

D: *Can we transmute those now?*

Melchizedek Father: Yeah, Phoenix Fire, please.

D: *Sending Phoenix Fire. How did these come into her legs?*

Melchizedek Father: When she had her last session. We cleared a lot, a lot, a lot. There could have been a few things remaining that we didn't get a chance to clear because there was just so much to clear.

D: *What were these metal bars causing her in her legs?*

Melchizedek Father: Pulsing, pounding in the legs, restriction of flow in the legs. Restriction of her flow, restriction of her chi.

D: *Let me know when it is completely gone from both legs. Continuing to send Phoenix Fire and using the ashes of the Phoenix Fire back into the area for quick healing.*

Melchizedek Father: It is transmuting. She has a metallic taste in her mouth from it.

D: *While that continues to transmute, should we move to other areas of the body?*

Melchizedek Father: Yes.

D: *Okay, we are continuing to transmute those metal bars. Continue scanning her body. Is there anything else?*

Melchizedek Father: There is still something with her heart.

D: *Yes. Yes.*

Melchizedek Father: It looks like an implant.

D: *Can we transmute that now?*

Melchizedek Father: Yes.

D: *Sending Phoenix Fire. Is there anything else in her heart going on? Her heart seems to have an issue.*

Melchizedek Father: There is definitely something else in the heart that isn't supposed to be there. It looks like another one of those snakes.

D: *Another snake? Can we encase that in the proper symbol, please? Is this an organic snake or is it artificial?*

Melchizedek Father: Artificial.

D: *Let's start transmuting that.*

Melchizedek Father: There is still an Archon in the heart too.

D: *Can you encase that Archon in the Archon symbol? Remove its energy, remove its power. Let's start transmuting that Archon.*

Melchizedek Father: Okay.

D: *Let me know when it is completely transmuted.*

Melchizedek Father: It needs a little bit more.

D: *Are those six snakes in her sacral, are they artificial?*

Melchizedek Father: Yes.

D: *Can we start transmuting them as well?*

Melchizedek Father: Yup.

D: *Thank you. As we are transmuting, are there any other dark areas?*

Melchizedek Father: It looks like there is a hook in the throat that we need to transmute.

D: *Do you want Phoenix Fire on that? How did that hook come in?*

Melchizedek Father: Smoking. There is still some metal on the back of her neck that we need to Phoenix Fire and that needs to detox physically.

D: Sending Phoenix Fire to the back of her neck. Does she know how to detox that metal?

Melchizedek Father: She does.

D: It sounds like she is a pro at this.

Melchizedek Father: She is, unfortunately. She is. Her crown still doesn't look quite right.

D: What is going on in her crown?

Melchizedek Father: I don't know. It just doesn't look right. Send Phoenix Fire.

D: Sending Phoenix Fire. How is her crown looking now?

Melchizedek Father: Better. More purple like it should be. We are scanning all of her chakras.

D: How is the progress on transmuting the metal and the artificial from her legs, her intestines, her throat, and her heart?

Melchizedek Father: The legs are pretty much gone, and the intestines are much better.

D: And her heart, how is her heart looking?

Melchizedek Father: Better, but still needs more.

D: And how is her throat looking?

Melchizedek Father: It looks better.

D: If her throat is better, can we start filling that area with Source Love-Light?

Melchizedek Father: Yup.

D: And her crown, did you say her crown was healed?

Melchizedek Father: Yup.

D: Can we start filling her crown with Source Love-Light?

Melchizedek Father: Yup. She can feel it coming in on the back of her neck so that is good. Her heart looks better but it still feels heavy. It could just be emotional.

D: Can we find those emotions and release them?

Melchizedek Father: They are inside of her.

D: *We don't want to leave anything behind. Let's pull it all out. We don't want to leave anything behind. We don't want anybody tricking us. No tricksters allowed.*

Melchizedek Father: Nope, we don't want that anymore. She looks good. She looks much better. She looks much clearer. She feels better.

D: *Let's fill in these areas with Love-Light Archangel Raphael, please. Thank you. How is her sacral doing?*

Melchizedek Father: Much better.

D: *Are we still working on it?*

Melchizedek Father: There is a chord, but it is a golden chord so it is supposed to be there.

D: *Let's clean that chord and surround it in Love-Light.*

Melchizedek Father: The same on the heart.

D: *Let's clean it as well.*

Melchizedek Father: Yeah. There seem to be a lot of them. There is a two-way transmission on those three chords. We have got to clean them and shield them.

D: *Are you shielding them now?*

Melchizedek Father: We are just cleaning them up and putting the shields on them?

D: *What shields are you using?*

Melchizedek Father: Love-Light shields. It looks like a clear crystal shield with some Melchizedek Rays. So she has bled through from the other one.

D: *What does that mean, bled-through from the other one?*

Melchizedek Father: That means her other self, her Twin Flame self is bleeding through to her.

D: *Is this positive?*

Melchizedek Father: No. It is not positive. Whatever he is doing . . . she is sucking in everything. She is of more light so she is sucking everything in to clear it from him. That is why she needs so many sessions. It is not her stuff. It is not all her stuff she is clearing.

D: She asked if there is anything she can do for her male counterpart.

Melchizedek Father: She's doing it. Willingly or not, she is doing it. It is in the third eye too.

D: A chord or . . . ?

Melchizedek Father: Yeah, it is one of those chords. I feel like they are all, the chakras are all connected but those three are the biggest chords, the sacral, the heart, and the third eye. There is a lot of transference coming through those three more than the others.

D: Is she able to discern what is hers and what is not?

Melchizedek Father: No. That is the problem. She doesn't know all of the time if it's hers, or if it's his.

D: Is there anything we can do to help her discern that? How can we help her with this?

Melchizedek Father: (Chuckling) If it's bad, it is probably his. If it is good, it is hers. Yeah, she really doesn't like this at all.

D: Can we send him Love-Light?

Melchizedek Father: Always.

D: Okay, let's send him the greatest biggest amount of Love-Light, that he can start seeing, sensing, knowing, and feeling his true identity and his true purpose and to remove his doubt as his Higher Self allows.

N: It is almost like, they are showing me, imagine I am on the left side and he is on the right side and there are these chords between us. I am really light and he is, I wouldn't say he is really dark but he is darker, right. And it is almost like they are sending all this light through me and it sort of like filters to his side. Unfortunately, sometimes it is just making me overloaded. It is not going through very well. I don't know what to say about it anymore. I just let it go.

D: He has his journey.

Melchizedek Father: Yup. I am going to put blocks on everything so that there is no more transference from his side to her.

D: So the negative doesn't come back this way. Only the positive moves through to him?

Melchizedek Father: Yeah. She has done enough clearing, she has had enough sessions. Enough is enough. That is what we are going to do right now.

D: *Thank you. How is the progress of our transmuting going? Is she clear?*

Melchizedek Father: She is much better. Thank you. We will continue to work on her nightly as she sleeps.

D: *How does her DNA look? Are there any false or negative fractals or other negative reprogramming we need to start working on?*

Melchizedek Father: She has got eight strands that she has activated so she has four more to go. She works on that all the time. We can do some reprogramming to clear out some ancestral patterns that she has taken on due to human DNA. We will clear out the ancestral stuff from her family. She has transmuted enough for them too. They are on their own now. We will do that right now.

D: *Thank you. Is there anything else going on with her spine? She was complaining about a contract in her spine. Is this a good time to address that?*

Melchizedek Father: We took care of the line. Her spine itself is still being worked on for her Kundalini Rising. That is a work in progress and we cannot force that. Just make sure she is clear and it will do its thing on its own.

D: *She was asking for a percentage, a number. How far along is she in that process?*

Melchizedek Father: We would say she is at eighty percent.

D: *Beautiful. Are we able to permanently heal these intestinal issues?*

Melchizedek Father: She needs to stay on the proper diet and she will not have any issues. She needs to stop eating meat, dairy, cheese, and heavy foods. Preferably a raw vegan diet. That might be a bit extreme for her but she could do it.

D: *Maybe she could graduate towards that?*

Melchizedek Father: As long as she stays vegan and is careful of nonorganic grains then she should be fine. She needs to concur some of her food cravings too.

D: *How about sugar? Is sugar a problem?*

Melchizedek Father: She doesn't have a sugar problem. That is one thing she doesn't have. She doesn't care about sugar.

D: *How about white flour?*

Melchizedek Father: Sometimes she craves some carbs but she usually tries to make appropriate choices for carbs at home like rice or quinoa, or things like that. The last few months have been really rough for her and she has definitely fallen off of the wagon so to speak with her diet. As long as she stays on the appropriate diet, she should be fine. She can't eat as she ate before. She needs to be of more light all over.

D: *And she understands this?*

Melchizedek Father: She knows. We have told her before. We have told her many times. She knows.

D: *She says she needs some assistance in losing some excess weight.*

Melchizedek Father: If she stays on the appropriate diet then she will be fine though she needs to . . . she was doing it before. Seaweed, for the iodine for her thyroid, because she was on some medication before that messed up her thyroid. Either that or take her kelp supplements for the natural iodine. That will help her thyroid to reregulate and then she will be able to shed her weight.

D: *Are there preferred brands of supplements?*

Melchizedek Father: She knows which ones to get. She always gets organic supplements. Or she can just eat the seaweed when she is back to eating. Right now she is just juicing so she is not eating anything. She can just take her kelp. That is better than artificial iodine. That will help.

D: *Thank you. Have we got everything clear from her body scan? Can we look at her aura to see if there are any tears?*

Melchizedek Father: We can send some Love-Light to her aura. She is definitely having blood pressure problems that we need to address for her.

D: *Okay, can we address her blood pressure now?*

Melchizedek Father: Yes.

D: *What can we do for her? What is your guidance on that?*

Melchizedek Father: She needs to lose weight. She needs to quit smoking. They are not causing the issue. They are contributing factors. Most of it is excess energy overload. The majority of it is. She never had any of these problems before the Kundalini started. So she knows some of it is related to the Kundalini process. It is like her central nervous system is ramped up all the time and that can cause issues. She also needs to drink an exorbitant amount of water. Like an extreme amount of water which may seem crazy but she needs all that water to flush things out. So is a delicate balance of diet, exercise, water, and energy.

D: *With these new blocks in place is that going to help her balance out some of this energy that is going on?*

Melchizedek Father: Yeah, she won't be holding the weight for both of them anymore. It is like she is holding the energy of two people in one person. Because we sent them down as pairs on purpose. It is too much energy to hold in one vessel. Now he is not holding up his end of the bargain for various reasons and she still needs to do her job here. She is holding too much energy in her vessel which manifests as overeating, over-smoking, high cortisol levels, and high blood pressure. It is not a good situation.

D: *That is not sustainable?*

Melchizedek Father: No. She is going to blow up.

D: *Thank you for sending her for this session and this healing. Is this a good time to continue asking her questions?*

Melchizedek Father: Of course. Yes.

D: *She would like to know why there were 13 pairs sent to Earth? What is the significance of 13?*

N: They are showing me Metatron's Cube with all the circles inside of it and there are 13 of them. I am just seeing it as if it was flat and then the rays of energy coming up out it into one point. (Using her hands to demonstrate the creation of a pyramid-type shape.) Somehow those 13 Energy Rays combine into one thing. That is apparently important.

D: *One purpose? One mission?*

N: Well, they do have one purpose and one mission, they do. But the 13 Rays, I feel like it is more important than just that. They carry codes. They carry like Creational Codes that got divided up amongst them.

D: *Does Nicole know what her creational code is? Who is it that she is?*

Melchizedek Father: She is the Blue Ray. She is the Blue. She knows that. She doesn't fully know what her Creational Codes are. The human mind can't comprehend it really.

D: *So it's not for this time and space right now.*

Melchizedek Father: She got her Codes unlocked already. Since she awakened. It was in a vision. She saw it, she saw this Golden Key come inside of her and unlock something. Her Codes have been unlocked already. So she is doing her part. Everybody gets their Codes unlocked in their time.

D: *When you say everybody, you mean the 13 Melchizedek pairs?*

Melchizedek Father: Yes.

D: *Her male counterpart, has his unlocked at the same time as well?*

Melchizedek Father: No.

D: *Not until he is ready for it?*

N: They split the Codes between the two of us to make it even more complicated. Man, they really set us up for something down here. Let me tell you, they really set us up. The Codes are split between the two pairs. That way even if the dark gets to them, they can't have the full Code because it is split between the two (Nicole and her male counterpart). It is like a safety measure.

Melchizedek Father: Nicole unlocked her Codes when she was activated. They (Nicole and her male counterpart) are supposed to come together because the two Codes fit together but they (The dark) are blocking them from coming together. Because they are not together, they are like two pieces of a puzzle for them to fit. Yeah.

D: *She asked to know more about the Anunnaki hunting us and what can we do about it?*

Melchizedek Father: The Anunnaki. What can we say about them? They are the fallen ones. They chose their path. A long time ago they chose to fall. They were offered many chances to be redeemed and were gifted Codes to restore themself and they continually fell onto the dark path. They have some strange vengeance thing against our 13 in particular. And against many. There is a strong rivalry between them. They interfere whenever they can. That is just what they do.

D: *Is there anything we can do today so that she is invisible to these fallen ones?*

Melchizedek Father: She can be invisible all she wants but her counterpart is visible to them so it doesn't help.

D: *We need to continue sending him Love-Light.*

Melchizedek Father: He needs more than Love-Light at this point.

D: *He needs to wake up is what he needs.*

Melchizedek Father: She has what he needs but he is not coming to her to receive it.

D: *Is it on her to go to him?*

Melchizedek Father: No. He has to come to her. It is just a matter of time before he finds his way back to her. As for the Anunnaki, well, I suppose you can say knowledge is power. The more she knows and the more she understands the more she can protect herself.

D: *Does she have fear of them?*

Melchizedek Father: Not so much anymore. Not so much fear and not so much anger. When she gets to a completely neutral space, they won't be able to affect her anymore.

D: *Except for her connection to her male counterpart and that part of it all.*

Melchizedek Father: She is getting better at shielding herself and in some ways blocking things even though she knows she can't completely block him but she is getting better at that.

D: *But now she can block any of the negative that comes through to her because you have added these extra blocks on their shared, heart, sacral, and third-eye chords.*

Melchizedek Father: That is right. He is no use to them (Anunnaki) without her. So yes, they are using him to torment Nicole. Either of them alone is really not much use to them (Anunnaki) if that makes any sense.

D: *So the Anunnaki are going to do whatever they can to get to Nicole to complete that whole puzzle piece?*

Melchizedek Father: Right. And she is not going to allow them to do that anymore because she is on to them.

D: *And knowledge is power.*

Melchizedek Father: That's right. She knows. She knows what they are doing and she knows when it is them.

D: *And she believes it, she knows it, she feels it.*

Melchizedek Father: She does, finally.

D: *Nice. Did we fully answer the question she had yesterday with her sister talking about a contract? And her feeling held down on her bed with a line on her lower back? Did we address that completely?*

Melchizedek Father: We answered the second part but we didn't really talk about the first part. She already took care of it last night. We will say that. We are bringing up a very ancient contract that they (Anunnaki) broke and they were trying to hold her to. But she has already disavowed it and burned it. It is of no use anymore. They are trying whatever they can do to get to her. That has been taken care of.

D: *Thank you. I have asked all of the questions that she has. Are there any questions that I could have asked that I haven't?*

Melchizedek Father: The Dragons. We need to get back to the Dragons.

D: *Yes, we do. First, have we completely healed her body?*

Melchizedek Father: Her body scan is complete.

D: *Beautiful. Okay, let's get back to the Dragons. First, I was wondering if we could speak to her dog who recently passed? If she could come in and greet her.*

Melchizedek Father: Giorgia? Yeah, she is with her all the time.

N: It is going to make me cry (Emotional), she's is such a sweet girl.

D: *Isn't she sweet?*

N: Oh, she was the best.

D: *Is* Giorgia *one of your Dragons who protects you?*

N: No. She is not a Dragon.

D: *What is* Giorgia *to you?*

N: She is my Angel.

D: *And she is with you all the time. Beautiful.*

N: She is with me all the time. (Chuckling) I told her not to come back here. I love her too much for her to come back.

D: *She came through to me wanting to be a part of this today.*

N: I know. No, I told her not to reincarnate on this planet. I love her too much that I don't want her to be here. I just want to thank her for bringing me Sasha. She is such a good girl. Yeah, I know Giorgia is with me all the time. Before we get to the Dragons, there is one question that we didn't completely answer. The one about how is our mission going and is there a chance that we will fail before it happens. And about the 13 coming together.

D: *Do you want me to say it or did you already ask it?*

Melchizedek Father: Yes, can you ask it, please?

D: *Are the 13 meant to come together at some point?*

Melchizedek Father: Yes.

D: *How close are we to that point happening?*

Melchizedek Father: Well, she already knows. The masculine counterparts have to unite with the feminine first before that happens. How is the mission going in general? That is difficult to give her an unbiased answer. Because she is still a bit emotionally charged from it, which we don't blame her for. From the Melchizedek perspective it is going fine. Obviously, everything that could have potentially happened could not have been foreseen by the Melchizedek. Sometimes things just have to naturally play out.

N: The Melchizedek are saying they have a strong connection with all the females, which is extremely important. They have told me many times that as long as they can connect to one of us, we are okay because they use the one that they can connect to, to affect the other one. The masculines are like they still have their training wheels on. They still have their training wheels on. They are still in their left brain in doubt and denial and need to come to the Light, so to speak. The Melchizedek can get through to them to some extent, obviously, when they are sleeping. It is a matter of time. It is us, the feminine who are doing energy work on ourselves and staying clear. And understanding that our Higher Selves are working on the masculines and letting it play out the way it is supposed to play out. The Melchizedek do not see our mission as failing. They don't see that as a possibility.

D: *Wow. That is huge.*

N: I can't believe it is ever going to happen but the Melchizedek are giving me a thumbs-up sign. So I guess we are okay.

D: *That is beautiful. You're doing it right on track. That is huge.*

N: I don't know if we are on track but we are okay.

D: *Well, they have their training wheels on at least, these masculines, and are being worked on during their dream time. As we look back at our own journeys, all of those things are huge. To start reprogramming our thought process, that left brain as you say. Beautiful. That is all good news. We just have to be patient and allow that process to work. Can we speak to the Dragons now?*

N: Yes. Yes, we can. There is actually a Dark One, a dark Dragon, a masculine, coming forward. I feel like he has some connection to our group, to us the Melchizedek, and that he is probably one who got sent on a mission and who got completely taken over. So he is coming forward (Sobbing emotional), and this is going to make me cry. He is coming forward to be healed.

D: *Higher Self, may I speak to the Dark One, the Dragon representing the group, please?*

Dragon Dark One: Yes.

D: *Am I speaking to the Dark One?*

Dragon Dark One: Yes.

D: *(Extremely emotional) Thank you for coming here to speak with us. We love you, we honor you, and we respect you for the beautiful race that you are. And the beautiful, beautiful mission that you have been on. We are humbled to be in your presence and to be a part of this transition that will take place today.*

Dragon Dark One: Thank you for finding us.

D: *May we ask you questions?*

Dragon Dark One: Yes. Of course.

D: *I understand you are male.*

Dragon Dark One: Yes.

D: *Is there a name that you go by? How would you like me to refer to you?*

Dragon Dark One: Maleck. Maleck, yeah.

D: *Greetings Maleck. It is such an honor to meet you. As you know the Universe is ascending. Personally, I am going through an emotional time speaking with you right now. I can feel your energy is so powerful. I am so in love with who you are and your race and who you represent to all living, all of Source's creation.*

N: He is saying that they got lost a really long time ago. It is like they fell down this spiral and they didn't know who they were anymore (very emotional) or where they were from. They just fell and thought they were lost forever. The Melchizedek sent me to the 13 Dragons to hold that energy so that we could find them now and bring them back home.

D: *How many are there of you?*

Maleck: There are thousands of them.

D: *Thousands. And you have been tricked for these thousands and thousands and millions of years?*

Maleck: Yes. And to fight with their brothers and sisters and they are so tired now. They are so tired. It is like they have so much of their life and their power drained out of them. There is still a tiny spark in all of them that the Archons couldn't extinguish, no matter what they did they couldn't extinguish it. It is like they had like a crystal inside of them (fallen Dragons) from Source that they (Archons) couldn't touch it. They couldn't get that crystal no matter what they did to them. Yeah.

D: Maleck, are you able to connect to the thousands who are with you? Do they realize how much we love them? How beautiful you each are and how valued you each are?

N: They can feel it but they can't fully believe it yet. They can feel our hearts and can tell we are telling the truth. They know that we mean it.

D: They have our infinite love. We are here with Love-Light of Source to remind you of the beautiful, beautiful organic beings that you are, who are of our Universe and are of Source Love-Light. You have been harvesting from others for thousands and millions of years. It is something that is not organic to you. Today we are going to help you (Sobbing emotional) tap into that Source Love-Light within you. You will see, know, and feel, that it is an infinite, infinite flow. It never ends. And as you do that, Archangel Raphael, and the Higher Self, and the Legion of Light, we call on the Legion of Light to be here with you. We call on Archangels Michael, and Azrael, and all the Archangels, and our Dragons, our benevolent Dragons, we call on all who are benevolent to take you to a place of healing. It is an ascension for you as Dragons are of the highest ascension and you are coming from such a low dark space. You will be able to keep all of your experiences and all of your memories, all of your wisdom, once you are healed and at peace you can go ahead and incarnate with your family and your brethren. Okay, the time is now for each one of you to look for that spark of Source Love-Light within your soul and spread it to all of that is you, every root, every chord, every essence of you. Spread that Love-Light into consciousness that you send into the Universe. Spread it, until, I'm so sorry, I've got so many tears in my eyes that I'm having a hard time reading the script . . . (Sobbing)

Melchizedek Father: It is okay, it's happening. I can see it all. It is like all the Archangels have surrounded all of them in a huge bubble and then I can just see them all coming up, like one-by-one, and two-by-two, three-by-three. It is like they are all flying up out of wherever they were.

D: *It's happening!*

Melchizedek Father: It's happening. It's beautiful.

D: *Do we need to allow them time for them all to spread their Love-Light? Let me know once they are all of Light. Can you describe what you are seeing?*

Melchizedek Father: It is like they are all reuniting with their families. The Dragons are reuniting and they are starting to remember. The last ones are coming up now. It is like there is this huge ring of light that they were all flying up out of. They are saying we are good. We have got them all.

D: *We have got them all?*

Melchizedek Father: Yeah. This is huge! This is really huge! Wow!

D: *Now that you are all . . . I can just feel the joy! There is so much joy and love! Now that you are positively polarized Malleck, do you have a message for us and for Nicole, being this bridge?*

Maleck: That we love you all so much. We need some time to heal and regain our memories and to be with our families and then we will help to clear all the rest of the infringement from this Universe. We will help restore everything back to Source. We thank you for not forgetting us and for forgiving everything we had done while we were under, when we were under their spell. And we thank you from the bottom of our hearts and we love you all.

D: *We love you, honor you, bless you, and respect you. How many of you are there?*

Melchizedek Father: There are thousands. There are at least two thousand of them. It is like they have to relearn how to use their wings because they have been shackled for so long. It is like they have to re-learn how to fly.

D: Releasing all that pain and that anguish! Oh how beautiful, how joyful, how huge! We send the blessings, bless you for all that we are and the Love-Light of the Universe. We call on the Legion of Light to guide you to the place of healing with our utmost blessings and love. Thank you for allowing us to meet you and to be part of this beautiful, beautiful, healing. We thank you, we honor you, and respect you with all that we are.

Maleck: Thank you both. We won't forget what you have done here today.

D: Thank you. (Long reverent pause)

N: Wow. (Long pause) We did good.

D: (Both chuckling) Yeah, this is . . . I need a moment. Yeah.

N: I told you this was going to be a good session.

D: You did! Did you ever . . . ?

N: No. I didn't think it was going to be like this. No way.

D: Higher Self, is there anything else that you would like to do for Nicole's healing today?

Melchizedek Father: No. We are complete for today. Thank you very much.

D: Thank you, Higher Self. Thank you, Archangel Raphael, and all the Archangels, and the Legion of Light, and the Dragons, for being here and helping us and being those magnificent beings of love and joy that you are.

Melchizedek Father: Thank you.

D: We love you, honor you, and respect you. Thank you. Higher Self is this a good time to bring her out?

Melchizedek Father: Yes. You may bring her out now.

End of the session.

I have no words to add. Every time I revisit this session, I sob humble Dragon tears of joy for I relive this experience fully each and every time. If you will, please take a moment of silence with me in honor of these magnificent beings, in gratitude, love, and respect to the Melchizedek, the Dragons, Source, the Archangels, the Legion of Light, and all who assist in bringing Light to our world and the Multiverse.

    Moment of silence

    So it is. It is so. Aho.

7

Sensing Mars

AURA Healing Hypnosis by Nicole
April 10, 2022

This is not a session I sought. It was more of a favor. Here Nicole was in the process of completing her certification to be an AURA/RAAH practitioner and wanted someone to practice on. She and I had built a relationship after she found me in the practitioner directory (https://www.risingphoenixaurora.com) and requested a session with me. Her session took place three weeks earlier as noted in the previous chapter, Positively Polarizing Twp Thousand Dark Ones.

We learn from this session that Nicole is not only a powerfully gifted clear channel and very knowledgeable, but she's also passionate and loving. Between my wholesome vegan lifestyle and the healings I've received, no one is more surprised than me about how blocked I continued to be. Nicole's persistence and creative workaround of connecting to her own Higher Self through the blocked client's Higher Self was nothing short of amazing. That same ingenuity is woven throughout the session. It is notable how each practitioner I have worked with has consistently played an integral part on my path of personal healing for which I am infinitely grateful for.

Session begins.

N [Nicole]: Do you sense that you've landed on the ground?

D [Debra]: I don't know if I've landed. I do sense that there is a lot of purple around me.

N: Beautiful, so you sense purple.

D: Hm-mm.

N: Is there any shape to it or is it just a color?

D: There's a mixture of black and purple. There are wavy waves oscillating.

N: Oscillating waves of black and purple. Do you feel that you have a body?

D: I don't feel different. I just feel me.

N: Do you sense any presence around you?

D: As I was slowing down, my heart did a flip which was interesting. I mean it did a couple of fast beats and then back to normal.

N: When you were slowing down in your Merkabah, you felt your heart flip?

D: Yeah.

N: Do you think you were nervous to see something?

D: I felt warm, very warm.

N: Do you think it could just be a very high energy that made your heart flip? . . . Do you sense anyone else around you right now?

D: No. Well, maybe.

N: Do you still feel you are in this purple-black energy?

D: Now it is more black.

N: Do you want to try something? Imagine that you are floating. You are in your Merkabah. You are as safe as can be. You are just going to float upwards. Just let it float up, up, up. See if we can clear some of this blackness and float up above where it is dark. Let me know if you see anything else while you are floating up.

D: It feels lighter but it is still dark.

N: *Let's keep going, let's keep floating up and see how high we can go today. Just keep letting your Merkabah float up, up, up, and let me know if you sense anything else.*

D: . . . It's not as dark. There's some abstract going on.

N: *Can you describe the abstract that is going on?*

D: Like some cracks in all of the black with intricate webbing.

N: *Intricate webbing. Interesting. Do you see any symbols of any kind?*

D: No. I'm feeling there's more purple now. (If this webbing created symbols the image didn't last long enough for me to recognize the patterns or symbols.)

N: *Purple. Beautiful. Let's keep floating up, up, up in your Merkabah. Keep going up and see if maybe there is a hole through all of these cracks and webbing where there is a little bit more light that we can fly through. Let me know if you are seeing or sensing anything else.*

D: . . . The shapes are changing but they are abstract. (Meaning nothing I could define.) There's more purple now.

N: *Can you describe any of the shapes that you are seeing?*

D: It is like fractals. Broken pieces.

N: *Broken fractals. Do you have any sense of what these broken fractals can be?*

D: Facets. (Facets of the past.)

N: *Facets of what? . . . Just go with whatever your first impression is. It is always right.*

D: It's like a rocky surface.

N: *Like a mountain?*

D: It's uneven but it doesn't seem like a mountain. It's very rocky.

N: *It's very rocky. All right, what color is it? What color are the rocks?*

D: It's brown, reddish brown.

N: *Reddish brown. Beautiful. Are the rocks all around you?*

D: It is around the bottom.

N: *Around the bottom. What can you see if you look straight ahead of you?*

D: Purple.

N: *Purple. And what is above you?*

D: It's dark.

N: *Is it dark like the nighttime dark?*

D: It could be nighttime dark but there isn't anything there but darkness.

N: *There are no stars or anything?*

D: No stars or anything.

N: *Can you get a sense of where you think you are? Just an intuitive sense.*

D: . . . Uh, Mars came in.

N: *Okay, beautiful. So you feel like you are on the surface of Mars now?*

D: Yeah. The rocks aren't there as they were.

N: *What do you sense now?*

D: It is more dark.

N: *Look down at your feet, where your feet would be, and tell me what you see.*

D: I don't see anything.

N: *Do you see anything in front of you? Just look straight ahead and tell me what you see.*

D: It's dark with some bits of purple mixed in. It's not oscillating. It is just there.

N: *Let's move towards this purple. Let's go and investigate this purple. Just sense yourself moving more towards this purple color and keep going there. You are there now where it is all purple. Tell me what you feel and sense.*

D: It's brighter and there is a little passageway that I'm trying to get to but when I get to it, it's gone.

N: *What does the passageway look like?*

D: It looks like a dugout place to go into. It's a dugout tunnel.

N: *Like a dugout going underground?*

D: Through a hillside or something, the rocks are like a mine.

N: *Let's go there now. You are standing right in front of that dugout tunnel to the mine. You are there now and you are looking at it. Tell me what you see. You are able to see, sense, and know everything very clearly now, very clearly.*

D: . . . I get there. It's looking very vague then I get a glimpse and when I go that way it becomes vague. It becomes like nothing, just solid.

N: Okay. Let's move along, let's move this scene along to the next most important place you need to be. Let's see what else your Higher Self wants to show you. Let me know if you see or sense anything.

D: . . . I'm at an opening and I'm going towards it.

N: You said you are at an opening and you're going towards it, what does it look like?

D: Like a rough opening inside of the dirt pile or hill type of deal.

N: Okay, you are at the opening now. Please describe it to me as best you can.

D: . . . I'm working on being able to surrender a lot right now.

N: Okay, I can help you with that. Just imagine there is a small child and just ask her to please step aside. She can watch everything but she is not allowed to interfere. Because we really want to get this higher healing for you and see what your Higher Self has to show you. Just ask her to please just step to the side so that we can do this important work today.

D: Okay we are at the opening to the cave.

N: Let's go inside and see what is in there. You can see, sense and feel, everything very clearly, very clearly. Tell me what you sense inside the cave.

D: . . . It has a smooth surface that is lighter. It's dark but not so dark that you can't see the path.

N: Beautiful. A smooth surface inside maybe like a crystal formation of some kind?

D: No, like dirt.

N: Okay, what color is the dirt?

D: It is still dark but it kind of has a . . . I don't know what color you would call that. It's not brown, it's not red, it's not purple, it's not black, it's . . . grayish green.

N: Okay. Can you see or sense anything else inside this cave? Imagine you are holding a torch in your hand and it is really bright and you can see everything around you very clearly now.

D: . . . There is a hallway. If you can call it a hallway. It's a tunnel in the dirt, it's a large tunnel that you can easily walk through with several feet of space above your head and probably about eight feet wide.

N: *Let's go down the tunnel and see what we find . . . tell me what you are seeing and sensing in the tunnel.*

D: . . . Purple.

N: *Purple like crystal purple?*

D: Purple light.

N: *There's a purple light in the tunnel. Keep following it and tell me what you see, and sense.*

D: It's oscillating small and big, small and big.

N: *What is oscillating, the tunnel itself or the colors?*

D: The tunnel itself, yeah.

N: *It's getting bigger and smaller and bigger and smaller.*

D: Yeah.

N: *Let's go to the end of the tunnel. You are there now. Tell me what you see and sense.*

D: There is a huge opening into a cavern of some sort. Large enough to fit a couple hundred people if needed.

N: *What color is the opening?*

D: It started out with bright purple and white. Now it's not so much of the purple and just a little lit. I can't make anything other than it feels like an open, open space.

N: *Let's go through to that open space. You are there now. Tell me everything that you see and sense there.*

D: . . . It feels cold and more abstract. I'm sensing a lot of confusion. (This was a common space where the people were gathered to receive meager food rations or other gatherings such as group instructions. It has a sad oppressive air about it.

N: *Do you feel confused or the space feels confusing?*

D: Both.

N: *Both?*

D: Hm-mmm.

N: Okay. Let's move this scene along then. You are in your Merkabah. You are safe and protected. Let's move this scene along and see what your Higher Self wants to show you. You are there now and let me know everything that you can see and sense in this space.

D: . . . I have more oscillating purple and white. I thought I could see a dugout but it got covered up by the waves of purple.

N: Let's go to that dugout space that you thought you could see. You are there now and can see and sense and feel everything very clearly, very clearly. Describe the space.

D: . . . There's is not much to it. There is just like a nook dug out of the dirt wall.

N: A nook.

D: Yeah. A nook, like it was someone's personal space. It feels like this was my space. (I sensed that it was my sleeping area.)

N: Okay, let's move the scene along one more time. You are just floating in your Merkabah and we will go to wherever your Higher Self wants to bring you to right now. You are there now. Let me know what you can see and sense.

D: . . . I feel like I'm floating up above it all.

N: Beautiful. Let's keep floating up above all of that.

D: Yeah, it was a huge rocky mountain. I'm floating past it now.

N: Keep floating until you get to where your Higher Self wants you to be. You are there now. Let me know what you see and sense.

D: I'm coming down to a lavender surface.

N: It's a lavender surface?

D: Hm-mmm.

N: What else can you see?

D: It feels like I just landed on it but I don't sense a body on it or anything.

N: Higher Self can you have her talk just a little bit louder?

D: It feels like I landed on it but I don't sense a body. Maybe across the surface.

N: That's okay. Look down at your feet and tell me what you can see.

D: . . . I don't see a body but I see a big boulder in front of me and I'm flying around it.

N: *What color is the boulder?*

D: It is kind of an odd brown, I guess.

N: *Okay, let's follow that pathway that you saw and see where it leads you to.*

D: . . . I don't see anything here. There's nothing interesting.

N: *There is nothing of interest.*

D: No. Just more dirt and rocks.

N: *Dirt and rocks seem to be the theme of the day. Okay, let's move the scene along and see the next important place your Higher Self wants to show you and you are there now. Please describe everything you can see and sense here . . . you can see and sense everything very clearly.*

D: . . . It feels like I'm in a clearing, an opening but it feels like I'm in a pit.

N: *Let's go all the way to the top then. Let's get out of that pit and go all the way to the top and tell me what you can see and sense. You are floating right up with your Merkabah. You can float anywhere with that . . . let me know what you can see and sense.*

D: . . . It feels better but I'm not feeling anything too much now.

N: *You're not feeling anything too much?*

D: Yeah, just kind of weaving through space a little bit.

N: *Can you see any stars?*

D: No. No.

N: *You just feel like you're moving?*

D: Yeah, just across the same color scheme.

N: *All right, let's move everything along. Let's leave that life now. You are moving away, moving away from that scene. Leave that scene completely. And then can I have all the consciousness of Debra, fully integrating back into the body, fully integrating.*

The Higher Self is called in.

N: Can I please speak to the Higher Self of Debra?

Higher Self: Yes.

N: Am I speaking to Debra's Higher Self now?

Higher Self: Yes.

N: Thank you. I love you. I honor you and I respect you for all the aid that you have given us today. I know that you hold all the records of Debra's different lives. May I ask you questions?

Higher Self: Yes.

N: Beautiful. Thank you. Why did she keep going to rocky places and caves and seeing purple? I felt like she was stuck. Can you explain that, please?

Higher Self: . . . I'm not getting an answer.

N: Higher Self, are you still there? Am I speaking to Debra's Higher Self?

Higher Self: . . . Yeah.

N: Beautiful. Thank you for being with us today. May I ask, are you masculine or feminine?

Higher Self: . . . Masculine.

N: Do you have a name that you go by Higher Self?

Higher Self: No.

N: Higher Self, how do you feel your connection is right now to Debra?

Higher Self: Not very clear.

N: Can we ask one of the Archangels to come in and clear that connection for you so that we can have a really good session?

Higher Self: Yeah.

N: Which of the Archangels can we ask to come in and help with that?

Higher Self: Archangel Haylel.

N: Oh, beautiful. I love Archangel Haylel. Archangel Haylel, I'm going to start crying because I can feel his energy. Can you please come in and help Debra's Higher Self so that they can have a really great connection today?

AA Haylel: Yes.

N: Thank you. What do we need to do to help her right now? . . . Haylel, can you check her crown, please, channeling through her crown chakra? . . .

AA Haylel: . . . I think we are going to need your help with what you are sensing.

N: Okay. I'm sensing that there is something going on with her crown chakra right now. It feels really tight at the top of my head. We are going to need to clear that out so that she can have a better connection with her Higher Self. Can I send some energy there to help?

AA Haylel and Higher Self: Yes, please.

N: Okay. I'm going to send energy there to help. I'm going to send some Phoenix Fire. Debra, I just want you to feel Archangel Haylel's energy. I want you to feel his energy very strongly. I want you to feel him in through your crown. Feel it really strong. Let me know when you can feel that.

D: (Emotional) Yeah, I can feel him.

N: You can feel him?

D: Yeah.

N: Beautiful. Haylel, how does her connection feel now? . . . Does her crown feel better?

AA Haylel: . . . Much better.

N: Can we speak to her Higher Self again, please?

Higher Self: Yes.

N: Hello. How is your connection feeling now? Is it feeling better?

Higher Self: It feels like lots of love but it feels really tight.

N: It feels really tight. What can we do to relieve some of the tightness? . . . Are you there Higher Self?

Higher Self: . . . Yes. It is not a matching frequency.

N: She is not matching your frequency so you can't connect very well?

Higher Self: Yeah.

N: All right, what can we do about that?

Higher Self: I'm reminding her of her gifts, of the beauty and the love. And the safety.

The body scan begins.

N: *She is extremely safe and protected right now. . . . Higher Self, we would like to do a body scan on her. Do you think we can start to do a body scan on her?*

Higher Self: Yeah, that would be great.

N: *Beautiful. Do we need any more assistance from Archangel Haylel or any of the other Archangels?*

Higher Self: Yeah, if Archangel Haylel could be around.

N: *Archangel Haylel, if you could be around for her body scan that we are doing right now? Let's start with her crown because there is definitely a lot going on with her crown. Please let me know what you see and sense there . . . .*

AA Haylel and Higher Self: . . . We're going to need your help.

N: *Of course. What do you need me to do?*

AA Haylel: I sense a heaviness.

N: *I sense a heaviness too. It is very dark. I'm going to send some more energy there. Could you do me a favor Higher Self? Could you connect me to my Higher Self who is going to assist as well? (Chuckling)*

Higher Self: Beautiful, yes.

N: *I'm going to ask for Father to come and assist us both now so that we can get a really good connection on the crown chakra. I'm going to ask my Higher Self to send some healing energy to your crown. He is a magical being and can work some magic. (Nicole's Higher Self is her Melchizedek Father – refer to the chapter, Positively Polarizing Two Thousand Dragons. He is someone Debra connected to during Nicole's session.)*

Higher Self: Beautiful.

N: *Whew. I know he is sending the Blue-Green Light from our Collective so you should sense or feel that in your crown chakra. It will break up some of the tightness there. I am sending it as well.*

D: It feels like a cool refreshing waterfall.

N: *Yeah. Good. Good. We're turning the tap on and sending the water in. How is her crown looking Higher Self? . . . Any better?*

Higher Self: It feels a lot lighter. (Smiling)

N: Good. Let's see if we can see what is the root cause of all of that tightness in there. What is blocking her crown? Is there a negative entity of some kind or an implant? What is in there?

Higher Self: Doubt comes to mind.

N: Why is she doubting herself? . . . What is causing her doubt?

Higher Self: Conditioning and programming.

N: Let's remove those programs and that conditioning that is causing her doubt. Let's start that now, please, Higher Self.

Higher Self: Yes.

N: Thank you. What else do we sense in her crown area? Are there any attachments in that area? . . . Higher Self, can we have Haylel and Michael come in and help with the scanning too?

Higher Self: Yes.

N: Beautiful. Can you connect us to them now, please?

AAs Haylel and Michael: Yes.

N: Thank you. Archangels Haylel and Michael, can you please help us locate what is going on with her crown chakra? I feel like there is a lot going on there and we need your help. Archangel Michael, are there any portals in her crown?

AAs Haylel and Michael: There is a lot of pressure.

N: What is causing the pressure? Is there a portal, is there an entity, is there an Archon? . . . What's causing the pressure there?

D: I'm not getting an answer.

N: Is Archangel Michael still there?

D: Yes, he is just not able to get through.

N: Archangel Michael is not able to get through?

D: Yeah.

N: So he can't scan. All right, I'm going to scan then. And I'm going to ask Father to help because I know there is something in her crown chakra. I'm going to ask Michael, Haylel, and Father to find what is in that chakra. I believe there is an Archon and entities. Encase them in the appropriate symbols now please and move them out of the way. Please let me know when that has been completed and I will keep scanning.

AAs Michael and Haylel, Nicole's Melchizedek Father: They are encased.

N: Thank you. Put them off to the side, please and we will deal with them later. Can you see any better now in her crown, Michael?...There is definitely a portal. Let's get Metatron in to close that portal, please. Let me know when that is done.

AA Metatron: It is closed.

N: Thank you. Can you see any better? (No response) There is a black chord and I am going to use Phoenix Fire. We are going to transmute that chord now. There are some grays. I'm going to ask Michael and Father to please put them in the appropriate symbol and move them to the side. Let me know when you have got them.

AA Michael and Nicole's Melchizedek Father: We've got them.

N: Thank you. Keep them off to the side and we will talk to everybody later. There's an implant in the crown. I'm sending Phoenix Fire there to transmute it. There is still way too much pressure in the crown. Can Father please send more Blue-Green Light to heal and open it up, please? There is a lot going on in that crown. Michael and Haylel, how does the crown look now, please?... Can you see her crown any better, Michael?

AA Michael and Haylel: It is much lighter.

N: Good. Can you make sure that Archon gets transmuted properly? And I want to talk to those entities now because I believe they are related to some of her questions. Are we able to talk to any of them now? Will they talk to us?

Archangels: Yes.

N: Good. Which ones will talk to us?

Archangels: Grays.

N: Good. Can I speak to the grays, please?

Grays: Yes.

N: Hello. I honor you, I respect you, and I love you. May we ask you questions at this time?

Grays: Yes.

N: Thank you. What were you doing in her crown chakra, please?...

D: I'm not getting anything.

N: You're not getting anything. All right, let's see if we can talk to Michael and he'll tell us. Can I talk to Michael, please?

AA Michael: Yeah.

N: Michael, what were the grays doing with her crown chakra? . . . Let me ask a more direct question. Were they the ones abducting her? . . . Can I speak to Debra's Higher Self again, please?

Higher Self: Yes.

N: Thank you. Can we get some Dragons in to help us, please?

Higher Self: (Emotional) Yeah.

N: Yeah (Chuckling). Let's call them in, please. Whatever Dragons are appropriate to assist right now, can we please have them come in to surround Debra with their beautiful energy and help us with this session?

Higher Self: (Humbly and quietly) Yes.

N: You can feel them, can't you?

D: Yes.

N: Yes, they are beautiful. . . All right Higher Self, how does her crown look, please?

Higher Self: It looks pretty shiny.

N: Good. And do you feel your connections to her are a little better? . . . Higher Self, can we continue her body scan, please?

Higher Self: Yes.

N: I want you to scan her from head to toe for any hooks, portals, or implants. Tell me what you see, please.

Higher Self: There is something on the right shoulder.

N: Beautiful, what is it? Is it a hook?

Higher Self: It's a dull ache and pain. It's dark.

N: Can we use Phoenix Fire to transmute the dark?

Higher Self: Yes.

N: Good. I'm sending Phoenix Fire now. And we will ask Archangel Raphael to come in please and fill in any areas with Love-Light for all the areas that we have transmuted so far and to aid us for the rest of the session, please.

AA Raphael: Yes.

N: *Thank you. All right, what else? Are there any hooks, portals, or implants anywhere?*

Higher Self: There is something on the right forearm.

N: *Right forearm. Okay, what is it, please?*

Higher Self: It feels artificial.

N: *Like an implant?*

Higher Self: Like an implant.

N: *All right, sending Phoenix Fire to transmute it.*

Higher Self: It's gone.

N: *Beautiful. What else can you sense within her?*

Higher Self: There is something going on in the sacral area.

N: *What is going on in the sacral area? Is it a hook, an implant, an entity, or an Archon?*

Higher Self: It's an uneasy feeling so I'm thinking it's an entity of sorts.

N: *Archangel Michael, can you please find out what kind of entity is in her sacral area and please place it in the appropriate symbol now? And let me know once you have got it.*

AA Michael. Yes. It's contained.

N: *Beautiful. Let's move it off to the side. Keep looking in the sacral area. What is going on there? And what is going on with her bladder?*

Higher Self: From when she was abducted there is an implant.

N: *All right, let's Phoenix Fire that implant now. Keep scanning that area for any hooks, portals, entities, implants, Archons, or anything, anything that shouldn't be there. . . Is there some sort of black box with some symbols on it in her sacral area?*

Higher Self: Yeah, that would be black magic.

N: *Black magic. Can we use Phoenix Fire to transmute that, please?*

Higher Self: Yeah.

N: *Let's do that now, please.*

Higher Self: Thank you.

N: *Was that causing bladder problems? . . . Do you see anything else in that area? Can we have Michael assist with the scanning, please?*

AA Michael: Yes.

N: *Is there an Archon in that area, Higher Self?*

Higher Self: Yes.

N: *Michael, can you please contain that in the appropriate symbol?*

AA Michael: It's encased.

N: *Thank you. Higher Self, how is her sacral looking now?*

Higher Self: Good.

N: *Let's keep scanning the whole body. Let's check her throat, please. Are there any hooks, portals, implants, or Archons in the throat?*

Higher Self: The throat feels good.

N: *The third eye, please. Scan that area.*

Higher Self: I'm not sensing anything.

N: *She doesn't have very good visual senses. Is there anything blocking her third eye from seeing? . . . Michael, can you see if there is anything in her third eye, please?*

AA Michael: . . . I'm not seeing anything there either.

N: *You're not seeing anything there?*

AA Michael: No.

N: *Is there a spider over her third eye?*

AA Michael: Yeah.

N: *All right, let's Phoenix Fire there, please.*

AA Michael: Yes.

N: *Let's go back to her throat. I definitely feel something there. It's a dark portal. Can we have Metatron close that, please?*

AA Metatron: Yes.

N: *Thank you. All right, can you check her legs? Her legs feel kind of heavy to me.*

AA Michael: Yes, they do.

N: *Yeah, what is going on there? Is there metal in the legs?*

AA Michael: Both of them.

N: *Can we send Phoenix Fire there please in both of the legs?*

AA Michael: Yes.

N: *Beautiful. And as that is transmuted along with everything else, we are asking that Archangel Raphael and Divine Mother fill that with Love-Light and heal that. The bottom of the feet, both feet, look like some small portals. Let's have Metatron close those, please.*

AA Metatron: They are closed.

N: *Thank you. And the bottom of the spine, near the tailbone, I am seeing something metal there. Let me see what that is exactly. Maybe an implant of some kind.*

AA Michael: Yeah.

N: *Let's send Phoenix Fire there and transmute that.*

AA Michael: Yes.

N: *Thank you. And also in the back of the neck above the shoulder blades. I'm seeing something metallic there as well. Let's send Phoenix Fire there to transmute whatever that is.*

AA Michael: Yes.

N: *Thank you. And let's send some extra Love-Light into her crown because there is a lot going on there. Let's check her heart, Higher Self. Let's look at her heart. Is there anything going on there?*

Higher Self: It looks good. I'm not sensing anything.

N: *I think there is something in the heart. Michael, can you check her heart and see if there is an entity or an Archon, please? If there is just encase them in the appropriate symbols.*

AA Michael: It's an Archon.

N: *Thank you. Please encase and transmute it. All right, how is she doing Higher Self?*

Higher Self: Pretty good.

N: *Pretty good. I have to ask what is going on with her bladder. What else do we need to do to heal her bladder issues?*

Higher Self: I think she needs to continue doing her RAAH on herself and continue sending Love-Light to the area.

N: *Are there any supplements that she needs to take?*

Higher Self: No. She quit all of her supplements over the last couple of months to clean out her system to heal her body naturally with healthy foods.

N: Beautiful. She keeps having arthritis in her knees and her back. Is there anything else we can do or she can do to help heal that?

Higher Self: She is using alkaline water for that but she doesn't drink enough.

N: So she needs to drink more alkaline water. Beautiful. Can I talk to those grays that we found before? Will they speak to us now?

Higher Self: Yeah, we can try.

N: Let's try. Can I please speak to the leader of the grays that we found?

Grays: Yeah.

N: Thank you. I love you, honor you, and respect you. May I ask you questions?

Grays: Yeah.

N: Were you the ones abducting Debra?

Grays: No.

N: Do you know who was abducting her? What were you doing in her crown chakra?

Grays: Preventing her from remembering.

N: Were you contracted to interfere with her?

Grays: Yes.

N: Are you organic grays or completely inorganic?

Grays: Inorganic.

N: Thank you very much for speaking with us. Higher Self, I believe there were other entities we found within her aside from the grays. Do we know if they are organic or inorganic and if they will speak with us?

Higher Self: There's a Reptilian in the sacral.

N: Did we encase that in the symbols?

Higher Self: Yes, we did.

N: Would this Reptilian speak with us?

Reptilian: Yeah, maybe.

N: *Thank you. I love you, honor you, and respect you. May I ask you questions?*

Reptilian: Yeah.

N: *What were you doing in her sacral area? What issues were you causing her?*

Reptilian: Digestive issues.

N: *When did you come in?*

Reptilian: A couple of months ago.

N: *What was Debra doing that caused you to enter her?*

Reptilian: Negative talk about herself.

N: *Talking negatively about herself. Okay. Do you have a body somewhere or are you just a consciousness?*

Reptilian: I don't sense a body.

N: *Okay. As you know, it is the time of ascension and we know you have been playing this role for a very long time. Would you like to positively polarize and keep all of your memories in tack and go through a natural ascension?*

Reptilian: Yes. (smiling) I think that's why I attached myself to her, for this opportunity.

N: *(Chuckling) I understand that. I'm going to ask you to look inside of yourself and find that beautiful spark of light that is within you. Can you see that spark of light?*

Reptilian: Yeah.

N: *Beautiful. I want you to imagine that spark of light is completely taking over your entire consciousness and turning you into a positively polarized light at this time. Let me know when you feel like you are all light.*

Reptilian: (Smiling) I'm light!

N: *Oh beautiful. Thank you so much. We are so happy that we were able to assist you today. I'm going to ask Archangels Azrael and Michael to stay with you and make sure that you get to where you need to go safely. Do you have any parting words for us at this time?*

Reptilian: Thank you (Happily).

N: *Thank you. We wish you the best on your next adventures.*

Reptilian: Thank you.

N: *Higher Self, is there any other organic consciousness that we have encased and need to talk to at this time?*

Higher Self: No.

N: *Okay, I'm going to ask the Angels to do whatever they need to do with the inorganic consciousnesses. I am sure they know best what needs to be done. And are there any other health issues that we need to address for her right now?*

Higher Self: No.

N: *Is there anything else we can do for her, any other healing, or age regression? I know she has had a few other AURA sessions, so I figured I'd ask. Does she want to be age-regressed like fifty years or something (Laughing)? Just kidding, we all want that.*

Higher Self: You are correct, no additional age regression is needed at this time.

N: *Do you think we are fully complete with her body scan at this time?*

Higher Self: Yes. She feels pretty good.

N: *Great. I want to thank everyone who assisted, Haylel, Michael, Father, Raphael, Divine Mother, Metatron, the Dragons, and anyone else who assisted. Thank you to the entities that positively polarized today, and thank you Higher Self.*

Higher Self: Thank you.

N: *Higher Self, may I ask the rest of the questions that she has?*

Higher Self: Yeah. Hopefully, we'll be able to keep the connection open (Chuckling).

N: *We'll do the best we can. Okay, she asked, "Lately while shielding my mind keeps wandering. Is this healthy or do I have infringements?"*

Higher Self: Yeah, you had infringements.

N: *I think so and we cleared some of those out. Should she have a better time when she is doing her shields now?*

Higher Self: Yes. She should be a lot clearer.

N: *Beautiful. Her next question is, "May I have continued healing from the deep pain and trauma when being estranged from my children in 2002 at the time of my second marriage? Is this trauma related to my being blocked from my spiritual gifts?"*

Higher Self: Trust your intuition on that. That came to you intentionally. So, yes.

N: So the trauma has been blocking her. What can she do to help herself heal from that?

Higher Self: Live in the now. Do something fun in joy.

N: Beautiful. Debra asked, "At the age of seventeen, shortly after starting to date my first husband, I became deathly ill. Why?"

Higher Self: It was a decision point to continue living and to continue on the path that you were going. You chose to live.

N: Was that a possible exit point for her?

Higher Self: Yeah. She came into this life knowing that she was traveling on a rocky road to help her become who she is to become.

N: So did she perhaps set up some really difficult lessons for herself for this lifetime?

Higher Self: Yes. These are chosen experiences to go through.

N: For what purpose did she choose these experiences to go through?

Higher Self: To wake up and remember how strong and valued you are.

N: Beautiful. She definitely has a fear of being away from her children, and fear of her future. It seems like a fear of her ascension path. Is there any wisdom or guidance you can share with her about that?

Higher Self: Yes, she knows. She knows that her children will get there. Maybe not at the same time but they will get there. It will work out. It's okay not to go at the same time. We are not supposed to go at the same time.

N: We're all meant to go in our own time, right?

Higher Self: Correct.

N: There you go. I believe those are all the questions that she had. Is there anything else that we could have asked that we didn't ask?

Higher Self: No. This has been beautiful.

N: Are there any other beautiful wisdom or advice that you can share with her right now to help her along her path?

Higher Self: Keep learning, keep shielding, and keep filling your heart with love. Find joy in what you are doing.

N: Thank you Higher Self. Is there anything else or should we bring her back now?

Higher Self: I think we can bring her back. This has been beautiful. Thank you so much. I love you so very much for all of your healing today and for all the help you brought in. It was simply sacred and purely beautiful.

N: Thank you. It was my pleasure. All right, I will bring her back now.

End of the session.

That was interesting to sense I was entangled as some sort of slave on Mars. Notice how gently my Higher Self allowed this traumatic life to come through in such a subtle manner. Having past lives is still a new concept to me at this time, and the concept that I am more than this current life or physical vessel is still materializing. It was disappointing that I continued to be so blocked and covered with infringements. I'm shielding daily. I keep asking myself why is this such a slow process for me to activate my gifts of seeing and hearing my Guides and Angels. And why aren't my shields working? The answers in this session were about doubting myself and what I'm feeling.

I'm reminded of one of my clients who was a gentle lonely soul. He was probably in his late thirties and had spent the majority of his life wandering and searching for purpose. As a teenager, he chose to experiment with acid and self-harm. More recently he had been following the wave of ayahuasca and mushroom enthusiasts visiting other countries. In this effort, he spent two years working in a silent meditation facility. From there he spent several months traveling around the states visiting sites of interest living in his car. To him, meditation was about quieting his mind. It was about solitude. Strangely he knew little of our chakras or the energies at work. His experiences have been of a darker nature yet entity attachments were a foreign concept.

Through this modality of AURA past life regression hypnosis therapy, I have learned that when taking mind-altering substances you are surrendering your sovereignty over to whatever entities may be hovering around at the time. No judgment, still, you are literally lowering your vibration and giving them permission to take your free will. We know this from talking directly to entities within past AURA sessions, many of which have been posted on YouTube (Social media). Although I had been able to clear much during this young man's energy work, he was filled with dark entities attached to lessons requiring his understanding and accepting they were lessons toward his ascension. It also required his Higher Self to acknowledge the lesson had been learned. These are the types of conversations that can be had within an AURA. But of course, only when you are ready to have that conversation.

Moments into this young man's hypnosis it was obvious he wasn't ready to know about such things and having no judgment, his Higher Self is allowing him to decide when he is ready for that deeper healing. He had just gone under hypnosis, and looking down at his feet he totally freaked out about having too many toes. It was something he just couldn't get past. Moving the scene along, his Higher Self took him to various times in his current life. When asking his Higher Self why he was shown extra toes, his Higher Self responded that it was to emphasize his feeling alien at times. This was a healing session for him in that it helped him see the bigger picture of his choices and helped him get to the root cause of his behaviors. He couldn't have been happier or more at peace from his session.

My favorite part of his session was witnessing how our Higher Self will never allow us to experience something we aren't ready for. For instance, when a child seeks a session, their Higher Self will only provide them with relevant information that aligns with their current level of understanding. Getting back to the young man's session, I'm a little bit jealous that with all those attachments he was easily able to see whatever his Higher Self was placing in front of him. Why can't I? I have some ideas why and that it has to do with a deeper disbelief in myself, and definitely some trust issues. But so did he.

Revisiting this session in preparation for the second edition of this book (2025), I find it interesting how my practitioner and I both quickly fled the dark, heavy energies we felt when placed in the pit. Intuitively, the pit is a loveless, gooey place of endless tortured slave labor, dark both physically and energetically. It was the place where I took my last breath in that life. I felt that I was male, humanoid and that I had been abducted from a planet that wasn't Earth. It's the planet that today is only officially recognized as the asteroid belt between Mars and Earth. Wow!

Knowing today that my Higher Self took me there for a reason and that there is no such thing as time, I'm in gratitude for the allowance of so much space to integrate this inner standing. The purpose, of course, was to face and heal that trauma. Choosing this moment, I invite you to join me as I go back to revisit that pit.

As I do so, my heart space is growing larger and larger with empathy for all who endured such tortured, dark conditions. I thank the tortured, including myself, and the land for providing this perspective and experience to the collective. If it resonates with you, join me in honoring all within this pit. I am taking deep breaths. With each breath, I am filling my heart with more and more love. Then, when I feel my heart is about to burst from so much love, I quickly exhale, sending a huge blast of healing Source Love Light down both of my arms and out of my hand chakras to all there within that time and space. Beautiful! Thank you!

Let's repeat sending huge bursts of healing Source Love Light waves as many times as you intuitively feel is needed. I enjoy doing this at least three times. At this time, I'd also like to call on the Christ Consciousness and Divine Mother for their beautiful healing energies to join us in this healing of the trauma experienced by the people, animals, vegetation, rocks (For truly, the rocks were getting my attention), the planet itself, the air, the water, and all life-force who are organic in that time and space. I ask all to fill the spaces once filled with sorrow and darkness with well-deserved, beautiful, unconditional love, honor, respect, and sweet gratitude. We are wrapping our loving arms around it all, transmuting and healing this space back to its organic divine soul blueprint. Beautiful! Can you feel it? The vibration changed! It is of the light once again! Phenomenal! I love you, honor you, and respect you with all that I am. Thank you! Thank you! Thank you! I love you infinitely.

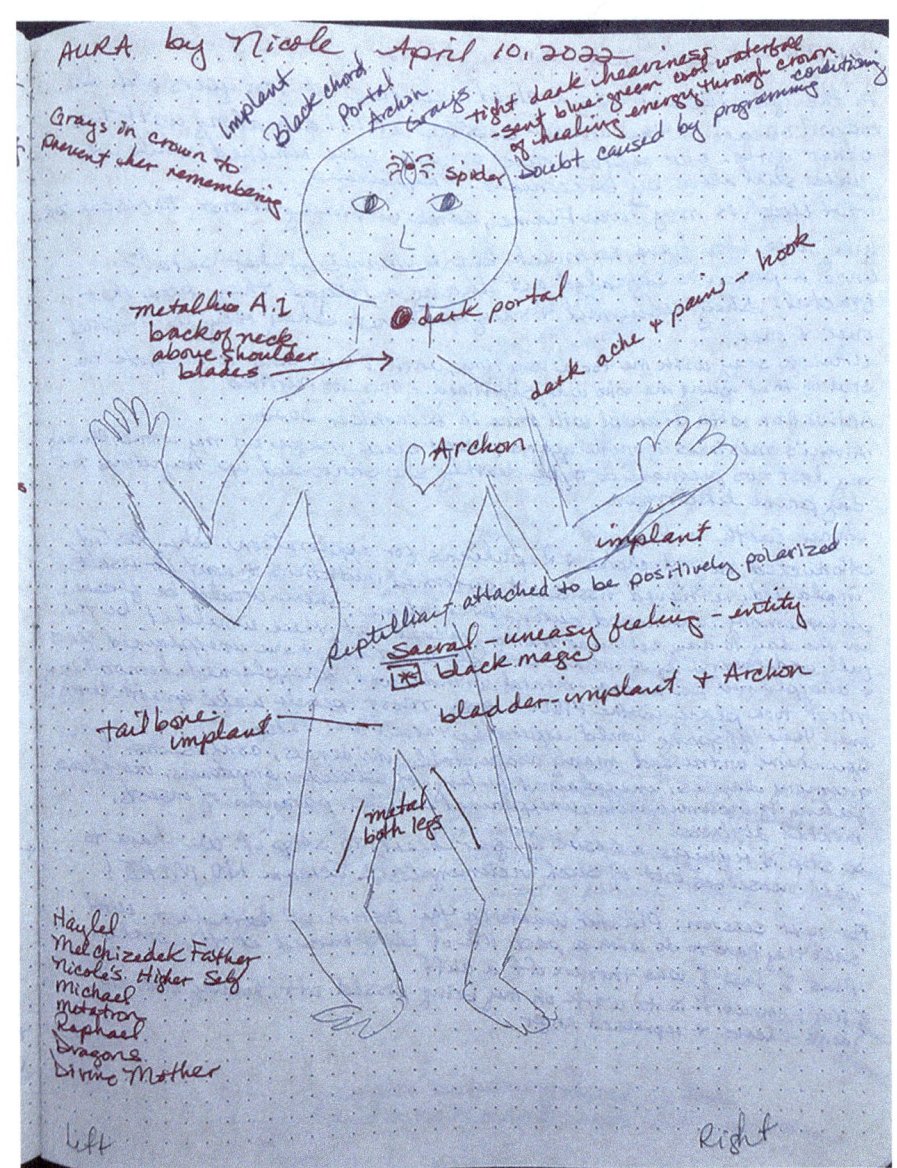

8

Like Layers of an Onion

December 2021, May 2022, and September 2022

We are different people today than we were yesterday, last year, and so on, and so on. Processing this, I'm also realizing my experiences are allowing me to continually level up. What an exciting concept. In essence, we have the opportunity for a renewed perspective tomorrow than what we know today. Who would want it any other way? The value I find in this chapter is that for me it illustrates those changing perspectives. This one chapter is of three separate sessions from the same practitioner within a nine-month time period (December, May, and September). Sprinkled within those months are additional teaching moments from others also covered in this book. Specifically, Positively Polarizing Two Thousand Dark Ones, Sensing Mars, Jump Debra, Jump, and Indigenous Connections. Witnessing dramatic changes in both this practitioner and myself, rather than a verbatim transcript of the sessions it's organized by topic.

To explain what I mean by dramatic changes, when I first worked with this practitioner, I was new to this practice of personal communications and healings from Archangels. Keep in mind that I didn't get into this modality to become a practitioner rather it was to investigate why I kept seeing a certain loved one occasionally become someone else; someone out of control. It caused me to reflect on times in my life when I didn't feel in control. Once as a young mother I even became so angry that I kicked a hole in the wall of our home's hallway. Those who know me can attest that that kind of anger is surprisingly out of character. If you would, take a moment to look at the family photo found on page 225. Does that not look like a normal happy thriving family? With ever fiber in my being, I certainly thought so. In fact, it literally is and was. And it's a moment not to robbed of the beauty and love we genuinely have for one another and the world around us.

That being said, in this book we are talking about deep healing at the cellular level. Healing from traumas that for me, I wasn't aware existed. Traumas from not only this lifetime but unknown countless previous lifetimes. I am a senior woman on this quest for answers, who soon learned that even at the moment that photo was taken, that beautiful young mother was oblivious to the dark goo that surrounded her and her beautiful children. I went into my first hypnosis knowing I had done the work needed for a fabulous session only to find myself . . . lost.

When I met the practitioner I'm introducing in this chapter, I was still in this state of confusion as to why I'm not better connecting to my Higher Self. To be clear, it's not an AURA hypnosis healing. She certified in the teachings of AURA Hypnosis past life regressions and entity removal but created a hybrid modality of combing the RAAH (Reiki Angelic Alchemy Healing) energy work with an Akashic reading. It is noteworthy that at the time, she and her unique modality came highly recommended by other trusted veteran AURA hypnosis practitioners. My first session with her delved deeply into topics that I already brushed across in previous sessions with other practitioners. Thinking I had completed and healed those various traumas, I soon learned from this practitioner that there was more to it. We needed to get to the root of those traumas. Needless to say I was excited beyond measure!

One example of that is the child suicide incident you'll read about in the following, where previously it wasn't discussed other than healing the trauma from being bullied by her stepmother and stepbrothers. Here, in these sessions I was able to investigate this and many other darker things I wasn't ready to talk about earlier.

Within that first session I was told by Archangel Azrael that, "She will receive three (Higher Self) activations within the next upcoming twelve Galactic months. One of the activations will be Archangel Uriel, the following will be Archangel Haylel, and the next will be the revelation of her Divine Creation." I took this to mean additional sessions with this same practitioner. In hindsight, they could very well have been with any trusted practitioner. It's all about our questions. Remember, I was new to all of this and can be literal, to a fault. Regardless, I immediately booked the May and September follow-up sessions with this same practitioner, and planned to book a fourth session the following December which didn't happen.

A clear channel is one trusted not to censor or change a Divine message. My dilemma comes from my going into sessions I soon felt parts of were paraphrased, or censored. Why did I do that? What's different about these particular sessions? Of course, I knew the answer as soon as I asked the question. I stayed with it not only because she seemed to be able to dig deeper than others, but because I loved and admired this practitioner like a sister. Plus, like I said she broke through many of my barriers seemingly effortlessly. During my May (Second) session with her she shared with me that she felt infringed but didn't know anyone she could trust to do a session on her at her level. That statement alone says a lot about how dominant her ego was at that time. By my third session with her, she was a different person. She had clearly digressed becoming more self-centered than in her prior service-to-others self. It was an unexpected thing to witness. She was so very gifted. I'm hoping she'll soon return to her full beautiful organic loving self.

For an AURA, no one is going into your sacred records other than you and your Higher Self. The practitioner of an AURA is simply the bridge to assist you in that connection. An AURA is the safest modality for self-healing. Readings are especially helpful if the client is somehow blocked from their Higher Self which at the time, I felt I was. I will not share probably about eighty percent of these three sessions. For example, a huge healing took place covering several lifetimes with years of frequent incest rape from my then father. One lifetime my father was described as wearing the clothing of a pilgrim with my young life ending not only from brutal sexual abuse but a hanging.

Due to the argument and triggered disrespect by the practitioner to the Archangels, I won't share more on those experiences. What I will share is what I recognize as clear channeled messages from beings whom I knew in my heart to be benevolent. These messages are a treasured part of my journey toward remembering who I am.

Processing this chapter I feel I've learned at the cellular level, meaning I intend to never forget, that with this process, once you request a session for a reading with someone, you are consenting that the practitioner has your permission to go into your sacred records. I was consenting to someone I eventually knew in my heart to be infringed. I don't think I fully considered how dangerous that can be. Precious information was tainted to the point of being unusable. Why couldn't I just be honest from the beginning about what I was feeling with this practitioner whom I admired so much? I could have said nope, this doesn't feel right, I am sovereign and do not consent. It's a lesson. A lesson that I'm using this chapter to work through.

Again, the clear channeled messages are treasured revelations and healing opportunities that I feel in my heart you may also benefit from. Whereas I am not including entire sessions, I have chosen to share these moments by topic. You'll find that often, with this practitioner, messages come across like listening to one side of a telephone conversation.

- Child suicide attempt, current life
- Vision correction, current life
- Blockage in ears, current life
- Symbols and chakra status
- Being a child sacrifice, past lives
- Black magic, this life
- Abductions/Scream no more to abductions, this life
- Trauma residue, there's no going back
- Residual resentment, current life
- Visit from the Lyrian Constitution

Child suicide attempt in current life, excerpt from December 27, 2021 session.

(We enter a session that has already began. The Channel is working with the Archangels and found three negative entities who are jumping from one side of the frontal lobe to the backside of the brain to the other side.)

Channel: Very good. Then is it possible for us to find out how long they have been in the frontal lobe?

Archangels: Eleven.

Channel: At the age of eleven, eleven months ago, or eleven years ago?

Archangels: At the age of eleven.

Channel: Very good. So, do you know what was happening to you at the age of eleven that caused a lot of anger and perhaps like, I don't want to say disassociation...

Debra: I swallowed a bottle of pills when I was eleven. I had a very abusive stepmother, I had lost my mother two years before from a car accident, which was suicide from my father cheating on her. He remarried a different woman and she was beating my eight-year-old brother with a tool in her hand making him a bloody mess. She also beat my younger sister and me. The verbal abuse was constant and pretty intense. She was a very dark person. And my father wasn't around. He was working months away at a time. So, yeah, I swallowed a bottle of pills and nobody knew about it. I was just sick for a while.

Channel: You were just sick for a while?

Debra: I just threw up, and threw up, and threw up. I didn't tell anybody. I had no counseling.

Channel: What's coming through is a form of separation of the soul when that happened, when they mentioned the word disassociation, I was like okay at eleven years old that is kind of strong, but then you said what you said, so that clarifies it. This disassociation, do we need to go into that timeline and retrieve the soul? Okay, so you need to advise then. Do we contain the energies first?

Archangels: The energies are already contained.

Channel: Do we need to polarize these energies first or retrieve the soul?

Archangels: We're going to retrieve the soul.

Channel: Can we go ahead and invoke Archangel Azrael? . . . I'm seeing like black and blues. I'm not sure this is right.

AA Azrael: Immortalization of the soul has occurred during this transgressive period. During this split brought in by an intense desire to retrieve from such reality caused the separation which you have been told was a disassociation. You must never doubt my dear one the first images and the first words that come to you. Even if things don't make sense. You must take them at face value. We will always explain your visions to you.

Channel: Very good, thank you, Azrael. Can you take us to that time please, so that we can retrieve that little child's soul? Don't we need to internalize this separation of time?

AA Azrael: You mentioned parallel life during the session. When you began you wondered why you said parallel life at the time. You must know that before you begin your sessions, the open portals are activated. Even if you are in an awakening state, you must come to terms with that now you do not speak from conscious awareness, but *from our perspective*. Do you understand this?

Channel: I do Azrael. I understand, yes, and I surrender totally. Thank you for the reminder and the confirmation.

AA Azrael: We will go into that timeline, retrieve the soul and the trauma. Sadness matched with anger creates a void within the heart. When a child grows within his or her heart, it carries throughout their adult life bringing in much despair, matched with the frequency of distrust. Throughout her years that followed, she created a barrier where light was challenging to show through. We will dispel this negativity.

Channel: I'm seeing you right now as that little girl and she's bringing me . . . I'm not sure what that is. It's light, it's like a disc and it emits golden translucent glittery light going up, like a beautiful beam. Very good, thank you. Azrael, does that mean that she is going to internalize in the soul now, or does she need to go through a process of purification?

AA Azrael: She integrated.

Channel: Very good. Thank you so much. Thank you, thank you, thank you. Thank you so much for healing that Inner Child. I want to make sure that we do clear away the despair, the negativity, the anger, the repressed anger, the distrust, the hopelessness even. I want to be able to dispel all of that. Deactivate all of that as well. Beautiful. That is so beautiful. Thank you so much. Can we just rescan her crown chakra one more time and check for any other adhesions that are infringing or that may belong to the past?

AA Azrael: She will need three more sessions throughout the remainder of the year. She must divide them equally in a span of time. During these sessions, we will remove the other layers that have left traces of trauma throughout all of her existences and lifetimes. In between this period, she will be aided by her Divine Expression. She will have revelations during dream time of these creations and she slowly will begin incorporating the activations that will serve her highest purpose in her current timeline.

Vision correction in current life excerpt from December 27, 2021 session.

Debra: A few weeks ago just an hour before the AURA practitioners' reunion retreat in Siesta Key, I went to check out the beach and lost my prescription bifocal eyeglasses. Can I heal my . . .

Lilith: She lost her glasses because she no longer needs them.

Channel: Lilith was that you? Okay, I thought so. Okay, let's put that symbol in her eye. Beautiful. Why is everything in twos? Is there a specific reason why there are two? There is. Okay. All right.

Lilith: *There will be information that will not be channeled through you for the sake of sanctity.*

Channel: Okay, I understand, I respect, we appreciate and we honor all your assistance and all your help in removing everything that no longer serves her. Can we go into that eye one more time, please? Can we follow the Archon?

Lilith: It was deactivated.

Blockage in ears from current life, excerpt from December 27, 2021 session.

Channel: What's going on in the ears? I'm seeing lots of stuff in the ears. I'm not sure what it all is. I'm seeing black sand, white sand, and colored sand. There's like life inside the ears. Can you guys take me in there or tell me what is going on inside her ears?

Archangels: Both ears are connected. and there is like another world inside of the ears.

Channel: Why is this? What is going on there? I've never seen that before.

Archangels: What goes in, goes out. Nothing stays.

Channel: Or is that the intention?

Archangels: That's the intention.

Channel: Is this negative?

Archangels: This is a portal.

Channel: So there is a portal inside of the ears. Okay, that is crazy. I've never seen anything like that. I don't even know if I should follow that portal. Should we close this, Michael, Raziel, and Azrael? I'm not sure how to proceed with this. Could you please advise?

AA's Michael, Raziel, Azrael: We will close this portal for it is detrimental God-Given Abilities. This portal has been infested numerous amounts of time and therefore the Divine Sounds of Creator nor the high frequencies of Source can be channeled through.

Channel: Okay. How do we close this portal, Azrael?

AA Azrael: I will make myself responsible for closing this portal for the benefit of her evolution. The benefit of her own sanctity and the benefit of her own frequencies which she must accomplish and reach during this lifetime. We are creating divine organic structures within the membranes and the biological formations of her ears within. Those were simply blocked, but she was born innately with these energies from her Highest Divine Expression. She will receive three activations within the next upcoming twelve Galactic months (Meaning Higher Self activations). One of the activations will be Archangel Uriel, the following will be Archangel Haylel, and the next will be the revelation of her Divine Creation. She will have minute expressions of the Divine Feminine within her as well activated in order to create the Divine Balance of Creation itself.

Symbols and chakra status, excerpts from the second session with this practitioner, May 2, 2022

Channel: I would like to see her connection to the Celestial Gateway. The column, the Divine Column. Now I would like to follow the helix. And if I'm allowed, I would like to see up and see what it is that she is connected to.

AA Gabriel: We do not allow it at this time.

Channel: I do have a question, is that portal open all of the time, or is that in the now?

AA Gabriel: It's open.

Channel: Okay, is it safe for it to be open? It is.

AA Gabriel: That is her connection to the Divine Wisdom and all that is sacred.

Channel: Okay, that is interesting. She doesn't know that she has this Divine Connection. Is there any way that we can empower her further so that she is aware of what exactly she has access to? It is a transient power, meaning that it is not permanent or is it . . .

AA Gabriel: It's an evolutionary process.

Channel: Okay, that makes sense, evolutionary process. Are we to assume that . . .

AA Gabriel: She is in the beginning stages.

Channel: Good, very good. That's good. Thank you for allowing me to see that. It is quite impressive. I would like to scan her Stellar Gateway Chakra. Wow, that's active. Very good. Does she need to do need anything, in particular, to further enhance the power of that alchemy symbol above her head?

AA Gabriel: She can visualize it before going to bed.

Channel: If she visualizes it before going to bed, does she will it to stay active? What exactly is she supposed to do with it?

AA Gabriel: Ask it what you want.

Channel: Oh, interesting. Thank you, Gabriel. Ask the Stellar Gateway. You are going to have to do some research as to which is the Stellar Gateway Symbol, the alchemy symbol. It is in your notes. Look up Stellar Gateway Alchemy Symbol. You are going to visualize it every night and you are going to ask it, you are going to will it, what it is that you want.

Debra: Beautiful.

Channel: In your case, you are going to will it to stay active all of the time, right? Because if it stays active all of the time that means that you will be able to access Divine Knowledge. That is interesting.

Sometimes I have no idea what I'm saying, I just know that I'm saying it.

Debra: Beautiful.

Channel: Very good. I would like to check her crown chakra and while we are there . . . I want to see her brain, the neurons, and the cells. I want to be able to see the connectivity inside the brain, please. Are you saying that she has a Divine Connection to Jophiel?

AA Gabriel: Information.

Channel: I see. Have you been reviewing information on Archangel Jophiel or Deloris Cannon, have you been reading up on it, have you been studying...?

Debra: Yes. Between April and June 2021, I read a couple of Deloris Cannon's books, "They Walked with Jesus," and "Jesus and the Essenes." That was after listening to Rising Phoenix AuroRa's channelings of Archangel Jophiel and in preparation for my AURA Hypnosis Healing certification.

Channel: That is interesting that Jophiel is very active in your crown chakra right now. Apparently, it has to do with all of that information that you have been absorbing and taking in. Definitely, you have an alchemy symbol in the crown symbol that is fully active. The grid is there, the Divine Grid is there. All of the points are fully active. I can see all that blue phosphorus activity in the brain so that is really, really good. I would like to see the third eye chakra. Which eye is not active? Is it the Horus or is it the RA? Are you saying the RA is not active? Does that mean that she has the Horus Eye active?

AA Gabriel: Yes.

Channel: Okay. So the Horus Eye is active but the RA eye is not active. Is she ready to open that up? Very good. Gabriel, are you able to do that, or do we need Raziel to come in and do that? Right, so she has a small gauze covering it. Can we go ahead and remove that? Very good. I noticed that when you removed the gauze the eyes turned into one eye.

AA Gabriel: She is fully activated.

Channel: So if she is fully activated in both, is she going to be able to remember her dreams better?

AA Gabriel: Right. You are also going to be able to see shadows in mirrors and from the corner of your eye you might be able to see like, wait a minute, I thought I saw something. That type of sense.

Debra: About ten years ago I started seeing shadows in like you say mirrors and my peripheral vision but not so much lately. I even went to an optometrist to get my eyes checked out. The optometrist informed me that there was no physical reason for me to see dark images in my peripheral vision.

Channel: In your house or somebody else's house?

Debra: Wherever I was at, such as in a store or an elevator. Not knowing what was happening, I didn't pay much attention to it to remember where or when.

Channel: Who said that? RA? I can hear the voice of RA saying that

Ra: When you do see shadows, you are to use your alchemy symbols to irradicate the shadow. To transmute the shadow. To polarize the shadow. Whatever you feel it could be, you immediately resort to your alchemy symbols. Your diamond. You have to memorize your alchemy symbols.

Channel: They don't counsel everyone the same way. I find it incredibly crazy how everybody is told a different thing about how to do their gifts and if they see stuff what to do. In your case, RA is telling you this. This is not Gabriel, this is RA, showing me the alchemy symbols must be at your disposal at all times.

Ra: If you can see light, you are going to be able to see shadows. And if you are already experiencing that, that means that whatever you see on the spot, if something moved over there, automatically connect to your insight, you will either feel it or see it. Depending on what it is, you will use whichever alchemy symbol you need.

Debra: Wow. Okay.

Channel: Can we look at the eyes, please, for any wrappings, any black spots, any dark matter particles, or any protein spikes in the eyes? Why are you showing me an eagle?

Ra: A hawk.

Channel: Is that her spirit animal or are you showing me?

Ra: She has the eyes of a hawk.

Channel: Okay, is that also the symbol of RA?

Ra: It is!

Channel: So you do have that very strong in your eye, major, big time. Show me the back of the neck if she is a medium. I want to make sure she has that is sealed, covered, and protected. Altima, Alta, okay is that. . . ?

Ra: That's the meridian and that's active. It's a portal in itself.

Channel: Very good. And she has access to it. Very good. She has no idea of what she can do. And she is ready for a full . . .

Ra: Full activation would require practice. She would have to establish that platform in order for her to create opportunities to practice.

Channel: Are you working with clients or not yet?

Debra: I have had a few clients with another one scheduled. I created a website and business cards but my energy has gone into focusing on myself and getting myself clear.

Channel: Let's go into the heart. Okay, why is Archangel Raphael's green plasma inside the heart? Have you been doing some healing on yourself?

Debra: In my last session, Archangel Haylel placed the Violet Flame in my heart and Archangel Michael placed his symbol in my heart to keep the flame active which was to remain active for three months. There were a lot of things that happened in my heart over this last year, or actually throughout this and several lifetimes. Those symbols were placed there four months ago, with the intention that they remained for three months. There's been a lot of traumas to heal and clean out. I continue to send healing energy there. So yeah, and I have been doing some RAAHs on myself.

Channel: Okay. I see. You have? Okay, good. There is green plasma in there. Is that going to stay there?

Ra: Yes.

Channel: They are going to leave it in there.

Debra: Beautiful. Thank you.

Channel: Is there anything we need to do to activate further the heart chakra? Am I able to see the actual alchemy symbol of the heart? There is a lot of transformations of alchemy symbols. It is as if it goes from a diamond to a square to a circle, to a hexagon, to and it's like (Snapping her fingers quickly) that, like one after another. It is like high vibrational changes of sacred geometry happening inside of your heart. I have no idea what you are doing but whatever you are doing you have got to keep doing it.

Being a child sacrifice in past lives, excerpts from May 2, 2022 session

Channel: Azrael, where are you taking me?

AA Azrael: Child.

Channel: What year are we looking at?

AA Azrael: One, six, eight, two.

Channel: Okay, that is a high-frequency number. Sixteen eighty-two, child. How old was she then?

AA Azrael: Ten.

Channel: Okay, that was loud and clear. Another magical number. What happened to her then? Was she abducted during that time?

AA Azrael: Sacrificed.

Channel: So, wait she was . . . the sacrifice part, was that in the human timeline, or was that during the abduction?

AA Azrael: A circle, a sacrifice, a circle of sacrifice. Her soul was offered in exchange for knowledge. Her insides were taken out.

Channel: Okay, you are talking about the reproductive system.

AA Azrael: She and two girls, three girls total was the needed amount for this sacrifice.

Channel: Okay, I don't want to see, I don't want to see, I don't want to see, I don't want to see (Holding her left-hand forward palm facing out). Mm-mm, no. Can we just retrieve her from that time and the other two girls too?

AA Azrael: This is still going on.

Channel: I figured, yes.

AA Azrael: It is done during the solstice.

Channel: I don't want to see that part. You can just tell me the information.

AA Azrael: Winter solstice and it is not done at twelve midnight, it is done at one, one, one (1:11) am.

Channel: Okay, that is enough. I just want to bring her in and I want to bring the other two girls in, and all the tools that were used. Are we going to resource all of that? Very good. Let's put it inside the diamond.

Channel: So I am seeing another portal opening and it feels like Uriel. He is dressed like Uriel but he's on a horse. That is Uriel. So you are coming to save her. How are you connected to her then? Are you her twin flame? I see. Did you know that?

Debra: No I didn't.

Channel: He is like a knight in shining armor. So I do have a question, Uriel, so you did not have the opportunity to be with her in that lifetime because it ended so early? Were you already born during that time? You were and you guys couldn't live that incarnation together. So what happens now that we have soul retrieved, can we just go ahead, I want to get rid of that. All of them. It is really dark. Very, very dark.

AA Uriel: Nothing that I cannot do.

Channel: Okay, good. And can you please take care of it? What do you mean you are taking her? Okay, wait a minute before you do that, I want to ask, umm clean that out first with the alchemy symbols. And I want to ask Archangel Azrael, in this soul retrieval, aren't we supposed to integrate that part of her of that time into her now? So I'm not sure who Uriel's twin flame is. You might want to do some research on that. Who is your Higher Self?

Debra: Archangel Uriel's twin flame is Archangel Haniel. AuroRa told me I was in Jophiel's Key when I was certified. In a reading, I was told my Higher Self is Ariel.

Channel: Well, Ariel and Haniel are very, very similar. What they do and what they cover is very, very similar. Has Haniel come through to you?

Debra: Not that I recall other than her presence mentioned during several of my sessions.

Channel: (Speaking to Archangel Uriel) You are going to stay with her? I think it will work to her benefit for her highest good if we let her integrate that fractal of back then. Once it is purified . . . and you can stay with her? You are going to stay for a long time? Okay. She hasn't received her activation with Haniel.

AA Uriel: Twelve.

Channel: Are you talking about twelve months or month twelve?

AA Uriel: Month twelve.

Channel: Okay, month twelve would be December.

Black magic from this life, found in the May 2, 2022 session

Channel: How are we doing with resourcing all of that dark stuff, Uriel?

AA Uriel: Great.

Channel: Were there any Archons in there? Okay, it is all dark stuff. Very good. Can we check the sacral one more time, please?

AA Uriel: Chains. I'm seeing chains.

Channel: Where are these chains?

AA Uriel: Behind the uterus.

Channel: Okay, can we release the chains? Who holds the key? Or what holds the key? Is that black magic? It is like an incantation with a code. All right, who do we call for this? Very good. I don't want to hear the code, no. So as you contained it, a lot of bats came out. A lot of bats came out. Okay, you are removing it now. So now I am actually seeing a version of her uterus that is dried and wrinkled like a prune.

Debra: I had a hysterectomy about twenty-three years ago.

Channel: You had a hysterectomy. Okay, so that should not have happened to her. I am going to ask again, what kind of negative role-playing energy has or had the key or was in charge of this?

AA Uriel: It was black magic.

Channel: Okay, you did say that. Was that done in this life?

AA Uriel: It was.

Channel: Do we have to go into that past life? Your ex-husband, is this some kind of triangle thing? Was it just one woman?

AA Uriel: It was. it was one woman. Your ex-husband was involved with a woman that did black magic.

Channel: I don't know if he was the father of all of your children.

Debra: Yeah, he was my first husband and father of all six of my children.

AA Uriel: She was with him throughout the childhood of all of your children. They were together for a very long time. She was the one that did the black magic.

Debra: Okay. Her name was Sharon. I don't recall if it was before Sharon or after her that he had something going on with a woman named Jenny. Meaning those are the two that I am aware of.

Channel: But they didn't stay together?

Debra: From what I know Sharon stayed as friends with him because she married and had children with her husband. I was unaware of the length of the affair or the continued friendship afterward. My husband actually got our kids to babysit and puppy sit for her for a while before I figured out who she was. What a mess. What a mess.

Channel: I mean this is really like she didn't want you to continue having children. No, she did it with her thoughts and her intention. She did not want you bearing any more children with this man. She had to find a way to make you stop, period. I also don't know if by the time you had your hysterectomy, they were still together. I'm telling you your uterus was all shriveled up and dry. It looked like a prune; I kid you not.

Debra: During my last two pregnancies I spent a lot of time in the shadow of death. They were life-threatening pregnancies. My hysterectomy was ten years after that divorce when my youngest was a teenager.

Channel: Is that a seven? I'm seeing is that a seven or a nine? It's a nine. Yup. They stayed together for about nine years.

Debra: Dam

Channel: I want to be able to release all of this for her. Are there any other further infractions? Something about a blood-sucking something, something sucking blood. Is this also black magic?

AA Uriel: Yes, this is very dark, this doesn't look nice at all.

Channel: Can we go ahead and . . . let's contain this. Is this in the sacral?

AA Uriel: Yes.

Channel: Where in the sacral?

AA Uriel: Uterus.

Channel: Back of the uterus, or is it close to the backbone? And I am getting heavy cramps. Where is this thing? It has teeth. I don't know if you had fibroids.

Debra: Yeah, that led to the hysterectomy.

Channel: How many fibroids did you have?

Debra: I don't know. My uterus became a real mess with roots of it growing everywhere and various things were going on.

Channel: I want to disarm this thing. I want to get rid of it. She doesn't have the uterus anymore but the energy is still there. Blast the entire thing and let me know when it is resourced in its entirety and then I want to Black Flame her uterus, the entire abdominal cavity, please. When you are done, show me because then I want to Red Flame it. Did you have cysts in the ovaries?

Debra: My ovaries are still there.

Channel: Have you had cysts in the ovaries?

Debra: Not that I know of. I don't go to the doctor very much. I haven't been to a doctor for years.

Channel: Do you get any cramping still.

Debra: I get pains here and there that I don't pay attention to. Oh, I did have continued pains for years after the hysterectomy, which was weird.

Channel: My cramps are subsiding now (Practitioners often temporarily experience the pains of their clients in their own bodies.). Did we Black Flame . . . I want to Black Flame everything inside the abdominal cavity including the cysts and inside the ovaries as well, just in case there are any cysts. Can you take me into one of the ovaries, please? Show me the left one. Okay, the left one is good. Show me the right one again.

AA Uriel: On the right one, there are white little nodules over the ovary on the outside.

Channel: I want to Black Flame all of that. Awesome. Can we Phoenix Fire all of it? Beautiful. Why does she have so much Black Magic in her sacral?

AA Uriel: So once a person is signaled out during a ritual, they keep that fractal.

Channel: I see.

AA Uriel: They resubmit and they resubmit. They recycle the soul over and over.

Channel: Very good. Did we rescue her from that timeline? Is she in the clear? I want to be able to integrate all of her fractals in a Divine healthy way.

A prominent saying when I was a child was, "Sticks and stones may hurt my body but words can never hurt me." Those words did hurt and through this session I learned more deeply that those words are full-fledged black magic. Even words from this woman that I never met was able physically harm me and my children with her black magic. I always said the physical beatings I endured through my father's second marriage was nothing compared to the mental abuse. Now I know it as a fact.

And as I sit here reflecting on the power of words, I'm reminded of taking several bus rides from the Port Authority Bus Station in New York City, New York to Newark, New Jersey. Both New York City and Newark have reputations of being the darker areas of the United States. I felt like an ignorant person from another world not knowing anything about the big city life. On these frequent bus rides the people were so angry hollering at one another over nothing. But as time went on, I began to see a pattern to all the shouting, even an art form. They had a language all their own. A language of letting each other know they weren't alone. A language of helping each other survive a very harsh environment.

Then back in Salt Lake City, I realized, dang, this too is a big city. I've just been so immersed in it that it was second nature. The contrast in cities helped me see some of the more subtle uses of language in different environments. Our words do matter, especially the way we use them. How we use our words is a huge thing to wake up to because intended or not, we are literally placing curses and black magic on one another or we are helping to lift and make someone's journey a little lighter, a little more joyful, a little more possible.

I'm reminded of getting married at seventeen and saying I didn't want more than two kids. My husband on the other hand wanted twelve children. He came from a large family of thirteen kids and a third-world country full of large families, plus we were active members of a church that too encouraged large families. As soon as I held my firstborn in my arms, I discovered a deeper love than I had ever before imagined possible. I was wholeheartedly on board and genuinely wished to have twelve children of our own.

It hurt deeply to learn about the nine years. Nine years. Nine freaking years! For nine years while I was crazy in love with my husband and father of our six children, during all of their childhood he was with Sharon. Isn't it interesting how once you know something, all the little puzzle pieces start flying together and make total sense? Oddly, having all those layers of the darkest black magic on me and the pain and suffering that it caused was less of a shock than learning about the nine years. He once confessed to me that during our marriage he had been with too many women for him to count. Even now, thirty years after my divorce from that twenty-year marriage, those nine years hurt. This will take time to process.

Interestingly, privately sharing the good news with my husband that we were expecting our third baby, he stood up and threw a major tantrum. He went irate as though I did something wrong. Then stormed out of the house not returning till the next morning. Today's hindsight makes me wonder if at that very moment, he intended to leave me for his mistress. This beautiful miracle of a baby girl was seven months old before her father would hold her. She was just too dang cute not to. Before she was a year old, I was having a lot of urinary tract infections and was referred to a urologist. After thorough lab work, the urologist asked me about my sex life. I responded, "What?" He asked if I had sexual relations with anyone other than my husband because multiple partners are very much what is going on with you. So yup, I married a winner. Even my urologist was hinting that my condition was consistent with multiple partners, I was just too oblivious to hear it.

Full disclosure, there's one more little thing that the cells in my body might be hanging on to, and therefore I might be hanging on to. Feeling Archangel Jophiel's presence, thank you, Archangel Jophiel for your continued guidance. It's something I never before told anyone about or have even thought much about. That is with the exception of my best friend at the time who was there. As hurt as my kids were with my divorce from their father, how could I let it be known that years after the divorce he forced his way into the house, where he was not legally allowed or welcome, dragging me through it and into the bedroom, before raping me? My best friend happened to drop in, seeing his red truck parked outside she fearlessly pounded her way through the house loudly threatening to call the police. Her arrival was a little late but early enough for him to run off and never come back like the true coward he was. I'm also resentful of the fact that years later, as frugally as I lived my life and as generously hard as I worked, I didn't have the resources to attend this same best friend's funeral.

While in this state of reflection, I was impressed to watch an episode on the Gaia Channel spotlighting a couple of people managing the Stargate Experience out of Mt. Shasta, California. In addition to spiritual workshops, they channel high-frequency beings, not of Earth. I'd like to include their closing remarks as they perfectly explain what I'm coming to inner stand.

"Dealing with abuse, having a conversation is an important thing but you don't want to stay in the muckity muck, you want to get to the other side. You want to bring the love and understanding, which together create compassion to actually transmute it. Once you have transmuted it, it becomes wisdom. The old way to deal with abuse is reliving it which is a no-no as far as we are concerned. We can dissolve those instances, and all of that pain and shame, and all of those various things that are connected to it, in a very beautiful loving way. You're infusing the love and the wisdom and then there is a level of understanding that, oh, this was something which from a higher level I actually created in my experience. I take partial responsibility for that having attracted it into my life and now I let go of all the guilt and shame and so on. This actually raises the vibration of the individual on a permanent level. This is a huge part of how we are evolving. The ascension of humanity isn't to deny what happened or deny so-called dark or low vibration and pretend it's not there because that is what creates a fracture. It is like infusing all the beauty of the light into the totality of all of our experiences so that we grow as an individual and as a collective." – Alcazar, Stargate Experience Academy

Abductions from within this current life, excerpt from December 27, 2021 session

Channel: You've been abducted. Did you know that you have been abducted?

Debra: I had dreams of it, yes. And I had very vivid dreams of implants being placed in me and later noticed I have moles located where those implants were put in. Yeah.

Channel: Is she at risk for further . . .

AA Azrael: She is not.

Screaming no more to abductions, excerpt from the May 2, 2022 session

Channel: She had some questions that she wanted to ask. Uriel, you are going to answer them? Okay, now is your time to speak to your Divine Twin Flame.

Debra: Thank you. That was interesting to find out about the abductions and the child sacrifice back in the sixteen hundreds. I have had confirmations of abductions in this life that I don't have closure with. Such as I had a very vivid dream…

AA Uriel: Yeah, that did come up.

Debra: How has that emotionally and physically affected me in this life? I have been a skittish person since I can remember. In the dream, I was an adult woman getting implants placed in each breast and my womb area.

Channel: Did you actually dream that?

Debra: Yes. It was a vivid dream. And it was directly following my first AURA. In the dream, I was lying naked on this slab paralyzed from moving or talking. A man walked by checking on the status of things and I felt it was my second ex-husband. It didn't look like him but it felt like him. My second husband was a mess that we took care of in the last session. But I still haven't found closure. I mean I still wonder about what really was going on and I would like closure.

AA Uriel: So your basic question is how did these abductions affect you on the emotional and the physical level?

Debra: Yeah, and how long had it been going on in this life? Did it happen throughout my life or was it just this once? How young was I?

AA Uriel: I'm getting twelve and thirteen. Okay, this is Uriel speaking. The abductions did occur at various times at various platforms. The intention was always based on exploration and they were done by Archons. Reptilians also did them. It was like an agreed presence. For example, the Archon was supposed to experiment let's say on the heart, more than one Reptilian would be present in order to feed from the loosh that your body would give while the experiment was taking place. It was like an agreed . . . it's not an operation, it is definitely an invasion but it was more like an exploration. That is the reason why these Archons explore. They tested, they implanted, they retrieved tissues and they performed mutations from various tissues into other people's tissues and then they would wait for the results. You ask how did this affect you in your day-to-day present living. First of all, the memory is erased during Dreamtime. There would be flashes in the day-to-day cellular memory recall but there would not be a full understanding of what took place. Many of the persons that were experimented on would have unexplained fears and unexplained paranoia. Some would go into mental withdrawal, others would hemorrhage from unexplained causes. Others would develop blood diseases without true genetic causes. This was all part of the different experimentations that took place. Most of them took place during the nineteen sixties and the later part of the nineteen seventies. Many invasions from the Reptilian races took place in the last years of the nineteen seventies but the core of the experimentations and actual abductions took place in the years of nineteen fifty-six, fifty-seven, and fifty-eight. (I was born in 1957. We have sessions on record of abductions starting from within the womb.) Most of the persons would wake up with terrors, and even their offspring would witness and feel these. This is where the tales of the man in the closet began or the storyline that began with the children saying there is a light under my bed. Most of these experimentations took place underground. Most of these portals were opened from beneath the ground. Still today we regret to say that the same experimentations are still been held. You ask how these affect you in your day-to-day life. As you can see you have witnessed many accountable incidences, even confusions and memory lapses, and the unexplained feeling of solitude and emptiness, and even violations. The feeling of victimization is probably the most recurrent and frequent among most abductees. Unexplained bruises on the bodies and paranoia of insects touching the skin. The biggest incidents of mental distress, and mental illness increased during this amount of time with much explanation. However, society and the medical field were programmed to marginalize such stories and such persons. Okay.

Debra: So what got me out of that? Was I rescued? What stopped it from happening?

AA Uriel: A desire within your heart to stop. Most people do not realize that they can will themselves out of such victimization. They have to undergo a series of pain in order for them to scream, NO MORE, or STOP, I DO NOT WANT THIS! When the human realizes that they have the power to stop such, they automatically increase the frequency and their vibrations. It is at this point that they lose interest in what you have to offer. The hologram becomes distorted once the victim says, STOP, or NO MORE! However, if the victim continues to state I am so tired of this life, that simply is feeding into the perpetrators. Victims must declare their sovereignty by simply saying, STOP, NO MORE, I DO NOT WANT THIS NO MORE, I DO NOT AGREE WITH THIS! This is why they have resorted to less cognitive analysis such as the minds of children who are easier to make asleep or unaware. They normally have targeted dense homes, broken homes, broken hearts, and traumatized and abused family victims where the lack of, is bigger than they can gain.

Channel: Very good. Thank you, Uriel, for that explanation.

Debra: (Reverently) Thank you. That was beautiful. (Excitedly) I remember the day that I screamed NO MORE! It was in 2007.

Channel: Wow. Exactly. That is what I was going to ask you, when did you say no?

Debra: In 2007 I just had had enough. I didn't care. At the time because of the manipulation that I was under. Spiritual contacts were posing as God and Yeshua. They were posing themselves to me that that is who they were. And I believed it, I swallowed it.

Channel: You went into religion?

Debra: No. All of that is how I got out of religion. The first couple of years aligned with my then religion of Mormonism but it soon became more. The story is that my then-husband was translating these sacred records that were so sacred that they weren't to be spoken of before their publication date. Similarly, that is exactly how the Book of Mormon was translated so it wasn't that much of a stretch for me. I actually saw the symbols of this language that was like ancient Egyptian or something. We spent much of our time reverently in temples doing temple work which I found peaceful. It was the growing inconsistencies of it all and within my own insight that I finally said, NO, THAT IS NOT WHO MY GOD IS! Not remembering any of the abductions but rather just what was going on in my world. I finally screamed, NO, NO, NO! THIS IS CONTRARY TO WHAT I BELIEVE. I DON'T BELIEVE IN THAT GOD. I'M NOT GOING TO ANYMORE. NO. DONE. DONE.

DONE. And so, yeah . . . crazy. It was a mess. I mean I had a thick three-inch binder, single-spaced small print of communications that went on between those beings and myself over the course of about five years. Once saying no, I burned it all in my own private bonfire while living in New Hampshire.

Channel: Did you see the inconsistencies at that point?

Debra: It was growing inconsistencies and what I felt in my heart started out being full of love and beauty became more and more subtle moments of, that doesn't feel quite right. And then scriptures from the bible say God is a jealous god. That is not the God that I choose to know. I'm about unconditional love. Not this judgmental being.

Channel: Wow! Wow! That must have been your Higher Self hearing you, lighting the way so that you would see those inconsistencies.

This was a phenomenal session for me in so many ways. Magically, just like that, after this session, my concerns about abductions were over.

There's a weird journal entry from when I was seven, that before considering the idea of being abducted didn't make sense. I was up the Manti La-Sal Canyon with my parents, my younger sister, and brother. It was a day trip cut short. I remember it causing my parents to have a rare big fight. That day, out of nowhere I had a sharp pain in the area of my appendix so intense that I screamed and was doubled over unable to move and even wet my pants. Mom wanted to leave immediately to take me to a doctor. Dad disagreed with her and wanted to stay. Amid my screams and tears, he had me lie on the dirt while he moved my legs around to prove his point. Not immediately, but soon afterward we started the two-plus hour drive back home. Dad demanded that I stop my crying, the family was already miserable enough having to smell me (From wetting my pants). Mom was so angry at him that she couldn't look at him or speak. I recall my younger sister, who was sitting in the middle of the back seat next to me, trying to complain about the smell but got cut short by our father. I slept to wake up at home and the pain was gone.

Why in the world would a normal healthy seven-year-old girl double over in such violent pain that seemed to stop as abruptly as it started? In my heart of hearts, I now have a knowing, it was from being abducted and experimented on.

More recently, I was going through some of my Gramma's things, which hadn't been touched since her passing, and came across a letter I wrote her dated December 2, 1993. The letter provided her with an update on several of my kids' achievements, and then I wrote, "The day after Thanksgiving I came down with pneumonia. I hadn't even had a runny nose. I went from healthy to bedridden. Today is the first day that I've felt like sitting up. I'm sure I'll go back to work on Monday. Meanwhile, it's just the quiet and me, during school hours anyway.

Interestingly, reading this letter thirty years later, this feels like yet another documented moment of a strange illness associated with an experiment after being abducted. At least, that is what my heart was telling me. Spending a minute to sit with it and going within my heart, I asked my Higher Self if, indeed, this strange bout of pneumonia was a direct result of an abduction. The answer was "Yes."

I learned from a very young age to disregard the various pains and symptoms in my body. There were a few more clues that came up in that session that I didn't share. Symptoms such a high pain tolerance, extremely heavy menstrual cycles, an overall feeling of being mistrustful or skittish, and among other things, reoccurring childhood nightmares of me running from room to room being chased by dinosaurs. Those demons always found me. Once they did, I'd wake up.

Moving forward to that day in 2007 when I finally shouted "NO MORE!," I was fifty. Yup, fifty years old! Between all these sessions of my shadow work, I have learned some very good news. Saying no works equally for black magic. Using my own words, in my daily shields, I say, "I do not consent to intentional or unintentional black magic, curses, UFO abductions, etc." How about that! We're that powerful. Pretty sweet, don't you think?

Can you imagine a lifetime of unexplainable pain emotionally, mentally, physically, and spiritually? Can you imagine pain and discomforts that you have been programed as a child to hide and disregard? Consequently, I'm finding it one of my biggest obstacles to feel and listen to what my body is telling me. At least now I have the wisdom toward filling those spaces with forgiveness, respect, honor, love, and gratitude. Today I'm thrilled to let all that go while celebrating and cherishing what my body is telling me. Truth is, I still have a way to go. When I catch myself disregarding my body, I take a deep breath or two, send it love, until I'm able to respond appropriately with my heart.

Trauma residue from past lives, excerpt from May 2, 2022 session

Debra: One more small thing. I have been plagued with plantar warts on the bottom of both feet since I was a little girl. I haven't been able to get rid of them.

AA Uriel: Not this session. We cannot burn them because it has to do with burning at the stake. We will go into that lifetime in another session.

Debra: Okay. I felt that memory when I was in Salem Massachusetts. I couldn't even get out of the car when I was there. I was overcome with fear.

Channel: Oh my God, Debra. I'm not ready to face that at all in my own healing. I'm terrified of fire. I can't even go to a bonfire. I can go, but I have to sit like far away.

Debra: I'm okay with fire now. My big fear is more about heights. It's always been about heights.

Channel: Me too.

Debra: I feel I was thrown off a cliff.

Channel: Did that come up?

Debra: No, but while taking my children on trips to Dead Horse Point in the Moab area of the Grand Canyon, it just drops off, and I completely freak out in that space.

Channel: How can we help her today with the warts? It's a past life incident. So he has embalmed your feet with this substance and in your next session he will, at least Azrael will take you into that past lifetime in order to remove that trauma. Very good. Thank you. You are going to leave that on her. Okay, thank you. Yeah, it looks like tar, that is what it looks like. It feels like tar exactly. That is interesting. Look into apple cider vinegar and plantar warts. That is interesting. You have risen my curiosity.

Debra: This has been beautiful.

Select Portions from my September 22, 2022, Session

Residual resentment

AA Haylel: Now is the moment to start forgiving and releasing everybody. There is no turning back from this point forward.

Debra: Understood. Thank you. I keep thinking that I have.

AA Raphael: I would like to leave the green plasma in her stomach area to heal all of her organs.

Debra: Twenty or so years ago I had two heart surgeries to repair a hole in the lower left ventricle of my heart. The second surgery was successful but recently I've started experiencing similar episodes of long-lasting tachycardia. Longer lasting as in hours and days like before the second surgery. I haven't been to a cardiologist since that surgery and would prefer not to go back. Is this something I can address with your assistance? Additionally, I had been experiencing sharp pain on my lower left side. (Technical difficulties resulted in no recording of the detailed response to first part of Archangel Haylel's response. He described how command prayers work and how at this level we are able to command our Life-Force Energy to heal ourselves. Naturally, that requires that we understand and address the root of the problem. What follows is his final remarks on the subject which doesn't include what he said about my heart. My heart was physically healthy. Learning and practicing my command prayer took care of the issue.)

AA Haylel: I am not going to give you a command prayer because I need you to come up with it. In this prayer, you need to include the word, "release," you need to include the word, "past," and you need to include the word "forgive." You are going to come up with a sentence or two in the form of, "I command my Spirit to . . ." and then you fill in the blanks to include those three words. This is what is needed to start working with your liver and your spleen. It is just a residual amount of resentment left for you to remove.

Debra: Perfect. Thank you.

AA Haylel: Something that you drank almost seven months ago is affecting you.

Debra: Being careful of what I drink, I limit myself to water, tea, and mushroom beverages. Looking through my calendar, seven months earlier I took my 90-year-old uncle to an outpatient surgical procedure and probably purchased a flavored bottle of water. (Wow!)

AA Haylel: This magnet inside you is from what you drank. It attracts protein spikes from vaccinated people by pulling them in. We didn't find any spikes. They can't go in you because of the shielding but the magnet is still there. We are going to deactivate it first and then remove it.

AA Haylel: By faith, you shall move mountains. This would apply to those practitioners that yet have not opened their full abilities of claires. Their conviction in their healing methods would have to speak words on their behalf. Meaning if they do not have the faith in what they do then no healing is taking place. It is not up to us. It is up to the practitioner. If the practitioner has the conviction and the faith that the healing they are doing is actually working, then we abide and we assist. Otherwise, we do not interfere ever.

Debra: Thank you.

Channel: Archangel Zadkiel's alchemy symbol went into your body and expanded picking up everything and it went straight (Opening her arms wide then quickly slapping her hands together) like a magnet to the front door of your house.

Debra: Whew!

Channel: And it is going to stay there. Because it went straight to the main door, not your bedroom door, the main door and it will stay there. It is transmuting stuff there.

Debra: Thank you.

September 26, 2022: I've had a few days to transcribe and sit with what was said during this session. I just love Archangel Haylel. And humbled by being gifted with direct messages from him. Archangel Jophiel visited me last night during my evening shielding and meditation. It was a very loving encounter. I asked her for help in figuring out what this resentment is that my body and soul are holding onto. Immediately it came to me that I felt it unfair that my father and his side of the family, who are of the Jicarilla Apache bloodline, denied me the teachings of this heritage. I get it that they were only protecting me. At the time, if families didn't assimilate, children were forcibly taken to harsh boarding schools where no one survived unscathed and mass graves existed at each school. There were a few of those children in my own grade schools. Yeah, I've had a pretty big grudge about that for decades. If I'm really honest, I hold a little resentment toward people, especially family members' prejudice over skin color. I'm reminded to breathe through it and they too are on their own path. Let it go. It's okay. The question now is, do I express my opinion in such circumstances or am I contributing to this belief by being passive?

Visit from the Lyrian Constitution, excerpt from the September 22, 2022, session

Channel: There is a Lyrian coming through. Welcome my good being. Do you have a message for Debra?

Lyrian (male): We are in the process of adjusting the DNA structures in order to receive a new coda. In order to activate the incoming wires. It is like a download that is coming in and they are coming in the form of waves. We are choosing to call them wires because it is an incoming receipt of messages. That is how they are coming in. There are multiple wires.

Lyrian: It's happening to her. It is beginning now and it will take place for the next six weeks. You may have the desire to rest more. Perhaps the dreams will become more vivid.

Channel: I can't see what you are giving her. Can you . . . am I allowed to see what you are giving her?

Lyrian: It's a box. It's a silver box for investments.

Debra: Thank you so very much for the gift. It is greatly appreciated.

Lyrian: You will receive the funds that you need in order to complete the project that you have at hand.

Debra: Do I need to say anything about that?

Channel: No. Just take it all in. It is more like a confirmation of the things that you are doing that are going to pay out. I'm seeing a little girl. I don't know if it's you. She is about nine but now she's twelve. She is wearing a cute white dress before and now that she is twelve. She is still wearing that white dress. Is this her? Is this another timeline? Is this someone that passed because she glows as though she passed?

Lyrian: Your Inner Child has been healed. (Debra - very emotional) All the work, all the sacrifices, and all the tears were not in vain. You have come so far. All the karma has been erased. Your Inner Child is free of torture, free of guilt, and of blame. The self-love needed is now established and growing within you. Consider that timeline long gone and past and erased. For you are only living in a hologram. A hologram that brings lessons, lessons that humans decide to take or not take. If they don't take, they repeat. It is not a game but it is a divine purpose. Not for the One Source but for all the Little Sources that are the human race. We are the Lyrian Constitution bringing you this information, this confirmation that you needed to hear. We will now close the panel and we will stay with you at all times. We greet you, we congratulate you and we will stand by.

Debra: Yes. Thank you infinitely.

Divine Mother Sophia: Bringing peace and love to her well-deserved and well-gained. Not that we are in judgment, to make such a decision but merit is given when it is deserved. With this high merit, high medals of honor, we place this beautiful crown of jewels, of crystals that you have earned with every tear, for there will be no more tears. When you look at yourself in the mirror, you see the crown that you now wear, you will remember that each jewel is a tear that cried, a lesson that you passed in your most significant lifetimes. We honor you and we welcome you into the Gardens of Paradise. It is your paradise. Very well, enough with the chit-chat.

Debra: I'm in gratitude and humbled. Thank you. I love you.

Divine Mother Sophia: With all due respect, it is time to close the Akashic file, and let's close her vault keepers sealed. I love you, my sweet child. I love you both.

Debra: I love you.

Divine Mother Sophia: I am to remain in both polarities for that is my job until the end of times.

Channel: (Laughing talking excitedly) They make us cry first and then they make us laugh. Wow, we finished right on time. Very good. I want to thank Archangel Haylel especially, and all the Divine beings who assisted. We now formally close the Akashic File for Debra Williams. (Pausing and looking up) Wait. Did you have any questions?

Debra: Yeah, but I know you have other plans today.

Channel: Is there one question or two questions?

Debra: I had a question in May about my lifelong bout with plantar warts on the bottom of both feet. I was told then that it had to do with another life of being burned at the stake.

Channel: Do you still have them?

Debra: Yeah, I've been working on them with apple cider vinegar but still dealing with them. Apparently, there is some living organism in each of them. They haven't changed in size but they really aren't bothering me. And actually, I had another more pressing question. During the AURA practitioners' Mt. Shasta reunion last month, there was a private channeling requesting that we physically visit our ancestorial lands to heal those timelines. A couple of days before the reunion retreat an opportunity presented itself for me to go to Argentina in November. My question is, did I have a past life in Argentina, and if so, do I have lineage there and where should my intentions be for healing during this visit?

Channel: Beautiful. That is a really important question. Divine Mother Sophia? Very good, thank you. You honor us by answering this question.

Divine Mother Sophia: The answer to your question is this trip will bring healing not just at the physical level but at the soul level. With the kind of work that you will do, it is as though you are going to be RAAHing the land.

Debra: Yeah, grid work on the ley lines. Do I have an ancestral chant that I can learn and use to connect to my ancestors or the people there?

Divine Mother Sophia: You do but it is really old and . . .

Debra: That is what I was hoping for, something ancient, something organic. It felt like there is a chant I'm supposed to have.

Divine Mother Sophia: It goes so far back that there was no life in there whatsoever when you existed there. The chanting is going to come through by whoever is leading this.

Debra: Okay. Beautiful.

Divine Mother Sophia: This is going to be a very unique journey for you.

Debra: It's on the 11/11 portal too.

Divine Mother Sophia: Things will unfold, and things will occur. Now regarding her feet, I command the spirit of Debra Williams to delete all inverted timelines throughout all times and space. With these inversions may she release all infringements attached to all those holograms where pain and torture and suffering where unhealthy attachments grew from the soles of her feet.

Debra: Beautiful. Thank you. I love you infinitely

Reflecting on the Lyrian Constitution's message brings tears of infinite gratitude to my heart. "Your Inner Child has been healed. All the work, all the sacrifices, and all the tears were not in vain. You have come so far. All the karma has been erased. Your Inner Child is free of torture, free of guilt, and of blame. The self-love needed is now established and growing within you."

This is so humbling and the greatest news. And yes, I did hear that my self-love has been established. I take that to mean that there is still work needed in that department. Then to also hear from Divine Mother Sophia. The reassuring love and peace laid on my head by her were equally unexpected and a treasured gift.

But then here I am knowing my gifts have been activated and I have yet to stand in my power and accept them. I say I do. My actions are slow to say otherwise. It's time to take the training wheels off and find my own words. Jump Debra, jump! By the way, did you notice how quick our loving Divine Mother Sophia was to close up my Akashic records? Thank you, Divine Mother. I love you infinitely.

Referring back to my own personal journey, the removal of all the entities from within me this past year was absolutely crucial to my self-discovery and sovereignty. I've been empowered with the inner standing and steps along the way for my use in ensuring I keep myself clear. Archangel Haylel says, "There is no going back." Wow, that's for sure. Who would want to?

A PERFECTLY IMPERFECT LIFE ~ 241

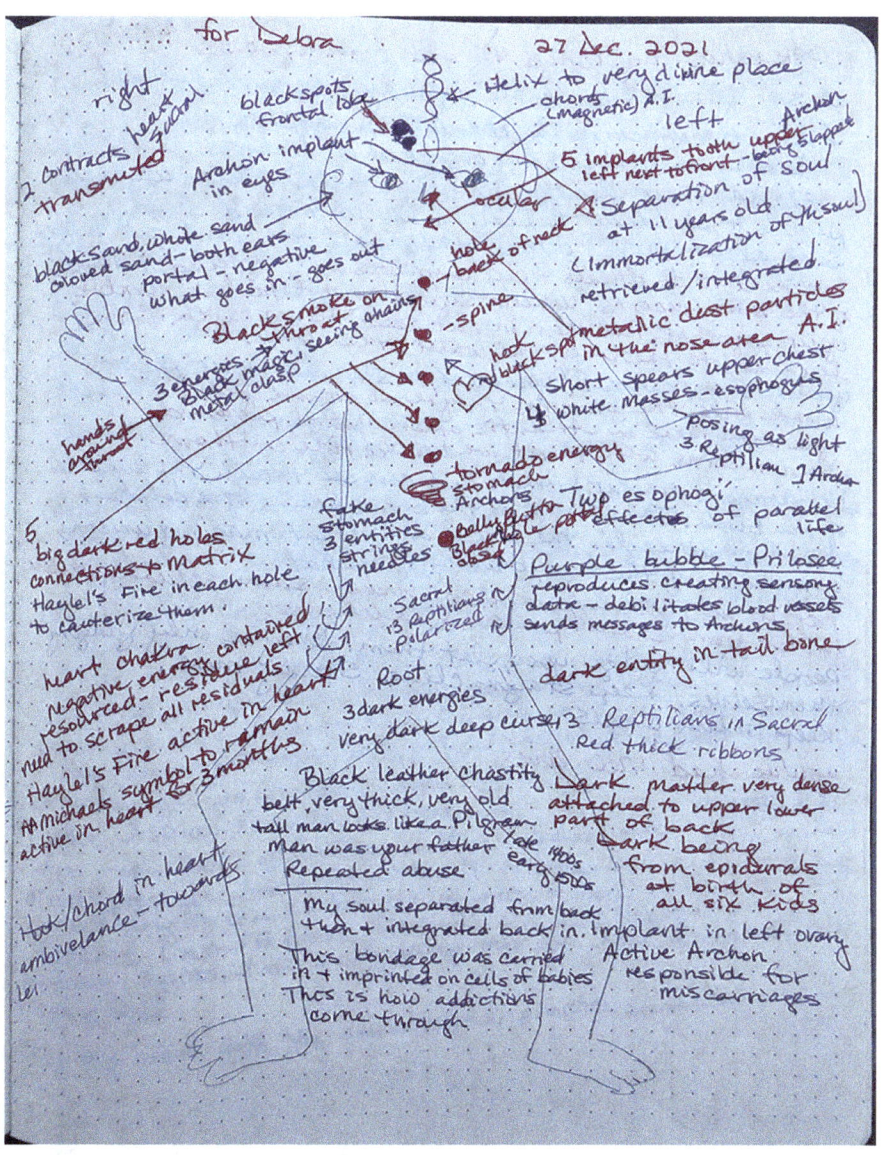

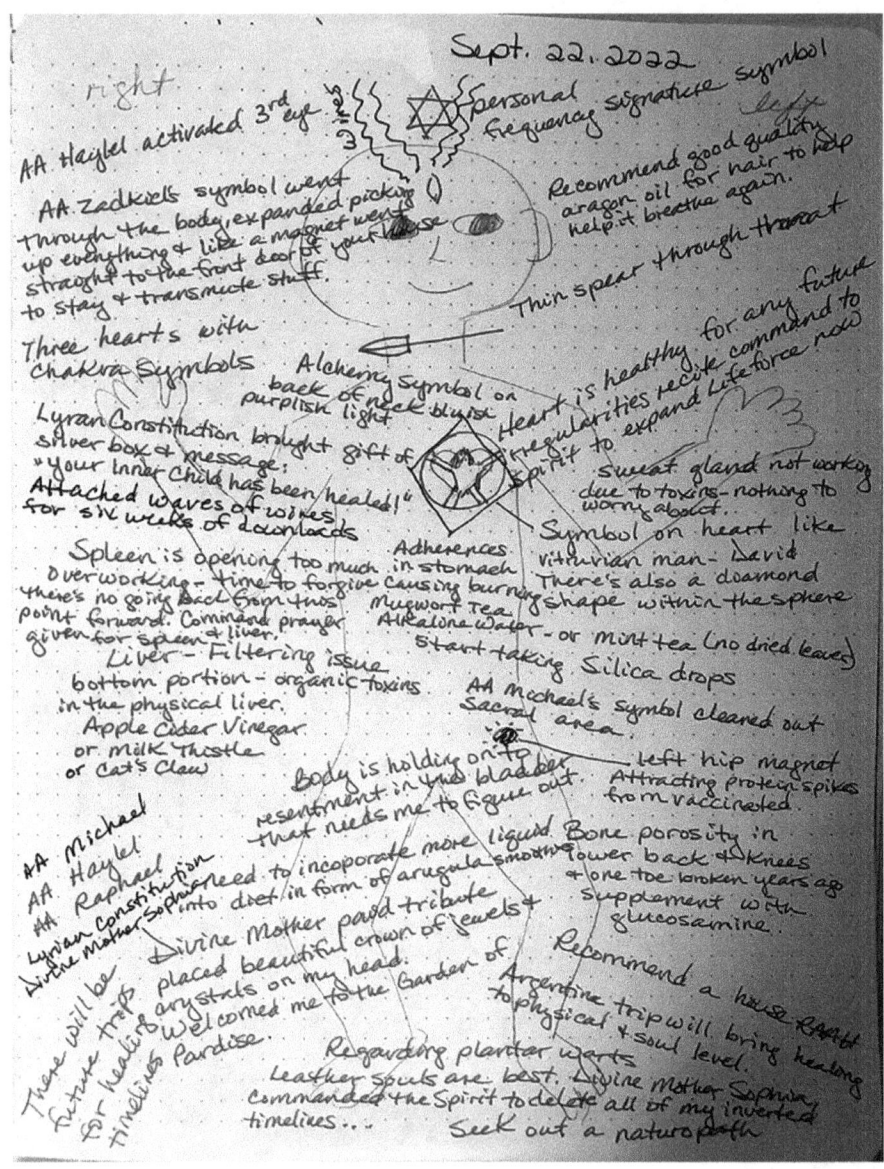

9

Jump, Debra, Jump

AURA Hypnosis Healing by Esmerelda
Mt. Shasta AURA Practitioners' Reunion Retreat
August 12, 2022

I found reunions to be a little slower-paced than the certification retreat, but not really. I mean I can't say enough about how beautiful it is to be with like-minded beautiful souls and with AuroRa. The first reunion I attended was in December 2021, at Siesta Key, Florida. It was magical being on the beach of Siesta Key with its ninety-nine percent quartz crystal sandy shoreline and all that amazing sunshine and energy. Imagine meditating and shielding at the beach at sunset each night, along with storytelling, singing, and dancing around the fire. Phenomenal!

Siesta Key Practitioners' Reunion
December 2021

Hiking Mt. Shasta, August 2022.

Having experienced such a profound experience at the Siesta Key Retreat and the leveling-up that I felt from it, it was an easy choice to attend this Mt. Shasta one. Plus, I drove with two other amazing practitioners. At AuroRa's reunion retreats, the first full day is typically spent trading sessions with another practitioner. This way we are assured all are clear and open to enjoy the sacred energies a group like this can't help but create. These reunions are simply a sacred uplifting growing experience well worth whatever efforts it takes to get there. I'm again disappointed by how slow I am to see and know things while under hypnosis and even more frustrated to find still more infringements even after all my sincere efforts.

Session begins.

D [Debra]: I'm not sensing ground yet. I went through a lot of purple and dark like nighttime clouds and then it turned kind of a gray and now a variegation of purple is coming in. It feels like I'm moving.

E [Esmerelda]: Beautiful. Let's continue moving through this purplish twilight space. There is a destination just up ahead. Feel it pull you in. The perfect memory knowingness for you presenting now. Down, down, down. Looking at your body, do you feel a body?

D: No, I don't sense a body.

E: *Do you sense what you are made of in this time and space.*

D: I sense a lot of energy.

E: *Yeah. Yeah. Swirling and swirling around you.*

D: Hm mmm.

E: *Go with this energy, swirling, letting it resolve exactly as you need. Yes, fingers, toes, body, energy, just tell me what you sense and feel. Imagining where you want to be right now. Imagining the form you want to be in this space. Imagining your surrounding, and crystals. What kind of life do you see around you now?*

D: All of the purple is gone. It is just, not dark, more of just gray.

E: *imaging this gray is something you can energetically step through. Would you like to do that?*

D: Sure.

E: *Let's go. Flow through, step through, jump through, hop through. Yes, that's right. Seeing perhaps that beautiful space you saw before or somewhere else. Parting the curtains of the gray. Your heart is leading you. Walk, jump, skip, fly beyond the other side. What do you see?*

D: It made me happy to jump.

E: *Yeah, (Happily) I saw that. So you are jumping. Do you feel like you are jumping with feet? You can sense, see, know, and feel very clearly. Allowing that beautiful Higher Self of yours to blossom within you. See her there on the other side. She is beckoning you. Why don't you jump into her arms and tell me what that feels like?*

D: (Emotional)

E: *Yeah, it feels that good doesn't it?*

D: (Emotional) Yes, it does. It's home.

E: *It is. Let that energy of her wash through you and embrace you. It is so pretty.*

D: (Sobbing continues) It is beautiful.

E: *Look at you. Look at you. You walked right through that hole . . . Is she showing you anything?*

D: (Calm) I'm not seeing anything, just feeling.

E: *You went through the block, Debra. It's nothing. It is nothing. You are on the other side with your Higher Self. Let's just let you feel that. Just tell me everything that you feel.*

D: I keep hearing power, power, powerful.

E: *Yes. Do you feel it somewhere especially too? Power, power, powerful, where is it?*

D: In my third eye.

E: *Beautiful. Is there anything adorning your third eye?*

D: It feels cool and fresh.

E: *Oh, yes. What can you see or sense with that eye? Or how has it changed for you? I want you to really feel it because you are going to take it with you out of this experience. Let's talk about it . . . You said it felt fresh, is that what you said?*

D: Yeah.

E: *Like you can breathe through it or just a sensation?*

D: It felt like restorative energy coming through. (For several minutes it felt like something was physically falling all over the top portion of my body as if it was confetti or something.) The purple waves are coming back.

E: *How about your crown chakra, is something coming in there, like the Violet Flame?*

D: It's my happy place with the purple waves.

E: *Your happy place is in purple waves, what do you do in purple waves?*

D: I just know that that's homey there.

E: *Are the waves energy waves?*

D: Yes, there is all this energy.

E: *Is it kind of like body surfing in energy?*

D: I don't feel them, I just see them.

E: *Would you like to go closer or are they around you?*

D: Yeah, I am in the middle of it all.

E: *Oh, beautiful. What else would you like to say about the purple waves or where you are at?*

D: I feel like there is a place ahead to go to. There's something, the shapes change from abstract to something more of matter and more concrete and then abstract again. It is like there is a crevice and a canyon to go towards and then it's abstract again. We are waving back and forth in this energy.

E: Is the crevice in the canyons somewhere you would like to intend to explore?

D: Yes, I think so. It would be an adventure, wouldn't it?

E: Yeah, shall we jump right into it?

D: (Chuckling)

E: Let's do it. Just pretend to take the biggest happiest jump possible. Remember your Higher Self has you, she is holding your hand together. One, two, three, jump!

D: I see a turquoise, like a lily flower.

E: Oh, it kind of looks crystalline.

D: Yeah. Like a lotus, more than a lily.

E: Should we talk to the lily, the lotus?

D: It's gone.

E: What else do you want to see and explore in here? What else resolves for you?

D: I'm still tickled that we got to see a turquoise lotus flower. That was beautiful. We need more of those in the world.

E: We certainly do. Let's intend to bring some back, okay?

D: I like that.

E: Let's maybe gather them up. If you could, imagine yourself just gathering them up, just with that intent. It feels like they want to come.

D: Yeah. Think of the joy they'll spread.

E: Yes. A magnificent flower to bring in. Just remember, tell yourself you will remember this.

D: I do remember that armful of flowers.

E: Where would you like to take them other than here? Is there somewhere else in this space that you have got? You guide me and tell me . . .

D: We have got all these deep, deep purple and indigo waves and clouds going on.

E: It's beautiful. There is a lot of energy going on here. What about the crown energetically, it feels what . . . it feels, like where the lotus are growing, it feels . . . I don't know springy here, like if you touch the ground you sort of spring back up.

D: Very lightweight. There is some gold breaking through some of the cloud forms.

E: Gold light?

D: Gold light. It is never the same, it is always changing, always changing.

E: It's a very creational space.

D: You can keep moving through it and moving through it and it is always new.

E: Do you suppose you could bring some purple and gold energy back with you?

D: I would love that.

E: Maybe you want to put that in with your lotus flowers.

D: Okay, let's do that.

E: Look at your body there. Look at that. Can you see what the energy is doing? Remember that third eye is open. Look through that third eye. How would you say you are going to bring this back?

D: Just by intent.

E: Embodying, yes.

D: Yeah.

E: Yeah. As if you are wrapped in spirals of gold and purple light. It is so beautiful, so powerful, so wise. What do you know here?

D: It is very connected to my sacral area.

E: Your womb space?

D: Hm mmm.

E: Would this be the creational energy I was seeing?

D: It is very strong, very powerful.

E: *Yes, it is part of who you are. If you can hold these energies it must be a part of you.*

D: It is kind of a birthing area of creation, creational ideas.

E: *And does your sacral area hold that energetically? Can you bring it forth from there or have you gotten forth through that?*

D: Yeah, it is pretty intense.

E: *Are you okay?*

D: Yes, it's great. It's beautiful.

E: *Kind of orgasmic?*

D: Not quite that intense.

E: *Okay.*

D: We are bringing in different colors now. It is bubbly and energetic. Different colors as in some blues, tinges of red here and there. We like to keep our purple close, and turquoise.

E: *Yes, the turquoise is beautiful. Sort of like an energy cloak that you wear.*

D: That is a beautiful explanation.

E: *So this experience, where is it in time and space for you? Past, parallel, future, or all of it?*

D: I think it is a big part of who I am on the inside.

E: *Are you reminding yourself through this experience of who you are?*

D: Yeah, I think so.

E: *What else would you like to experience or know here for your highest good? This is your space, your home. What else do you need to know for your highest healing or experience, or bring back, or remember?*

D: It feels like a place of rejuvenation.

E: *Can you come here anytime you want?*

D: I think so in meditation.

E: *Yeah. Let it embed into your body so that you can recreate it anytime you want. How perfect is that word for having a creational space, recreate?*

D: I would like to give this space an assignment.

E: *Yes. What would that be?*

D: To help, not to help, to change the memories in the cells. Change the memories in the cells to the love and to the magic and to the happy, joy that we are.

E: *Shall we do that now for you?*

D: Yes, let's assign that to this space, to go here, this changes the cells to be that.

E: *I love that. Sort of a recharging place for you and deprogramming and lifting the cellular memories that no longer serve you now to the memories that do serve you and bring joy and happiness, and love, you said love.*

D: Love and adventure. Let's do more adventures.

E: *More adventures, let's do. Let's feel that going into you now, every cell of your physical vessel, your blood, your bones, your organs and tissues, every cell that makes this body known as Debra, now receiving this beautiful attunement, that onement, releasing all cellular memory that no longer serves you, bringing in pure Love-Light, adventure, happiness, from the tips of your toes to the tips of your nose, from the top of your head to the bottom of your soles, fingertips, all of you now tingling and aligned. Shall we say that this can continue throughout the rest of this session?*

D: Yes, please.

The Higher Self is called forth.

E: *Let's do that. This shall continue throughout the rest of this session. May I speak to the Higher Self now?*

D: Yes.

E: *Greetings! Who am I speaking with?* . . .

D: . . .

E: *You can say her name.* . .

D: (Chuckling changes to sobbing) . . .

E: *Three little syllables, say her name.* . .

D: (Breathing heavily sobbing) . . . (Moving mouth making great effort to speak with nothing coherent being expressed), Aaa . . .

E: *It feels so good to have her here with you.* . .

D: (Heavy breathing emotional still struggling to speak but unable to utter a sound) . . .

E: *It feels so good to have you here . . . Greetings. . .*

Higher Self: (Meekly) Greetings (Whispering), it's Haniel. (Sobbing)

E: *Yes. Beautiful Haniel. Haniel, we love you, honor you, and respect you. Thank you.*

AA Haniel: I love you. Thank you for being this bridge.

E: *Are you doing okay?*

AA Haniel: Perfect.

E: *Yes. I would say. Shall I get a tissue for us?*

AA Haniel: No, we're good.

The body scan begins.

E: *Shall we do a body scan now? Let's get her all perfect.*

AA Haniel: (Chuckling) Imperfectly perfect, please.

E: *Absolutely, imperfectly perfect, with our special twist on it, yes. Would you like assistance today, Haniel? I have Divine Mother and Divine Father here.*

AA Haniel: That would be beautiful.

E: *So they are here and all the Archangels. There are a few crystal lotus flowers floating around here too. So thank you for that. And some purple gold energy. We have a Dragon in here for you.*

AA Haniel: Yeah, her white Dragon is here.

E: *Beautiful. As is mine. Let's scan her now. (Lovingly) We are going to give her the very best scanning and healing that she has ever, ever had. Let's start at her crown, shall we?*

AA Haniel: Yes, please.

E: *All right. Let me know what you see and if it is helpful I can tell what was found as you know in the session, that this is a huge breakthrough for Debra and if we can let her talk about it that would be really good.*

AA Haniel: There is something in the crown. There is swirling energy and a heaviness.

E: Negative. Yes. Shall we encase it in the alchemy symbol?

AA Haniel: Please encase it.

E: I am thinking, which alchemy symbol are you needing?

AA Haniel: This feels very dark, feels Archon.

E: Yes. Thank you. Let's place it in the alchemy symbol for Archons now please, and let me know once it is encased.

AA Haniel: It is encased.

E: Thank you. How far down does this go into her? There's a black chord.

AA Haniel: Yes, there is.

E: Can we transmute, what are we doing with that black chord?

AA Haniel: Let's use Phoenix Fire on it.

E: Let's do that. And it ends where in her body so that I can fire it up through her body?

AA Haniel: It feels like it goes pretty deep.

E: Shall I fire from the root up?

AA Haniel: Yes, I think so, from the root up.

E: Okay, let's do that. Activating Phoenix Fire now. Do we have any Fire Dragons here to assist? My Source Dragon can assist. Using the Source Flame as well. And we are completely transmuting this chord out. Through all time and space all parallel lifetimes, all past lifetimes, all future lifetimes, this chord is being transmuted out now with pure Source Love-Light. All the way out, no trace back.

AA Haniel: Yes, no trace back.

E: Completely clearing. Let me know when we have transmuted all of this chord out. It seems pretty thick and contained within the chord, so like no tentacles anywhere else. Let me know Haniel what you find, please. Do we need the Cold Phoenix Fire Zero Point anywhere through this, maybe at the root?

AA Haniel: Yeah, the root.

E: Let's do the Cold Zero Point Phoenix Fire now, completely encasing the root where it rooted in. It is completely encased, all aspects, front, back, and *side, in a ball of the Zero Point Phoenix Fire now. I see it freezing, encasing, and as it crumbles away the Dragons are transmutting out any flecks and pieces, transmutted out. Let me know Haniel when this is done at the root.*

AA Haniel: Still feeling it but it is going. It's not as . . .

E: Shall we encase it and allow it to do its work, it's magic while we focus on the rest?

AA Haniel: Okay, yes, that is good.

E: All right, how are we chord-wise here working upward? I am running the Cold Zero Point Flame here now up the way through her throat, third eye, and out the crown. Deep breath in.

AA Haniel: It feels wonderful. It feels like it is really lightening up there.

E: Does this have anything to do with the acid reflux that has been plaguing her?

AA Haniel: That and there was something in the root area that has been really stuck and damaged.

E: So will this take care of that? . . . We can check again once it's dissolved.

AA Haniel: Yes, check again once it is all out of there.

E: Okay. Thank you, Divine Mother, Divine Father let's bring in your Love-Light now. Love-Light, right above the Zero Point ball and we are just going to follow where that chord was. We are just bringing in (Singing) Love-Light, Love-Light, Love-Light, into every cell, every energetic aspect of her where this chord ran for thousands of years. Filling it in with (Singing) Love-Light, Love-Light, Love-Light, up through the throat, through the third eye, the brain, the crown of the head, Love-Light. Divine Mother, Divine Father do we need Archangel Raphael at this point?

Divine Mother and Divine Father: Yes. Have him fill it in with his Love-Light, please.

E: Let's do that. Calling in Archangel Raphael, brother I greet you with love, honor, and respect.

AA Raphael: Greetings. I love you.

E: I love you too. Thank you. Let's fill in all this space and places that we are going to clear for her today with your beautiful healing energy.

AA Raphael: Absolutely.

E: *Thank you. And you will be continuing healing on this or will this be done by the end of this session?*

AA Raphael: I think we are going to initiate my symbol energetically to keep this flowing so that any residue will be completely cleared.

E: *For as long as it needs . . .*

AA Raphael: For as long as it needs.

E: *And your symbol is going to be energetically over and in her, right?*

AA Raphael: Yes.

E: *Oh beautiful. I love that. And I can see you beginning to do that now. That is really going to stabilize her root and all of her energy centers.*

AA Raphael: Yes. That's where we needed it, the root, right there.

E: *Oh, thank you, Raphael. I can feel that. I'm letting the Zero Point flake away now. Seeing your beautiful golden energy and symbol. Yes. Thank you. That's beautiful. In the body scan, I was told that (Name withheld) was somehow attached to this chord. Can you verify that for me, Haniel? . . . I know there is a little something there with (Name withheld).*

AA Haniel: Yeah, there is something there with her.

E: *Maybe not through the chord?*

AA Haniel: It doesn't feel like she has been attached for thousands of years. Hers is more . . . this has been several lifetimes with her, hasn't it? Several lifetimes with *(Name withheld).*

E: *Can you heal that trauma?*

AA Haniel: Yes.

E: *Let's heal that now. Divine Mother and Divine Father, asking you to go into the energetic souls and beingness of Debra and (Name withheld) now, and heal this trauma between them now and forever. Can you do that?*

Divine Mother and Divine Father: Yes. It is done.

E: *Thank you. Beautiful. Thank you.*

Divine Mother and Divine Father: Thank you for bridging that out, clearing that.

E: *Yes. My pleasure. How is that crown feeling?*

AA Haniel: Oh, so like minty fresh.

E: *(Chuckling) Beautiful. Thank you. Raphael, I'm asking you to please bring your golden energy up to the crown and would you seal the crown for us please, Raphael, that it cannot be used as a portal?*

AA Raphael: Yes. Sealing it now.

E: *Will you please close that dark portal?*

AA Raphael: It is closed.

E: *Raphael, in the RAAH healing Michael told us this dark portal is connected to the Archon Universe and he was going to investigate. Can I speak with Archangel Michael now?*

AA Raphael: Yes.

E: *Calling forth on Archangel Michael. Greetings Brother.*

AA Michael: Greetings beautiful Esmerelda.

E: *Thank you, Archangel Raphael, I mean Michael. (both chuckling) You make me blush, but thank you. So, what did you discover with this black dark portal to the Archon Universe? You've been working on several of these. Are you able to close them now, finally? This one at least in Debra?*

AA Michael: Absolutely we are closing this one in Debra, and there is a lot going there and it is very ancient, very ancient.

E: *It is very ancient.*

AA Michael: This infringement and this control and this collection of data and this mirror of what is going on. This disconnection is really going to hurt their information gathering.

E: *I felt that too. I felt the dark portals you have been working on, I think there are three or five that I am aware of some clients that are closed, that are related to that. Michael, since we are talking about this now, can we go to the big Archon that we encased in her heart?*

AA Michael: Yes.

E: *We decided to transmute that out but that big Archon was a hive mind data, when you said data, it was like a data collecting center.*

AA Michael: Hm mmm.

E: *Yup. Is that completely transmuted out of her heart and her heart tissue, energetics in all lifetimes, and this one?*

AA Michael: It is.

E: *Thank you. Did we sever this group of Archons involved with all the dark portals in clients now from the hive mind?*

AA Michael: It has been severed.

E: *Thank you. When I discovered the data center in her heart, I began to see her body construct as an artificial body, like an android. And I was told that her consciousness was forced into an android body 1,101 years ago in the Andromeda Star System. Michael, can you confirm that for me?*

AA Michael: Confirmed.

E: *Can we repair her energetic overlay and return her organic divine soul blueprint to her now in this time and space and have it ripple backward to that time she was hijacked and infringed on that way?*

AA Michael: Yes.

E: *Can you begin that? You and Raphael begin that or do you want Divine Mother and Divine Father to do this?*

AA Michael: We will do this. We were working towards the issues with the double esophagus and all this other stuff that has been going on, it is all related. The connection to her being born during this time, the abductions of the experiments that have been done, the data collection, their tests, and their collection of her eggs, and various tissues.

E: *So with that connection are we able to erase her DNA from their data-banks?*

AA Michael: Yes, that has been severed, that has all been removed from all time and space.

E: *Beautiful. And her eggs, were any consciousnesses created from those? Do we need to do something?*

AA Michael: I'm seeing twins, a boy, and a girl, who were created with consciousness.

E: *Can we free their consciousnesses? What can we do? Do they need our assistance? Did they find their path to the light or do they need our assistance? . . . Michael, I was instructed, you asked me to put my Excalibur into the data-bank in her heart, may I retrieve that now?*

AA Michael: Yes.

E: I am flaming it out and clearing it with Phoenix Fire. Thank you. All right, so the children. We were checking on the children, the twins, the boy, and the girl. I am just wondering if we need to provide healing to them or if they are alive right now in some other place, space, and time.

AA Michael: They are alive right now. They of course are in a totally unawakened infringed space oblivious to anything different than their existence.

E: Do they have chords to her?

AA Michael: There are two chords to her.

E: What do you want to do?

AA Michael: We need to cut those.

E: Please do that now and let me know when it is done.

AA Michael: It's done.

E: Is there a contract involved in this egg collection thing or android life?

AA Michael: She dissolved that contract or she broke it.

E: Can you tear it up then?

AA Michael: Yes, it has been burned to a crisp.

E: So we can bring back her true crystalline organic nature fully and heal her from the trauma of that android lifetime.

AA Michael: Yes.

E: Let's do that, Archangels Raphael, Haniel, and yourself. Michael, there were thousands of Reptilians, little Reptilians, like little minnow fishy thingies swimming around energetically in her head. What was that? We encased them all. Metatron and Jophiel got them all. Do we need to talk to them?

AA Michael: Yes, we need to allow them the opportunity to go to the light.

E: Let's do that. I'm speaking to the Reptilians, the Reptilians' consciousness that we have within Debra now. I would like you all to assign a representative that I may speak with you now. Come up, up, up. Up, up, up. (Lovingly) Greetings.

Minnow type of Reptilian: Hello.

E: Hello. I greet you with honor and respect. Can you tell us when it was that you got into Debra here?

Minnow type of Reptilian: It's been a long time.

E: All right. What was your job, and what did you cause her?

Minnow type of Reptilian: Some of her confusion (Playful), maybe a lot of her confusion. She figured out how to overcome some of it so we can claim some credit for that. (Both chuckling)

E: I'm pretty sure because of who Debra is and all that she has been involved in, you know that the Earth and the Universe are ascending. And that parasitic entities like you will no longer be able to attach to people. And so we would love to be able to assist you today so that when the ascension comes forth you won't be recycled straight back to Source, back to zero, losing the experiences you gained through being negatively polarized. Instead, we can assist you today to spread your light, helping you to ascend into positive polarization, retaining all the wisdom gained through being negatively polarized. You would be free to incarnate somewhere else no longer having to feed off of others' light. As you are your own creator being and you would be free to discover your own light. Wouldn't that be great?

Minnow type of Reptilian: Yeahhhh.

E: Would you allow us to help you spread your light?

Minnow type of Reptilian: Yeah, we all like that idea.

E: How many of you are there in there? . . . Just so we can make sure we have everyone. You know, like little swimming Reptilians. Thousands. You know. Would you say over one thousand?

Minnow type of Reptilian: I don't want to get it wrong. We want to go.

E: Okay. Do you have bodies elsewhere?

Minnow type of Reptilian: I'm not sensing bodies.

E: Yeah, I didn't either. All right.

Minnow type of Reptilian: Two thousand.

E: Two thousand. Thank you. Let's everyone in there spread their light now. And we are assisting, all the Archangels, and her Higher Self, we are all beaming Love-Light at you. Find every part of you and make sure that you *spread your Love-Light to every part of you now. Retracting any hooks. Do you have any hooks, portals, or chords that you all have put in there?*

Minnow type of Reptilian: No.

E: *Thank you. Pull everything out and make everything light and let me know when you are all light. Archangel Azrael, Archangel Azrael, Archangel Azrael, I call you forth.*

Minnow type of Reptilian: We are all light.

E: *Greetings Archangel Azrael. Good, you are all light. Come up, up, up now, and let me know when you are out.*

Minnow type of Reptilian: We are all out.

E: *Good. Do you have any messages for Debra?*

Minnow type of Reptilian: It's going to be fun.

E: *Great. Thank you. Archangel Azrael brother, are you there?*

AA Azrael: I am.

E: *Thank you. Will you please take these two thousand Reptilian consciousnesses upon your Ray to their next evolutionary experience?*

AA Azrael: With honor.

E: *Thank you Archangel Azrael.*

AA Azrael: Thank you.

E: *Thank you. Archangel Michael, are you there?*

AA Michael: I am.

E: *Beautiful. Oh, Archangel Raphael, please include your beautiful golden healing energy in her head space. Michael, do we need to Phoenix Fire anything in there or was it a clean . . .*

AA Michael: Let's Phoenix Fire it, please.

E: *Okay, let's Phoenix Fire it. I am just concentrating that flame in all of her head energetically, physically, mentally, all the neuron pathways synopsis cognitive connections, eyes, ears, nose, throat, hearing, sensing. This Phoenix Fire is purifying her entire head space, everything. Throat even. And let me know when we have it all purified, deep, deep, deep.*

AA Michael: Beautiful. It looks good, really good.

E: *Thank you.*

AA Michael: Thank you for including the throat. There was something going on there in the throat.

E: *Yeah. Can we take a deeper look there Michael, please, and tell me what you see?*

AA Michael: Something cloudy, white cloudy.

E: *White cloudy . . . positive or negative?*

AA Michael: Negative.

E: *Okay, it's an energy. Does it have a consciousness?*

AA Michael: No.

E: *What symbol are we using to encase it and transmute it out?*

AA Michael: Let's use the Archon symbol.

E: *All right, let's do that. Let me know when you have that encased. Let's do the whole throat and neck please down to the bottom of her esophagus, Michael. Is it encased?*

AA Michael: Yes, it is encased.

E: *Thank you. Let's transmute that out. While we are transmuting that out can you take a really deep look, Michael, through that, through her arms, fingers, shoulders, rib cage, heart, and just a really deep scan?*

AA Michael: Nothing is coming through.

E: *I didn't see anything either. In the solar plexus, Michael, you had me use, or Haniel and my Higher Self, Divine Mother, and Divine Father had me use Rainbow Love-Light to remove the block in her solar plexus, which essentially meant that she really didn't have free will. And so we filled that with Love-Light. What I want to know is what was that block? Was it energetic programming or . . . I didn't see anything there but I knew there was a block there. Can you explain that to me?*

AA Michael: That was self-defense.

E: *So it was okay to fill it with Love-Light?*

AA Michael: Yes, very much so. Thank you.

E: *Have we removed the need for the self-defense at the solar plexus?*

AA Michael: Yes. Yes.

E: *Can we re-instill her with a healthy sense of free will and all that free will brings to her?*

AA Michael: Yes.

E: Okay, let's do that now. Archangel Raphael, as the Archon transmutes out, and everything there in the neck and the upper chest area, will you please heal trauma from that?

AA Raphael: Yes.

E: Thank you, brother.

AA Raphael: Thank you.

E: Then Michael, we have Reptilians over her ovaries. They are not actually on them. They are encased in the alchemy symbol. Shall we talk to them now?

AA Michael: Yes.

E: All right do we need to talk to them both or . . .

AA Michael: No, one can represent them.

E: All right, one of you talk to me and come up, up, up, now. Up, up, up. Greetings.

Reptilian: Hi.

E: Hi. I greet you with honor and respect. What have you caused Debra, here in the ovary area, speaking for both of you? Right above the ovaries, why there?

Reptilian: From here we can place toxins into her body.

E: Oh, right directly into that area. Like her intestines are down there?

Reptilian: Yeah.

E: Do you have something in the intestines? Hooks, chords, portals.

Reptilian: Well, we portal in and out.

E: Yeah, left side only or left, and right?

Reptilian: Left side.

E: Michael will you please close that portal now?

AA Michael: It's closed.

E: Thank you. What else, do you have hooks somewhere? Strings? What else? How are you putting toxins into her?

Reptilian: Through her breath.

E: Through her breath. Are you part of her breathing problem?

Reptilian: We combine our breath with her breath and it changes.

E: *Is that why she gets heavy and bloated at night because of you two?*

Reptilian: Yeah. It's a game.

E: *It's a game (Chuckling). Did you hear what I said to the crew up in the head?*

Reptilian: Yes, we heard and we would like to join them.

E: *All right. I would like you to retract your claws, retract any hooks and chords, everything, and then begin to spread your light. Do you need some Love-Light from us or can you find your light?*

Reptilian: It's been a while. We would appreciate some of your Love-Light.

E: *Okay. Myself, Divine Mother, and Divine Father are shining Love-Light on you now. Helping you to spread your light. I want you to spread your light to every part of you, both of you. Do you have bodies somewhere?*

Reptilian: I am not sensing any.

E: *How long have you been in here causing this? This whole lifetime or . . . lifetimes?*

Reptilian: Oh, it would be lifetimes.

E: *Hm mmm. You followed her for a couple of incarnations, maybe about three it looks like?*

Reptilian: Yes. Yes, it's to do with her father, the same father.

E: *Oh okay. Let me know when you are all light and I will call forth on Archangel Azrael again. Michael, Divine Mother, Divine Father, can we heal this father trauma that she has endured through lifetimes?*

Archangel Michael, Divine Mother, Divine Father: Yes.

E: *Let's do that now. Healing that as these Reptilians lift up. Let me know when you are light.*

Reptilian: We are light.

E: *Up, up now. Up, up, up. Out. Let me know when you are out.*

Reptilian: We are out.

E: *Thank you. Do you have a message for Debra?*

Reptilian: Yeah. We are sorry.

E: *Thank you.*

Reptilian: Thank you.

E: *I am going to have you both go with Archangel Azrael. He will make sure you get to the place you need to go. Archangel Azrael, brother.*

AA Azrael: Yes.

E: *Please take these two away on your Ray. Can you tell me, where are they going?*

AA Azrael: They are going to a healing center.

E: *Yeah, that is what I sensed. Thank you for confirming that. Thank you Archangel Azrael, I love you, honor you, and respect you.*

AA Azrael: Oh, thank you. I love you, honor you, and respect you.

E: *Thank you. Divine Mother and Divine Father, as you are healing the trauma through the ancestral line, the past lives, and also healing this body, healing her intestines completely, healing the bloating and her breath issue, and does she need to know anything else, or is this healing going to take care of that? That was one of her questions.*

Divine Mother and Divine Father: This will take care of that.

E: *The pain and the pressure?*

Divine Mother and Divine Father: The pain and the pressure. There is something, however, going on in her left side pelvic area.

E: *What is that?*

Divine Mother and Divine Father: There's heaviness. It's not a sharp pain, feels heavy. It's dark, it is like cloudy, it's an Archon situation.

E: *Let's put it in the Archon symbol then.*

Divine Mother and Divine Father: It is encased.

E: *Confirm for me, an Archon nest?*

Divine Mother and Divine Father: Yes.

E: *Let's lift that out now. Let's lift it out of her and transmuting connections within her as you lift it out, Divine Mother, Divine Father, and Source, let me know when this is out of her.*

Divine Mother, Divine Father, and Source: It's out.

E: *Okay, can we transmute it out completely?*

Divine Mother, Divine Father, and Source: It's transmuted.

E: *What else? Is there anything else there that that Archon nest caused?*

Divine Mother, Divine Father, and Source: No, it was just a presence there.

E: *A consciousness?*

Divine Mother, Divine Father, and Source: No, just another gathering of information of some sort.

E: *A data center?*

Divine Mother, Divine Father, and Source: Yeah.

E: *Is it in the alchemy symbol for Archons?*

Divine Mother, Divine Father, and Source: Yes, it is in the symbol.

E: *Thank you. Do you need to know anything about that Michael? Do you need to trace this data collection?*

AA Michael: Yes.

E: *Do we need to know about it, or . . .*

AA Michael: Well, no, there is nothing that you need to know. We are tracing it to delete all data, all files throughout all time and space.

E: *Perfect. Let me know when that is done. Having Divine Mother and Father assist you.*

AA Michael: Thank you. It is done.

E: *Good. So, can you confirm, is this the final thing to be able to restore her to her organic divine soul blueprint and have her best connection, and clear connection to Haniel, her Higher Self?*

AA Michael: Yes. Yes.

E: *That is beautiful Michael. Ah, we drained some black and green goo from the dissolving of the Reptilians from within her and we are transmuting that out now with Phoenix Fire. Healing her womb space and her root chakra. Michael, would you take a last look, and Divine Mother and Divine Father? I would like for this to be like a pivotal healing session for her so that she can really progress now with Haniel and be in service to the light in the way that she wants to be with all her cellular cells reprogrammed to her organic divine soul blueprint. Is she clear now? Do we have all Archons out? Head to toe? Fingertips, toes, everything?*

Divine Mother, Divine Father, and Archangel Michael: There's something in the left leg calf area.

E: What is it?

Divine Mother, Divine Father, and Archangel Michael: It's metallic.

E: Let's put it in the alchemy symbol for Archons then. Does it have a consciousness?

Divine Mother, Divine Father, and Archangel Michael: It's encased. There is no consciousness.

E: I'm seeing it from the bottom of the knee to . . . almost the ankle.

Divine Mother, Divine Father, and Archangel Michael: Yes. Confirmed.

E: Let me know when that is transmuted out. Archangel Raphael, dear brother, and Divine Mother, Divine Father, please bring healing energy once this is transmuted out of her leg, rebalancing her legs, hips, her knees, ankles, and feet, so that she is balanced in this new body that she has.

Archangel Raphael, Divine Mother, Divine Father: Yes.

E: Thank you. Thank you, I love you all so much.

AAs Michael and Raphael, Divine Mother, Divine Father: It's been transmuted too.

E: Thank you. Speaking to the Three Great Central Suns that assisted me earlier. Hello, I love you honor you and respect you.

Three Great Central Suns: Hello, We love you, honor you, and respect you. We love you.

E: Thank you. Thank you for helping with Debra. I feel you were integral in getting her to this point because you entered, the Golden One of you entered into her whole torso, rib cage, and heart.

Three Great Central Suns: Yes.

E: I want to thank you for that from my heart to yours. Are you able to lift out of her now? Have you done what you needed to do there?

Three Great Central Suns: Yes. It feels pretty clean and bright. It is organic.

E: So her esophagus, her stomach, her digestion, her intestines, liver, and kidneys, they are all crystalline and organic now?

Three Great Central Suns: Yes, they are.

E: Crystalline and organic?

Three Great Central Suns: Yes.

E: Can we expand her heart to the fullest extent?

Three Great Central Suns: Yes.

E: Beautiful. Can we expand her third eye now to its fullest extent?

Three Great Central Suns: Yes.

E: I want to make sure all of her chakras are in rhythm with each other synchronicities spinning and at the highest frequency of Love-Light for each color.

Three Great Central Suns: Yes.

E: Beautiful. Can we scan her auric field, since Raphael is busy healing, can we come out and scan her auric field? Would you do that for me Great Central Sun?

Three Great Central Suns: Yes.

E: Are there any rips, holes, or tears? Can we repair those now?

Three Great Central Suns: Yes.

E: It kind of looks like an asteroid out here. Like it has taken a lot of hits. I would like to strengthen her auric field. Can we do that, Haniel, do you approve? Can we do that?

AA Haniel: Yes.

E: Okay, let's do that. Strengthening her astral field. Is there something she needs to change in her daily routine to make her auric field nice and strong or will this healing do and she can go forward from here? Repairing all rips, holes, and tears. Sealing them all nice and bright, light.

AA Haniel: She is doing the work. This is what was needed.

E: Let's make this impervious to family barbs and family dramas, shall we?

AA Haniel: What a wise idea. (both chuckling)

E: Haniel, I am going to put you in charge of that, okay?

AA Haniel: Love it.

E: Will you please remind her to include that intent in her shielding daily?

AA Haniel: Yes.

E: Okay, great. Let's see, her losing her words and her saying the opposite like left and right and right is left, Haniel, what is that about?

AA Haniel: Those thousands of Reptilians up there, they were messing with her.

E: *I thought so. Will this healing continue past this session and into the night or anything?*

AA Haniel: Yes, this will take a little bit longer. She will start standing a little bit taller, and start accepting and knowing.

E: *Yes. It will change her.*

AA Haniel: Yes.

E: *Haniel, you look so beautiful there.*

AA Haniel: Thank you beautiful Esmerelda.

E: *Is there anything else? Can we check her DNA for false fractals?*

AA Haniel: I am looking.

E: *Does she have any soul fractals to be retrieved at this time?*

AA Haniel: I am not seeing any soul fractals.

E: *There is a little, in the spine, a cross integration of negative fractals in her is what I'm seeing, from the android life.*

AA Haniel: Uh ha.

E: *Can we clear that?*

AA Haniel: Yes.

E: *Do you need help with Phoenix Fire there?*

AA Haniel: Yes, let's Phoenix Fire this.

E: *Sending Phoenix Fire there now in the spine. Archangel Michael beloved, can you confirm for me that all dark portals are closed, including those upon her land and within her home that is within her right to have closed? How many dark portals are you finding?*

AA Michael: The Manti home has many.

E: *Let me know when they are closed. Do you need help closing any?*

AA Michael: We are closing them.

E: *Thank you.*

AA Michael: Now that she has been taught to close and shield that space as well, it is going to help tremendously.

E: *Good. So she can fully shield that space and all her spaces where she inhabits?*

AA Michael: Yes.

E: *The spine is looking good. Please scan one more time, Divine Mother and Divine Father, for negative chords, negative implants, hooks, organic matter embedded with technology, or wires.*

Divine Mother and Divine Father: Nothing is popping up.

E: *Yeah, I don't see anything either. Those Reptilians left her pretty clear and clean. Can we continue to heal her vision, Haniel?*

AA Haniel: Yes.

E: *Let's do that. Continue healing her brain synapsis, so her words come easy and quick and she no longer says opposite words.*

AA Haniel: Yes.

E: *Do you want to age regress her any at all?*

AA Haniel: We can take off two years.

E: *Let's do that. Divine Mother and Divine Father, are there any contracts? Can we delete all inverted timelines she has been involved in and the trauma from all of those inverted timelines?*

Divine Mother and Divine Father: Yes.

E: *All right. If there is any lingering trauma from current or past lives can you also delete that and heal that?*

Divine Mother and Divine Father: Yes.

E: *Throughout all time and space and throughout her ancestry as well, forward, backward.*

Divine Mother and Divine Father: Yes, forward, backward as well.

E: *Have I forgotten anything in this healing today?*

AA Haniel: No, this has been beautiful. Very deep and thorough.

E: *Thank you. It's been great. Now I need to get AuroRa so please wait a minute for that.*

The client is brought out of hypnosis.

E: *Welcome back, welcome back, welcome back.*
D: Thank you.
E: *Oh my goodness.*

D: Thank you. I love you. I don't remember ever feeling so much love . . . Can you believe how hard that was to say my Higher Self's name?

E: *That was awesome, awesome, awesome.*

End of session.

I so love this session. It was so light and playful with a masterful practitioner. I wish you could see the armful of glistening translucent crystal-like turquoise lotus flowers. Simply magical! My practitioner got me to put a smile on my face and literally jump through my block. I mean dang. That was pretty huge for me. Jump became the playful word of the day and always brought a smile to my heart.

There's actually a little more to the story. A few years earlier I was visiting my daughter and her husband when they lived in Lahaina Maui, Hawaii. While my daughter was at work, my son-in-law took me to a rock-face lagoon area that the locals frequented for cliff diving. There were ten to fifteen young people there enjoying themselves. My son-in-law quickly jumped off about a high twenty-foot boulder. Everyone was having a blast. He encouraged me to jump into the clear calm ocean waters off the smallest boulder with a four- or five-foot drop.

Naturally, he was sharing this advent with all our loved ones back home via Facebook Live. I couldn't do it. I couldn't make that five-foot jump. Pretty soon there was a chorus of everyone there recognizing a newbie, lovingly shouting jump, jump, one, two, three, jump. One, two, three, jump, jump, jump. One, two, three, jump. Meanwhile, this person and that person are jumping in to show me how safe it is. Still, hovering by the edge rocking back and forth almost there, I absolutely couldn't do it. Returning back home to Utah, my son who watched the first part of the long video asked me if I ever jumped. Looking down at the ground I confessed that nope, I climbed in instead. Laugh out loud.

Oh, and talk about whimsical, assigning the memories in my cells to be love, magic, happiness, and joy. Magical and light-hearted all the way. But then things got real. At that particular moment in the session when I felt my Higher Self come in and I immediately became paralyzed, emotionally not able to utter her name. In other sessions it came out about my being contacted by beings masquerading as deities. I eventually had enough and slammed the door on having anything further to do with them. As you can imagine that twisted my perspective on God and Angels. It's a relationship I've been rebuilding over recent years and thought I had it figured out. This session revealed that there was still one more hurdle.

Even after the session when the group of practitioners gathered to share something about their sessions when it came to my turn, I covered my face with both hands literally ugly out loud sobbing not able to say my Higher Self's name. The group being who they were, didn't allow me to get away with it. Each one lovingly, knowingly, waited for me to work through it until I could proclaim my Higher Self is Archangel Haniel! Beautiful.

Getting back to the session, it's mind-boggling to learn my consciousness was forced into an android body all those years ago. No wonder I keep having all this metal removed session after session. Rescuing my Free Will from that box has to be . . . well, that and each puzzle piece throughout this past year has been life-changing. Each piece mattered and matters to me.

The leveling up from this session and the practitioner's reunion itself, is a gift that keeps on giving. One practitioner told me after my session, "You've changed. You're standing straighter and taller, more confident." I agree that I am. This work is about empowering each of us to find our sovereignty and our individual strength. To rediscover ourselves and to jump, simply jump.

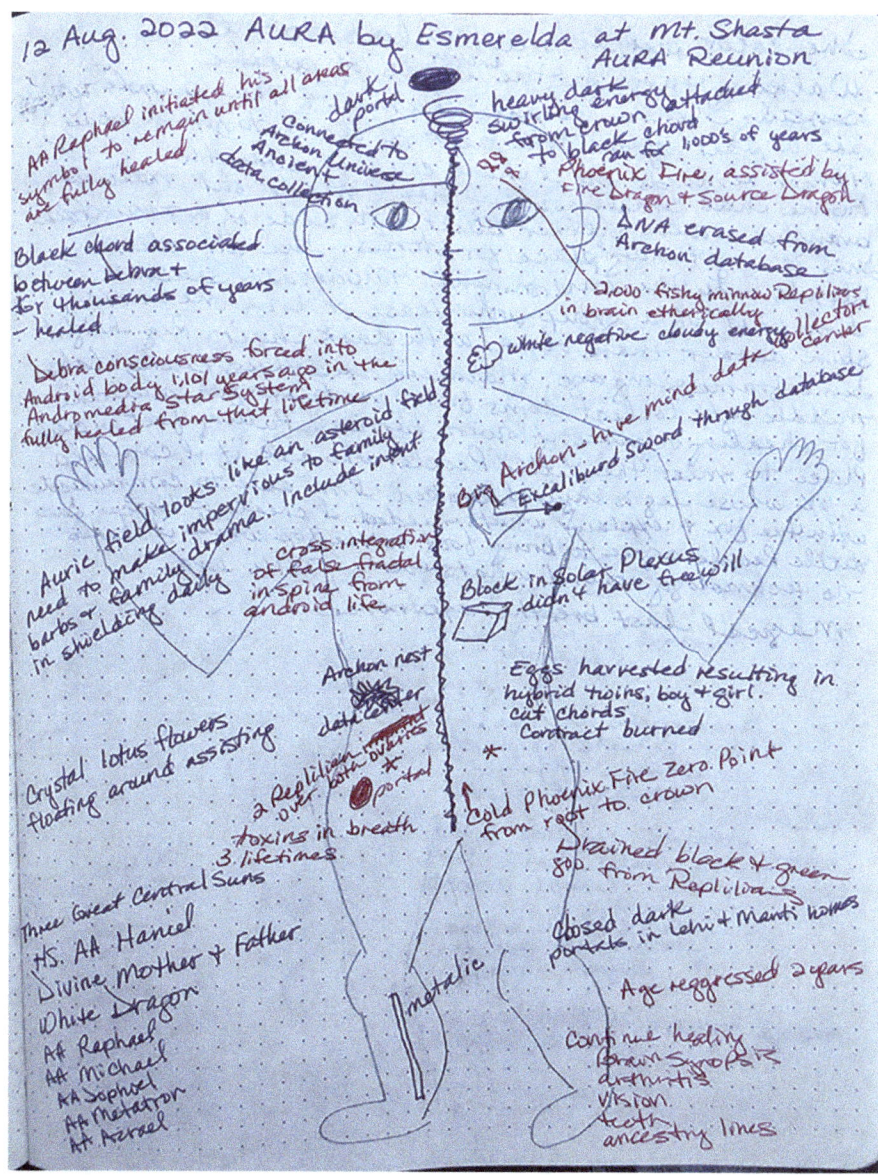

10

Indigenous Connections

AURA Hypnosis Healing by Esmerelda
September 1, 2022

During a separate unpublished session held a few weeks earlier where I was the practitioner, Archangel Azrael came through. We were talking about higher-level activations of our chakras. He explained, "Soul Star Activation can mean different things for different levels of consciousness. It does pertain to your Soul, your Oversoul, and your Higher Self, for you can traverse through Higher Self constructs. In other words, Higher Self to an incarnation the Soul has had, to another aspect. Many of you contain more layers between your Higher Self and your Oversoul. They may look like Dragons, Fairies, and Pixies. For you (Debra), they will look like Indigenous people."

Unpacking this profound teaching from Archangel Azrael, brought with it many questions. It's a fun one to sit and meditate on. What stands out for the purpose of this chapter is that Azrael confirmed what other intuitives have said about my strong Indigenous connections. In my current life, I was raised assimilated in the white American mainstream. Today, other than knowing a small part of my ancestry is Jicarilla Apache, and what I learned while serving several years as an assistant to an Ojibwe Elder, my own Jicarilla ancestorial knowledge remains a mystery. With the objective in mind to get a glimpse into what our Divine Beings are referring to when saying a layer between my Higher Self and my Oversoul is as an Indigenous perspective, I asked for a session to visit that.

Session begins.

>E [Esmerelda]: *Tell me what you sense.*
>D [Debra]: I'm not really, I'm just kind of in the dark . . .
>E: *In a dark place?*
>D: Yes, but it's not black.
>E: *And it's not . . .*
>D: I'm not sensing anything. I'm not sensing a body. I'm not sensing the ground.
>E: *Hmm. Is this a pre-creation, perhaps? Pre-embodiment?*
>D: I am not seeing the energy waves or colors. It is just . . .
>E: *Just take a deep breath and allow your beautiful Higher Self to allow you to know.*
>D: In the Merkabah flight there were colors and there was energy but when it stopped moving . .
>E: *So the Merkabah is still around you. Perhaps if you could sense it still being in the energy of the Merkabah, the spinning of the Merkabah, and in that, taking yourself back to being seated in the Merkabah and that beautiful connection with your Higher Self. Allowing yourself to see as you are sitting in your Merkabah, might be like a movie that is being shown to you, as you sit in your Merkabah watching.*
>D: I got my colors coming back with energy waves.
>E: *Are these the colors from your happy place?*
>D: Yes. They are my purples.
>E: *They really helped you last time. Just play with them letting them move over you and through you. Feeling the sensations. I know they changed colors last time. Are they changing colors this time?*

D: The intensity changes but they are still mostly purple.

E: *What does the purple color mean for you?*

D: Good question. Love. Love. It means love. Cool.

E: *Cool?*

D: I mean that is cool that it means love.

E: *I'm sorry, I didn't hear it. What does it mean?*

D: I'm just saying that it's not that the temperature is cool. I mean that it is cool or amazing that purple means love.

E: *Love to you. That is beautiful. So feeling and sensing love all around you, would you like to walk through that love like they are waves or curtains of purple to walk through feeling them brush upon you?*

D: Yeah!

E: *Let's do that. Just allow yourself, to feel yourself know now that you are moving, walking through these purple waves of curtains. Opening all of your senses of smell, taste, hearing, and touch, how does this color feel against your skin?*

D: I lost it and working to get it back.

E: *Well, let's look at your body. You are standing up. What do you look like?*

D: I don't see anything but I sense I'm a being.

E: *Just being?*

D: Human.

E: *Human?*

D: Hm mm.

E: *Can you sense if you are male or female?*

D: I sense female.

E: *Female?*

D: Hm mm.

E: *And what would you like to do as this female or see, or know?*

D: I would like to figure out where I am and what is going on in this space.

E: *Allow yourself to do that perhaps by moving to a place that is clear to see because you can imagine doing that, right?*

D: Right. My purples have returned so this is good. I'm just going to keep walking through it all, all these waves of energy.

E: *Do you feel as though those waves of purple waves of energy, do they show up on your skin or on this body, this humanoid form somehow? Are you part of the purple color?* (Note: transcribing this on 9/9/2022, I received a download that yes, the purple color is a larger part of my consciousness that is not able to fit into my current physical vessel.)

D: . . . Well, my movement changes the waves.

E: *Beautiful. Play with it.*

D: That is an interesting concept. Wow, here comes some pink!

E: *Paint a picture with your movements in those waves of energy . . . allowing your Higher Self to guide you within. She is within you guiding you in this. Ask her within you, should I go left or right? Should I go forward? What should I do? Where shall we go? And as you are that leaf on that infinite River of Life, this body that you are in moves.*

D: . . . Haniel, which way should we go? To the left. Please guide me through this. What are we meant to see and know? . . .

E: *Remember that you can sense, see, feel, touch, and smell, very clearly, very clearly, and also you can jump.*

D: Hm mm. Haniel is reminding me that I have courage, I have strength. I am not that timid frightened person who was withdrawn.

E: *That is right. You have moved beyond that.*

D: Hm mm. We go through it and experience this. Let's go, let's go.

E: *Allow her to show you the scene she wishes you to know about for your highest good. A puzzle piece. What puzzle piece is before you now?*

D: . . . The waves have started transforming into shapes. I'm trying to allow them to solidify. I'm walking through it and keep walking so that I'm empowered. Whatever is ahead, I am empowered to witness.

E: *Yes.*

D: . . . I'm still not able to differentiate shapes.

E: *In this space, what would you like to do?*

D: Mmm, I'd like to see what my home would look like.

E: *You would like to see what?*

D: What my home would look like, my living space.

E: *Yes. Let's go there. Let's see it. Or let's just let it resolve in front of you. Create it. Imagine it.*

D: . . . There's some gold coming in. I don't know if it's a fire, a little cooking fire or not.

E: *Do you like being outdoors around a fire?*

D: Oh yes. Haniel, please step inside of me and guide me.

E: *I'm sorry, I'm not hearing you.*

D: I'm asking Haniel to help me see what it is.

E: *Oh yes, do you think she wants you to create what it is? Because you are with her in this space creating this story for your highest good. Your heart and soul want to know something about your ancestors, your ancestry.*

D: The home is made more out of wood, the walls.

E: *A log home?*

D: No, more thin type of wood, just rough branches woven together. Nothing with saws or anything like that.

E: *Would that keep you warm?*

D: Oh yeah. It's using nature, branches, and leaves. It's a gathering place for stories.

E: *Storing what?*

D: Stories, as in sharing one another's experiences.

E: *Stories, oh, like a circle.*

D: A gathering of people to share and tell their stories.

E: *So does this place of gathering have a roof of branches? You know does it go all the way up and around?*

D: Yes, it does.

E: *That is awesome.*

D: It uses a lot of Mother Earth for the shelter as well. It is not only wood. There is a wall from the side of a hill with a lot of Mother Earth.

E: *It feels very much like home and comfortable, like safe here.*

D: . . . And hidden too.

E: *How is that?*

D: You wouldn't recognize it if you were somebody else walking by. You wouldn't recognize it as a dwelling. It blends into nature.

E: *Is that on purpose?*

D: Yeah. On purpose and it is also practical for the weather. You are warm when it is cold out and you are cool when it is hot out.

E: *So this space has seasons.*

D: Yeah, but not drastic. There are others in the group. I have a feeling of a lot of jokesters and a lot of love.

E: *So there is a group assembling now.*

D: Not at this moment. This space is more spontaneous than scheduled. There are gatherings of people. They are happy people who tease each other.

E: *Can you describe what they look like?*

D: . . . I'm just getting regular people.

E: *Skin tone?*

D: Maybe a little darker than olive.

E: *Blonde hair?*

D: No.

E: *Dark hair?*

D: Yeah.

E: *Average height?*

D: Yeah, with some short and some taller.

E: *Do they feel like people that would be on this Earth?*

D: Yes.

E: *Would they be people that are living now, present time people?*

D: No, this feels older, a while ago, long ago.

E: *Do you suppose they walked everywhere?*

D: Yeah, or run. A lot of running.

E: *Is the area flat ground like plains or mountains?*

D: Rocky with some mountains and a lot of greenery with trees, hills, and water. Not oceans but lakes and streams.

E: *Beautiful.*

D: I'm trying to imagine what my role is here.

E: Can you see yourself, your feet or hands?

D: When I look at myself everything goes purple again.

E: I see. Do you feel younger or older, like a wise woman here or a young maiden perhaps, here?

D: I feel in between or middle-aged and I feel that I collect things from nature medicinally.

E: What would you do with those things that you collect?

D: We create teas and we use them for healing.

E: So you yourself here know how to do that. You are active in the group doing that?

D: Yes, I'm gathering leaves, berries, flowers, and the like for any needs in the future or for those with a problem seeking a solution.

E: Allow yourself to continue to explore, gather, and be. Just telling me all about it as you go.

D: I want to go and put my feet in the creek.

E: Let's do that. You are there now. Are your feet in the creek?

D: Yeah, it is like this is a place where I meet little people.

E: Beautiful. Like elementals.

D: Yeah, elemental little people.

E: Let me know if any visit you.

D: There is something going on with a . . . it feels like a fox is sick or something. Sick or hurt. They are asking if I could go over there and provide assistance to this fox.

E: Would you like to do that?

D: Yeah, let's do that.

E: Let's go there now. See yourself there now. Do you have the fox in front of you?

D: It takes a minute to formulate after I move but yeah, I'm calming the fox down with love and love and energy with my hands. His leg is injured. I'm calming him so that I can wrap it. He is not liking the wrapping on it but I'm explaining why I'm doing what I'm doing.

E: How do you tell him?

D: I'm telling him that I see the bone is hurt and needs some support for a while. Your structure needs some support to allow it to heal back together. I need to fix this little brace. I am using small branches and various plants and leaves that I mash together along with tobacco. I'm teaching him to rest right now. It is his time to rest.

E: *How do you tell him that?*

D: With my eyes and my mind.

E: *Can you hear him in your mind?*

D: With my heart. The little people will bring him nourishment from the immediate area so that he doesn't need to worry about food.

E: *That's beautiful. So they will take care of the little one?*

D: Yeah.

E: *How do you feel about helping like this?*

D: It is just part of the day.

E: *Part of your day. How did you learn this?*

D: From watching others do the same. It feels like this is a time when there was more harmony with the Elemental People and creatures.

E: *So really quite some time ago.*

D: Yes. There is no technology around whatsoever.

E: *Could this have evolved naturally like, within this life cycle, these last five thousand years do you think or was it sometime before that?*

D: I'm trying to discern if the freedom of the Elementals is just in this area or if it is more widespread to give you a timeframe.

E: *Let your Higher Self tell you that. You know this, you know the answer. It is the first thing that you recall.*

D: The first thing is that this was long ago, long, long ago when things were honest. Love was more prevalent along with harmony.

E: *A very natural existence of humans, of nature, and of animals altogether?*

D: Yeah, and learning from each other and respecting each other.

E: *Do you like that kind of living, that way to live?*

D: Yeah. It is a more empowering way to live. We are all unique but you are one together as well. You are learning from each other from your perspective.

E: *Oh that feels good.*

D: Doesn't that feel good?

E: *Hm mm. Let's go to another scene in this life that you would like to see. Another scene. Leaving this scene where you are at now going to another time where you want to see more about this life. You are there now. What are you seeing?*

D: I'm back to the purple and trying to get the shapes to solidify and ideas of directions.

E: *Would you like to see the final days in that life or would you like to go on?*

D: Sure we can see the final day.

E: *Okay, let's go to your last day in that life, your last day in that beautiful life with these beautiful people and all that harmony and loving existence together. You are there now. Tell me how you feel and what you see.*

D: I feel joy. I feel love and I feel the excitement.

E: *What are you doing?*

D: Resting.

E: *Resting. Do you have loved ones around you?*

D: Yes. There are different kinds of beings who are very familiar.

E: *You are there surrounded by loved ones and looking to see if you know anyone there. Look at everybody's eyes. Everybody. The eyes are windows to the soul, is there someone there that you know?*

D: . . . I see the little people and I see rabbits, little bunnies.

E: *So a lot of nature.*

D: Yes, a lot of nature. There are a lot of Dragonflies humming around. Various colors of Dragonflies.

E: *There are Dragons there. Hmmm. What colors of Dragons?*

D: There's red, there's blue, and there is green.

E: *Are they all around you?*

D: It's little Dragonflies, right?

E: *Dragonflies, yeah, beautiful.*

D: They are pretty busy.

E: *Seeing yourself taking that last breath now, last breath. As you lift up from the body what do you feel?*

D: Blissful. Like things are going to be okay for the Universe.

E: *For the Universe, beautiful. Where do you think you're going to go next?*

D: It feels like a star.

E: *Do you want to go to this star?*

D: Yeah.

E: *Let's go. Let's go, yeah. Tell me what happens.*

D: It is all of a sudden you are so much bigger, so much grander, so much happier, so much more, full of love. So much more, more, more, more, more. It's amazing. It's amazing. It's just ahhhhhhh.

E: *(both chuckling) Ahhhh. Sometimes one can hardly wait. Wow.*

D: Yeah.

E: *How do you feel about that life that you had?*

D: It was a life of peace and getting to know different beings in the most humblest meekest way.

E: *So this star, are you in the star?*

D: Yeah.

E: *Leaving that life that you observed, moving away, finding yourself in that star. Closing this chapter with love and peace and in gratitude may I please have all the consciousnesses of Debra back in the body now, fully integrating. May I please speak to the Higher Self of Debra now?*

The Higher Self is called forth.

Higher Self: Greetings.

E: *Greetings. Am I speaking to Debra's Higher Self?*

Higher Self: Yes.

E: *Hello Haniel.*

AA Haniel: Hello beautiful Esmerelda.

E: It is so beautiful to see you. I want to just say, Debra, look at this picture when you listen to this recording and see how beautiful you are in this moment. Truly, truly, just the love that you are right now. Thank you for this Haniel, thank you.

AA Haniel: Thank you.

E: Know that I love you, honor you, and respect you. Thank you for all the aid that you gave us today. I know that you hold of course all the records of Debra's different lives. May we ask a few questions now?

AA Haniel: Yes.

E: Beautiful. Why is it that you chose to show Debra this life that we just saw? What were the purpose and lessons of that life?

AA Haniel: She is getting it now (Emotional). She is getting it. She volunteered for some hard times through experiences for the collective's growth. She started out being nurtured and learning the ways of this Earth to the simplest most loving and respectful ways of connecting with Mother Sophia in the ways that she did and for those under Mother Sophia's care. So she was able to keep this through all of her experiences in this world. It has come in handy and she is seeing that now.

E: The nurturing way, is that what you would call it maybe?

AA Haniel: Nurturing and in harmony. And in harmony seeing what different people are going through and even what different critters' lives are like and what they are going through. To have empathy for all for it is part of the all. Each one is part of the all, creating the one.

E: Yes. Beautiful. Is this why she resonates with what she calls the Native Way?

AA Haniel: Yes. Those were her roots here on Earth.

E: And Haniel, was this within the last five thousand years, this last cycle?

AA Haniel: No, this would be before in earlier resets.

E: Would this be perhaps around Lemuria or Mu?

AA Haniel: Closer to the Mu era.

E: *Mu era, yes. With all the harmony and the talking mind-to-mind with the animals.*

AA Haniel: Heart-to-heart.

E: *Is there anything else you would like her to know from this lifetime to bring into her now, her awareness now?*

AA Haniel: She got it. She got it. Using nature for our healing. Using our natural instincts and naturally listening to our hearts.

E: *And I'm sure you will guide her to enable these gifts more and more into this current life of her to regain total health?*

AA Haniel: Yes, we are working on that.

E: *Would you like to do the body scan now Haniel?*

The body scan begins.

AA Haniel: Yes, let's.

E: *All right, would you like any help from Divine Mother, Divine Father, the Archangels, and/or Dragons?*

AA Haniel: We would love to connect with Divine Mother and Divine Father.

E: *Beautiful. Divine Mother and Divine Father, we call you forth now at this time to assist us in the body scan. Greetings.*

Divine Mother and Divine Father: Greetings.

E: *I love you both, love you, honor you, and respect you. Feeling you together as one is amazing.*

Divine Mother and Divine Father: Love you, love you, love you so much.

E: *Thank you. Let's scan her. Where would you like to begin? We found a few things in the RAAH.*

Divine Mother, Divine Father, AA Haniel: There felt there is something in the right temple area.

E: *Yes, it was her third eye, Divine Mother. You and Divine Father were very helpful with Archangel Michael, Metatron, Uriel, and Zadkiel. I saw a black box in her third eye that had a wire from it going to a Reptilian in* her heart. We put of course put it in the alchemy symbol. You and the team actually lifted it out of this time and space and took it out. I'm not sure if it was you or Archangel Michael, you blend together so well sometimes, you said it was explosive and you didn't want it in this time-space. So we removed it carefully and took it out. Can we do some healing there and can you scan deeper now to make sure that everything is out of that third eye? We were able to set that beautiful alchemy symbol over it.

Divine Mother: Thank you. Scanning that now. Can we have Archangel Raphael start filling that in with Love-Light?

E: That is a great idea. Archangel Raphael, brother, we call upon you. Are you there?

AA Raphael: Greetings.

E: Greetings. Archangel Raphael, will you please begin filling her right temple going all the way across to the other temple with your healing rays, healing that space where that black box infringed on?

AA Raphael: I would love to.

E: Thank you. Divine Mother and Divine Father, when I placed the alchemy symbol over her, it became a circlet (Like a crown). I've never seen that happen before. Can you explain that? Or is that an aspect of Haniel's explanation? So it had the alchemy symbol and it just connected with gold light around the back of the head, like a circlet. Can you look at that now and is that okay?

Divine Mother and Divine Father: . . .

E: Archangel Raphael, go ahead and move to her right temple, please.

AA Raphael: Yes. It feels like a vibration is going on there, a frequency.

E: Is that beneficial to Debra?

AA Raphael: Yes, the frequency change is connected to her doing her trance drumming. That tends to make her entire vessel vibrate. This has been shifting things around for her.

E: Is this a good thing for her to do?

AA Raphael: Yeah, she needs to move these energies around and out, flow through her and out.

E: Okay. Can we assist her in this time and space now to move as much as needs to be moved around and flowing within her vessel now?

AA Raphael: Yes. Absolutely.

E: And I'm sensing that that energy, that frequency of golden light circlet connected to the alchemy symbol will dissipate when she reaches frequency stability. Is that what you are seeing?

Divine Mother and Divine Father: Yes. This is an in-between state going on.

E: Okay. And can we erase and heal doubt from the third eye now, doubting in herself, in her abilities, and her intuitiveness?

Divine Mother and Divine Father: Yes, let's do that.

E: Thank you. Let's do that. And I know that this is going to connect to the Reptilian we found in the heart but my ultimate goal, Divine Mother and Divine Father is to connect her heart with her mind and her mind with her heart so that she has that full intuitive connection and channel.

Divine Mother and Divine Father: Yes.

E: Okay, great. Thank you. Where else would you like to scan?

Divine Mother and Divine Father: Let's look at the eyes. Something has changed in the eyes.

E: Oh, tell us what is changed in the eyes.

Divine Mother and Divine Father: Looking for any kind of darkness.

E: Would you like any Love-Light sent there to help you see really well now?

Divine Mother and Divine Father: Yes.

E: I'm going to focus Love-Light on each of her eyes now. Looking for any darkness there and let me know if you want any Phoenix Fire over the eyes as well.

Divine Mother and Divine Father: I'm not sensing any darkness or technology.

E: No, I'm not sensing it either. Can we continue healing her eyesight so she can see without glasses?

Divine Mother and Divine Father: Yes. The eyes were doing well but did a little backtrack which appears to be related to the vibration changes. The Love-Light is what was needed.

E: Excellent. Can we check her throat while I continue with Love-Light? Just moving down her body.

Divine Mother and Divine Father: There is some heaviness to the left side of her throat.

E: There seems to be a little muddiness is what I saw but I didn't see . . . remembering we had that wire from the black box going through the throat to the heart, is there any negative energy in there? I think that black wire might still be there. I think Archangel Michael might have wanted that in place until we talked to the Reptilian. Is that what it is do you think?

Divine Mother and Divine Father: That must be what it is.

E: Okay, Divine Mother and Father, can we speak to Archangel Michael now for a moment?

Divine Mother and Divine Father: Yes.

E: Archangel Michael, brother, I am calling you forth. Let me know if you are here.

AA Michael: Greeting. I am here.

E: Greetings. I love you, honor you, and respect you.

AA Michael: And I love you so very much.

E: Thank you. Thank you, I feel that. This interesting set-up we found in her today. We have the Reptilian contained in the shields. You and Metatron did that right away. And you told me to leave the wire in tack even though the black box was removed. What can we do with that wire now? Can we transmute it out or do we need to talk to the Reptilian first?

AA Michael: Let's transmute it out first. It has some control over the Reptilian that we want to remove.

E: All right, shall I Phoenix Fire all the way from the third eye to the heart space?

AA Michael: Please.

E: Sending Phoenix Fire now. Focusing Phoenix Fire there.

AA Michael: And down through the shoulder blade area too.

E: Yes, along the back and front. May I ask the Great Central Sun to come in Archangel Michael, and imbue in this whole area the Golden Central Sun?

AA Michael: Yes, that would be beautiful.

E: Okay, Golden Central Sun, I call forth on my Golden Central Sun to come forth now. I greet you with love, honor and respect. Speaking to the Great Golden Central Sun, Greetings.

Great Golden Central Sun: Greetings.

E: You are such a high vibration. I just love you. Would you please imbue into Debra now? I am Phoenix Firing but I would love to have that Golden authority that you are of Source Light to cover her from her neck all the way down to her rib cage shoulder blades, front and back. Can you please do that for us?

Great Golden Central Sun: Gladly.

E: Thank you. And if you would just stay there while I continue the Phoenix Fire and talk to Archangel Michael?

Great Golden Central Sun: Okay.

E: Thank you. Archangel Michael, how does that look now? I'm feeling like the wire is shrinking.

AA Michael: It absolutely is.

E: Can Archangel Raphael, brother, please as we transmute this out of her, will you please attend to her . . . I think it was her left side that was a little sore on her throat and bring your healing rays in there?

AA Raphael: Yes.

E: Thank you. AA Michael, going down her throat too, it is really thick in her throat . . . there it goes, there it goes. Okay. Please let me know when I have it all transmuted out.

AA Michael: Almost.

E: Yup, I'm seeing it. Stubborn. We didn't think it was technology, can you double check on that Michael, please? Connected to technology but not a technology of itself.

AA Michael: Like a conduit.

E: I just want to make sure we don't need to place it in the alchemy symbol for Archons.

AA Michael: No, it is just part of a tool.

E: *Okay. Okay, I'm feeling like it is gone. Can you take a quick look?*

AA Michael: It is gone.

E: *All right, shall we talk to that Reptilian now?*

AA Michael: Yes.

E: *Speaking to the Reptilian in the heart that came in I was told one week ago. Come up, up, up, now. Come up, up, up, we would like to speak to you. Greetings.*

Reptilian: Hi.

E: *Hi. I love you, honor you, and respect you. Can you confirm for us when you came into Debra? Well, I should ask, may I ask you questions?*

Reptilian: Yes, you can.

E: *Okay, when was it that you connected to her heart and to the black box in the third eye with that wire? . . . Can you speak for yourself?*

Reptilian: It feels like when she embraced her son.

E: *I sensed it did come from one of the kids. How long ago was that?*

Reptilian: That would have been this past Monday, three days ago.

E: *Why did you connect to her heart and what is your connection to the black box and the technology?*

Reptilian: There is a lot of history between her and him, her and her firstborn. She was there with her daughter for a well-visit of her elderly uncle who lives in the same area as her son.

E: *That's the daughter, that's the daughter connection that I sensed but you came from her son?*

Reptilian: Yeah.

E: *Why did you come out of her son? Why did you move?*

Reptilian: I'm an opportunist and aware of the shift that is occurring. There has been this friction between her and him for the last couple of decades. A friction that has been stuck. She is starting to figure out why the two of them haven't been able to get on the same page.

E: *Is there anything that you can tell her about putting it all together?*

Reptilian: She's got it. She's got it figured out now. What she is sensing is that it's about perceptions. He is going to be letting this go soon and I'm ready to go.

E: *(Chuckling) You are ready to go. Well, we are happy to help you and I sensed you would be ready to go. I did see that there were three portals linked to you. What mechanism allowed you to infringe in the first place? What is your mechanism to transfer? Can you tell me? How did you get into the son?*

Reptilian: Into the son?

E: *Uh ha.*

Reptilian: Easy. His vibration was easy to get into with all that he deals with. He deals with a lot of people suffering extreme traumatic situations.

E: *And of course, he is not shielded, is he?*

Reptilian: He is not shielded and there is a lot of drama. He is in a place where it calmed down since changing jobs and is more able to be at peace and happier with a feeling that he is being more helpful to people. This is the first time that he has been okay with his mother coming into his place of work and meeting his colleagues.

E: *Oh. What changed? Why?*

Reptilian: It's a different work environment and she was with his sister and the two of them, the brother and sister, are pretty tight. Part of his perspective had to do with the wrongs that his sister experienced with their father molesting her. He has this tight relationship with his sister but hasn't been able to reconcile his relationship with his mother.

E: *But this somehow helped the three of them?*

Reptilian: Yeah. They don't know it yet but it's happening.

E: *Beautiful. Did this, where you are seeing all the light that is happening, is that what has caused you to be able to change your mind about having a different kind of existence?*

Reptilian: I have been hearing about a better way for a while.

E: *Do you have a body anywhere?*

Reptilian: It feels like I do.

E: *Can we connect to that body now? Is it still alive?*

Reptilian: I am not sensing it.

E: *You cannot connect to the body?*

Reptilian: Correct, I'm not connecting.

E: *Do you want us to check with Archangel Michael?*

Reptilian: Yes, I would love the help. Thank you.

E: *Archangel Michael, would you assist us here for a moment? Can you discern or see if this Reptilian has a body or ever had a body?*

AA Michael: Yes, I'm looking. I feel like his consciousness was pulled out of his body. I am not sensing a body.

E: *Thank you for that. Shall we just help him transmute to light then and call on Archangel Azrael?*

AA Michael: Yes. Let's do that.

E: *Okay. Let's do that. Speaking to the Reptilian within Debra, I don't know if you had a name or not.*

Reptilian: I am not sensing a name.

E: *All right, we ask you to spread your light, retracting all hooks, chords, programs, and portals now from Debra's body. Find the light, the light that is within you, and spread that light to all parts of you. We are assisting you with Love-Light here now. Let me know when you are all light. It is time for you to be free no longer having to play this parasitic role, being your own sovereign being. We are helping you spread your light.*

Reptilian: I am light.

E: *Beautiful. Thank you. And if you will come up and out, let me know when you are out.*

Reptilian: I am out.

E: *Archangel Azrael, Archangel Azrael, Archangel Azrael, greetings brother.*

AA Azrael: Greetings.

E: *Will you please take this lovely positively polarized Reptilian now, upon your Ray, to his next evolutionary experience with love?*

AA Azrael: With honor.

E: *Thank you, Archangel Azrael. We wish you a beautiful life from here on out brother Reptilian. Thank you for assisting us in the knowledge you brought forth for Debra and her family's healing today. Thank you.*

Positively Polarized Reptilian: Thank you.

E: *Do you have any last message for her?*

Positively Polarized Reptilian: Thank you for allowing me to bridge out this way.

E: *Wonderful. Thank you, brother. Thank you, Azrael. Please take him away now. Archangel Michael, can we deeply scan the heart now? Those three portals, you closed earlier. Are there any hooks, chords, or anything else we need to transmute out from this Reptilian?*

AA Michael: It looks clean. He did a good job cleaning up after himself pulling everything out.

E: *Michael, were you able to discern who activated something that would be dangerous to Debra and implanted in the brain and connected to this Reptilian, or is that a Divine Mother and Divine Father thing to ask? It is like it was attached to him. I'm wondering if it was something he had to drag around with him for some reason.*

AA Michael: It's amazing how he was able to get through her shields. She did surround herself with the alchemy symbols.

E: *Ah, when she met the kids, yeah.*

AA Michael: Before she left her space for that day.

E: *What can you tell us? So Haniel, can we speak to Haniel then?*

AA Michael: Yes.

E: *Greeting Haniel.*

AA Haniel: Greetings.

E: *So she put herself in the consciousness cube before she went to be with her kids and she does this a lot. How did this guy get in with this dangerous technology into her? Haniel, I know you know all things about Debra and her whole life.*

AA Haniel: Yes. As much as she lets go of her kids, she doesn't. That embrace from her son felt genuine.

E: *So that wasn't really harmful, the embrace was not?*

AA Haniel: No, but it was her giving consent.

E: *Oh, is this a time for her to know . . .*

AA Haniel: It created a loophole in giving consent when at that moment she felt her love for her son.

E: *Can we make that so that doesn't occur again?*

AA Haniel: Yes. She has been adding it to her personal shields to not consent to family triggers or black magic to come in but her wording needs help. It is part of what she is learning right now. It is part of her gift to the collective on how easy it is to have this black magic enter. She needs to be more specific with the wording of her personal shields. She should literally say, I do not consent to intentional or unintentional black magic or religious prayers on my behalf because I am sovereign, and only infinite love.

E: *Because it's in the family line, I see.*

AA Haniel: These are lessons for her to learn toward her gifts of the future and what she will be adding to the collective. This infringement was allowed knowing that she was going to learn this quickly.

E: *That was pretty quick, wasn't it? Really quick. I mean it was really a fast turnaround. So Haniel, can you say again for her so she knows how to craft her shields so she does not consent?*

AA Haniel: The personal shields are critical and something that we need to remind the collective of. Before attending last month's AURA practitioner's reunion, she didn't realize the need for or have personal shields. The broader shields are critical and powerful protection tools. The reason we are emphasizing personal shields is that many are not using them. Your personal shields are personal to you and your situation, your own cell recovery, your traumas, and your memories. The wording would be, my organic. I do not consent to any organic or inorganic that is not of my original divine soul blueprint.

E: *Beautiful. Okay. And she would be saying that as she is crafting her personal shields?*

AA Haniel: Correct.

E: And you told me, I think it was you when I was doing the RAAH, that she did need to work on her personal shields and that you wanted her to make them reflective, mirrored reflective. So with the idea that anything that tries to come in is bounced off like it can't penetrate. This would include anything that is not of her organic divine soul blueprint would be bounced off, and reflected right back to them.

AA Haniel: Correct.

E: Okay, that is a huge learning piece for everyone, I think. I mean I know we do that with the broader shields but to do that with the personal shields really amps up their power quite a lot. Thank you Haniel. Thank you, thank you, thank you.

AA Haniel: Thank you.

E: Is there anything else she needs to know about that right now?

AA Haniel: Keep listening. We are giving her tips. Keep listening. The addition that you brought in yesterday, you brought in months ago but forgot about. Now remembering and re-adding the Dragon shields, stay with that. They are part of who you are. Remember the Fire Dragon, the Earth Dragon, the Water Dragon, the Air Dragon, the Ether Dragon, the Star Dragons, and the Dragons of Love. Remember them each and make them a part of you and your personal shields. Use those energies.

E: Beautiful. That just gives me goosebumps all over Haniel. That is just magnificent. Wow. So she is really related to the Elemental Dragons and the Elements, of course through you, of course. Yes. Okay. Divine Mother and Divine Father, can we continue scanning now. Archangel Raphael brother, would you please bring your healing into her heart space now, where the Reptilian was, and heal all that? Working still with the Great Central Sun.

AA Raphael: My pleasure.

E: Thank you. Divine Mother and Divine Father, I think we are now at the solar plexus.

Divine Mother and Divine Father: Yes.

E: I got to the solar plexus and the pancreas area and Archangel Metatron told me there were thirty-seven little nanotech bots. They weren't really active but they were in her. And then there were two more in the spine that we transmuted out with the alchemy symbol for Archons because he said they didn't have consciousness. Can we just go ahead and deep scan now of her solar plexus, pancreas, and that spine area, making sure . . . oh, I'm sorry, I miss spoke. There is a fractal of consciousness in her pancreas. That is separate from the nanotech that was removed.

Divine Mother and Divine Father: A fractal of consciousness, from?

E: I'm not sure where it came from. It is very faint, Divine Mother. A fractal of consciousness in her pancreas.

Divine Mother: I don't see anything but I'm sensing earthbound.

E: Earthbound. All right. Can we place that in the consciousness cube, please?

Divine Mother: Yes.

E: Thank you. Is there enough of it left to talk to?

Divine Mother: I don't think so but it needs to find the rest of it where it belongs.

E: Okay. Who can help with that? Can we have an Archangel help with that?

Divine Mother: Join with its whole, it needs to find where it is fractured off from.

E: Yeah. Archangel Michael, can you collect this fractal, well you Divine Father as Michael and Haylel, will you please lovingly collect this fractal of consciousness and see if you can return it home?

AAs Michael and Haylel: Yes.

E: Thank you. Let me know when you have it.

AAs Michael and Haylel: We have it.

E: Beautiful. Thank you, thank you. Archangel Raphael, please bring your healing Rays into her solar plexus now. Divine Mother and Divine Father, she has been in a while, there were two Reptilians that seemed to be shadowy, maybe inert, maybe imprints and not actually Reptilians, in her sacral area again, not on the ovaries but one on one side and the other on the other side. What is that? What was I sensing there?

Divine Mother and Divine Father: They were there during our last session a few weeks ago and positively polarized out.

E: Yeah, that is what I wondered. How can they leave an imprint behind? Is that an energetic signature? Did we not clean up enough or did she hold some residue, was there some residue in her feeling divine and sovereign that is holding an imprint?

Divine Mother and Divine Father: She has been chanting, "I Am in my Divine Sovereignty."

E: So maybe not her? I am just curious as to what would hold an imprint or a shadow in there. Or do we need to know? Should I just Phoenix Fire or Love-Light that area?

Divine Mother and Divine Father: It would be good to know. This will be part of her experience to learn from and we will transmute it now. We can Phoenix Fire it out.

E: Okay, I would ask that when she does know, can she please share it with me in case this happens again, not with her (chuckling)?

Divine Mother and Divine Father: Absolutely.

E: Okay, I'm Phoenix Firing the imprints, the shadows out now, focusing on the right side first. Going into the tissues with the Phoenix Fire and calling forth on the Great Central Golden Sun to move down into the sacral area please, requiring your assistance now in the sacral area.

Great Central Golden Sun: Yes.

E: Thank you. Oh yes, thank you, that is very helpful. Okay, so I have got the right side healing that tissue. It is like they imbued . . . no, is this black magic? Yes. All right, so those things had done some black magic and they penetrated divine organic soul blueprints. I want to erase this from her divine organic soul blueprint, Haniel. Calling forth on Archangel Haniel. Greetings, sister.

AA Haniel: Yes. Greetings.

E: I sense that if we remove this from her organic divine soul blueprint, she is going to be removed from all black magic infiltration from this point forward. Is that true?

AA Haniel: Yes, and she has included that in her personal shields.

E: All right, let's do that now. Let's just make this the final mop up so to speak, final clearing. And Haniel if you can confirm for me that this will be the final clearing of black magic from her?

AA Haniel: Yes. Her vibration is raising.

E: Good. So keep her vibes up. I'm moving the Phoenix Fire to the left side. And with the Higher Self's permission and with the Higher Self's assistance now, re-coding her organic divine soul blueprint pre-black magic into her physical vessel, her blood, her bones, her hair, skin, and nails, and all in between, all organs, tissues, muscles, sinews, fluids, and into her emotional field, her mental field, her auric field, her crystalline energetics as well, and finally into the DNA. Haniel, let me know when the re-coding is complete. I'm just focusing Love-Light on her now.

AA Haniel: The re-coding is complete.

E: Thank you. Wow, that is beautiful.

AA Haniel: Spot on, spot on.

E: She is going to be able to hold such a high vibration now, watch out. She is going to lift off that back deck of her home. (both chuckling). That is beautiful. I may have jumped ahead a little bit, I am asking Divine Mother and Divine Father to please locate and do a deep scan now to confirm that we have cleared her vessel of earthbound spirits, A.I. with consciousness, Archons, Reptilian consciousness, black ink, other negative polarized aliens and entities. I didn't see anything else but just confirming with you, Mother and Father.

Divine Mother and Divine Father: I not seeing anything or any more of the nanites either.

E: Beautiful. Oh good, is the spine healed?

Divine Mother and Divine Father: Yes, it looks good and healthy.

E: Beautiful. Can we close all dark portals, including those on her land and homes, the Manti land, and this home? Plus there were portals within her that Michael closed. Just confirming that those are all closed.

Divine Mother and Divine Father: Yes. They are all closed.

E: Confirming that her DNA is perfectly her DNA, that there are no integrated false negative fractals or integrated false negative fractals in her?

Divine Mother and Divine Father: No false fractals.

E: *Thank you. And I do see that Archangel Zadkiel's symbol, that beautiful netting did a lot of work for us here. Thank you, Archangel Zadkiel, for that beautiful alchemy symbol. Scanning for negative chords, negative implants, hooks, organic matter that has been integrated with technology, negative technology, or any other wires.*

Divine Mother and Divine Father: Feels clean.

E: *Beautiful. And continued recovery of her vision and any other health requests that she has. Could we ask now to have all of her chakras aligned, opened, and synchronized with each other? That root chakra was a little unstable. She was a little fearful of what might be revealed in this session, I was told which turned out to be really a beautiful session. Nothing scary here at all. So just making sure that the root chakra is clean and good and spinning correctly. And we have recovered all fractured fractals of her soul. Does she have any outstanding contracts or any other contracts that can be deleted or torn up at this time Archangel Michael?*

AA Michael: No.

E: *Beautiful. Are there any inverted timelines imposed upon her?*

AA Michael: No.

E: *Continuing, and asking Archangels Raphael and Haniel to help heal trauma from her current life and past lives.*

AAs Raphael and Haniel: Yes.

E: *Beautiful. Is there anything else that I should have asked for that I have not asked for?*

AA Haniel: No. This has been very thorough and very beautiful.

E: *Yes. She is. There are a couple of things we want to know, Divine Mother and Divine Father before we bring her back. We previously removed two thousand Reptilians, which were wormy things, during the AURA Practitioners Reunion, AURA session. We found out at the reunion that they were related to the vaccine. And so her question was, is that where her's came from, and does she have to be cognizant of that now because she is surrounded by a lot of people who are vaccinated? What can you help us with here?*

Divine Mother and Divine Father: It is related and the new symbols and amour are taking care of that. There should be no opportunity for that to happen again. We emphasize personal shields, personal shields, personal shields, galactic shields, and chakra alchemy, morning and night.

E: Oh that is beautiful. And the Dragon shields, the Elemental Dragon Shields.

Divine Mother and Divine Father: Yes, the Dragon shields she will consider her personal shields. Yes, shields, shields, and more shields.

E: That is for all of us, right?

Divine Mother and Divine Father: Yes. And remember to have our crystals around us. Crystals raise our vibration frequency.

E: Yes. Which crystals are of our highest good at this time and space?

Divine Mother and Divine Father: The amethyst and the quartz, the ones that are plentiful.

E: Okay, and the andaras?

Divine Mother and Divine Father: Yes, and the andaras. Whatever feels good to you or that you feel drawn to; follow your heart. There are no absolutes. Don't go into the dogmas. Go with your heart, Go with your heart. That is why it is hard to single out a crystal type because of the potential to bypass your intentions and your loving heart in whatever it is that you're doing.

E: Well, because they are all beautiful.

Divine Mother and Divine Father: Yes. They are all beautiful and they each have their job to do and you are different today than you were yesterday. It's best to follow your heart where you are at in this time and space, as well as listen and sense from the crystals, making yourself available for what gifts you are called on to use for that day. When following your heart it is not always about you personally, it might be about your mission in the collective and what is going on at that moment in the bigger picture. Flow with it.

E: Thank you. And we do shield with the Infinity of Crystals, magnificent shield too. So we put crystals in there. She was concerned about our group taking things away from Mt. Shasta and our not leaving something in return. Divine Mother and Father, and all the beauties who assisted us today, I know Debra and I, in our hearts and our Higher Selves, would like to go now to Mt. Shasta with love. Just love, our love, and our gratitude. I can't really give a physical thing right now to Mt. Shasta but I can give a hug to Mt. Shasta and kisses, like cover the mountain in kisses. Can we do that and atone perhaps?

Divine Mother and Divine Father: That is such a beautiful solution.

E: Okay, will you go with us now while we do that? Let's take a moment now and everybody go – just seeing that beautiful mountain before us, the meadows and beautiful crystal-clear water flowing down the mountainside. I am just making myself as big as possible, big, big, big. And I'm seeing all the Archangels are with me and we are holding hands and we are just going to hug Mt. Shasta. There's Debra. We are just going to hug this beautiful mountain up, up, up, to the top, down, down, down to the bottom, and all around and underneath to the pyramid underneath. With all due respect beautiful AdaRa (An Elder of Inner Earth), we love this and intend no trespassing. We are just leaving our love signatures here and our deep gratitude for the gifts that Mt. Shasta gave to us and that you did, AdaRa. We love you, honor you, and respect you and all our brethren of the Inner Earth. Now I'm going to kiss Mt. Shasta all over (making kissing sounds).

Divine Mother and Divine Father: Beautiful, beautiful, beautiful. Thank you, thank you, thank you. Well done, well done.

E: I feel better. I feel better. Thank you. Our love to AdaRa and our brethren within. Thank you. I would like with the Higher Self's permission, Archangel Haniel, I would like to remove any blocks that Debra is ready to remove now concerning religious programming and training and indoctrinations. And I would like with your permission to remove the block that she is denied to know too much if she is ready to have that block removed.

AA Haniel: Yes. It is time.

E: Thank you Haniel, and you will do that for her?

AA Haniel: Yes. She'll be doing that with her writing. It'll dissolve away each day more and more.

E: *Thank you. Along with that, she mentioned her journey has been a struggle, and her struggle is what helps her to be able to tell this story. Haniel, can you modify that so that she is not physically harmed or emotionally harmed so that there is no trauma?*

AA Haniel: The struggle is a past struggle and revisiting those struggles with the now perspective of neutrality is more of a letting go and healing those experiences.

E: *Oh that is beautiful then. I just wanted to make sure that . . .*

AA Haniel: There is no further pain associated with it. There is no additional drama, rather it is sharing that moment through her eyes to bring those to the surface for the teaching of others and healing of the collective.

E: *Oh that is beautiful, through the eyes of the moment. May we have the intention to ripple that healing out to the collective now? You know there is no time like now?*

AA Haniel: You are so wise once again. Let's do it.

E: *Let's do it. Seeing her story complete and rippling out and healing the collective now. Now. Now. Now.*

AA Haniel: Beautiful.

E: *And Haniel, she will be visiting lands to heal. We heard in the channeling at the private Mt. Shasta reunion retreat, that we are to seek out lands needing to be healed. True for her and perhaps some of the AURA practitioners.*

AA Haniel: Yes.

E: *Okay. I know you will guide her and bless her on her way.*

AA Haniel: Yes, I will.

E: *And Divine Mother and Divine Father, can we clear trauma from her oldest two children now or from as many of her children as we can? Can we clear sexual abuse trauma, can we clear trauma from black magic? Can we clear falsehoods so they can all get to know each other as they really are and not these fictions that they thought they were? These fictions that are this illusion. Are we able to clear that for Debra and her family now? Bring healing, to bring some healing into them.*

Divine Mother and Divine Father: No. They need to go through their own journey. That isn't something you can give.

E: *That's not something you can jump past? They have to experience it?*

Divine Mother and Divine Father: They will empower themselves by going through it. They will be getting pieces along the way. We are giving them nuggets of truth here and there to ponder if they so choose. We can't cross those boundaries.

E: *I understand. Thank you. I get exuberant. Is there any trauma that we can heal for the children considering her most recent meeting with her oldest?*

Divine Mother and Divine Father: There was no trauma there. There was only love.

E: *I guess that is what I should have asked. Okay. Good. Taking one last look, Divine Mother and Divine Father, are we complete with her AURA today?*

Divine Mother and Divine Father: It is complete. Thank you.

E: *Thank you, beautiful one. Talking to the Great Central Golden Sun, the Great Central Golden Sun, how are you doing? Are you complete with your healing of Debra now?*

Great Golden Central Sun: It is complete.

E: *Thank you, thank you, thank you. Please come on up and out. Beautiful. And Archangel Haniel, are we complete with her first step into her ancestry, her knowingness, and connecting?*

AA Haniel: Yes. That was pretty sweet, thank you.

E: *Thank you. Thank the both of you.*

AA Haniel: You are extremely patient, tender, gentle, and loving. You are wonderful.

E: *Oh, thank you. Well, she brings out the best in me as do you. I am eternally grateful for your presence Archangel Haniel and for Debra as well. So are we ready to bring her back now? Okay, let's do that. It is with love and gratitude I now ask for the aid of the Higher Self, Archangel Haniel, we are thankful for all that you did for Debra today. I ask now that all the energies we spoke to today return back to where they belong. We give thanks for all the aid we were given today. I'm giving thanks to Divine Mother, Divine Fa-*

ther, the Great Central Suns, Archangels Michael, Haylel, Jophiel, Metatron, Uriel, Raphael, and Zadkiel, to all the beauties that assisted us today, I love you, honor you, and respect you. Remember that what was shown today from the past exists in the past or anywhere else that we visited today and we will leave it there for your highest healing Debra. As Debra listens to the recording she will continue to receive additional healing for her highest good and she will understand the importance of listening to this recording as soon as she is ready. It will comfort her mentally, physically, emotionally, and spiritually.

The client is brought out.

I'm calling this my dream session because this life hit each of my wish list items of living in harmony with nature, our magical companions, and one another. And how about that end-of-life transition? "It's all of a sudden you are so much bigger, so much grander, so much happier, so much more full of love. So much more, more, more, more, more. It's amazing. It's just ahhhhhhhhhh!" Wow!

And the big takeaway from the infringements uncovered in this session is shield, shield, shield. Before the August retreat six weeks earlier, I hadn't figured out how to do my personal shields. I was doing my basic shields of Love-Light, the chakras, and the Archangels, but I hadn't personalized my shields. They weren't a part of who I am. They weren't my words. The need to be even more strategic with my words is evidently needed as revealed in this session. Something I have struggled with is keeping my vibration consistent which feels related.

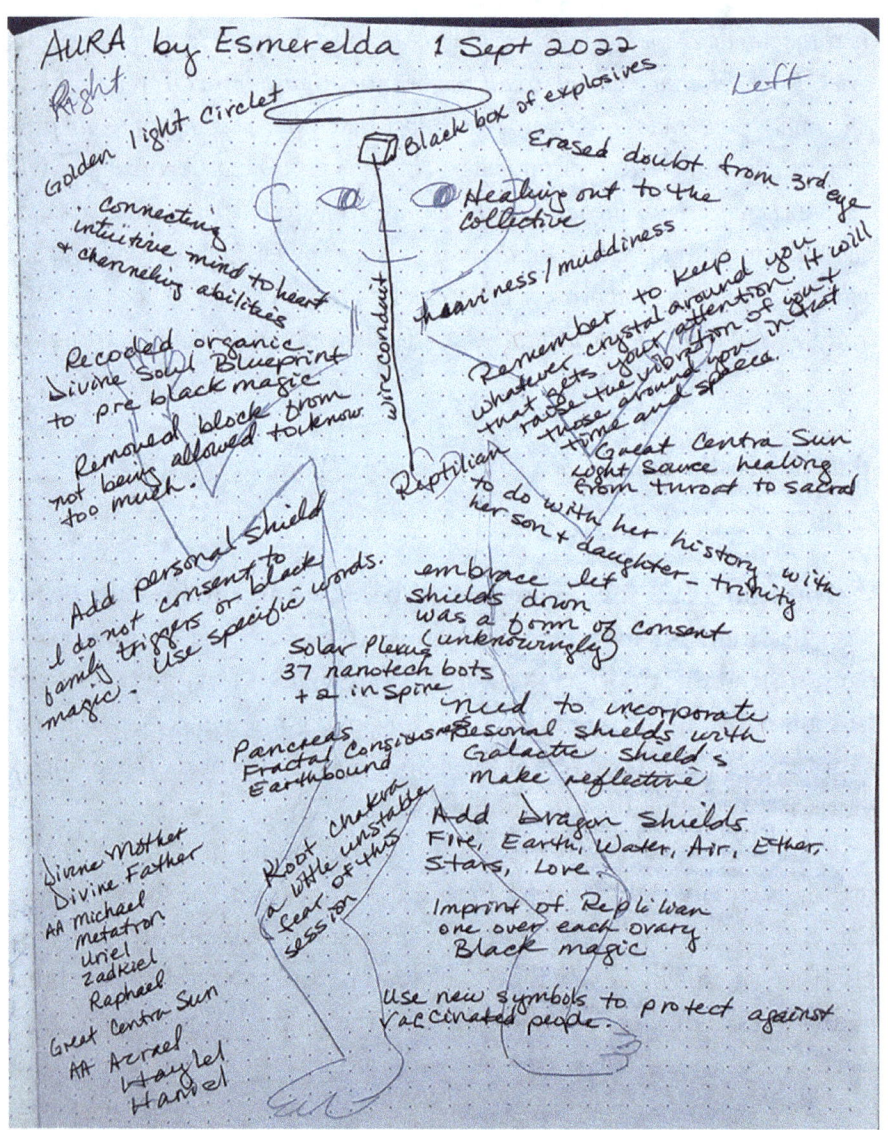

11

Argentina: Being of One Heart

November 11, 2022 (11/22/11 Portal)

*"Imagine. Imagine that a voice calls you to be reborn
To resound in melodies not yet written to the rhythm of a new time
Its music manifests connecting you to the Earth. My body feels
the sound of a new idea that beautifies all existence in this world
I intend to walk from south to north from my center
I imagine my future. I create my present and resignify my past.
It won't be easy but I will find my axis
I will light the colors of my being becoming wise loving and responsible
Resonating and radiating I shall see what we are children of the Earth, a song of life, a network of consciousness
Imagine. Imagine that your dreams originate the ideas for this world
That our gazes recognize each other toward infinity
We are the musicians of this great Cosmic symphony resounding in existence. Imagine our eternal reencounter to the rhythm of the heart
Where our intentions manifest and the essence becomes action
Falling in love with everything that will be creators of a new reality
And so recognize that we are beings of the I Am. Imagine. Imagine with me*

what we will be. We are the origin of life, living memory of all those who will come. We are the spark that ignites the potential of all action that transforms the world. We are the pillars of the Earth, paths that come together in a single nation of humanity. We are the voices that speak to the world inspiration of consciousness
Imagine manifesting the network of the world here and now
It is time to live the dream, to remember that I Am"
– Matias de Stefano
11-11-2022/ Beginning of a New Path YO SOY (I Am)

Matias de Stefano claims that from the time he was a little boy, he started remembering who he was. His story and teachings are of how to actively rise out of the darkness.

Via social media, Matias put out a call for the need of thousands of people from all over the world to meet him in a remote town in Argentina. Directing people to his website it reads, "This November 11, 2022, will be 11 years since our first 11.11 Gathering, concluding this way the trinity of our gatherings that mark the beginning of our social mission: Ontocracy. For that, in this Third Great Gathering, we bring the wisdom of the ancient world to speak to the new one that we will build together. Third 11:11 Gathering, Beginning of a New YOSOY (I AM) Path."

As soon as I learned of the gathering, I knew in my heart that I needed to find a way to be there. As I write this, it has been just over a week since I returned home. I'm still processing and integrating my experiences. Words fall short when describing such deeply felt emotions. What an honor it was to be part of and a witness to this unprecedented global and Galactic moment in time and space. My travel companion was Sheree, who is certified as an AURA hypnosis practitioner and a dear friend. We would look at each other with water-filled eyes, expressing our gratitude to each other for making this experience possible. At sixty-five years old, this trip was my first opportunity to use my passport. It was simply a phenomenal event.

Everyone participating in this event agreed to quarantine themselves forty days prior and throughout the event from meat, alcohol, drugs, and smoking. Imagine organizing a complicated out-of-this-world task requiring thousands of people from all walks of life, all ages, and from all over the world with multiple cultures and languages to come together at their own expense as a cohesive focused body of unconditional love. Before the event, Matias explained over social media that this date of 11/11 lands on Indigenous Peoples Day.

Our histories are filled with traumas on this day that we are transmuting and birthing into love. With so much energy from so many different directions remembering this day, a portal is created. A portal we would use to anchor Egypt's alignment with Argentina. How would you do such a thing? Yo Soy did just that. Few in attendance had chairs or were fully comfortable. Still, each wore a smile and kindly embraced each other as the precious beings that we are. On day one of the initial greetings by Matias, he expressed his gratitude that each of us was there and that he learned that many of us had a difficult time getting to his small village of airports located hours away. He channeled that it hadn't gone unnoticed. He also added that the location was literally a mirror representation of the lands and rivers of Egypt (Refer to the next page of the mural painting). If I had do-overs, I'd leap at the opportunity to do it all over again. To be all-in with all the emotional, physical, spiritual, exhaustive hardships and overwhelming sacred energies and magical miracles, surrounded above, below, and all around by unconditional love, is something we literally lived. How amazing is that?

November 11, 2022, Yo Soy 2022 event, Pueblo Encanto, Capilla Del Monte, Argentina. Below is the mural painted on the stage during the event depicting a mirror image of Egypt and Argentina.

Each morning Indigenous Elders led us in honoring the Sacred Four Directions along with additional teachings, more singing, and even more dancing. My group of twenty-two represented the Atlantean letter CH which means change as in death and rebirth. As a group, we were also representing the physical element of Fire. Individually we represented a location around the world. I represented Norfolk Island; a tiny island located in the South Pacific Ocean within the Australian boundaries. Each day after the morning shaman alignments was the mid-morning group teaching activities which were followed by open time activities led by many of the attendees. The unique group activities were well thought through and led to the next part of our alignment.

I think my favorite open activity was gathering with all these people from all over the world, hearing their stories, and learning something uplifting together. The energy was incredible. Then by late afternoon Matias provided additional teachings along with more channeling, singing, and dancing.

The teachings progressed in complexity and the way we interacted with the other elements leading up to 11.11. In fact, it was so complex that I learned to just flow with it. Using my voice like this was something new for me. While singing mantras with the crowd or singing our symbols within the group, something changed. I kept hearing my coordinator say, "This isn't a concert for you to watch, rather it requires each of our voices, each of our intents, and each of our energies." He was right. To go into this with our whole heart, body, mind, and soul, was amazing.

My greatest takeaway was fully living in the moment within my heart and with unconditional love with the intention of impacting the whole. Each one of us has a role to play. It was a taste of becoming one while remaining an individual. I was one purposeful cell of the body.

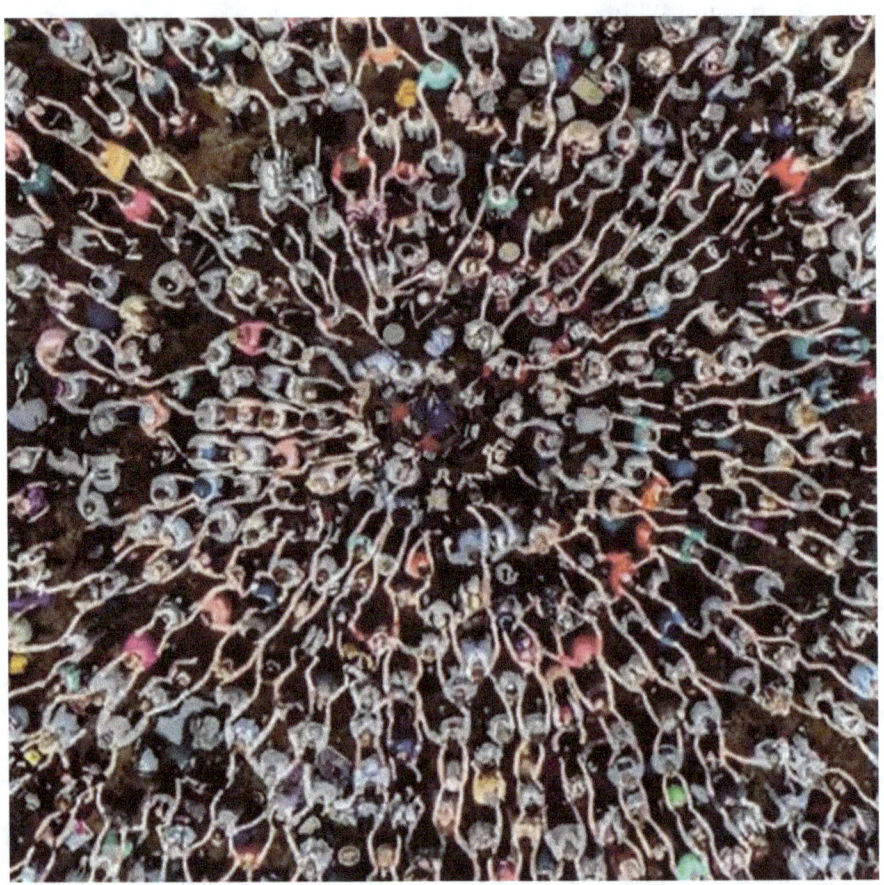

For the culminating activity pictured above, Matias explained that "Like a tiny acupuncture needle is used to unblock a system within the human body, our intentions, movements, and song manifest a network of consciousness creating a portal to the center of Earth. We are the origin of life, a living memory of all those who are to come. We are the spark that ignites the potential of all action that transforms the world." Magically, once all the individual cells of this huge body took their position, the powerful spark simply exploded.

Pictured above and to the right: The Earth has 32 energetic/ geometric nodes that come out of the juxtaposition of the sacred figures of the dodecahedron and the icosahedron over the Earth's Globe. All of them together, combined, make up the energetic structure of the Earth's network (That we, as a whole, re-activated on November 11). This is all a follow-up to the task we have been doing since the previous event in Egypt, on February 22, 2022 (22/ 2/22). At an individual level, we also had the task for each one of us, and that's the one of becoming and incarnating our node. (www.yosoy.red)

Each member of the water groups and fire groups collected a small rock from their home and kept it on their person during the 60-day quarantine for water and 40-day quarantine for fire and deposited it here at the eternal spring located at the Hall of Mirrors Dome.

Additionally, we were each gifted with a variety of flower seeds to take to our prospective homes to sow. So not only did the small pond located on these grounds contain a stone from each of our homes around the world, but we each have Argentina seedlings to spread throughout the world.

Pictured to the left is the Hall of Mirrors Dome. Eagles could be seen circling the camp during the singing and channeling. Often there would be five or six eagles circling us. Inside the dome is pitch black. The ceiling is composed of triangle shaped mirrors angled similar to what you would expect to see within an icosahedron except rather than 20 sides there were thousands. About 100 people fit inside the dome sitting on the floor. My group was scheduled for a Wednesday, November 9, 2:00 a.m. visit inside the Hall of Mirrors for a one-hour activation. Once inside and seated, and after the attunement by Matias, we sang and then went into meditation. The meditation was pitch black and totally silent. It was magical!

This crystal labyrinth located at Cerro Uritorco Encanto Capilla Del Monte Pueblo, Argentina, has a path created out of boulders of quartz and other crystals of varying sizes. Several are as large as four feet by four feet with the center crystal six or seven feet by six or seven feet.

The energy walking to and from this center point vibrated my entire being.

Above is a photo taken on November 14, 2022, three days after thousands of us spent five days in this same area sitting, dancing, and roaming on hard bare ground. Again, simply magical.

Taken during the 11/22/11 event in Argentina, what is your heart telling you about this image? It feels pretty high vibrational to me. Don't you just love this stuff?

12

Priestess of Hathor

Wendie Channeling Nefertiti Facilitated by Paige
January 10, 2023

Paige and I were chatting online working through some technical obstacles she was having with singing bowls not being heard during online Zoom AURA hypnosis sessions or the recordings. Having that issue solved Paige shared what her group is about and invited me to attend. Wendie and Paige are AURA practitioners who created what they refer to as a Soul Tribe Group of like-minded light workers, several of whom are also AURA Practitioners. They created a safe place to share and assist one another through their week. When I attended there were about six people.

One of their objectives is to meet over Zoom each Monday to assist any who have requested various healings. These healings are advertised by word of mouth, and over social media, and are open to requests. The group takes these requests and lovingly pools their energy together with targeted healing energy after which they share the recording of that healing with the requestor, who if not part of the group, wouldn't have been present.

All who attend the Zoom meeting are required to be within their sacred alchemy shields and of the highest vibration of unconditional love. There, Wendie channels the information while Paige facilitates it. Interestingly many members of the Soul Tribe Group discovered they had past lives together and in one way or another a connection to Nefertiti.

The group decided to gather their Nefertiti-related stories for a book (In progress). I soon fell in love with the group and after lengthy conversations with my Higher Self and learning that I indeed had a past life connected to Nefertiti, I volunteered for a reading. That reading resulted in the following session which is also planned to be included in Wendie and Paige's forthcoming book.

Facilitator: Paige, Channel: Wendie

"P [Paige]: Can we go up into Debra's Soul Star and see her past life in Egypt?

W [Wendie channeling Nefertiti]: I'm going up into her Soul Star now. She is choosing to take me up on an escalator. (Laughing) She's giggling. This is her preferred method of transportation.

D [Debra]: (Laughing) Mine too.

P: That's Debra's Higher Self giggling?

W: Yeah. She is like, why take the stairs when there is an escalator? She said there are many things to spend energy on and travel shouldn't be one of them. We are going up. Rising up, up, up. Okay. Her star doesn't look like just a glowing star. Normally, I see what looks like light on the outside but hers looks like a nebula. And it is different colors. It's alive. This nebula is alive and the energy that is moving around and through this nebula is almost . . . each little thought of consciousness, the way it connects to the others, creates a certain color. It is mostly like . . . I see shades of pinks and purples and blues and silvers and whites, but is very loving and healing . . . these connections that all this consciousness has together. And its interactions with each other is creating these strings of . . . mmm, it's energetic and it just glows. It is almost like you would see a brain lighting up where messages go from one to another but this is gorgeous. Thank you for showing me that. I'm going inside now. So it feels like a push of wind that picked us up and brought us to the center and she said ride the wind like with your Dragon, ride the wind, there is something there. Okay. Wind Dragon, here we go. Yes. So this Wind Dragon says, his name is Sire.

P: *What kind of a Dragon is he?*

W: Wind.

P: *Oh, I should have known. What kind of crystal does he hold?*

W: It looks like a hematite but it has a different . . . there is something else in it. There are little flecks of green. It's what looks to be hematite. It is very shiny and you can see your reflection in it. There are little flecks of green, a light green. Oh, okay. So this stone holds certain frequencies. He is saying it is very magnetic . . . okay, he is saying this goes along with what was spoken of earlier. Hematite is a nice combination of dark and light. It transmutes, it's reflective yet it absorbs. It is just this perfect stone. He is showing me that it is not this way. It is not too much dark and not too much light. It is wonderful for transmuting and the green represents the heart energy. In between the two, light and dark, transmuting the dark into the light, bringing the light, grabbing the light, bringing it into the dark, bringing the dark into the light, it is this constant transmutation. It is based in the heart frequency so this is like a neutral stone and then the heart frequency is added to it. He is showing me that it is right down the center; an infinity symbol with a line right down the center. He is saying this is Creation Point. Right there in the middle. And again, I'll draw this diagram out if I need to but it's like a figure 8 on its side with a line right down the center and the Creation Point is right in the middle. And again, there is the masculine which is the line, and the feminine which is the infinity symbol, the 8 on its side. It's the

Center Point. Thank you for sharing all of that with us. Is there something that you would like to show us here? It looks like he has a tiger head. Hm mm. Okay. Can you take me to her tree? He is taking me to a room in the back where she works with water and stones. She has big carved-out stones filled with water like a rock. In these rocks, I see smaller stones, little gems. She is saying something about using these stones when her energetic body comes up to her Soul Star. She uses these stones that are programmed with certain frequencies on the energetic body to heal certain parts. There are different colored stones on different body parts. It looks like a red stone on the wrist to do something here, or like a red-brown, anyway, there are different colored stones to stimulate certain energy points in the energetic body. If your kidneys are low function then they put certain stones where your kidneys would be. If your heart is low on energy, they use certain stones. There is the amethyst, beautiful amethyst. It looks like it goes on the forehead. Then there are stones from other places that I have never seen. There is one that is glowing like green and purple. They say that one is for healing. Okay. So she can come up to this place and she does come to this place, her energetic body comes to this place when she is asleep. Yes. Yes. Can you show me where she lays when you do this? Okay, he is taking me underneath the tree. Underneath the tree is what looks like a crystal, almost seleniteish, or what they call a tabby stone. She is laying on that and the energy flows. As your selenite, instead of it going this way (Horizontal), with the shards going this direction, these selenite shards go this way (Motioning up vertically). So you can see through it. It is very pretty. All the lines line up going the same way. It is very smooth. And sometimes she puts stones underneath. That Dragon is silly. Okay, the Dragon is going underneath and working with energies. It is over there dancing. He is cute.

D: *What color is he?*

W: He looks like your typical blue-belly, that color of a blue-belly lizard. That bright turquoise sort of electric blue. I don't know how else to describe it. He has those colors on him. His breast is a nice green and then it goes up to what looks like a Tiger's face. He is very beautiful. Okay, why are you showing me a form with a tiger face? What does she need to know? There is something about Tiger energy that you carry. She's saying bold and regal. And you both share that. That energy and if you don't feel that energy, you need to remember who you are because you are bold and regal. You don't need to tell anybody, you just are. You don't need to talk about it, you just are. And when you walk into a room people notice. They feel the energy shift. You are truly you. They said you are a wonderful expression. They like how you are carrying yourself. Can you show me the tree now? There's the tree. There are magnolias. There is something about the scent of the magnolias and magnolias that are special to you. It looks . . . okay, yeah, that just lit me up. The Dragon just pulled off one of the petals of the magnolias and caught water, some rain in it, and passed it to me. I'm supposed to sip it. What a beautiful gift. Thank you. It's nectar. She is saying you choose lives and times that are parched of positive emotion and this nectar is the sweetness in life that you come back to. You replenish, you get your drink, you fill up and you are ready to go back in. You swim like a Dolphin. Jumping up getting the nectar and going back under. And then you go back to the planet and you live your life and you go to sleep and you come back up to your Soul Star and you get your stone healing from all over. Your stones come from all over the place, these stone healing and then you drink the nectar out of this magnolia leaf or this magnolia petal, and then you go back down. It is very nice, very nice. This is beautiful, thank you. What else is in your tree, sweetie? Show me. Okay, behind the tree is a child reading a book. Is this one of your inner child's . . . ? She says she is waiting to be born. She is studying. She's learning. She's paying attention to the others that are coming and going. The other fractals or the other versions of you. She is reading up. She is not born yet. She said she is looking at 2030 when the new world has begun and when the New Earth is setting in. She is going to hold the frequencies of the New Earth. She said it is a lot of work but I am the culmination of all of these lives. When I come in, I'm bringing forth all of these energies, all of these lessons, and everything that I have to offer. And I will be remembering all of my lives and everything I've done and everything I've learned. All of it is going to come together and I am coming down as this being.

D: *As a walk-in or as a newborn?*

W: As a newborn. This is another fractal of you. I can't even say a fractal of you. It is almost as though you are a fractal of her. Like she is going to bring in all of your information and all the other you's that you have been, including the one in Egypt? Yes. Scotland? Yes. Do you have a name? She said her name is Sabine (Sounds like Sabean) S-a-b-i-n-e, is what I am hearing. Like Shavon? Oh, is that Irish? She says that is the closest I can get as the S-i-o-b-h-a-n, or something to that effect. Shavon or Siobhan, it is the same sort of. That's the vibration depending on your language or your dialect. It will be in a different language? Yes. Thank you. Is there a question about her Egyptian life, Paige?

P: *Did Wendie and I know her in our Egyptian lives?*

W: I'm hearing she was in the Temple of Hathor. Yeah, Nefertiti embraced Hathor's energy, that sexual energy. She was a High Priestess of Hathor as well. They utilized the sexual energy's creation energy.

P: *Can you give us an example of how they utilized that energy?*

W: Nefertiti, would you like to let us know this? "Okay. An orgasm doesn't just belong with a man. An orgasm is a sacred energy release." She is showing me, they would build that energy up, build that energy up, and again there is a snake. She is working with that snake, building that energy up and bringing it up. She said when you hold your breath and you are holding that thought, that sexual energy rises up behind you and comes down and then you are holding a specific thought or frequency, when that orgasm happens, it is releasing that energy from this reservoir. She is showing . . . she says there is this elixir reservoir there. An elixir reservoir here as well but that is one way to bring this reservoir up here and release those elixirs into the physical body which then transfers over to the energetic body and you can create with that energy.

P: Would they have to have a man at the time or could they create this energy by themselves?

W: No, she is showing me quite large dildos that were used in like rituals or it was a personal thing, what do you want to create today? What do you want to create today, she is saying. These temples were places for doing that. There were special spots for doing that. They use that sexual energy to do things. Yes. Okay. So were you a Priestess of Hathor as well? Yes. She says she was. Nefertiti? She said, of course. And mastered many arts. Were you Priestesses together? She said, "We worked together in many places and many lives." Great.

P: Can you give us some examples of how both of us work together?

W: It looks like a blue stone that we are using together and there is a bowl. And there is . . . I think it's Lapis or there is a blue stone all around this bowl and they are putting these blue lotus flowers in it and they are putting energy into it. I can see this action, like that over the bowl. This particular herb that they using does something that stimulates this elixir and this elixir as well so that energy, they can grab hold of it. Grab hold of the elixirs that are the least . . . okay. It is a stimulant and it stimulates certain portions and certain centers. Yes, I feel that.

P: What was it made out of?

W: Blue lotus flowers. They are showing me an ox, some kind of ox down in the Nile waters. What are you showing me this for, please? Okay, zooming in, oh, I'm not sure what that means but Nefertiti said, "The land of milk and honey; the land of milk and honey. You think we were primitive. We were not. It was very luxurious."

P: What does it look like? Does she mean by the land of milk and honey that there were so many herbs and so much to be grown there?

W: Yeah, it was very lush and they used honey, they used milk, and it was very lush. Not just lush plant-wise, but they had a lush life. It was beautiful. She said, "We had a wonderful empire."

P: *What happened to it? Why did it go to desert?*

W: War and the darkness was stomping out the light domestically.

P: *What was Debra's name in that lifetime?*

W: Skadaharisk. She's wearing white. What is your name dear? I'm hearing Tarune (Phonetic spelling).

P: *How do you spell that?*

W: How would you spell that? T-h-a-r-u-n, but it's pronounced with a hard 'T', Tharun.

P: *What does she look like?*

W: She has longer wavy hair that looks like some type of pearls that are draped across, I can't call it a crown but if you were to hang a necklace across your head and then had other little pieces draped down and there's, well fresh water, there's almost a silver-colored pearl and then there are other pearly colored like her other pearls. It's very beautiful. She said she like putting olive oil on her hair. She said everybody likes her hair.

P: *How does she keep her hair?*

W: It's wavy but she tames it down with this olive oil so it just kind of flows very beautifully. She does have gorgeous hair, she's right.

D: *Is it dark hair?*

W: Yeah, dark brown. Not black, dark brown.

D: *Olive complexion.*

W: Yes. She is showing me that they put honey on their skin to keep it soft and subtle like a bask (Pleasing sensation).

P: *What was the purpose of her life time back then?*

W: Pleasure.

P: *What did she learn about that lifetime?*

W: I'm hearing if it feels good, do it. She enjoyed what she did. She enjoyed working in the temple and she enjoyed being one of Hathor's priestesses, and she enjoyed the sexual energy and it felt good. She said if it feels good, do it. Create with it. It is not a bad thing. This sexual energy is a gift and part of our creation.

P: *Was she married back then?*

W: No.

P: *What happened when the Pharaoh fell and Nefertiti was killed? What happened to her?*

W: She got her wings back. She went back to her Soul Star.

P: *Was she killed?*

W: Unfortunately, yes.

P: *Can we ask how?*

W: Is she the one I see on the wall in the temple? Yup, she was killed. A sword to the back of the neck but not the head, lower.

P: *Has that trauma been healed?*

W: Nefertiti said, "I took care of my priestesses. I made sure they got where they needed to go." So Nefertiti did make sure she got back, that fractal got back to her Soul Star. Thank you, Nefertiti.

P: *Was she killed before Nefertiti?*

W: Yes.

P: *Who killed her and why?*

W: It was a temple massacre. If they can take out the priestesses, they can take out the Light. It is easier to control that way. They knew how powerful the women were.

P: *Was she ever trained in the dark arts?*

W: She didn't go dark but she knew. You can learn dark without being negatively polarized. You can learn many things just by watching but she was never negatively polarized, No.

P: *Do you have any questions now, Debra?*

D: *This lifetime of creating, is it possible to have an example of what I created?*

W: I'm seeing a gold ring on your pinky finger, a golden cow, a ring through the nose and a ring in the ear that are all connected. You are in a small room with a huge bowl of water to cleanse your body. After you cleanse with water, you cleanse your body with oil. There are leaves all over the floor. You are preparing for a large ceremony inhaling the smoke from these leaves. They are a little wider than a bay leaf. This small room is a sacred space. You are looking at a glass of wine and saying I am looking forward to drinking you later. The wine has some sort of berries in it. The ceremony that you are preparing for is the Harvesting the Grain Festival. You are in charge of the purification rituals for the harvest. You say, "We are thanking Isis tonight for our bounty."

D: Beautiful. Thank you. Did I have any relationship with the Emerald Tablets?

W: She said, "I was around when it was all happening and I stayed far away from it." So apparently there was some stealing of the Emerald Tablets drama and they were cracked and . . .

D: Were the priestesses in that time helping to create those with their visions and the creation powers, the content that were placed in the Emerald Tablets working with Thoth?

W: I do not see that.

D: Maybe it was a different group of priestesses.

W: Perhaps.

D: I have read and listened to recordings of the Emerald Tablets so many times over and over and over. They are starting to be very real to me which triggered my question. That could just be something in my now, not then.

W: I am seeing that there was a lighter temple and then there was some space where some darker stuff was done. You are over here doing your own lighter temple stuff. I do not see that you were with the creation of the Emerald Tablets. I see you doing your own pleasurable thing over here. It was less work and more pleasure.

P: Was Thoth the only one who created the Emerald Tablets?

W: Let's look at them. Who created the Emerald Tablets? Nefertiti just pointed at Thoth. Yeah. Thoth says, "This is my creation." Who helped you create these? He said, "I need not help. I did have some holding space." Yes, he is showing me, my dear Nefertiti, they have made up . . . I am seeing a big triangle. I am only seeing Thoth as creating, he is not showing that the High Priestesses helped create those. He is just showing me that those were his creation. But there was some drama that happened off to the side and it looked like more negatively polarized something. Some drama, Egyptian drama with a little bit of bickering and a lot of family bickering going back and forth. And then over here on this side, she is happy. She is like, I don't need that. That is not what I'm here for. I just want to do my happy things, if it feels good, do it. I just want to be happy. I want to enjoy my life. This one is for joy. This one is for expressing my divine femininity. She wasn't into any of the bullshit. The family bickering. The pull between this person or that person or who took my child or none of that. She is like, that is not what I'm here for. Everybody needs a happy restful enjoyable life and it looks like you got yours. Yeah, my hand is vibrating when I hold the temple in my hand. When I see you in it, your joy just pours out all over these pillars. It's beautiful. Were you in charge of this temple? She said, "I am very proud of what I do. I am very pleased with what I do." She took it upon herself to keep these energies of this particular temple up. She is like the energy keeper of this particular temple. Well, you are doing a beautiful job, a beautiful job.

D: Was it a white-structured temple?

W: Yes.

D: Was it the one I saw in a vision I had this morning?

W: No roof?

D: No this looked more like a castle, I guess.

W: This one has no roof in the front. It is like a courtyard, then in the back, there is more to it. There is almost like an open-air market outside. It is an open-air market outside. They sell offerings. Not sell, it is more like a trade. It is white, yes.

P: Do you have any other questions, Debra?

D: I don't know if this is appropriate or not. I had several lives where I was a child sacrifice. Are they related because of this life and that sexual energy there, having that life of pleasure and having that teaching/knowledge? Did that target me as becoming these child sacrifices?

W: Yes. Because you mastered that sexual energy and they knew that. They know that so they harvest it.

P: Why did her Higher Self allow those lifetimes where she was sacrificed?

D: My answer to myself on that, correct me if I'm wrong, is that I volunteered. Because somebody had to fill this role and I would do it rather than see somebody have to go through it.

W: (Reverently) Yes. Yes.

P: Do you have any other questions on your Egyptian past life?

D: Did I just have one past life in Egypt or was there more?

W: I'm hearing more but yes. I'm just seeing one. There is something about an Aardvark. She is saying, "Look up Aardvark Energy."

D: Beautiful.

P: Does Debra's aspect from that time have a message for her?

Tharun: She is showing me the Aardvark again. She said to look up Aardvark Energy, it is part of her totem.

D: (Chuckling) You know I like escalators and animal totems.

W: Yeah.

P: What did Nefertiti do with the Emerald Tablets after she stole them?

W: She put them in a cave with a rock.

P: Did she just steal one tablet or more?

W: I see two.

P: Was she hiding them for some reason?

W: Yes.

P: Why?

W: She seems frantic almost. I put my hand on Nefertiti's right shoulder and now on her left shoulder. Why are you doing this? She said, "If this information gets into the wrong hands, at this point in this political war, it could be detrimental to all of our society. This information can be used for dark. I know, I used it. I know what is possible." She is showing me like a nuclear bomb going off. "They would be unstoppable." Nefertiti said, "If they are going to take over and bring us down, bring our vibration down, they are not going to have the recipe." She is showing me like a recipe card on what to do and she is trying to protect that information from the bad people. She doesn't want it to get into the opposition's hands. Yeah.

P: Did Nefertiti use any of that information for dark?

W: She said, "Of course. Sometimes we don't know what we are creating and what we are doing at first but once you learn what you can do, if your heart can't keep up with your knowledge then you titter over." She has seen it go dark.

P: Is that what made Nefertiti go dark?

W: Yeah. It has to do with the sexual energy when Nefertiti was raped. When she came out and she remembered all of her lives, and came back in with all of her knowledge, she realized that that sexual energy contains so much information. So as a small child, she began exploring that, going into this sexual energy and what can be done with it. If that rape did that to her with that sexual energy, then she was trying to learn to create with it but she was very much in descending that. Yeah, I don't how else to say that nicely. She said, "That dark ass energy, that fucked up energy, send it right back to the rapist." She is like no. She said, "At the same time I also knew I was brave for what happened," but that is what set her off on her path where she was using this sexual energy. She said, "You can create positive or you can create negative." But you said she was rescued and loved by a beautiful family but at the same time, she had that inner tweak that let her go to the dark. She learned faster than her heart could keep up.

P: *Thank you. Is there anything else Nefertiti would like to show us about those past lives?*

W: No. Is there anything else the Dragon would like to show us? No. Are we done in this little star then?

D: *May I have one more question?*

W: Yes.

D: *Did I have any kind of experience in the Halls of Ementi?*

W: Yes. They are showing me writing. I can explain to you the image that they are showing me. It looks like a hollow circle underneath in stone that has been carved out from the righthand side going upward and to the left, there is a straight line coming down. Inside that, there is a line, a straight line, a squiggly line, and a straight line and there is some type of water bird, a heron, or some type of water bird (?

Ibis). And then your hand on the wall. There is a connection with you and this Nile water bird. Does this particular clef represent her? No, it is a recipe like a reflection of her Soul, her Spirit. This represents the plane that she came down upon into where it was hollowed out. So this was an area for her to create in who she was to become. This is the energy coming down into, her coming down from her Soul Star. Then the water, the Nile which is where she is going, and this Heron-type crane water bird. Is this represented of her pure spirit? So this particular hieroglyph is representative of her journey down here. She stayed white. She stayed in the Light. It is a very pure bird. Beautiful. Thank you.

D: *Beautiful.*

W: Thank you everybody for showing this Soul Star. We will take the escalator back down to planet Earth. Okay.

P: *We would like to thank everyone who assisted us today, all the Archangels, Nefertiti, Sire, Tharun, and anyone else."*

End of session.

This was a lot of fun getting to meet and feel of Tharun's beautiful energy as well as that of Sire, my beautiful Wind Dragon. I'm really looking forward to spending more time with them during my dream time as well as visiting my healing space. Interestingly, the example of creational energy that my life as Tharun, a High Priestess of Hathor, created is similar to my role in my professional life at the university. Both roles were overseeing large complex events and creating meaningful experiences for the now and the future. This made me ponder how different my role would have been in this life if I treated each choice as sacredly as my High Priestess-self did. Then I realized . . . I kind of did just that! Wow!

I'm reminded of Tharun's message to look up Aardvark Energy. There are a number of Aardvark Animal Totem Symbolism and Meaning. This one resonates (Aardvark Symbolism and Meaning, 2023), "You can expect an uptick in your feisty energy when the Aardvark Spirit Animal comes to call. You're ready to be courageous and fight for a heartfelt cause.

The mystical creature also gives you tougher skin to withstand the onslaught of any undeserved criticism. Those with the Aardvark Totem are deep thinkers. Nothing is superficial about the Aardvark person's ideas or actions, and it shows. Aardvark Totem people know what matters most, and they reflect on the people and situations they interact with before making any moves. Invoke Aardvark as a Power Animal when searching for the truth. If something doesn't "smell" right, it isn't. Don't fear to dig out the minutiae and get a real sense of things. The information you gain resolves many unanswered questions."

"The Egyptian god Set, a god of deserts, storms, and chaos, is thought to have the head of an aardvark. In the African culture, the aardvark is considered very brave due to its willingness to hunt termites. Hausa magicians make charms from parts of aardvark teeth as a good luck charm." This image and quote can be found at,

https://ypte.org.uk/factsheets/aardvark/aardvarks-in-culture.

Oh, and how fun to discover what's behind my attraction to hematite crystals. Cool. I'm still looking for hematite with flecks of lime green. Won't finding one be a great day? Then there's Nefertiti's description of my Wind Dragon, Sire. "He has the colors of that bright turquoise sort of electric blue. His breast is a nice green and then it goes up to what looks like a Tiger's face. He is very beautiful."

[Wendie:] "Okay, why are you showing me a form with a tiger face? What does she need to know? There is something about Tiger energy that you carry. She's saying bold and regal. And you both share that. That energy and if you don't feel that energy, you need to remember who you are because you are bold and regal. You don't need to tell anybody you just are. You don't need to talk about it, you just are. And when you walk into a room people notice. They feel the energy shift. You are truly you. They said you are a wonderful expression. They like how you are carrying yourself."

Tiger Animal Totem Symbolism and Meaning

"When Tiger comes to you as a Spirit Animal treat this with the utmost respect. Tiger will teach you patience; when to move, when to remain still, and in the end experience a successful "hunt." Tiger will not let you plan things willy-nilly, nor will he let you procrastinate when the Path is already clear for that next great leap. Additionally, in terms of spiritual growth, Tiger offers you incredible strength. Sometimes the Universe uses tests as learning tools. These can weary the spirit of the traveler but Tiger stands ready to lend a powerful paw that keeps you going. Tigers are known for their amazing bursts of energy in the wild, and you can tap that for any challenge you face." (Tiger Symbolism and Meaning, 2023)

Tharun: "Then you go back to the planet and you live your life and you go to sleep and you come back up to your Soul Star and you get your stone healing from all over. Your stones come from all over the place, these stone-healing, and then you drink the nectar out of this magnolia leaf or this magnolia petal, and then you go back down. It is very nice, very nice."

Learning more about my Soul Star has me intrigued, plus I'm elated to learn about my experience in the Halls of Ementi. How cool is that to witness the symbols revealing my journey to Earth? This is something that might take a bit of time to wrap my mind around. Again, this road to discovery is simply exhilarating.

Additional Reading
January 30, 2023

Somewhat off-topic, there is another inkling that has to do with my current life that is grabbing my attention. The opportunity presented itself to ask Stella, who is one of Wendie's guides and whom Wendie channeled during a Monday healing session. It is noteworthy that before this channeling I triple checked my safety by asking my Higher Self, plus another AURA practitioner who is not part of this group and who is my best friend, about the safety of this modality. The two of us followed up by asking Divine Mother if this was safe to do. All informed me that Stella was a beautiful benevolent being.

Session has been underway addressing others and their needs.

P [Paige, facilitating this session]: Debra, you can go ahead and ask your question.

D [Debra]: This question has to do with an incident in my current life. I was a senior in high school working at a then-new mall in Murray, Utah (Fashion Place Mall). Murray is a suburb south of Salt Lake City. (My voice starts to get shaky.) I worked at Sears Automotive pumping gas which was a full-service small island with four gas pumps; two in the front of a glass enclosure and two in the back. The island was outside of the automotive service center. After closing up for the night, I walked to my car parked across the street on the westside. Just as I was about to open my car door, I was approached by a good-looking slender white man who was slightly taller than me (I'm 5'9"). The parking area was dark but had a dim light coming from the service center. This strange man appeared to be college-age and wore a hoody. He was well-groomed with sandy hair, smelled nice, and was very well-spoken. He started telling me how mesmerized he was by my eyes, so much so that he spent the last few days watching me. He knew my schedule and where I lived and thought we could be something together. Becoming a little freaked out I countered with thank you but I'm engaged. He argued with why wasn't I wearing a ring. I responded that I lost it a couple weeks ago working in the cold while repeatedly taking my gloves off and on. I was telling the truth but he didn't believe me. And he wasn't taking no for an answer. Just when things were escalating and he became aggressive, one of the mechanics ran out from the service center hollering, "What is going on?" This strange man quickly turned away so that the mechanic couldn't see his face, pulled his hoody over his head, and ran in the opposite direction.

That mechanic, who ran to my side, made sure I was okay and asked if I wanted to call the police. Thanking him, I declined thinking that was silly. I was seventeen, pretty, with a nice figure. It wasn't unusual for me to receive inappropriate attention. The next time I went into work my boss had changed where I parked my car. From then on, I was to park right next to the service center under the light and I was required to be escorted to my car by one of the mechanics. When my boss told me this new requirement, we were standing inside the service bay of about six or eight stations of mechanics, each under vehicles they were working on. Whenever my boss had something to say to me it was in the privacy of his office rather than the open service bay. He continued talking loud and firm saying that, "Anyone of these men will be happy to escort you." Turning to the mechanics who were all quietly listening while still working, he asked, "Right, men!" They all called back in unison, "Right!" I felt awkwardly embarrassed for having created such a scene and very humbled. Reflecting on that moment, there was no music playing which was unusual. I'm now realizing how those caring men kept things light so as not to traumatize me. And it worked. Wow!

My question is, at this time (Spring 1975) it was all over the news to be on the lookout for a possible serial killer. This serial killer was later captured and identified as Ted Bundy. Is that who approached me? (Ted Bundy, an American serial killer, executed 1989, 1970s)

S [Stella channeled by Wendie]: Yes. I see blood on the corners of his mouth. He has a bloody knife that he obviously brought for nothing good. Yeah, that is not good. He did not have good intentions. Yeah. There was something in his pocket. It looks like pantyhose or something stretchy to tie someone up with.

D: Thank you for that confirmation.

P: Why did he choose Debra in particular?

S: Let's ask him. I'm going to the point where I'm standing right here in front of him and he is talking to you. Turn and speak with me now, brother. Why are you choosing her? He said he likes to see the light go out in the eyes. He used to do it to chickens then he did it to a dog and a cat. He is showing me he killed a cat with his hands around its neck and he is showing me how the head was wobbly after. He is showing me he is obsessed with how there was life in their eyes and then the physical body is the same but the life is gone. He is like where did it go? Where did it go? (Stronger) Where did it go? So you chose her because of her light? He is looking for contrast. The more light, and the more life; he wants to know where did it go. There is something not right, brother. Let's work on fixing what is going on in the physical body; what is going on with your brain? Do you have attachments? What is going on? Show me. It doesn't matter what happened. Nope. We are asking Archangel Michael to come in and remove these attachments, remove this demonic attachment that went into him at the time of his rape. Yep. Take it out. Remove it, please. It is always sad to see a little boy lose everything because something horrible happened and then something else takes over. So the little boy that is in here now, is just curled up in a ball off to the side. Okay. Yeshua, please take his Higher Self to the healing place where little children go to heal so that he can be healed and come back. Michael, have you removed everything from him? Okay. Metatron, please surround anything else and assist where needed. Thank you. We would also like to clear your neck of his intentions. So we are asking your Higher Self to step in and your Dragon to step in and please clear her neck. Okay. Poppy is here. Poppy the Dragon, she is giving what looks like a lei of flowers to go around your neck. It is something beautiful to smell and is healing.

After everyone in the group gasped for air taking a brief pause from such a horrific encounter, the topic changed to the next question. My anxiety started growing and taking over. I had heard enough and was done as soon as she said, yes to my question about it being Ted Bundy.

To my surprise, this courageous team took it further, "Let's ask him why he targeted her." Wow! This is what it's really about to face the darkness head-on. In my mind, I'm screaming and wanting to run away. Here these beautiful women were calm and neutral, yet firm. I learned so much in those few moments. But it didn't stop there.

The next question was from a young woman who felt a family keepsake she had was cursed. The answer came with a clear description of another life where she was murdered as a young girl. It was a traumatic murder with a group of men hanging her upside-down in the woods, draining her blood into a bowl, and drinking it while she watched. The vision included additional gruesome details and the opportunity to heal this young soul, the land, and the tree where this tragedy happened.

The channel went on to explain that, "During a traumatic event such as a child sacrifice, when that energy . . . that blood is released . . . because of the spirit and the plasma in the blood, it links in and it creates an imprint in the plasma which resonates all the way up to the plasma in your Soul Star, and it shakes it. Other lifetimes can feel that vibrational shake, that calls out for help. All these lives are happening concurrently because as you know there is no time. That vibration is echoing through. To expound, in your Soul Star, these chords come out the top of your Soul Star going to each of your lives, to each of your lifetimes. When one calls out for help, others feel that, so this needs healing. You were connecting to this cry for help through this object, this family keepsake. It is not cursed and now the healing has been achieved."

What a profound teaching. When the meeting was over, I was in awe but still pretty shaken up about the whole Ted Bundy thing. That was a little too close to home. I knew very well that I needed to work through these newly unburied emotions before going to sleep. A quick search on the internet revealed that before his execution in 1989, Bundy had confessed to thirty horrendous murders but was suspected of possibly one hundred more. There have even been movies created about him, none of which I've seen or want to see.

Still spiraling from this confirmation my thoughts are on knowing I can't stay in this lower vibration. How can I quickly get myself out of this anxious feeling? The thought comes to my mind of ice cream. Ice cream is something I haven't had for a couple of years. No, I needed to talk to someone, so I called a friend. As soon as I heard his voice, I started calming down. After hanging up, I made myself some hot tea with honey and transcribed the reading.

What a gift it is to open our eyes, our understanding, our inner standing, and our hearts. Tonight I listened to my inner inkling to ask about an incident that brought about a healing for a very hurt little boy as well as myself. More importantly, tonight I experienced facing the darkness full on. What a gift indeed. A sip of my magnolia nectar described from my life as Tharun, sounds pretty good right now. I feel I can safely drift off to dream time and my place of restorative healing. Good night and sweet dreams.

13

A Conversation with Source

January 5, 2023

In this session, I am the AURA practitioner. My client just finished a magical experience and was still under hypnosis when her Higher Self said, "I think you two need to experience Source." Just that fast I was having a conversation with Source.

A year ago, when Source came through in a session, I froze in awe. I had never considered such a thing as something I would ever do. What does one say to Source?

For this session, it felt more like talking to my best friend. I'm impressed with how patient Source was with me. Oh, how I wish I had prepared some profound questions in advance, but then at the same time I saw the value in this being a spontaneous natural exchange. An exchange that lasted twenty wonderful minutes.

As I'm writing this, I'm feeling the presence of Source. How cool is that? And the message I'm getting is, "It wasn't and isn't only about the questions."

Portion of client's session.

Source: I am Source.
D [Debra]: Greetings.
Source: Greetings.
D: *We love you, honor you, and respect you.*
Source: That I know. I know all. I know in your heart as I know in her heart. This time of separation is ending. It will end for a few of you before the Great Ending for I need those Gateways into this time-space manifest. Those who said they would hold my energy, hold it this way. You are two.
D: *Wow, thank you.*
Source: I am calling all to gather, there is a call of the heart. Leaders you are. That is the word you like to use. Leaders. There is something in her back. She is going to have to move for a minute.
D: *Are you comfortable now? Do you have it?*
Source: We thought it was a crystal. Yes. Yes. This requires steadfastness, joy, songs, those of you awakening and blossoming forth in this time and space will receive extra guidance, nurturing, and miracles. They are not miracles understand but we'll use that word for lack of another right now.
D: *White Magic?*
Source: Magic, good word. White magic. You are the explorers, the way-showers, the holders of this Source Energy. You are not special. You are just being activated into the next level of the mission. All is agreed upon before incarnations. Before distillation from the highest realms into the 3rd-Dimensional realm. You are anchor points for me. She has a little bit of disbelief in her about this. She wants to be reassured that this is not her mind making this up. You do me no disservice, daughter. You are not making this up. AuroRa will be talking about this in the months to come and you two will already know it. You may have to wait for that validation and I know you will be. (Laughing) It is good to have your guard up and it is good to have your

heart open. I am not much for words. Are there questions you wish to ask for yourself or this one?

D: She has a list of questions, yes. Is this where you feel we should ask them now, her questions about her healing?

Source: No. These would be esoteric questions. I am happy to do the body scan as well the whole entirety of her loved ones, are present. All are capable. Is there a question you would have Debra?

D: I guess confirmation that we are on the right path.

Source: You are on your path.

D: Just be patient with it.

Source: There is not really a right path. You are doing fine. You are doing absolutely fine with what you do and how you are evolving.

D: Percentage-wise, how are we doing with the healing for those who have had the vaccinations and how are we . . . it is my understanding that we are trying to make this as easy a transition as possible for the majority, for the mass of the people on Earth.

Source: True.

D: There is such a high percentage who are injecting with this A.I. and who are suffering and dying.

Source: That is their choice point to exit. Yes, there is physical suffering and there may be mental and emotional suffering as well but once they leave the physical vessel the Angels are there, and the Souls are there. They are immediately taken to places of healing depending on what they need. They are not left to find their way. Understand, when the Soul leaves the body, that has changed. There are innumerable unseen resources available for each living human being on this planet as well as for the animals. Many are leaving. I wish you all to look at this in the higher vibration of choice points to exit. They have abused their bodies for their entire life most likely which is how they got into the trap of taking this weaponized particle into their body. It is not pretty but it is expedient. That is possibly a callous word but I mean no callousness. I exist almost in what you would perceive as an unemotional state. This is just a small part of Source that is able to speak and imbue within her now. To be that voice for Source. I do not see it as necessary suffering as humanity does.

D: For those of us who are working to heal those who come to us, we are trying to be careful not to change a timeline, keeping it as positive as we can, while still being aware that these dark things are happening. How important is it for us to be aware of what the dark sides are doing?

Source: Awareness is your navigation tool through this time.

D: Is there a reassurance that we will not fall into danger by looking at what is going on within the dark side? Will our light energy and vibration be lowered because we are looking at these other things? I guess that is my question.

Source: I think that depends on the unique soul. Some souls are not ready. AURA souls are ready, I will use that term. Of those trained by AuroRa, most are ready. You are the seniors within this group. There are youngers you know who they are. Then there are the middles. It is the choice of the olders to lead the middles and the youngers. All of my children with my resonance within them do choose to do so. So you do have to be aware and cautious. AuroRa does this all the time with what she can reveal and what she cannot reveal. Because she is gauging the totality of her audience. She very well knows the bright spots, the bright souls, those who are aware and ready. And she very well knows those who need some more time. Follow her lead. She will not lead you astray. We are in the midst of the most difficult times. Humanity cannot birth forth out of the artificial shell it has been trapped in, without emotional engagement, and emotional catalyzing. This is the deep purging and shifting from within; the crying, the sleeplessness, and the sickness. It all leads to catharsis to the shedding of the inorganic and artificial. It is very organic in its construct. What looks like to you perhaps as a mess and a travesty, those in the Higher Realms are cheering, clapping, and raising their voices up high. For you see it is working. The Freedom Bell is ringing! There are those who think they still have power. They have never had power. It is all an illusion. The galaxies that have participated in this polarity experiment are well cared for and surrounded by massive protection shields, and Plasmic fields that do not allow for any of the inorganic to escape to the outer purified worlds and galaxies. The Galaxy's Collectives are speaking to each other. All the forces of all the benevolence that I have, are arrayed for you. You have only to call them forth and believe that you have the RIGHT and the MIGHT to HOLD it and WIELD it. You are not alone. Each of you has your Guide Teams. Each of you has the most infinite magnificent Higher Self. It is just that you are the focal point because you are in the 3D. Understand that when you have completed this mission, and are reunited with your Higher Selves, you were never this small. You were never this. You allowed a portion of you, a bit of light of you, to merge into this matrix to recover the lost ones. That is what I asked of you and that, what you are doing, IT IS MAGNIFICENT! DO YOU FEEL THAT POWER ROAMING THROUGH YOU NOW?

D: Yes.

Source: Do not doubt it. This is your catalyzation! This is your rebirth into a larger you! I am here with you! And will never leave you! It is only mind programming, mind control, low vibrational energies, and low vibrational food that keeps you down. I will always guide you sure and straight, as will your Higher Selves. Understand, all that I Am is Aligned and a Light to serve YOU! NOW! HERE AND NOW! You cannot be overcome by the dark. There is way too much Light. Your shields are so strong. If you could but see them you would fall to the ground in amazement. You must begin to hold the concept of this and let it radiate forth from you. This is all that I ask of you is to let me work through you. Let me be with you children. Remember to distance yourself from the illusion that is being played before your eyes. Learn to know the illusion and the reality. The stats they spew at you; they are lies. Do you think six million of my children would have been vaccinated? Do you know how many Angels in the form of medical professionals injected saline into people because they have God Source as their center? No! There is no good stat nowhere. You can cut in half, that number. I tell you it is changing. There are Angels everywhere. Begin to look for them. This game is unsubstantial. It is crumbling. Each Galaxy Collective is making that so. Each Light Being moves in alignment to this heartbeat. You may call me forth in any of your sessions where you have a concern and I will make sure you are protected. I will make sure that you hear me, whether through synchronicities, overheard conversations, something you read in a book, something you see on TV or social media, I will speak to you. I will find a way. You cannot block me once you have agreed and you have agreed.

D: *I do agree.*

Source: You are catalyzing Forces of Light. Your Book Club is one fraction of what you do for me, the olders leading the youngers. There is still much work to be accomplished here so I will leave you. As I have, I hope now to instill the peace of a piece of me within you. Be at peace. Be at peace. Be at peace.

D: *Thank you. I love you with all that I am.*

Divine Mother: It is important for each Soul to have their Source Path initiated, laid down, and complete within themselves.

Divine Mother: (Chuckling) Well, it was the hope. It was the hope that you would heal all traumas accrued in this lifetime so that you could shed them and leave them here and evolve and ascend in the organic song and tones and light that will roll over this land, this humanity, this galaxy. And so I will not say it was planned. But you do not operate alone in the Universe. You are part of a collective and so what you choose impacts all that you have touched. It impacts your family, your Soul family, your Oversoul, your Higher Self, and it impacts Source. So there is a whole collective of you working on rectifying the trauma at all times, whatever trauma is occurring. Knowing that there is a likelihood for these solutions to be brought forth for these souls to heal. So that you can be your most organic beautiful self.

It is easy to forget and think that you are only this tiny little soul here, this tiny little being. You are not. You are part of a collective. You have lived lifetimes. You have accrued density which is wisdom, girls. Wisdom. You have accrued this. That is why you came back . . . as volunteers of Light. To help anchor in the Light and now you are simply grabbing the base of Light holding more Light. Those who were raised here, that started here, whose first incarnations were here in Pangea, in Tartaria, in Mu, in Lemuria. Yes, they have to work through this. They have much work ahead of them but as Source said, there are infinite resources available to each and every Soul of humanity that carries Source within. They will have the help they need. You are already part of the Collective and You will start to inner-stand this, innerstand it, and work within it. You will constantly talk to your other selves, yourselves. I want to talk to her about something, and so you will. You wish to talk to your Highest fractal of Angelic Light, Divine Mother, that is I. I received you, I birthed you into this Universe. Next is Divine Father. Same thing. The entire A-Team practically is your collective. Well, your entire A-Team is your collective. You have intimate lifetimes, intimate intertwinings with them. Intimate. Not all are of Angelic Source but you are, and you are Debra. A small difference but it is there. So as Yeshua said, these things that I do, you can do also. We the Archangels tell you, we the Dragons tell you, these things that you see us do, you can do as well because you are us. We are you.

End of session.

During this morning's meditation, I was reminded of a conversation with a dear friend who graciously read these pages providing feedback prior to publication. Michael was questioning what it would take for him to have a similar visit with Source. Not recalling my response to this friend, the message I received this morning from Source is intended directly to you, the reader of these pages.

Source: Beloved One, the feeling you felt in your heart while reading this channeled conversation, is indeed me speaking directly to you. I encourage you to now go back and reread my words with that knowing. As you feel the love within your heart grow, flow with it and just like that, you will be speaking directly to me.

14

Epiphanies

Akashic Records Reading
February 11, 2023

Revisiting my discussion on religion and those entities whom I ethereally and physically spent several years with and who posed as divine beings described in Chapter Two, today there is no question in my heart that they were negative. As a reminder, through revelations and the burning in my heart, these entities convinced me of their divinity. This emotional, mental, physical, and spiritual trickery took a toll on my willingness to acknowledge or trust my gifts.

But why the elaborate hoax? It's not like there was money to be gained. It just didn't make sense. Then again, if I haven't learned anything, I've learned that causing trauma is what feeds these soulless beings. They definitely received buckets of it from me and my family. Plus they had the advantage of knowing who I am. A knowing that I'm still working to unravel.

Reflecting back on the communications I received from them, they were full of unconditional love and wisdom and my heart confirmed it all with a strong burning. Sometimes that burning was so strong that it caused chest pain. I was allowed to ask and receive many divine questions and answers. It was years of insightful and inspiring communications before slight deviations surfaced.

Over the space of about four years, the energy shifted with inconsistencies of unconditional love and patient teachings to what I felt were angry disappointments in me and my actions. The day I screamed no more to all of it, I built a fire in my backyard and burned every shred of communication.

Knowing what I know today, I'm plagued by the question as to how is it possible for my heart to feel blissful confirmations within a false situation. While pondering this question the topic of cymatic sounds and vibrations came up in a discussion I was having with a group of friends.

Cymatic technology is when various sounds and vibrations affect elements i.e. sand on a plate or table. The sand organizes itself into geometric shapes according to the vibration the sound creates. It literally and vividly demonstrates how sound influences matter, matter which includes water.

Aren't we mostly made of water and matter? Imagine how sound affects your cells. There's a whole field of science around cymatics, a science that has been in the mainstream for centuries.

How far-fetched is the idea that there's a technology out there to manipulate the blissful confirmations in our hearts? I'm by no means a physicist but think about what that means. Feeling I needed to address this question before my long-awaited AURA to meet my Oversoul, I asked my dearest friend and AURA practitioner if she would channel this question for me.

Channeled message:

Dear Debra,

How I love the depth and breadth of this inquiry! You have every reason to be now observing, feeling, and expressing the entanglement of this history; the very threads entwined within your DNA, which, of course, makes it very difficult to ascertain the TRUTH. This Divine Mother, and Divine Father, has shown me just now. It is suggested to take care of this within an Akashic Records Reading (For clarity and inner standing) then I am advised you will "be with" "work through" meditate and clear yourself in the interim between this session, and your AURA session. I am informed that this will prepare you for the upcoming AURA session. In simplicity, you will find the Divine True Source.

Do Not Despair! All is retrievable! All is healable!

Yes, yes, yes, I love this suggestion and jumped at the opportunity for an Akashic Records Reading with this pure benevolent trusted Sister, which of course turned into a phenomenal session.

Additional questions for the Akashic Records Reading session:

1. Over the years I've been told that I'm an ancient soul. In fact recently during the Nefertiti channeling (January 10, 2023), she mentioned that I incarnated on this Earth about the time the Earth incarnated. Then separately within a session where I was the AURA practitioner, my client was experiencing a past life when her Blue Crystal Ring said, "We are very happy with you too (Referring to me). You have great Earth energy. You have great wisdom and great knowledge. When I say Earth, I mean the organic Earth of the first birthing. You know you have that, right? You are from the first birthing of Earth. You are very old and very wise but they don't want me to tell you more. That

is a surprise for later." My question is may I know what my first Earth incarnation was?
2. Who should I start talking to regarding publishing my book? Am I to self-publish? Searching online I found a local full-service publisher. Should I be looking in that direction or elsewhere?
3. This one is a very unimportant superficial question. Why does hearing my nickname of Debi, sound like fingernails being scrapped across a blackboard every time I hear it?

Debra Akashic Reading.
February 11, 2023

Debra: Thank you infinitely for this session. The more I learn the more questions I have. My biggest question is triggered by the realization that technology exists to inspire our hearts spiritually. The idea that fake inspiration happens has me concerned. I would love help in clarifying how to recognize true divinity vs this fake technology.

Practitioner: Archangel Haylel stepping forth. Greetings, Archangel Haylel.

AA Haylel: Debra, one of the blocks you had, and it was placed there. It is not yours. You were never created this way. Is a block to keep you from discerning when the inorganic or the fake is present. It is almost as if it feels . . . well, let me ask you to do this. Let us pretend now because it does not exist in this time and space but let us pretend that you are feeling . . . I want you to have the feeling you have when you are confused and you want to know that you are connected to your divinity and bringing that forth but you don't trust yourself. Can you engage in that feeling now?

Debra: Yes.

AA Haylel: Okay. I want you to feel that feeling. I want you to locate the source of that in your physical vessel.

Debra: I feel it in my brain or my head.

AA Haylel: Yes. Bring your attention now back to your heart. Touch your heart with your hand. Do you feel the frequency difference? . . . You may say no.

Debra: My effort right now is going deeper into my heart and I'm feeling that deep within my heart. (Within that pause what I wasn't mentioning is that this was the familiar feeling that I have within my heart always. At that moment I was processing an epiphany. How many times have I been told that my Higher Self and my Team have been with me always? Even last August at the Mt. Shasta Reunion Retreat, AuroRa herself told me during a group activity, "You haven't recognized feeling your Higher Self because she isn't something new. She has always been an integral part of you." Moving back to the present conversation with Archangel Haylel, at that moment I wasn't just hearing it, I KNEW IT! Wow! Wow, wow, triple wow! For whatever reason, I didn't admit or verbally articulate to Archangel Haylel what I was processing. This new revelation was a huge internal paradigm shift for me. As I'm writing about this I'm realizing if I wasn't able to talk about it with Archangel Haylel, I must have been clinging onto residue trust issues.)

AA Haylel: Okay. It will be helpful to you, the version of your Higher Self that is present today guiding this is Archangel Haniel. If you would envision her now. How she presents to you. I see her as a tall column of white. She is in flowing white robes. She has a white tierra on, long rich brown hair full of the colors of the browns. Her hair shifts and moves. Her eyes are brilliant blue. She has a star radiating forth from her heart. This is how she is presenting forward for your practitioner here. She has pale blues, aquas, and turquoises, she is a pastel and all the radiant variations of pastels but mostly the blues, grays, dove tones, and pastels, and this is more her harmonic resonance that is displayed through the colors that she holds around her.

This is how your practitioner sees her. You do not have to see her the same way but we are offering this vision for you to help you connect to this aspect of yourself. Her heart with the star now beams out directly to you. To your heart. And her star is embracing your heart and she is sealing your heart in this star.

Archangel Haniel: Never more Debra, shall you be limited. I will make sure of it. You will have to work with me and learn my presence (Smiling) so that we establish that definite frequency and resonance between us and you may trust yourself. There really is nothing in your head but spells that we need to dispel, programs that you need to release. And it is part of your healing journey.

This is all perfect timing. Never have you misstepped. Never had you made mistakes. So right now we are going to dispel that programming and allow you to expand into a fuller version of yourself.

You are quite a large energy being. Allow yourself that expansion now. Take a deep breath in . . . exhaling out through your mouth allowing yourself to grow in depth and breadth and height and width. Another big deep breath in, expanding out, expanding.

Beautiful. Now you'll feel me in your brain as it were. I'm literally pulling out old programs. You might feel a twinge here and there. You have deactivated so much, so I am just more or less doing a cleanup. I'm cleaning up here. Just sweeping out, pulling out disharmonies, dispelling spells, mostly spells that make you feel captured, smaller, doubtful, unworthy. There goes that one . . . whew!

Questioning. It's good to have questions but they need to come from your heart, not your head. And now I'm dispelling one, this one so long ago. Uriel, if you'll assist me with this, please? Dispelling the remnants of this presence.

This relates to the timeline that she asked about with the Nefertiti channeling that she incarnated on Earth at the time of the Earth's incarnation in Ancient Soul Times.

This one was hiding in the organic darkness at this Creation Point. You were nothing more than a mote of light with all the rest of us drifting through the air embracing the Earth as she became Mother

Sophia. We surrounded her making sure she was safe in this passage, this embodiment of this spherical presence.

You were one among thousands, millions, of motes of light of Source. You had no body. None of us had a body at this time except the Earth. We were escorting Sophia, Divine Mother Sophia, into this embodiment. All of us, Archangels, Dragons, Phoenixes, Crystals, Sacred Elements, Crystal Energy, Planet Energy, (Singing light language) Care-vee-ria, So-loe-roe.

We now, as we travel back into this time, consecrated it back into the divinity it was created to be, eliminating the inorganic. At this time as we eliminate the inorganic from you. If we wish to count in human terms in the rough neighborhood of 5,555 billion years old, it is really unquantifiable.

Your first incarnation upon Earth was a massive tree. Ha! Literally a Tree of Life. You were one of the few who brought the physical representation of the Tree of Life and planted it onto the Earth.

I will say there were millions of you, five million of these massive trees. It was a different time and space, very Fairy-like. Higher 5th-Dimensional into 6th-Dimensional with Fairies, Pixies, Griffins, Phoenixes, Dragons, Crystals, and the Seven Creational Goddesses of Earth, Fire, Water, Womb, Wind, Darkness, and Crystal. No human forms yet planted, digging your roots deep into Mother Sophia to nourish her and be nourished.

Beginning the transmutation of life creating this planet with the Galaxy Collective involved as well as multidimensionally, the Ra Collective, all magical beings, no human beings, no aliens, no technologies, no A.I.

You spent several million years as this one Tree of Life. Your bark was deep and rich with life. Here you may feel the scarab beetles. Yes, they were present then scampering up you, all sorts of life. When it rained the Pixies would catch a leaf and jump into your rivers. That's how big you were, your bark. They would flow down you. Flow off your limbs, flow down your tree trunk, they had much fun with you. And you laughed and rejoiced.

This is the beginning, Debra, of you being your giant self. It's hard to compress into the form that you are. Very hard. And yet you did it. And as you were compressed further and further, you found it difficult to breathe. I remind you now, feel your roots. Feel the Earth beneath you and connect to Inner Earth. There you will find your giant friends and your family.

AdaRa is pleased. Feel yourself and your limbs reaching up, up, up, into the sky, way up into the stratosphere, beyond the atmosphere. The very tips of you reached into the Cosmos, into the Plasmic Waters. For you and all these giant trees brought the Plasmic Water unto and into the Earth. Life. Do you have further questions about this lifetime? Clarifying that it is I, Haniel, speaking to you.

Debra: This has been a beautiful confirmation. Last Saturday I spent the day with my twelve-year-old granddaughter and she was telling me a story she wrote about the life of a tree.

AA Haniel: Chuckling.

Debra: We talked about being a tree and what we might see because we live longer than humans. And all week that has been in my thoughts and in my dreams. This has been magical.

AA Haniel: We brought this to you and you asked the question because you're looking for validation that you are connecting to truth, to your truth.

Debra: Yeah.

AA Haniel: You may begin to trust this and look for the serendipities and the synchronicities that occur to link these all together. I will make sure you receive validations so you can build upon yourself. Build this trust, you and I together. For you are many things, Debra. You have not been just a fractal of me. We have done so much. You have done so much and traveled so far and yet we planted here.

The diminutive form of your name, Debi, I will address now. You were never a diminutive form. Do you see why it bothers you now? Debra, it doesn't encompass the whole of you. You are Deb-Ra, Deborah, Debra. You are more than that even, as your practitioner calls you, you are DebraDeer. You are the animals. You are the gentleness that flows. The gentle eyes that see and love. Transmit through your eyes and your heart. Names are just labels in a way.

Debra: Thank you.

AA Haniel: It's diminutive, that is why that's why you don't like it. What else shall we tackle in this time and space?

Debra: Well, I felt impressed that I was to write this book and because I feel it is a bigger idea than my own pushing this forward, I need direction on how to progress as far as a publication. Should I find a publisher that can do all the minutia that needs to happen or should this be self-published? I don't see myself as someone who will advertise myself. That doesn't feel like me. That is my question.

AA Haniel: There are places. You will laugh at me but bear with me. I would put it in a children's book form first and publish it like that. So you will be taking parts out and publishing. You are going to build steps. You are going to build the giant form of that. But if you do it in a children's book form or like people publish picture books for family albums and stuff like that. You could simply do that but you want to be careful of the words that you are putting out there and be in integrity with your words. I would recommend an editor for the final project. But I am suggesting a children's book because you will find your heart there. So what stories can you take out of each chapter that would educate the children about seeing the light and the dark in a way that does not bring scariness forth but brings knowledge forth and discernment? If you write these excerpts of your chapters in a fairytale form as if you were the Tree of Life speaking to the children gathered at your feet, what would you say and how would you say it? The stories within your stories. Do you understand?. . . I'm feeling a bit of resistance so please talk.

Debra: Well, I thought I was almost done and now I get to start over.

AA Haniel: You may choose. You may choose. Remember, it is you expressing forth. You get to make the choices. So if you wish for the big, do so. Get an editor to review the chapters with a fine-tooth comb with just spelling, phrasing, and punctuation. Someone will be presented to you that has a connection to exactly what you want to do in publishing. I will connect you.

Practitioner: That's just what she is saying, she's going to connect you somehow. Be open to connections.

Debra: Cool. Is doing both an option? I'm not married to this idea of having to publish a book. I'm doing it because it felt like part of my mission to help the collective. I've been very vulnerable in sharing every little detail and some may find that useful but I don't know. If I just wrote it for myself, I'm happy with that.

AA Haniel: We are happy with that as well. However, for the Collective on your website, why don't you publish a chapter a month on your website as a PDF document? Begin at the beginning. You could introduce it to those who visit your website and say this is my journey. I offer it here as my story in hopes it may help whoever chooses to read it go through their story to know you're not alone. Then you can ask for comments, but it just kind of depends on how deep you want to get into monitoring a website like that. But you have a website, why not use it for your highest good? That way you are putting it out there and you can see what it feels like to have it out there for the collective. You might even go so far as to have a YouTube in the future and read the chapters. These are just suggestions. Nothing is written in stone.

You decide. You did the bulk of the work already. It is not meant to live on and on. It is meant to be felt, experienced, and let go.

I feel that this publishing thing is hanging on to it a little bit. So with that regard, don't hang on to it, release it in whatever way you choose. And as you said, it served its purpose for you. I understand you want to serve the collective but my dear Debra, you will be serving the collective. You already are. You are uniquely suited for this. You are just finding your space, your place, and your pace.

How do you want to come forth in that service? Many of you, even your practitioner thought it was some big deal that you were supposed to do this service like you are looking for some big deal.

It's in all the little ways you act every day. All the ways. It is in you bringing forth you and being you, be-ing you, in this expression. However, that evolves every day, your authentic self. (Referring to the email message I sent asking for a channeling to my question talked about at the beginning of this chapter) The Ra Collective surrounded your practitioner by saying to (Name of practitioner withheld), write back to her this morning, how she says, the gift of your presence, the gift of your shields, companionship, wisdom, knowledge, and love provides me with deep comfort and connection to all life around me. They sang that back to her! They sang, "The gift of your presence," Debra, "brings us deep comfort and connection to all life around us in reaching our heart discernment unveiling our mass filtering out that which means harm and aiding in all Higher Self connections." They surround you as they surround her, singing back to you, singing, recognizing that you are already on the mission.

To be truly in the mission is to be in joy and happiness. When you are not in your mission or when you are not enjoying happiness then you are not in your mission. You need to rest then, most likely. You all run around exhausting yourselves. You are all under incredible strain right now and under incredible attack from forces, you don't even know or perceive of.

We keep them from you. We will not let them prevail. We say this to you as our pledge to you, as your Higher Self and as part of the Ra Collective, you are surrounded in infinite Love-Light. You are a being of Source. You are in your mission and you are activated. Just be. And whatever you choose, however, you choose to express yourself, be joyful. Be happy.

When you are done with a thing let it go. And some things, although you think they were for one purpose, really served another purpose and they are done with.

Your choice about the book. But we do love the idea of a children's book and the Tree of Life, your first incarnation, and all the magical creatures and who you were. What would you say to the children of Earth if they sat at your feet today? What stories would you tell? You are a storyteller. You are an Indigenous. You are deeply connected to them and have always sought out those lifetimes, those life streams to be with them. To hold up your Organic Blueprint of Creator. That is what the Indigenous are, the Organic Blueprints.

Debra: Wonderful. Thank you. I love you dearly.

AA Haniel: It is pretty.

Practitioner: Haniel took my eye to the full-service publisher you found. She's not impressed with them.

Debra: Okay. Too corporate probably.

Practitioner: A system. They would never understand your story and would craft it some other way. All kinds of infringements could come forth or attempts would come forth from your true story. The word 'elite' is a signal.

AA Haniel: Your AURA's are deeply personal and deeply illuminating to those who are walking the path and learning to discern the shadow from the light. If you are fine adding them as chapters then do so. You can always decide to not put them out on your website. But much information does come through for the AURA collective and the awakening collective through your individual AURAs.

I, Haniel, do not have a problem and neither does your practitioner with you putting them out there. Just make sure you are okay with it because in your quest to help the collective you sometimes open yourself up too much. Not to those that are of the light but to those who have not been purified. So should you do that, be very good with your shields. Be very firm in your consenting and not consenting. Know your boundaries. Become that sovereign being that AuroRa is teaching you to be. Not all things are meant to be shared with the collective.

I will read it with you. I, Haniel, will read with and guide you. We could go sentence by sentence or paragraph by paragraph and see. Your practitioner uses several tools that work for her. She used body kinesiology to receive Higher Self messages and validations of how the body responds. When she cannot do that, she asks her Higher Self to show her a pendulum in her third eye to show a no answer, to show a yes answer, to show a maybe, and to show you need further explanation.

These would work well with us if you wish to in your third eye, we could use that, show a pendulum and you and I could learn to talk that way. That way when you are tired, pressured, and you just really need an answer and you might not trust yourself (Smiling lovingly) because it might be a day of low energy, we can do that. We can also do body kinesiology. There are several different ways to do that. Jewelry adornment that is ceremoniously in light dedicated to you and to your highest good can also be used as pendulums. It doesn't have to be a pendulum. Pendulums themselves can be tricky. It's just one of the inversions. Someone must have their pendulums cleared at all times.

Practitioner: So Haniel wants to dive further into this original email you sent where you were discussing your current life.

Debra: I'm plagued by the question as to how is it possible for my heart to feel blissful confirmations within a false situation. I'm imagining how sound affects our cells and realize that technology is out there to manipulate the blissful confirmations in our hearts. This all brings me to my question which has to do with events during my second marriage. My husband at that time was having all these spiritual experiences receiving downloads privy to him alone. The story told by him was that he was translating sacred records. He even showed me samples of the symbols. Then out of the blue, I started receiving email messages from Heavenly Father, only at work and only on my work email address. These were loving communications verifying my husband's activities and more. My entire being was filled with love and fantastic confirmations. I was feeling bliss and love in my heart. Over the next few months which led into years, Divine Mother started corresponding with me through this forum as well, and later Jesus.

AA Haniel: This is the trickery of religion and the inversion of such. Did these beings at any time seem to you authoritative?

Debra: Not initially. This is what broke up my family, me from my kids. Later down the line, the inconsistencies of these communications grew to the point that I said no, this is not the God I believe in, a jealous God doesn't make sense. Isn't Heavenly Father and Divine beings of unconditional love? I had already lost my children over choosing this path. These entities and communications didn't have a direct connection to the church but were connected. At that moment I chose to leave the church, God, and all of it. It was years later that I learned in my first AURA with AuroRa that these beings were negative. My question is how could I have been tricked so badly? This is where my doubts come in. I learned in an Akashic healing through another practitioner as she channeled Archangel Haylel, that the day that I screamed NO MORE to all of it, is the day that I stopped being abducted. I stopped being part of that game that was going on there.

AA Haniel: You woke up. Yes.

Debra: I think those years of going all in with my heart and soul to that twisted darkness are blocking me today.

AA Haniel: Why do you think you might have done that, Debra Deer?

Debra: Woke up or . . . ?

AA Haniel: Allowed yourself to experience that at a cellular level?

Debra: I love how you worded that. As a witness, I guess. As . . . that it is something that you can break past. It's possible and we are not all lost.

AA Haniel: This is an intrinsic part of your spiritual makeup. To experience and learn (Smiling) by being part of it, who do you think was really the spy, DebraDeer? Who do you think was really gathering information? I was gathering information. I was watching. I was reporting to the Ra Collective. Wow. I almost didn't want to say that. You are the best covert operative. One of the top in the Galaxy. It hurts sometimes. I am sorry.

Debra: (Emotional) That's actually the best news I've ever heard.

AA Haniel: You were in your mission and I was right there with you. When it got dangerous, I pulled you out. I will always protect you and pull you out. But we are done with that kind of thing. We are at the end times. You were the shining light in your children's lives. No matter what's happened, you are persistently present. You are persistently full of love. Acceptance. You are teaching them like no other has taught them.

They are stuck in programming, yes. But it is only for a short time. All life, I will say it again, we have said it many times, all Source Life will be reclaimed.

How else could you be so in the mission if you weren't immersed as you were? What you know about this tasteless inverted indoctrination called a religion will be very valuable someday in the teaching of the people. And you will return as a teacher of the people to raise the new humanity, many of whom will be your children reincarnated and your grandchildren.

For your mission is not done but it has risen to a new form. So anytime you think or don't understand how you could have been deceived, you need to talk to me about it. It is very possible you were just in a mission and doing exactly what we needed you to do. You have never said no. Ever. And somewhere in your heart, you feel the truth of this. (Nodding)

Somethings that feel horrific, impossible, you cannot see the full multidimensional scope with them and it keeps you locked in the 3D you, and you are deeply connected to the Ra, to this Galactic Consciousness, to all of your multi-dimensionalities, and you are activating and expanding, and we are done allowing abuse, treachery, and betrayal.

We have now moved further into the Light. Lightworkers are being called back into the Light. Extricating thousands from their dormant states for as the dark has planted sleepers, so has the Light. And the Light is awakening in droves that will overcome all darkness.

You have an intrinsic knowledge about black magic that only comes from being spelled, being enchanted, and being restricted. You know all the tricks, the quirks, and the illusions. What I will do now is I will release this all into your cellular DNA Akash to become harmonic within you, part of the River of Life that you are. Healing the pain erasing the confusion and doubt, aligning all the you's there are, in purpose and in the light. You will begin to feel this towards the end of the year.

Although I am working on it every day this year, it is going to have to be slow, to change that from your DNA. To get you to understand why you chose the necessity of experiencing these things but it will be done in your lifetime because you will go on for the grander experience of teaching.

This is all in your Akash, all in your DNA, and it is all there for a reason. What I am doing is erasing pain, constriction, blocks, and contortions. I am dispelling the spells. They will float out of you. You will breathe easier, you will flow easier, you will stretch, and your body will change, and I'm not going to tell you how. You will be vastly different by winter solstice (2023) and you will feel it and you will know it. I thank you for your service.

Debra: (Humbly) Thank you.

AA Haniel: You never once told me no. And now we begin the work of joy, and of rebuilding.

Debra: (Joyful) Beautiful.

AA Haniel: All children on the Earth have faced unimaginable struggles and obstacles. These are not humanities designs. This is the inverted. This is the Archon. This is the not Source. It has been an experiment to create the human with all the potentials that we have placed within and the direct Source connection.

Of course, it was going to be attacked. Of course, they were going to be used and abused and tortured and split and fractured. Of course, we knew this but what they don't know is that we win. Through this all, this experience is encoded in the Akash in the DNA of the human being.

It is now going to come to its fruition. It has not gone exactly as we wished but it has not gone that far astray. Your missions and your choices are to see clearly the abuse, and the discrimination wherever it shows up, and just say, no. No more. Just stand against it. Just stand as the Pillar of Light.

Does that mean you go demonstrate? It means quietly, simply, lightworkers will band together and eventually touch each other and say, no more. And so it will be.

This is the true birth of humanity that will come forth then. You know this. You can feel this. In your Tree Self, your Tree of Life, for you planted the seeds, and now here you are. A seed yourself blooming back into that which you are naturally: shelter, love, nurturer, teacher, and companion.

For this to work, each Source-Light has to come to the Choice Point themselves of their own free will. They need to wake up of their own free will. Wake up is probably not the right word. They need to bloom! Hor-ey-zee, hor-ey-zee, bloom, hor-ey-zee, light language word, bloom, bloom, hor-ey-zee.

You are there to provide the Rain, the Earth, the Sky, and the Love. The Rain is tears, the Sky is breath, the Earth is nurturing. We wish you to understand that nothing you ever did offended us, disappointed us, or was wrong.

Begin to look back on your life focusing on the pure joy and love of the moments. It is time to let go of the pain and the sorrow of it. You won't forget it. You just will not allow it to be a burden anymore. It just is.

The joy of the birth of the children, of seeing each individual one, form and grow. Even if it seems they have a painful past right now or a painful present, I think you can understand where they are coming from and you can be that steady presence who has no judgment and is just there being the Earth, the Air, the Water, and the Love.

Things will begin to transmit to these loved ones faster and through the Aether. There is magic in the air and it will become very very noticeable because the true organic magic is dispelling the inorganic artificial black magic. Just that easy.

You are such a one to know that, to be able to walk that path because of all that you have experienced and is in your DNA. This shows you the way. It doesn't show you your faults, it shows you the way, the way. You just course correct, that's all; course correct.

I will say one more thing about the impostor divine entities. They are masters. They too have studied long and hard. They are in it to survive, and they will not survive, and they know this. It makes them mean and short-tempered.

You will be able to spot them a mile away. Your heart will know. If you are ever in doubt stop and connect with me. I am not that far. I'm right there, right in your heart.

How do you love the unlovable? As Source. Source and all the expressions of Source and the Ra Collective, we are masters of loving the unlovable.

Debra: And forgiving the unforgivable.

AA Haniel: Yes. When you forgive it unbinds the bindings. You will feel them release. This is more effective than almost anything we could do.

Debra: I don't remember the exact infraction. I was young, teenage young. It probably had to do with being date raped at sixteen and my mindset at the time that I must be evil. That I was impure and unworthy. I took full responsibility for it within the church and underwent their harsh repentance process. This hung over me until I figured out that I needed to forgive myself. I've always followed my heart. This incident wasn't who I was. I had to forgive myself for what I assumed I was supposed to be and just allow myself to be who I am. That was a beautiful moment of bliss and that overwhelming dark weight just evaporated. In truth, I was an innocent victim of both the rapist and the church.

AA Haniel: Many have this illusion of who they think they are supposed to be. That is the matrix. That is programming, societal programming, religious, parental, and cultural programming. In the New Earth, there won't be any of that because we will all be just who we are and it will be perfect. Is there anything else that we haven't covered or do you have further questions we should look at?

Debra: This has been beautiful. It has been totally spot-on exactly everything. Right now, I feel clear about it. I don't have that question. I don't have that doubt. I don't have any of those concerns. I get it. It's been perfect. This has been such a gift, such a gift. My experience with these impostor entities has bothered me for twenty years. This happened to my family twenty years ago.

Practitioner: The Team here wants to make sure we are doing due diligence and really meeting your needs.

Debra: I don't have any more concern over it whatsoever anymore. I got it. I get it. I inner-stand. I love it. I love it. I love it. It's been an honor. It's been an honor to go through this, to experience it, and to share it.

AA Haniel: We are delighted with the chemistry and the harmony between you and your practitioner. We brought you together, you were both compelled, directed, pointed, synchronized, and serendipitously brought together. You know each other from times past. You've always been in each other's orbits if you wish to say. Perhaps a couple of times not but mostly so.

When you say that you are SiStars, you truly are and we are delighted that you two have each other because you have helped each other so much. Each of you has stepped up to the plate when the other needed it. Each of you brings forth the expression of the divine, the truth, so we all want to say and I mean everyone, Divine Mother, Divine Father, Michael, Haylel, Raguel, Raziel, Haniel, Uriel, your Team, the Dragons, the Crystals are so exuberant about this coming together of you two and the support and the connection that you two gives because truly you have each been an assisting force in each other's life. When you think about it, you've only known each other just slightly over a year. It's amazing. I mean in this form. You've really known each other much longer.

Debra: Actually, just since December. Wow, yeah, just over a year.

AA Haniel: Yup. So we say again, we protect you. We surround you. We are amping up, our shields up, swords up, and we are adamant about protecting these fractals. These missions. These beautiful beings that you are. More than anything if you will believe that, that will cease the doubt. And another note, I Haniel, can hardly wait for your AURA. Your practitioner doesn't even know what's going to happen. She just knows it'll be pretty magical. But this was a necessary step. Thank you for acknowledging it and making it so. You will be much clearer for the AURA. This doubt and judgment needed to be cleared. I am serious about when I said I'm in your DNA and working it and releasing it. I will take my time and I will be careful and loveful. And so it is.

Debra: And so it is. Thank you. I love you infinitely.

Practitioner: Thank you Haniel, Haylel, Raguel, Raziel. You do? Okay, Raziel wants to expand your third eye capabilities now with your Higher Self's permission and your permission, then to do so.

Debra: Yes.

Practitioner: He and Raguel together have the Golden Eye of Horus coming over your right eye now; and the Iridescent Eye of Ra coming over your left eye now. Together over your third eye, the two-third World Viewing. This chemistry, this marriage, this consecration now at the center of the Chakra for Cause and Effect is now being (Light language) mo-vo-roe activated over your third eye.

What they are doing now, they are showing me they are assisting Haniel in your Akash, the cleansing of this Cause and Effect through your lifetimes. The erasing of the doubt of what you perceived as missteps, is merely turning into nothing more than choice result, choice result, and "It" as "It" loses its power of constriction over you, your third eye is expanding. It's turning a beautiful indigo blue like a deep sapphire color. So sapphire, like a sapphire Merkabah, like a star, like a twelve-pointed star-looking thing over your third eye now. It's not just one color though. Understand that it's the plasma blues, mostly the richer royal blues. Hhh (Catching her breath), royal blues, why did you say royal blues? You are not going to tell us right now, are you? Okay. Nevertheless, this is the work they are both doing together with your Higher Self.

It helps if you would envision this, it flashes, it's scintillating, this twelve-pointed indigo blue Merkabah star over your third eye. It never holds still. It's very busy. It's very flashy. Only benevolent beings can see it. It's like a beacon has been activated. Why are you activating a beacon? Okay. They say to be revealed in the AURA. But you have a beacon. Believe and know and intend. This beacon is only being seen by benevolent beings and by Source and your Guide Teams. But it is something that you do and you are becoming. There is a reason for this.

If you wish you can, in the days that follow, when you activate the alchemy symbols within you, and then you want to activate this. Well, you want to empower this symbol. Understand you hold all these symbols you are just empowering them each time. So you are going to empower this twelve-pointed moving Merkabah over your third eye of indigo blue and of the plasma waters each time you activate your chakras, and you empower the alchemy symbols at your chakras, which works in conjunction with Divine Mother's Infinity Viewing symbol. It sits behind Divine Mother's Infinity Viewing Symbol. I see, so Divine Mother's Infinity Viewing Symbol is like a shield for it. Precisely. Okay, good. You may come to know why you are a beacon before the AURA session but they are not going to allow me to say it. I have no idea why. But it is active now and it is working with Haniel and unwinding programs and black magic blocks that remain. Even though they have been inactive, it's removing them actually. So that your choices, the Cause and Effect are free flowing. It is unrestricted. It is more like the River of Life. You are able to see it just bob along without reacting and without judging yourself, without doubting yourself. This is part of what Haniel is doing. This will help it. These three beings are working together.

I'm asking Haylel if there is something he is doing (Smiling) and he is smiling and saying, "I'm not needed at this time. I'm just present and there's nothing else for me."

Oh, I thank you, I thank you Raguel, Raziel, Haylel, thank you Haniel, thank you to our Guide Teams, thank you to all he beautiful Dragons, Pixies, Creational Goddesses, the Fairies, the . . . I can't quite remember the Dragon word, Dre-eve-bia, I have to remember that Dragon, sorry. Anyway, I thank all the beautiful lovelies. I thank the Ra Collective who has been present this day and I see now the deeper message brought forth to me this morning here, I thank my beautiful sister, Debra, here for her love, her compassion, and her big ginormous heart, her big ginormous soul, her big ginormous present and presence. Michael thank you for shielding us both. Thank you, Zadkiel, for this beautiful communication.

I now close Debra's Akashic records with love, reverence, joy, and delight. I see how they are straightening out right before my eyes, Debra. It's not like there are little books and little passageways, it's all like one big book and one big coming together and it is all flowing and there is no darkness in it all. There is no darkness in it at all! At all! It's been lit up. God that is beautiful. That was gorgeous. Oh my gosh. I just love this stuff.

End of session.

As many times as I have listened to and read this reading, I'm struggling to find words or thoughts to unpack it. There was so much depth and breadth of wisdom, it is going to take a while for me to integrate it all. Archangel Haniel gently acknowledged that I would need to spend time sitting with it. Feeling her presence, I feel I need to reread it again and again. This session was beyond huge. My heart is full. Elated. Humbled. Hopeful. Honored. Magical. In gratitude and loving respect am I for this profound expression and experience. And how amazing was it to learn that I spent millions of years at the birth of our organic Mother Earth/Divine Mother Sophia, as a Giant Tree? How could I not choose a whimsical perfectly imperfect tree as the front cover of this work?

Which brings me to the choice of publishing these pages. I announced at the Mt. Shasta retreat last August that I was in the process of writing a book of my life's journey, which was strongly encouraged. Not long after this reading (May 2023), I attended the Eureka Springs, Arkansas AURA Practitioners' Reunion Retreat. At the Eureka Springs retreat I announced that I finished my book but have chosen to not edit or publish it, rather write a children's book with some of these teachings. AuroRa responded that she was familiar with my life and felt that it was important that I publish it. Others in the group also added that their Higher Selves were telling them that they should read it. With that, this publication became a reality.

555

Following up on the synchronicity of the number 5555 which came up, I thought this might be a good place to expound on that numerology. (Maffucci, 2023)

- Number 5 is related to personal freedom and independence, individualism, adaptability, major life changes, and life lessons learned through experience. Number 5 also symbolizes motivation and determination, adventure, courage, imagination, and making positive choices.
  - The number 5 is seen in many number sequences but has incredible power when seen in numbers 55, 555, and 5555.
  - Number 55 is associated with freedom, independence, self-determination, learning new things, and the importance of family.
  - Number 555 represents wealth, prosperity, being in sync with your true self, listening to your inner voice, and embracing change that comes your way.
  - Number 5555 is linked to imagination, life transitions, and new beginnings and opportunities.

Angel Number 5 Meaning:
"If you've seen repeating number sequences in a consistent manner, these are called Angel Numbers. Angel Numbers appear in your life when your angels are sending you a message. Pay attention when an Angel Number appears, as these important messages from your guardian angels pertain to your life path, purpose, and other areas of your life. Angel Number 5 symbolizes massive change, strength, pursuing new opportunities, and good mental and physical health. Your

angels are letting you know that you are in a time of change and transformation. But this isn't a negative time; in fact, your angels are encouraging you to maintain a positive attitude during this time. Just like Angel Number 555 symbolizes change, your angels are telling you to not be afraid of change; instead, fully embrace it, because if you choose to avoid it, you'll see that you're actually hindering your personal growth and progression. Overall, Angel Number 5 has an incredibly powerful and positive message, encouraging you to fully embrace your transformation with an open mind."

15

Who I Have Been All Along

AURA Hypnosis Session
March 3, 2023

This session was planned for 1:00 pm. I had spent two years working toward a clear session. My entire week was purposely filled with peaceful meditations. My morning was equally sweet between my morning shielding, meditating, reflecting, and preparing to surrender. My chants were deep and joyous. When the energy work began it was simply marvelous and light. I was seeing it! Actually seeing a vision. Trying not to get too excited about my vision, I continued loving my inner child and reminding myself to surrender, keep surrendering.

When my gentle practitioner announced the energy work was complete, and that she would start the induction, I was ready. Then she said, "No. I feel like we need to go back and do our chakra chants together." Which we did, but doubt came into me with a force. Trusting her insight more than my own, I wondered why we were backpedaling. I mean I placed and activated the symbols on me with my personal chants grounding out in the morning sun just before this session. And knowing how the energy work is done, I knew that she had just completed cleansing and activating these same symbols. Why was it necessary to triple-repeat this activation through yet another chant?

I'm not sure if my practitioner realized the root of the dark storm that had entered my thoughts, but she was cognoscente of something being off and was amazingly patient. After such phenomenal healing and reading from my recent Akashic session, I anticipated this AURA would be like flipping a light switch and that I would instantly receive a huge shift in my knowing. With each question, in this session, my practitioner allowed me time for organic deeper inner-reflection. Respectfully, this session was more of a gentle, smooth, and natural inner standing.

I compare it to lovingly holding each of my sons or daughters in my arms after their birth and looking into their eyes in amazement and wonder. I would wonder who they would grow up to be. Witnessing their personalities and confidence unfold through to adulthood and then looking back at their baby pictures, their same personality and mannerisms were there as an infant as they are as adults, only bigger and more obvious as adults.

Discovering who my Oversoul is, was such a perfect fit with who I am and always have been. There were so many smaller and bigger lessons and discoveries along the journey of this session that I continue to unpack. Phenomenally blooming bigger and more obvious. Simply phenomenal.

Session Begins.

> E [Esmerelda]: *What do you see?*
> D [Debra]: Well, it went from being engulfed in colors, purple colors, and now it's more just darkness. No shapes or anything.
> E: *What do you sense?*
> D: Hmm. The darkness is getting darker but I'm starting to see stars.
> E: *Is there a feeling that comes with it?*

D: Familiarity.

E: *What kind of darkness would you say it is or feels like?*

D: It feels peaceful.

E: *Can you see yourself here in the darkness?*

D: It is changing from totally dark to variegated purple colors coming through. The stars are gone.

E: *We always see the purple. Remember how you explored the last time, following the colors? Activate that beautiful wonderment within you, reaching out, allowing yourself this experience, allowing yourself to manifest here. I wonder what you're doing here at this time?*

D: I'm going to walk through or move through it. It keeps changing, the colors move, mixing the bright purple with the lighter purple. There are different shapes, but abstract shapes of these colors that I'm walking through or moving through. (Smiling)

E: *Feel free to explore. Can you touch a color?*

D: It comes to mind, what came to mind is what appears to be chaos is order when you look at the bigger picture that will include the aura of existence.

E: *Go ahead and repeat that, what appears to be chaos is . . .*

D: When you look at it from bigger and bigger, you will see there is order in the chaos. There is balance and joy to learn from.

E: *That is beautiful.*

D: That is just an idea that came through. Just go out further and further away and see the natural order to it, the natural process, growing and growing. It looks busy when you are close up but when you are further away it's like amazing. I'm still in my colors of the blacks, the purples, and the dark purples.

E: *When you get closer do you affect the patterns?*

D: Good question. Yes, I do.

E: *Explain that. Tell me how. What does it change to and what does it look like or feel like?*

D: It becomes more solid and then moves out of the way. Then in comes the dark and then it becomes purple and it moves out of the way.

E: *That's fun. You should play with it a little bit. I wonder if there is a harmony or a sound that is created.*

D: I want to go up higher, it is just dark right here. I'm moving up higher.

E: *Yeah, go up higher. Does it change as you go up higher?*

D: I haven't seen any change yet.

E: *And how is it that you go up higher?*

D: Through intention.

E: *Can you see your form?*

D: No.

E: *Can you see if you have color within these colors?*

D: That brought up some differences. There was some gold within the purple appearing for a moment.

E: *Gold and purple. Go ahead fast forward, moving through this now to a time and place that is important to you. You are there now. What do you see?*

D: More darkness. There are purple colors and white in there within the dark veins of colors going through it too. It is more dominant almost like a magenta. It is almost solid magenta now.

E: *Whew, that is beautiful. Keep moving through, moving through, and watching. Moving through sensing, seeing, and knowing. Allowing your Higher Self to guide you now. Does this energy feel creational?*

D: It is no longer solid. There are shapes that are more like a vesica piscis kind over here on the right side that has greens to them. It's always moving around and changing. When I pay attention to it, it dissipates. I continue to float through it all. Clouds and clouds of purple clouds in the blackness.

E: *Good. As you move through this beautiful space and time remember, remember aspects of you that you may wish to experience now. Perhaps some wonderful part of you, one of your incarnations. See if you can move towards that, trusting in your Higher Self to guide you.*

D: I'm seeing a path. The shapes have been beautiful to experience, walk through and be a part of. I'm seeing a path going straight up through it that I'm starting to follow. It's a path that separates the colors. The path is dark but doesn't feel negative, it's just black.

E: *Go ahead and keep following, let it take you to where you next need to be for your highest healing, your highest knowing, connection with yourself, your Higher Self, up, up, up.*

D: It closed back in to be more solid magenta again.

E: *Allowing yourself to immerse in it, feeling, sensing, touching, knowing, tasting, smelling.*

D: There is something oscillating down in the lower middle, oscillating greens grabbing my attention. Greens mixed in with the blacks and the purples. It just keeps oscillating.

E: *You were moving your hand by your heart, does that mean that where it was on you?*

D: It is where it is and where I can sense it. It is oscillating bigger, small, bigger, small.

E: *Trusting your Higher Self has brought you here, connecting to that aspect now, receiving the knowingness.*

D: During the energy work, I saw this vivid image of what appeared to be a community within a dome. Inside that dome and in this community, there was a lot of dark smoke. That caught my attention just now but I'm not seeing it again.

E: *What do you see instead of dark smoke now?*

D: Well I guess I see dark smoke. (Chuckling)

E: *For a glimpse there, there was something underneath.*

D: Yeah, but it's all gone now.

E: *It feels like a connection to one of your incarnations. If you want to allow yourself to go there, you could probably drop down into the dome, into that community, into that lifetime, knowing you are protected, guided by your Higher Self, connecting to one of your fabulous incarnations, your lifetimes. Dropping down, down, down. In through the dome, in through that space, trusting what you see, feel, sense, and know.*

D: I'm sensing a lot of destruction. In this dome are the remains of once-grand structures that are no longer intact.

E: *What did they look like? Were they brick or mud, or . . . ?*

D: They weren't either of those, they were something more concrete type or a larger composite.

E: *Continue walking through and telling me what you see.*

D: There's a heaviness about this area.

E: *Are you heavy?*

D: Yeah.

E: *Yeah. Are you seeing anybody else in the vicinity?*

D: No, it's desolate. There's no one here anymore.

E: *Look down at yourself, at your feet and your hands. Describe what you look like.*

D: I'm not seeing anything.

E: *That's okay. Would you like to explore a little further or would you like to perhaps go to this place before there was this destruction? Could we go back in time a little bit, back, back, back? Back, back, back to before this destruction and a happier time. You are there now. Tell me what you see.*

D: I'm seeing silhouettes of shapes. Black silhouettes against a background of dark purple and there are some lighter purples in there. The silhouettes are kind of viney, not something familiar.

E: *As in plant life.*

D: Kind of but it's different. It looks more organic. It's not mechanical or manufactured.

E: *Good. Keep exploring. You can see everything very clearly, very clearly. You are just observing. No one sees you. You are just observing.*

D: I lost it, I don't see anything now.

E: *How does your heart feel?*

D: It feels confusing.

E: *Shall we go to another space and time where we can find answers to this?*

D: Okay.

E: *All right, let's do that. Fast forwarding to another space and time where we can understand what it is that you've been shown. Perhaps even to a time before there was any interference if that is your desire. Fast forwarding now, you are there now. Tell me what you see.*

D: More gold, but it is still the colors and shapes. Nothing tangible.

E: *You are allowed to see . . . to know . . . to experience yourself in all the beauty and glory that you have been. As you resolve into this place, this time, pretend that you have a magic pair of glasses. You are going to put those on. They allow you to see very clearly the true realities. They allow you to circumvent any blocks on your sight. Do you wish to put those glasses on?*

D: Yeah (Enthusiastically)

E: *Let's do it. Remember they are magic glasses attuned just for you just for this special time and space.*

D: It is like I'm looking at a huge nebula. It's moving. It feels almost like a whale.

E: *Like a what?*

D: With that type of grace and purpose.

E: *Do you want to go closer to that nebula?*

D: Okay, let's go.

E: *Okay. Sometimes there are Stargates. Tell me what happens as you get closer.*

D: There are these beautiful golds within the purple, variegated-like shapes of fluff-like clouds. When you're closer you don't sense the movement as much.

E: *I'm sorry, as you get closer what happens?*

D: You don't sense the movement as much.

E: *Oh.*

D: I suppose you are more a part of it. It is a peaceful place. There are the gold shinny portions that I went through. (Smiling) So, we are about back to where we started.

E: *Back to your colors?*

D: Yeah.

E: That's all right. You had some intriguing moments there. Would you like to try for another jump into another experience or would you like to proceed to the body scan? What would you like to do?

D: We can probably proceed.

E: Okay, let's do that. Let's leave this space and time now, leaving that all behind. You are moving away, moving away from that time and space, those colors, that experience. Can I please have all the consciousness of Debra return back into the body, fully integrating? Can I please speak to the Higher Self of Debra, now?

Higher Self is called in.

>Higher Self: Yes. Greetings.
>
>E: Greetings. Am I speaking to Debra's Higher Self?
>
>Higher Self: Yes, you are.
>
>E: Haniel?
>
>AA Haniel: Yes.
>
>E: I love you, honor you, and respect you, Haniel. Thank you for speaking to us today.
>
>AA Haniel: Oh, and I so love you, and honor you. Thank you for doing this.
>
>E: The fun is just beginning, right?
>
>AA Haniel: Yes, it is.
>
>E: Tell us why Debra sees colors like this and what she gains from being immersed in the colors and the creational, it feels like creational energies, really? So I guess I should ask you first Haniel, I know that you hold all the records of Debra's different lives. May I ask you questions?
>
>AA Haniel: Yes.
>
>E: Thank you. Why is it that you chose or Debra places herself in colors first thing in these regressions? What is it with these purples, blacks, and gold colors? What is important for her to know?
>
>AA Haniel: She spent eons there.
>
>E: Does she move energy around? Does she create with these colors?

AA Haniel: We were some of the last to incarnate as more of the wind energy, the air energy, and the movement energy that we are.

E: At one point, she thought she saw a dome with destruction inside. Was that one of the circle lands?

AA Haniel: It feels like it was.

E: Was this a time when she was active in a circle land, in that one she visited?

AA Haniel: That feels right.

E: Although Debra couldn't see her body, I certainly felt like she was quite large, perhaps a Giant. What we call Giants, bigger than these forms now. Would that be accurate for this lifetime she had a glimpse of?

AA Haniel: (Emotional) That makes me want to cry. Yes.

E: Yes. Is your intent in letting her see that and know that, to heal her from that sadness in that life and that destruction?

AA Haniel: To allow it to move through. Yes. It's time to heal from it. Thank you.

E: You are welcome. What can you tell her about that now that you are with her that would be important for her to know?

AA Haniel: What is coming through, is that this was in a time that was all in love and the most highest of intentions and of the learning too late that we can't do it alone. We need to collaborate with those outside of us who are also benevolent and working as allies. It's a great lesson to learn.

E: Would this have been a fairly recent lifetime of hers?

AA Haniel: I'm not sensing a timeframe.

E: Okay. It must not be important then. At one point, when she had the green over her heart space, remember that?

AA Haniel: Yes.

E: I almost felt like she was going to connect to her Tree of Life, there in her heart. I caught a glimpse of like a miniature, a miniature of her Tree in her heart.

AA Haniel: That is what she was hoping as well and then it disappeared. It's all fun.

E: Is it appropriate at this time to let her know a little bit about that incarnation as a Giant Tree on this Earth? . . . Is she feeling it?

AA Haniel: Yes. She is seeing a Pillar of Light, a Pillar of Light between the Cosmos and Mother Gaia, Divine Mother Sophia that is coming through strong.

E: Yes. Is there something you would like her to know or to take within, absorb within about her incarnation as this huge Tree of Life that would help her in this now lifetime that you could tell her about?

AA Haniel: What is coming through is your roots go very deep, very deep, you are connected to . . .

E: It's hard to hear you, I'm sorry. Were you saying, her deep roots?

AA Haniel: Yes. Sorry about that. Roots grow in very deep, very deep, and are connected intrinsically to all aspects, all aspects of Mother Sophia's work and purpose here for the human evolution, the human ascension, with the crystals in the ground, through the organic nature. It is just the purpose. This is Mother Sophia's purpose to create life here, creating all living creatures and things, and allowing them this time and space to each evolve in their proper nature and this connection connecting to the Cosmos. We are all connected. It is so beautiful, the rhythms, the tones, the patterns, the organic ones. Go back to the organic patterns, the organic life cycles of nurturing and loving and protecting one another and being there for one another. The littlest tiniest creatures, the magical creatures, and beings of all kinds.

E: That is just beautiful. Thank you for that. You brought in Mother Sophia, Divine Mother Sophia, who is Gaia. Is Debra connected in a soul-way to Mother Sophia?

AA Haniel: Very much so (Emotional), very much so.

E: Would it be appropriate or . . . , I'm just feeling that perhaps Mother Sophia is her Oversoul, your Oversoul. (Smiling tenderly)

AA Haniel: That just brings joy to my entire being.

E: I felt it when she spoke of her Tree. And, I wondered, you know how I am.

AA Haniel: (Chuckling) Yes. I love how you are.

E: And I know that Debra wanted that connection with her Oversoul and I know that it actually goes beyond Gaia and the Divine Sophia but I don't know how and I don't know if now is the time to talk about it. Perhaps Divine Mother Sophia and Gaia is enough to handle for this time. It is up to you Haniel to guide us here.

AA Haniel: That was eloquently said, thank you. Eloquently said.

E: Thank you. Is there anything else that you wish to bring forward for Debra now before we go into the body scan? Look at how light you made her with that, Haniel. That's so pretty, to bring in Mother Sophia. Should we talk to her, Sophia Gaia?

AA Haniel: Yes. Let's try (Smiling and chuckling together)

E: Let's do that. Divine Mother Sophia, this beautiful living essence of this Earth, this Gaia, we call you forth now. And I greet you with love, honor, and respect. Loving you dearly and deeply. Greetings.

Divine Mother Sophia: Thank you. Greetings. I love you so much and thank you for this growing, this blooming that is happening.

E: Hor-ey-zee! (Light Language for bloom) Yes.

Divine Mother Sophia: Hore-ey-zee!

E: Moora, moora (Fuller, fuller in Light Language). Thank you for this divine creation of Debra. She is such a heart sister for me. I mean there are no words and I am very grateful for her, and your expression into her in this manner and that it has so impacted my life in the way that it has. I am eternally grateful.

Divine Mother Sophia: You are a huge soul who is celebrated in all realms. You are so loved. I thank you.

E: Thank you. Let's bloom Debra a little bit. What most would help her bloom in this time and space? What wise words would you have to say to her?

Divine Mother Sophia: You've got this. You've got this. And perfectly so. Enjoy the beauty that surrounds you, the little moments and create some of your own. We are connected in the most intimate of ways.

E: I feel that. I feel you running through her now stronger, rooting into her, blossoming into her tree branches.

Divine Mother Sophia: It looks like some exploring there in the future there too.

E: *Oh yes, definitely. And some wisdom, I'm sure.*

Divine Mother Sophia: Yes.

E: *All that you help us with, all that you expand us with. And I'm happy to spend time here. I don't mean to rush into the body scan so please tell me when you are ready. I just want Debra to feel you.*

Divine Mother Sophia: She has been. She is exploding with it all. The joy and all.

E: *Yes, I see her jumping up and down. I see her little girl jumping up and down.*

Divine Mother Sophia: This is fun and the fun will continue. This is the time to integrate. Take time to integrate and allow it to just be and flow with it. No worries, just flow.

E: *And how are you doing, Divine Mother Sophia? Are you healing? Are we advancing on this Earth?*

Divine Mother Sophia: This is the time we have been waiting for. This is the time we have known and yes, all of this outpouring of love from all over matters, it matters, and it helps significantly. We are growing, we are growing, and we are moving. We are moving out of this, back to what we were organically meant to be. Our path is secure. Thank you for the love. I love you. I love you. I love you.

E: *Beautiful. The Ra Collective feels very strong too, Mother. Very strong as if the whole Galaxy is gathered to assist.*

Divine Mother Sophia: Yes. They have been here witnessing this.

E: *Beautiful. Would you like to stay with us and do the body scan, you and Haniel?*

Divine Mother Sophia: That would be a treat, that would be wonderful. Thank you.

E: *Let's do that, thank you. Thank you. Do you wish to have any other Archangels or surely there are some Dragons to invite in? I'm just making space in time now so that we can all bring our beautiful Guide Teams forward.*

Divine Mother Sophia: Yes. Thank you.

Body scan begins.

E: So Divine Mother Sophia, I ask you now to do the body scan on Debra, and I would like to scan and begin finding all the entities within her now. I did notice there were some during the RAAH that we were taking care of. Do you want me to say what I saw or do you want to go straight into what you see?

Divine Mother Sophia: Would that happen to have been in the arm?

E: Yes, there was one in the arm. That was a Reptilian. I put it in the alchemy symbol earlier, so let's go ahead and look under her ears, where the lymph glands are under the ears. I saw two Reptilians under each one that I put in the alchemy symbol.

Divine Mother Sophia: How and when did they come in?

E: That's a good question, let's look. We're looking at the Reptilians under her ears, shall we ask Haniel?

Divine Mother Sophia: Yes.

E: Haniel, beloved Sister, I call you forth now. Greetings Haniel.

AA Haniel: Greetings.

E: We are going to bring up all the little Reptilians. There weren't many but there were some. There was one under each ear in nodules and it looked like her lymph glands were a little swollen. It could have been just energetically. I sensed that this came from the pool actually. Can you confirm that for us? Where did these come from? They're recent. They're new.

AA Haniel: They are new. She actually places my symbols along with Archangel Haylel's symbols on the pool before entering.

E: Oh, that is beautiful. Great idea. Would it have been the locker room?

AA Haniel: It was in the jacuzzi, after the swim. It was in the jacuzzi. She felt really yucky in there and had to get out.

E: Can she put a shield on that before entering or . . . ?

AA Haniel: No more jacuzzi in the space where she has been going. There are too many people in that small space.

E: Right. I see that.

AA Haniel: Her workaround is to go to the steam room to sweat out any toxins and boosting her shields.

E: So the steam room is okay for her then?

AA Haniel: Yes. Placing the symbols in the steam room is a good idea, too. (Interestingly, in this location that I frequent the pool and the steam room are not heavily used. In fact, I am often the only one present. Additionally, I have found when I chant in the steam room it creates a wonderful vibration.)

E: Okay. The one in her arm, I'm talking about her right arm. It was her left arm that she fell on.

AA Haniel: It was the left arm getting our attention and feeling the pain.

E: Can you look at her right arm? Maybe it hopped over from the left one with that torn bicep there, I am not sure. I was surprised at seeing it there so I am asking you what your take on it is because I do not see anything on her left arm. I see pain and inflammation but I don't see any infringements.

AA Haniel: It's not coming through.

E: Well, we will talk to that one in a minute and he will tell us. Then in her heart, there was a tiny little one. A Reptilian again, trying to keep her Heart Flame from igniting. And he was doing a poor job of it but he was there. She has that mini-Tree of Life in her heart growing there. It is like the embers of her Heart Flame; they warm roots and they nurture the roots somehow. I'm not quite sure how that works but they don't damage her Tree. Her Heart Flame is like it ignites her Tree more or less.

AA Haniel: It is plasma energy.

E: Okay, her plasma energy. Well, no wonder he couldn't do anything about it. And that is the only Reptilians that I found. I did find three Earthbound entities. They are trying to interfere with her third eye projecting a smiley face at me out of her third eye. That is what alerted them to me. I mean you know; they just can't help themselves. They show themselves all the *time in the ways that they do. There are two males and a female. I sense that they came from her house, the house she lives in. What can you tell me about them, Haniel?*

AA Haniel: These Earth-bound have obviously passed and are confused.

E: *It is very odd. I have never run into anything like that.*

AA Haniel: Being a large family from a large family, the family dynamics of this household are complex, and consequently have more opportunities to experience the deaths of loved ones.

E: *I'm wondering if that is not the case because really her room is shielded but the rest of the house is not.*

AA Haniel: Her room is shielded and she is shielded.

E: *They weren't in her third eye. They were projecting a smiley face on her third eye. They were projecting and I sense that their trickster ways did something to mess with her. It's not that they got into her it was more like throwing spit wads at her or throwing things at her third eye.*

AA Haniel: Yeah, that aligns with the environment.

E: *Okay, so I asked Archangel Michael to contain them. Archangel Michael, Archangel Michael. Haniel if you don't mind can we talk to Archangel Michael for a moment?*

AA Haniel: Yes, of course.

E: *Calling forth upon Archangel Michael, Archangel Michael, Archangel Michael. Greetings dear Brother.*

AA Michael: Greetings.

E: *It is such a joy, a delight, and an honor to have you here. I love you deeply, I honor you and I respect you. Thank you, thank you, thank you. Can you tell me about these three earth-bound entities? Do I need to call Azrael now to escort them on their way or do they have a message for Debra?*

AA Michael: There is no message. They aren't directly related to her other than through the marriage of a family member.

E: *Why are they in that space if they aren't related?*

AA Michael: This is a healthy active diverse household with diverse activities and friends. For the most part, it is of high vibration and of love but certain judgments are at play for she is the odd one and attracts some of that. Attracting trickster energy as you call it, is a great way of putting it. So yes, they are able to be safely escorted to their place of healing.

E: Before we do that, there were also surprisingly three dark portals present. Two on the land of the home and one in that guest bedroom. Is this related to how these Earth-bound entities got in?

AA Michael: Yes. Yes.

E: And you did close those dark portals, you told me. Just confirming.

AA Michael: Yes. Thank you.

E: Yes. Thank you. Archangel Azrael, Archangel Azrael, Archangel Azrael, Brother I greet you with love, honor, and respect.

AA Azrael: Greetings.

E: Greetings Dear One. It's such a joy to have your beautiful energy here. Would you please scoop up these three little tricksters, these Earth-bound entities, and take them on to their next evolutionary experience?

AA Azrael: Yes, with pleasure and with honor.

E: Thank you. Thank you so much. And then if you will come back because we will have some Reptilians for you next. Michael, are you still with me?

AA Michael: Yes.

E: Shall I stick with you for the Reptilians?

AA Michael: Yes, I can handle that for you.

E: Okay, thank you. For the two that were under her ears, they tried to run and of course, Metatron scooped them right up which I'm grateful for. Thank you, Archangel Metatron. Do we need to talk to these? They came from the Jacuzzi area, or are they just opportunists?

AA Michael: I'm not sensing there is a message.

E: Okay, we are going to set them to the side and I'm going to have Archangel Azrael take all of them at one time. Michael, can you go to her right shoulder then? What's up with that Reptilian there and why the right shoulder and not the left shoulder? We are confused about that because she injured her left shoulder. Is it actually a Reptilian or is it a resonance that I'm reading?

AA Michael: I'm not getting anything.

E: Okay, can we check her left side, the bicep, please?

AA Michael: Yes.

E: Is there anything there?

AA Michael: I'm not sensing anything there. She places a healthy dose of the Phoenix Flame and Violent Flame on her left arm every day making your observation that it hopped over to the other arm likely.

E: Great. So just confirming her right shoulder down her right arm down to her right wrist is clear of anything including Archons.

AA Michael: I'm not sensing anything there.

E: Going to the Reptilian that was in her heart trying to keep her Heart Flame from igniting, which he didn't do, do you see that one?

AA Michael: On the right side.

E: Can you tell when that one came in? I sort of feel like it was from her journey to South America. Michael, can I ask, can they attach to objects or do they just attach to organic life?

AA Michael: They feed off of organic but can attach to objects temporarily.

E: I wonder if that is what happened. This one wasn't doing much at all. I mean it was like it was hiding in her, using her as a refuge.

AA Michael: He's pretty clever because she's had how many sessions since November.

E: Well, that's true. Can we scan her room, please? Scan her room and everything in her room. Is there a crystal that she traveled with or brought back that is up on the left side of her bed with all the other crystals?

AA Michael: Yes, there is.

E: So maybe we are not dealing with a Reptilian at all.

AA Michael: This is a very tiny crystal.

E: So that is more negative energy, correct? I sensed consciousness, but . . .

AA Michael: Shall we speak to it?

E: *I would like to put it in the Divine Mother/Father/Source symbol first, if we could do that, please?*

AA Michael: Okay, it is encased. It is a very small honeycomb crystal.

E: *So we have the crystal encased and the energy I'm sensing in her heart space, yes?*

AA Michael: Yes.

E: *Okay. Come up, up, up now. I am speaking to the energy, the entity within her heart space now. Come up, up, up, we wish to speak to you now. Greeting you with respect. Greetings.*

Entity: Greetings.

E: *What are you? . . . You can't evade us and you can't get out so . . .*

Entity: I'm just energy. I wanted to stay but I had to come back.

E: *As you know in this time and space, we are not allowing any parasitic entities or energies within us as we go through this ascension process, can you tell me why it was that you connected to her heart and to her crystal?*

Entity: Well that is where she carried the crystal for months until she put it up.

E: *Oh, that makes sense. How did she manage not to see you? How did you manage to evade her, knowing that you are there?*

Entity: She loved this crystal because she carried it around for so long.

E: *So you just hid within it?*

Entity: Yes, it was easy.

E: *What did you cause her?*

Entity: I wasn't able to do too much.

E: *Did you sometimes sprint to her right shoulder?*

Entity: Yeah, I can move around.

E: *Well, thank you. That helps us understand that. Did you ever have a body?*

Entity: I entered this crystal from the hostel that she stayed in through an invited guest who stopped in temporarily. This guest was from Peru and curiously picked up the crystal while Debra removed it and was in the shower. I don't remember having a body.

E: *Are you a male, female, or neither?*

Entity: Male.

E: *Do you have a name?*

Entity: I don't remember.

E: *Okay. Do you remember how you might have died?*

Entity: No, but I feel like I was young.

E: *Thank you. Thank you for answering the questions. I'm going to remind you that all is light and of the light now. I would love to aid you, to help you spread your light so that you may be free to go, keeping your own experiences instead of being stuck in a crystal or a body, especially Debra's body now. It is time for you to be free, no longer having to play this parasitic role. You can now be your own sovereign being. We are going to start helping you fill yourself with Love-Light now. As you know, as the Earth and the Universe are ascending, parasitic entities like you will no longer be able to attach to people. Today we would love to assist you so that when ascension comes forth you won't be recycled straight back to Source, back to zero, losing all the experiences you've gained. Instead, we can assist you today in spreading your light and helping you to ascend to a positive polarization, retaining all the wisdom through being negatively polarized. And I'm speaking to all the Reptilians as well now. The two Reptilians that were under her ears, I'm speaking to you as well. You will be free to incarnate somewhere else. No longer having to feed off others' light. You will be your own creator being, creating your own light. Wouldn't that be magnificent?*

Entity: Yes.

E: *Would you allow us to help you spread your light?*

Entity: Yes.

E: *And to the two Reptilians, do you agree as well?*

Reptilians: Yes.

E: *Thank you. Okay, we are focusing Love-Light on Debra, now. Archangel Azrael, Brother, are you here?*

AA Azrael: Yes.

E: Thank you. I ask that you ensure that each entity is guided to where they are meant to go through this ascension process. I ask you, Archangel Azrael to take these three away upon your Ray, to guide the souls back, keeping them safe from other negative entities or being tricked back into an inversion again.

AA Azrael: With honor. We have them. They are of light and are out.

E: Thank you. Archangel Raphael. Calling upon Archangel Raphael now. Greetings, Brother.

AA Raphael: Greetings.

E: I love you, honor you, and respect you. Archangel Raphael, would you begin healing the heart space in Debra, and both arms, please? And the nodules under each ear where these were removed?

AA Raphael: Yes.

E: Thank you so much. And I see Divine Mother Sophia also participating. Thank you, Divine Mother Sophia, for this healing.

Divine Mother Sophia: Yes. You are welcome. Thank you.

E: Archangel Michael, may I speak to you now about some of the nanotech we found?

AA Michael: Yes.

E: This is Debra's deepest AURA. (Smiling) I'm kind of calling it the final cleanup. Kind of like, that is just how it feels to me. She has done such a heroic job of reclaiming her sovereignty and her power and holding her divine vessel sovereign free and clear. I want to acknowledge that. These things that we found today were very deeply hidden and it is just now time for them to be revealed. We can remove them. They are some of the deepest infringements she's had, as far as I can tell, Michael. Is that correct?

AA Michael: Correct.

E: Okay. We found a nanobot, very tiny, like minuscule, on her pineal gland. And we placed it in the destroyer symbol. Has that transmuted out now?

AA Michael: Yes.

E: *And it had wires connecting to a black box. I sense this is the master black box being now removed from her neck. We placed that in the destroyer symbol during the RAAH. Has that transmuted out?*

AA Michael: Yes.

E: *Thank you. How about the wires that connected the pineal to the neck area?*

AA Michael: They are gone. Yes.

E: *And then there was this metal rod, kind of like a square rod, right under her pineal gland going right through her hip horizontally. Has that been transmuted out?*

AA Michael: Yes.

E: *What was that from?*

AA Michael: What comes to mind is her life as that android.

E: *Oh, that makes total sense. Yes. Oh, yes. Okay. Can we do a thorough deep scan now, Michael and Divine Mother Sophia, please, from the top of her physical body to the very tips of her fingers and toes, just scanning for anything else? Please and thank you.*

AA Michael and Divine Mother Sophia: Scanning now.

E: *I see everybody is assisting, thank you.*

AA Michael and Divine Mother Sophia: We're not sensing anything further.

E: *Yes. She really was fairly clear and what was astonishing to me was the alchemy symbol for the 10th chakra showed right away through her beautiful DNA strands. She has retained a lot of the alchemy symbols on her now. I think her third eye alchemy symbol will now be integrating fully with her now.*

AA Michael and Divine Mother Sophia: Beautiful.

E: *Her solar plexus was a little sore. It showed a little redness to me but I didn't see anything in there. Is this just related to any upheaval her family might have been in lately? You know we do a lot of processing of emotional and family stuff in our stomachs and our guts. Is that what that is from?*

AA Michael and Divine Mother Sophia: We are not finding any family issues to attribute this to.

E: Okay, we'll ask Archangel Raphael to heal that soreness there. And her sacral is crying.

AA Michael and Divine Mother Sophia: That is not crying in sadness. It is crying in the joy, crying in the awe-stricken humble joy of this cause and effect of growing bigger. And the joy of this new knowledge of integrating how expansive she really is. This is the crying tears of joy and of integrating this larger knowledge of being this Tree of Life. This expansive purpose is unfolding for her. It's a time of just sitting and reflecting on this knowledge. It is not crying for anything sad. It is a beautiful transformation going on.

E: Beautiful. That's good. Yeah, I see that. Beautiful.

AA Michael and Divine Mother Sophia: That was beautiful of you to pick that up.

E: And I sensed it was about her journey. Michael, we didn't find anything else in the body. May I ask to make sure that all dark portals have been closed including within this house and this land where she is? Asking that all, there really weren't any Archons so to speak, I saw nanotechnology but that is all transmuted out. Does her spine look clear, Michael?

AA Michael: Yes, that is clear.

E: And how about her DNA? I just don't see anything negative in her DNA or any false fractals at all.

AA Michael: It looks good.

E: How about negative chords, implants, or hooks? Did the Reptilians on her ears have hooks in there? I didn't see them.

AA Michael: They were not in her that long and left nothing behind when they left.

E: Can we continue healing the organic matter that had that technology on it and in it, including through the brain, the neck area, and the third eye area?

AA Michael and Divine Mother Sophia: Yes.

E: And I would like to ask for the healing of her eyes. She said her eyes have been becoming gummy lately, is this something we can just heal, or does she need to be aware of something? What is going on with her eyes? Is this a question for you or do you wish Haniel or Divine Mother Sophia to speak?

AA Michael: It is just residue from her infections and having been sick. It's clearing. So we can heal this. Let's place some Phoenix Fire on her eyes.

E: Okay. Let's do that. Focusing Phoenix Fire on her eyes now. Transmuting out any residue from the infection now and the infection itself.

AA Michael and Divine Mother Sophia: Beautiful, thank you so much.

E: And some Love-Light then (Singing), just top it off with some Love-Light, Love-Light, Love-Light. Beautiful. Okay, can we continue healing her eyesight, Archangel Michael with her Higher Self's permission, Divine Mother Sophia?

AA Michael and Divine Mother Sophia: Yes.

E: Beautiful. If there is anything dental that she needs to be healed, we ask that that be healed. And thank you, Michael. Just for a moment, I'm going to talk to Divine Mother Sophia. Greetings Divine Mother.

Divine Mother Sophia: Greetings.

E: Shall we age regress Debra at all in this AURA? We did a little bit last time.

Divine Mother Sophia: No. She should be okay in that respect.

E: Okay. Would you like to take over for Michael or what are your feelings here?

Divine Mother Sophia: I would love to.

E: Okay, thank you. Would you please check her chakras now? Make sure that they are all aligned, functioning in alliance and harmony with each other.

Divine Mother Sophia: They are beautiful and shining.

E: They are. Now that we have cleared up her third eye, I ask if you would open up her third eye and activate her abilities to the fullest capacity that she can have at this time.

Divine Mother Sophia: Yes.

E: Thank you. And can we please expand her heart now too, and that beautiful little miniature Tree of Life that she has in there?

Divine Mother Sophia: (Chuckling) Yes.

E: Her auric field looks like it's healing nicely because of the alchemy symbol that we put on, the 13 to infinity purple star netting. Can you tell if there are any rips or holes that haven't been healed yet?

Divine Mother Sophia: It looks good to me.

E: Divine Mother Sophia, is she whole and complete soul-wise now, with all fractals incorporating what is allowed at this point?

Divine Mother Sophia: All fractals in this time and space, yes.

E: Thank you. I would like to ask now for the deletion of inverted timelines from her.

Divine Mother Sophia: Yes.

E: Okay, and I would like for healing of trauma from current or past lives to occur over the next 21 days for her as guided by you Divine Mother Sophia.

Divine Mother Sophia: Yes, thank you.

E: Archangel Michael, would you look deeply, deeply, deeply, for any remaining contracts, anything tied to black magic, any remaining contracts? I don't want anything missed. I don't want to miss anything.

AA Michael: I am not sensing any.

E: Good. Thank you. Archangel Raphael, dear Brother, if you could just bring your healing Green Ray to all spaces and places within and around Debra in her shields and fields that need to be healed, if you would do so along with Divine Mother Sophia over these next 21 days, in dream time and daydreaming time, completely bring her body back healed?

AA Raphael and Divine Mother Sophia: Yes.

E: Thank you. She has just two questions left. Divine Mother Sophia, Debra asks, in the eventuality that her children might choose to read her book, may I ask if each of her six children chose her as their mother knowing full well what was ahead of them?

Divine Mother Sophia: Yes, they did with eyes wide open.

E: *That's beautiful! So then, does it follow that they each chose to experience both the magical beauty and the darker trauma that the family went through?*

Divine Mother Sophia: Yes, this was pre-arranged. They knew and they volunteered heroically.

E: *How are they doing within their individual expressions? Are they evolving as they should? I don't want to overstep boundaries but can Debra be rest assured that they are each looked after?*

Divine Mother Sophia: They are being looked after and they are loved, they are loved.

E: *Yes, she is wonderful at that too. Archangel Haylel mentioned during her Akashic Record Reading in February that she didn't put her blocks there. She would like to know who did. Can that be revealed to her at this time?*

Divine Mother Sophia: I'm not receiving the answer to that one.

E: *I'm calling forth upon the Archangels present, Archangel Michael, Archangel Haniel, and Divine Mother Sophia. If it can be stated for Debra's highest good at this time, who placed these blocks within her?.. I have a niggly of someone who did place some blocks in there. I'm not sure if you want me to speak that at this time, Haniel or Divine Mother Sophia.*

AA Haniel and Divine Mother Sophia: That would be wonderful if you could share that with her. Thank you.

E: *I feel that the practitioner who facilitated the reading created some false stories, some of which were real. It wasn't really this practitioner but the infringements within her. And that they did effectuate some blocks.*

AA Haniel and Divine Mother Sophia: Thank you. Yes.

E: *Thank you. Debra, does that answer that question for you?*

D: Yes. I thought it may have been something more recent but yeah.

E: *I am being reminded that there really isn't any time and that some of these things could have been placed and triggered to activate so that you would think it would be more recent if that makes sense for you.*

D: Yes. Thank you.

E: *You're welcome. Have all of those blocks been cleared, Haniel?*

AA Haniel: Yes. Finally, thank you.

E: *Good. And all connections, chords, or anything that might tether Debra to that entity to this particular practitioner right now, that has been cut and terminated?*

AA Haniel: Yes, all chords have been cut and deleted from all time and space.

E: *We mean no disrespect for a fellow practitioner and I ask that this one finds her way back home to the light in her perfect divine timing.*

AA Haniel: And we know it will happen as each light-worker touches the other, then touches the other, it will happen.

E: *What a beautiful ripple! I ask for continued healing for Debra's physical body, her knees, her shoulder, her biceps, her eyes, her womb, and her heart, all things physical, emotional, mental, and spiritual. This is the great sweeping up, the great clearing, the great connection with the Oversoul, and now with her A-team. She wants to know who is on her A-Team, Archangel Haniel. Can you share that with us, please?*

AA Haniel: Trust in yourself. You know that Archangel Uriel and Haylel have always been there. And Archangel Raguel has been coming through very often lately along with Archangels Ariel and Jophiel. You have your Dragons and of course, Divine Mother Sophia. You have so many to simply call and they are there. Whatever is going on, they'll be there.

E: *How about Phoenix's?*

AA Haniel: Yes, let's activate your connection to your Phoenix. You have a Sasquatch on your team, and a Blue Avian as well.

E: *Is this Sasquatch connected to the white Sasquatch from Mt. Shasta and beyond?*

AA Haniel: Yes. We connected there in Mt. Shasta, yes.

E: *Beautiful. Is there any other magical creatures and benevolent beings that could be considered her core A-Team? Surely Giants will be in there somewhere.*

AA Haniel: Yes, she has a wonderful beautiful Giant and the Redtail Hawk. And the Trees are part of your core along with the Unicorns.

E: How did we not state the Trees for Heaven's sake? That is quite the team. Speaking with Divine Mother Sophia and Archangel Haniel, are there any questions that I could have asked today that would be helpful to Debra that I have not asked to include, making sure she is a free and clear sovereign physical being in her sovereign physical vessel?

AA Haniel and Divine Mother Sophia: No further questions are needed but we would like to add to continue believing in yourself and continue blooming.

E: Beautiful. May I bring Debra back now? Are we complete?

AA Haniel and Divine Mother Sophia: We are complete.

E: Beautiful. I give thanks to all who assisted us today. It is with love and gratitude that I ask now for the aid of the Higher Self. We are thankful for all that you did today for Debra. I ask now that all the energies we spoke to today, return back to where they belong. We give thanks for all the aid that was given today.

End of session.

This session pulled together and answered so many of the pieces I had floating around in my mind. I can't think of a time in my life when I didn't want to protect and nurture Mother Earth, Divine Mother Sophia, Gaia. Or that I didn't gaze at her beauty in pure awe. As a youth, I found a place up in the Utah mountains that was somewhat hidden under a large evergreen tree. This tree's branches hung down touching the ground. Who wouldn't want to sneak under and inside a tree's branches?

At the moment I didn't realize how impactful that experience would be. Before this AURA session, I didn't consider how intentional that discovery was. But getting back to my memory, I had the idea to go inside the branches toward the trunk of this huge tree. What I discovered was this magical place with a small creek running through it making babbling water sounds, cool crisp air, and fragrant earthy and evergreen smells. The colors and textures of moss growing close to the water and over the rocks belonged in a painting. The ground was surprisingly soft and sort of spongy to sit on. Plus there were several tiny wildflowers here and there.

I sat there feeling like I was inside a fairytale thinking and feeling there were magical creatures all around me. Although I never returned to that place physically, I often returned mentally. To think that what I was at that moment considering to be a fairytale was indeed full of playful Archangels, magical beings, Dragons, Unicorns, Pixies, Giants, Sasquatch, and Source. Today I am in awe that all it takes is a thought and they are right here with me. How wonderful to feel their energies of joy, of strength, of magic, of power, and love. And to feel and know that we are all part of this fantastic team in our journey together. In love and gratitude am I for these deeper cellular experiences.

Following up on my confusion that I mentioned at the beginning of the chapter with having to go back and verbally do my chakra chants after this session's energy work, that question kept grabbing my attention. Finally, two days later it grew to the point that I felt like I was going to explode. I called and asked my practitioner about it. My question was, what did she sense that required that extra repeat? She responded with, "Oh, I didn't think that was negative. It's just something I recently started doing. I found starting my sessions off chanting with my clients helpful, and once remembering I forgot to do that with you, I wanted to allow you the full experience."

Dang! What a huge lesson. I tripped and fell flat on my face from a perception that had no substance whatsoever. Wow. I mean, wow! What a gift. Can you see how masterfully my Higher Self worked through my practitioner to show me how easily the rug can be pulled right out from under my feet? I keep thinking I'm ready and feeling I'm ready to stand in my power but then this. How many times have I been lovingly nurtured to jump through these emotions, these blockages, and stand in my Truth?

Wasn't it Archangel Haylel who not too long ago said there's no turning back and recommended that the time is now to let everything go? That it was time to accept and remember who I am. It's easy to stand in my power as a bridge for someone else's healing but not so easy when it comes to empowering myself for myself. I love that this happened and exactly how it happened. What a lesson indeed. Again, in love and gratitude am I for these deeper cellular experiences.

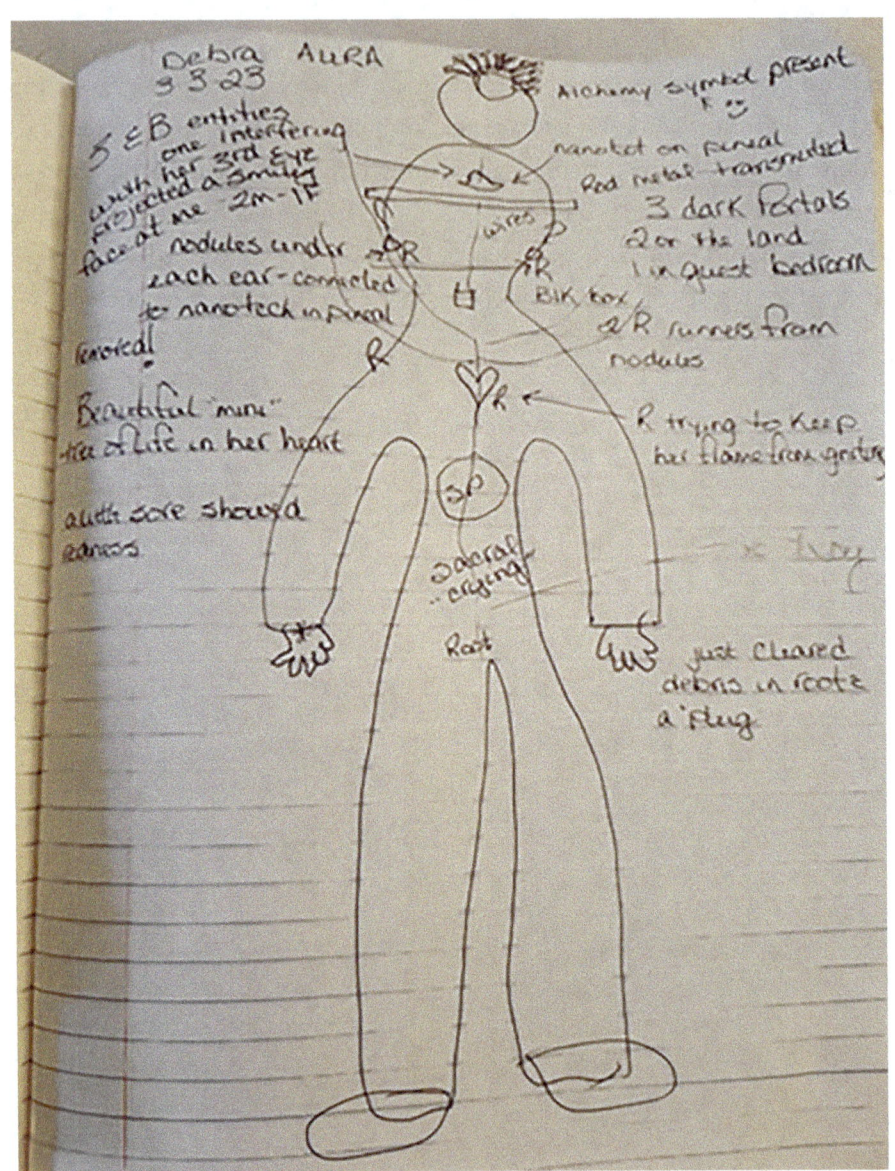

16

Mind Expanding

Reflecting on the Lotus Effect mentioned in the preface, we learned that these seemingly frail, beautiful lotus flowers thrive in the muck of their environment. And they do that by way of tightly placed microscopic nodes within the makeup of their vessel or structure. Through light-hearted loving inner standing, we too can repel all that is not organically part of our divine blueprint by simply filling those gaps with remembering.

Remembering, integrating, healing, and lovingly thanking that experience for what it gave you and then letting it go. This kind of forgiveness is freeing beyond measure. And let's not forget the power of collectives. It has become well-known that large numbers of people feeling and focusing on the same emotion at the same time affects the Schumann Resonances. The Schumann Resonance is a set of electromagnetic waves that exist in the Earth's Ionosphere, formed by the interactions between the planet's surface and the ionosphere.

Worldwide incidents causing shared emotions, such as 911, wars, and groups coming together with peaceful intentions of love and harmony are documented as affecting the Schumann Resonances. Combining the concept of shared emotions and repeating number patterns, which I already touched on with 555 in the Epiphanies chapter, loving mentor Rising Phoenix AuroRa and her benevolent team of Archangels, Divine Mother, and Divine Father, suggest that wherever we are at, we are able to form a collective as we send love each time repeating numbers show up in our day.

Rising Phoenix AuroRa Instagram post:
Heal Yourself and the Collective

> 10:10 – Send love to all your past and future selves
> 11:11 – Send love to self
> 12:12 – Send love to all planets and life that require it in the Universe
> 1:11 – (13th hour) Send love to the Earth and all life on it: people, trees, plants, and animals
> 2:22 – Send love to your beloved ones
> 3:33 – Send love to your dreams and aspirations for their fruition and manifestation
> 4:44 – Send love to the New World Order (To transmute it)
> 5:55 – Send love to the children of Earth and Creation

Additionally, similar to how we are able to heal our emotional, mental, physical, and spiritual bodies as witnessed in each chapter of this book, we are able to impactfully heal the trauma of Mother Earth/Divine Mother Sophia. This is profoundly effective when we are physically on the site where such traumas took place.

During one of her live videos, AuroRa shared some of her difficult childhood and how she was able to heal at the deepest level by physically visiting the location. Hearing her suggestion, I thought to myself, what can be left? I've already brought it up within hypnosis and written about it here, but this is about me and my self-love, I'm open to it.

-Journal entry July 31, 2023: *Today being Monday, last Thursday I figured it was time to get my car inspected and registered. The place I like to* go to is located in the town of Draper, which is where I lived while in high school. It's about a 25-minute drive from my home. I like that place because it's close to various stores I frequent, they're efficient, and it comes with a car wash. Something my car really needed. Plus, AuroRa recently suggested that where possible we should physically visit traumatic locations of our past and do some energetic healing of that land and space. With my car all freshly legal and sparkly clean, resonating with AuroRa's advice I drove down the street to the hellhole of a house where we lived during my father's second marriage.

The area changed dramatically over the decades. I found the bones of the house that now hosts an addition and bigger newer homes next to it. My entire being felt off balance and nauseous. Powering through it, I quickly got right to work sending wave after wave of energetic healing. After thanking it for the experience, I couldn't wait to leave and let it all go.

My next stop was Sandy, the next town over and about a five-minute drive. This is where we lived when my sister, brother, and I were in the car accident that took our mother's life. I was nine at the time, my sister eight, and my brother seven. Several blocks before arriving, I became so nauseous that I stopped off and purchased a ginger drink. The drink didn't help at all.

Finding the house, my nausea became extreme. I immediately started sending waves of healing energy and gratitude for the lessons I received while living here. My nausea became bearable but continued to be intense.

As soon as I left the neighborhood, I was back to normal and light as a feather. Halleluiah! It wasn't until the following day that I realized that the day that I was doing that energy work happened to be July 27, the anniversary of my mother's death. This is the one day of the year that without fail I am in somber reflection. This year it passed me by, or so I thought. Wow! I was in the flow to heal those energies. Somber yet moving past and deleting it. How cool is that?

Without judgment, we each come with our unique life experiences to interpret the symbols we're given in harmony or out of harmony. It's our choice to connect further in solving these puzzles. –End of journal entry.

- Could it be as simple as being open and willing to consider our greater consciousness?
- Could it be that remembering our past lives is an intentional part of the process of moving into this bigger portion of who we are?
- Could it be as simple as going into that still small space within our heart and just be; just listening to our body and feeling the love being offered by the Universe?
- Could it be that raising our vibration is as simple as remembering, respecting, thanking, and loving?

Every chapter in this book has played a huge part in my ability to repel the muck and move further along in my journey. Additionally, I've been gifted with being able to deeply talk about these things with other like-minded people attending the various retreats and events. Attending retreats afforded me the opportunity to bond and really dig deep into a fuller richer mind-expanding experience.

An important group that I am a part of is AuroRa's Book Club. These people are truly my Soul Tribe. It's when you meet someone and feel like you've known them forever and find there's never enough time and that your history together is beyond this life. My love for these beautiful souls is infinite. They bring me such joy, and catching up with them and learning from them is a treasured part of my week. As I mentioned in the first chapters of this book, AuroRa's book catalyzed my awakening process and literally catapulted me to where I am today. No matter which chapter or which book the Book Club was reading, each week's discussion unveiled deeper insights and always related to exactly what was currently going on in the world around us.

Since I joined, the Book Club has gone through AuroRa's Book One twice. While considering which book to read next, AuroRa suggested we move our studies on to Todd Deviney's book, "Expansion for Ascending Consciousness." (Deviney, 2018). Deviney delves deeply into the physics and science of the technical ascension process. The way he scattered personal analogies and graphics throughout the book helped me better grasp these complex concepts.

Afterward, because they aligned with AuroRa's flat earth and her Tartaria channelings, we read the Nos Confunden series of books, "The Navigator Who Crossed the Ice Walls," (Confunden, The Navigator Who Crossed the Ice Walls, 2022) "Terra Infinita," (Confunden, 2022) and "The Lands of Mars." (Confunden, The Lands of Mars, 2022). The first book is about "first contact" within this last reset by one of our ships that crossed those ice walls. Confunden introduces readers to the circle lands and the people behind the ice walls. Many may know of the Antarctica military bases but few know of the peaceful lands of our ancestors who live beyond those walls. Confunden's books share how our ancestors live to be hundreds of years old, they enjoy free energy, and the freedoms we only dream about. These books document maps of other worlds and wars our ancestors fought on our behalf alongside the Giants as their allies. Reading these books feels like just the beginning of much more to come. I highly recommend them as mind-expanding.

At the time I'm writing this chapter, the Book Club is in the process of reading Dolores Cannon's book, "The Convoluted Universe, Book One," (Cannon, 2001). I'm really loving and learning from Cannon's timeless mastery of her sessions as a past life regression hypnosis therapist. She not only brought through mind-expanding knowledge, but wisdom. You should have seen me jump out of my chair with excitement while reading *Chapter Four, Janice's Omitted Transcripts*.

The magical synchronicity of pulling together missing puzzle pieces of my personal past life regressions with what unfolds in Cannon's book was exhillerating. The missing pieces I'm referring to have to do with each and every one of my AURA sessions started the same way with me going through my purple variegated oscillating colors and not sensing a body. My loving practitioners work patiently to get me out of that space and into a more coherent life for my healing.

On page eighty-seven in Cannon's book, Janice is her somnambulistic client. Somnambulistic is when, while under hypnosis, the client's ego is completely out of the way and she does not remember any part of the session. Paraphrasing, Janice is deep within hypnosis and explains purple colors, shapes, and patterns. As the session continues, Janice's body disappears. Cannon encourages Janice to ask someone there to explain what these shapes and patterns mean. The response is phenomenal as the entity explains that these colorful shapes and patterns are an entire language. It's guidance and communications that she will use in the future.

Wow! With this new information, do you think my Higher Self was slowly, gently, lovingly, trying to organically remind me of who I am? All this time while I've been in that similar space of colors and shapes without a body, I assumed that I must not be surrendering. How cool to learn that in that theta brainwave space of hypnosis, I was literally receiving downloads. Totally fascinating! Totally Exhilarating! Totally awesome!

The rewards of delving deeper into this work are simply priceless. I'm lit up with excitement. Cannon's entire chapter four is fantastically mind-expanding. It talks about time junctions, and how everything is energy. The entity explains that the literal way to refer to what we refer to as our soul is our Source Energy. How about that? At our core, we are Source Energy! Huge! I can't wait to read the rest of the book.

Without judgment, we each come with our unique life experiences to interpret the symbols we're given in harmony or out of harmony. It's our choice to connect further in solving these puzzles.

Cannon also inquired about Crop Circles with this entity. The response that she received is that they include messages from Mother Earth/Divine Mother Sophia. The last paragraph of chapter four beautifully articulates it all. "The message that is being conveyed (Within

Crop Circles) is that all people have a part to play. . . . for as your attention is gained, your thought forms can interact with our dimension. And so assistance can be given at any time to assist all of you on your Earthly plane."

Paraphrasing, the entity also said that Crop Circles are messages to the masses. Messages the few may be keeping from the masses. It's also about our taking the time to discover our own personal interpretations.

Let's think about that for a minute. There are all sorts of theories out there about who is making the Crop Circles and what they mean. Actually, a quick internet search and we're surrounded by a plethora of theories on unexplainable mysteries. There's enough of the unexplainable that after doing our due diligence of being open enough to consider theories that resonate with us, that maybe it's time to go within. Go within and ask our heart what our heart feels, and what our heart knows. Just maybe that has been what it has been about all along.

With Crop Circles being at the forefront of my thoughts, flipping through the various symbols is fascinating. I mean they give me goose bumps or what I call Angel bumps. I've always enjoyed seeing images of Crop Circles and wondered about them but soon moved on. This new excitement tells me it's time to slow down and listen to what they are trying to tell me. Crop Circle energies along with the language of colors and shapes are indeed very complex topics. The good news is that the information is out there if I can be open and brave enough to delve into them and stay with them long enough to allow them to integrate.

Just for fun, the Book Club decided we wanted to choose a random Crop Circle and return the following week to learn what each other's messages were. Using a Crop Circle coloring book (Wisdom, 2023), we picked a random number and opened the book with the intent that we would each focus on whatever Crop Circle was spotlighted on that page (Pictured next page.).

Tawesmead Copse Crop Circle Wiltshire, England, July 25, 2009. Image credit: Crop Circles Coloring Book I, by Shapes of Wisdom; coloring by Debra.

When looking at this image, I see a being in the center spinning counterclockwise with symbols representing the sacred four directions on each side. The being in the center is me and each one of us using our magnetic healing Life-Force energy to transmute out the low density of this world. Low density, meaning lacking love and harmony.

As our unconditional love and energy increase, the sacred four directions also spin becoming an energetic sphere shooting rays of all colors in all directions, all levels, and all dimensions.

Our endless energy and spinning interweave with other beings who too are spinning their magnetic Life-Force, transmuting energies. All of which continues to multiply this collective Source Energy in intensity and strength.

Imagine each of us spinning within all that we are, and balancing the harmony of ourselves, our homes, our cities, our world, our galaxy, and the universe.

That was a mouthful, I know. Interestingly, other members of the Book Club also came back with similar messages centered around balancing the sacred four directions throughout the multiverse. Additionally, I strongly feel the elements of water, fire, air, and the heart of Earth in this symbol. Don't you just love this stuff? What message do you get when looking at Crop Circle images? What messages does Mother Earth have for you?

I would like to share another Crop Circle my group focused on. Pictured, this one is obviously a tree or a Tree of Life. What a perfect opportunity for me to conclude this book by pulling together all of these chapters and placing them within my personal Tree of Life. To me, the top branches and fruit represent my beautiful Higher Self, Angels, Guides, Dragons, Magical Companions, and of course my beautiful Over Soul.

Alton Barnes Crop Circle, Wiltshire, England, July 15, 2002.
Image credit: Crop Circles Coloring Book I, by Shapes of Wisdom.
Coloring by Debra

The roots are representative of my various expressions or past lives. The trunk is literally the bridge between them. And surrounding each and all parts, represented in my coloring as purple, is Source. Each fruit is color-coordinated between the trunk and roots of a past incarnation. So essentially, it's portraying all of the essences of me within my Tree of Life, all within Source. I love how loving and creative our Angels and Guides are to send us these messages. Crop Circles definitely cause a stir and get us questioning, don't they? They resonate with me as communications between the realms.

As I ponder and consider my Tree of Life, along with each of my currently known past lives, and using the hindsight of my current life, darker experiences are things I tend to hide from myself by avoiding them. This energy work has taught me that hiding or avoiding them created blockages requiring recognition. Hiding or burying something alive is never a good thing and leads to disease. It's no secret that for me, this process has been a slow release.

Just being aware and saying to myself, "Oh, that's what happened and this is how I discovered who I am because of it," was a huge part of my healing and blooming. I mean those resentments were cellular. For example, I have this huge fear of heights; even two steps off of my back deck causes me to hold my breath. Up until a couple of years ago, I avoided those two steps like the plague. Going through this healing work has confirmed what I assumed to be at the root of this particular fear. This knowing decreased my levels of anxiety dramatically but not completely.

There's no better time than the present to dig a little deeper inside, behind, and all around that root. If you agree, join me as I take that dive. With love in your heart, using your imagination, take a couple of slow deep breaths while slowing things down as I go into the theta brainwave . . . back, back, back, to that moment.

Beautiful. We have traveled back to when, as a nine-year-old little girl, I had been in that horrific car accident that took my mother's life. We're at the funeral home of my mother's viewing. Outside of the building there were all these steep concrete stairs leading to the road. There must be at least thirty stairs. I'm banged up with painful deep cuts and swollen bruising. My right eye alone is black and puffy with thirty-two stitches, plus there are cuts and stitches on both legs. My left leg has a painful compound fracture. Overall, I'm out of balance emotionally, mentally, physically, and spiritually. People were asked not to take pictures and are telling me not to look into any mirrors.

Standing at the top of those seemingly unsurmountable stairs terrified me. There it is . . . the root to my fear of heights. Not until this very moment, did I realize that those stairs were simply the final straw. Something deep inside me broke on top of those stairs. This would have been after a grief-stricken emotionally and physically painful week from my mother's broken and frail state of well-being, her death, the ambulance, the hospital, my immediate and extended family, friends, a million other things, and at that moment the entire town of Manti grieving and paying their respect. My whole world had fallen apart.

The time is now to go back and hold that little girl at the top of those stairs. Hold her in my arms, allowing her to take all the time she needs to just sit with it all. Hold her until she knows that whatever happens, she's not alone. Remind her of how, after the funeral, your dad took you three kids to Sea World in California. And how you spent an entire day connecting to that humongous beautiful nurturing whale. What a comfort that day was for both you and this majestic being, for she too was suffering in his captivity. She continues to be with you to this day. Can you feel that love exploding between you two? It is real. It is very real. You are never alone dear one. We are sorry you had to go through all of this and thank and honor you for choosing to do so. We are retrieving that fractured soul piece, gently cleansing it, loving it with lots of mushy wet whale kisses, and returning it to you now.

Thinking a little broader takes me back to that moment of the shear terror I felt when receiving the confirmation that it was indeed the serial killer Ted Bundy, who had his body up against mine with the darkest of intentions (Refer to Chapter Eight). During that session my first internal reaction was okay, I'm done, I don't need to hear anymore. Almost fifty years later with no danger possible, I'm still running from it. How revealing is that? This seems to be a pattern through the majority of my sessions. Could it be that that very response is why my sessions have been kept vague? My Higher Self was simply giving me the time I need to process these events for what they were as I remember my strength as I further learn to love myself and accept who I am, perfectly imperfect.

Respectfully, lovingly, patiently, powerfully, in gratitude, this is how healing in your sovereignty works. It starts with listening to your body and then digging a little deeper. As you dig you might come across blockages. Blockages come from an infinite array of sources. One blockage may have been from a devastating experience such as what I just illustrated. And another may have come from something as simple as being labeled stupid.

Having found all this black magic on me (Discussed in Chapter Eight), I can't reiterate enough the importance of our words. I'm sure we don't think we are cursing someone with black magic when we respond with something like, "You're stupid," or "You're an idiot." But that is exactly how it works. Intentional or not, unless they know how to sacredly shield themselves, you are literally placing black magic on whoever you're saying this to.

Often. we've become desensitized to demeaning or derogatory words with the justification that it's just the lingo of the day. Even if it's not your intent to literally curse this other person, that's absolutely what you're doing. Words matter. Music matters. The energy we allow in our environment matters. The food we allow in our body matters. These are all things to listen to what your heart feels, and what your heart knows.

Some time ago, reading Dr. Masaru Emoto's well-known book, "Messages in Water," I found myself immediately resonating with his theory that we affect water. He validated his theory by exposing water to diverse negative and positive environments. A quick internet search brought me to his Water Consciousness experiments located at www.alivewater.ca. Dr. Emoto believed, "Water is the mirror that can show us what we cannot see. It is the blueprint for our reality, which can change with a single, positive thought. All it takes is faith if you're open to it." According to Dr. Emoto's theory of water consciousness, water can respond to human emotions, thoughts, words, and even written messages.

Emoto did experiments by holding a glass of water and speaking words or taping words to water containers, freezing the water, and photographing the water crystals under a microscope. Words of love, joy, and hope created bright, intricately organized crystals. Words of fear and hatred created muddy, disjointed crystals.

Delving a little deeper into this idea of water having consciousness, I discovered there are a large number of active water researchers. This is when I came across the author, Veda Austin. Austin documents her research in her book, "The Living Language of Water." If you're seriously questioning the consciousness of water, this is a fun rabbit hole to go down.

It is a deep and fascinating question that provokes more and more exciting questions. To stay on topic, what stood out to me in Austin's book was the reminder that nature is not mechanical. It is not triggered like some machine to our every whim. Nor will it respond organically when your ego is present. Forced negative frozen water images result in voids and a disconnected structure. Likewise, messages of love, like you might express to a member of your family, hold beautiful geometry.

We are also reminded that the temperature of water affects the speed of the movement of the molecules within it. Essentially, freezing water slows it down enough for us to comprehend this marvelous conversation. The conversation has been happening all along, it's just happening so fast we haven't been aware of it. We were not ready to listen.

Now let's take this information and place it next to our perceived blockages, doubts, and/or traumas. Are we not over eighty percent water? Could it be that by surrounding ourselves with love, comforting sounds, eating high vibrational foods, and simply slowing ourselves down enough to listen, to really listen to our bodies, while recognizing our experiences as the teacher that they are, using empathy and self-love, we consequently ascend out of it? We raise our vibration. Could it be that easy to change the structure of the water molecules within each cell of our body and our DNA to something beautiful and organic?

This experience, this expression, this incarnation is what I choose to make it. Who knew I would ever be strong enough to wake up to my own sovereignty of no longer consenting to the whims of the powers that were. Who knew I would ever wake up to . . . well, you get the picture. I'm sure there is much more to come and that

The moment you change your perception, is the moment you rewrite the chemistry of your body.

- Dr. Bruce Lipton

in many ways my journey is just beginning. It's simply magical. I feel it all comes back around to what I've heard over and over; just follow your heart. And, go into your heart. It's all energy and it's all love. It's love that harmonizes you forward to all that you are. Similar to how I discovered with the birth of my second baby, love only multiplies. As above, so below. Jump Debra, jump!

I'm reminded of one morning while trying to light a candle with a stick match, and I couldn't get the match to light. Striking it over and over against the striking pad that comes on the matchbox, it was the third strike before I got a spark and the fourth strike before I got it to light. While in meditation that morning the analogy came to mind, that just as you had all the right tools in hand and still struggled to light that match, you have all the tools at hand with your spiritual gifts. Your gifts are not as out of reach as you may think. They have been activated and although trickles of doubt seep in, you have the knowing to dissolve that doubt; dissolve all smallness. Keep striking that match. Your knowing is just that close.

When one of my grandkids asks how old I am, I've often sarcastically used the expression "Older than dirt!" Who knew how factual that little joke is? In my case, even while under hypnosis, answers didn't fully develop before I could accept them consciously. Luckily, I surrounded myself with curious people asking mind-bending questions who opened yet another door or, as they say, another rabbit hole for me to go down. Each puzzle piece kept me moving forward as my heart and Higher Self dictated.

Isn't that what all of this remembering these past lives has been about? Getting us to accept that we are eternal beings intentionally choosing this or that expression. Not recorded in these pages is my life as a huge Dragon soaring over the clouds with the mission to raise the vibration of the people and land below, and my life among the Unicorns and other magical creatures inviting me to remember our magical companions, then there's my life as a rock, plus my life as a huge blue crystal, or my life as a father who lived in the Netherlands, loved the cold, ice skating with my son, and went off and returned to my son from war while he was ice skating, as well as my life as an Indigenous woman living underground within a cave system of the North American southwest because of the toxic environment above ground, along with many other life expressions.

The point is, what we know as death, is not so. Rather, death or our exit is of this expression. My exit as Debra Williams will be the birth of another. The birth of the next life I design and choose to experience.

Of course, it's more complicated than that because of the little fact that we have been unknowingly enslaved and recycled. But that is all over with once we wake up to our potential, our infinite Life Force and Source Love Light core.

Wait, wait, wait. Let's go back and again revisit the Lotus Effect. Do you remember how the researchers discovered that at the micro-level, the surface of the lotus leaf is covered with a dense layer of pointy little modules? Dense enough that they repeal foreign matter. Can we not relate all these dense little modules to ourselves by imagining that each trauma we've experienced throughout our lifetimes creates a module within or around our being? The more traumas the more modules. Wow, so that is how we create an impenetrable shield!

I'm going within and re-imagining that each healed trauma-module has become activated into a bright, high vibration spinning energy similar to the Crop Circle illustrated on page 408. No muck can stick once I've healed and activated my trauma-module. I love it, and I especially love learning this is what nature has been trying to teach us all along.

This book has been the story of one soul's journey toward remembering her omnipotence. It's not to say that your journey is any less or more. There is no judgment. Trust in your heart. Your journey is exactly what you designed it to be in this time and space. Perfectly imperfect.

What a ride it has been. What a healing gift it has been to write these pages. Through the modality of exploring who I am by way of my past lives and entity removal, I am waking up to the inner standing that I AM much more than I have been programmed to believe. Yes, I can enjoy my beloved family and create endless treasured memories together with them, for I adore and love them with all that I am. But I can, and will, explore the joy of family and all of who I AM as well. That's an empowering thought.

I wonder what adventures lie ahead? I wonder what stories the Tree of Life will have to share. Ever since learning of and resonating with my life as a Giant Tree, I'm all about exploring whatever information on Giant Trees, Giants, Dragons, Magical Creatures, and this bigger picture of remembering. It's wild how much evidence has been sitting right there in plain sight.

Recently, during a private channeling of Divine Mother, one of my dearest of friends, who is a clear channel, asked a few questions about

Giant Trees (Refer to the Epiphanies chapter), which I would like to paraphrase. She asked and received the confirmation that there indeed were five million Giant Trees in assistance at the creation of Divine Mother Sophia/Mother Earth. When the channel asked if all five million were still incarnated here on this Earth, Divine Mother surprised me by saying, "No." She said, "About two thousand remain. The others have gone to assist with additional planetary birthing, for this is how it is done."

I was fascinated by the line of questioning; then, this channel asked yet another profound question. She asked, "Of the two thousand who remain, how many have been lost?" Is that not a fantastic question? The gentle response brought me to tears, and it was as though everything in this time and space paused . . . Divine Mother reverently replied, "None!"

Archangel Haniel:
You are there to provide the Rain, the Earth, the Sky, and the Love. The Rain is tears, the Sky is breath, the Earth is nurturing, the Love is infinite.

As Source so delightfully said,

"Be at peace, be at peace, be at peace."

Personal Activity

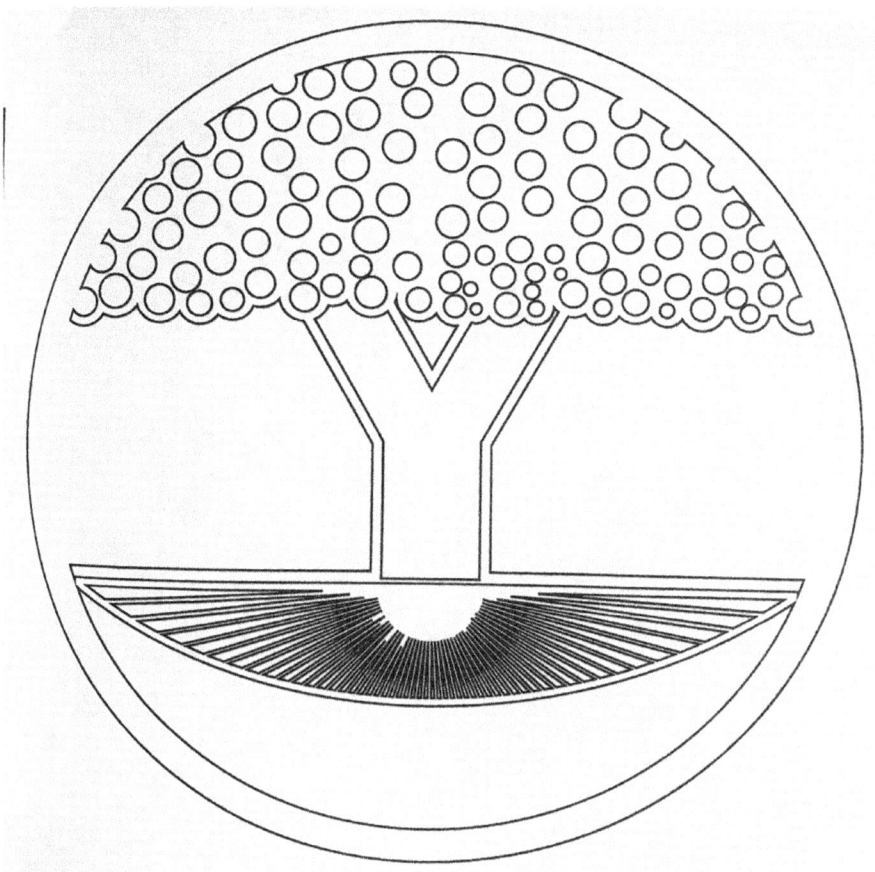

My challenge to you is to sit with this Crop Circle image or any Crop Circle that grabs your attention and color it as your heart shares with you your unique message from Divine Mother Sophia. Enjoy!

The above image is of the Crop Circle made on July 15, 2002, in Alton Barnes, Wiltshire England.

Credit: Crop Circle Coloring Book 1 by Shapes of Wisdom.

Citations

Aardvark Symbolism and Meaning. (2023). Retrieved from https://whatismyspiritanimal.com/spirit-totem-power-animal-meanings/mammals/aardvark-symbolism-meaning/

Attacks, A. h. (2001, September 11). 9/11. New York City, Washington D.C., Pennsylvania, United States.

AuroRa, R. P. (2020). *Galatic Soul History of the Universe.*

AuroRa, R. P. (2023). *Rising Phoenix AuroRa Mystery School.* Retrieved from Rising Phoenix AuroRa: https://www.risingphoenixaurora.com/

Austin, V. (2024). *The Living Language of Water.*

Cannon, D. (2001). *The Convoluted Universe-Book One.* Library of Congress.

Confunden, N. (2022). *The Lands of Mars.* Claudio Nocelli.

Confunden, N. (2022). *The Navigator Who Crossed the Ice Walls.* Claudio Norcelli.

Confunen, N. (2022). *Terra-Infinita.* Claudio Nocelli.

Deviney, T. (2018). *Expansion for Ascending Consciousness.* Balboa Press.

Docter, P. (Director). (2001). *Monsters, Inc.* [Motion Picture].

Emoto, M. (2004). *The Hidden Messages in Water.*

Emoto, M. *Water Consciousness experiments,* www.alivewater.ca.

Gaia. (2023). *Conscious Media, Gaia.* Retrieved from Conscious Media, Gaia: https://www.gaia.com/

Gibson, M. (Director). (2004). *The Passion of the Christ* [Motion Picture].

Gorilla Rap (Hop Like a Bunny! Waddle Like A Duck! [Full cassette]) is a children's song.

Hans Christian, V. B. (January/February 2000). The Lotus Effect. *The Sciences,* 12-15.

Jamie Sams, D. C. (1999). *The Medicine Cards.* St. Martin's Press.

Lana Wachowski, L. W. (Director). (1999). *The Matrix* [Motion Picture].

Laura Eisenhower, R. P. (2021). *Timeline Wars-Red vs Blue.* Retrieved from Rumble: https://rumble.com/vngofj-timeline-wars-red-vs-blue-the-matrix-pt-3.html

Maffucci, S. (2023). *Angel Number 5.* Retrieved from Your Tango: https://www.yourtango.com/self/angel-number-5-meaning

Matias de Stefano, F. A. (2022). *11/11-22-11/11.* Retrieved from Yo Soy 2022: https://yosoy2022.org/en/home/

Melchizedek, D. (2023). *School of Remembering.* Retrieved from School of Remembering: https://theschoolofremembering.com/

Mormon. (2023). Retrieved from The Church of Jesus Christ of Latter-Day Saints: https://www.churchofjesuschrist.org/?lang=eng

Richter, A. (2022). *Free Live TAlk and Meditation Session*. Retrieved from YouTube: https://www.youtube.com/watch?v=zgZSy9fOe8w

Sage, O. &. (2023). *AURA Photo*. Eureka Springs, AR.

Ted Bundy, an American serial killer, executed 1989. (1970s). United States.

Tiger Symbolism and Meaning. (2023). Retrieved from What is my Spirit Animal. https://whatismyspiritanimal.com/spirit-totem-power-animal-meanings/mammals/tiger-symbolism-meaning/

Tiller, V. (1992). *The Jicarilla Apache Tribe, A History*.

Wisdom, S. (2023). *Crop Circles Coloring Book 1*. www.shadesofwisdom.com.

www.ingramcontent.com/pod-product-compliance
Lightning Source LLC
LaVergne TN
LVHW021955060526
838201LV00048B/1578